Managerial

Communications

Dale A. Level, Jr.
Professor of Management
College of Business Administration
University of Arkansas, Fayetteville

William P. Galle, Jr.
Professor and Chairman
Department of Management
University of New Orleans

1988

BUSINESS PUBLICATIONS, INC.
Plano, Texas   75075

Acquisitions editor: John R. Weimeister
Developmental editor: Rhonda K. Harris
Production editor: Karen Smith
Copyediting coordinator: Jean Roberts
Production manager: Bette Ittersagen
Compositor: The Clarinda Company
Typeface: 10/12 Baskerville
Printer: R. R. Donnelley & Sons Company

ISBN 0-256-03730-2
Library of Congress Catalog Card No. 87-72017

Printed in the United States of America

1 2 3 4 5 6 7 8 9 0 DO 5 4 3 2 1 0 9 8

We dedicate this book to all communication scholars—
past, present, and future

Preface

The field of business communication has been in a steady state of transition over the past 20 years or so. At one time it was sufficient to teach business students how to construct letters and reports which met certain standards of grammatical acceptability and form. This was also the time when it was sufficient to teach students how to use a standard mechanical typewriter and a ten-key adding machine. The revolution in electronics and computers has, of course, put those times behind us to stay. As a result, the knowledge and behaviors required to generate and process information have drastically changed.

In much the same fashion, the rapid changes and development which have overtaken most organizations now require more sophisticated managers. And at the top of the list of survival skills for these managers is effective communication. There is significant testimony to this fact in the chronic complaints and repeated cries from corporate America for business college graduates who can communicate effectively. The validity of these complaints and cries is manifested in the many new communication courses being offered in both university and corporate classrooms.

What is interesting about these new courses is that they no longer focus just on writing letters, memos, and reports. Of necessity, they are taking a much more comprehensive view of communication. Appropriately labeled "organizational communication," these courses not only stress written forms but also look at the total organizational communication system. This has been a necessary expansion of the role and content of the business communication course.

An even more contemporary viewpoint is that information is the lifeblood of the organization and must be properly managed, like every other resource. The central figure in the sharing of organizational information is the manager. To effectively manage the organization's communication system, he/she must engage in certain activities—i.e., managerial communication.

This textbook takes a broad look at organizational communication from the perspective of the manager and the managing of the organization's information-sharing process. We begin with the view that managers must understand the languages they use—both verbal and nonverbal. Without a sufficient grasp of the power and effects of language, the manager cannot operate optimally.

In addition to understanding language use, the manager must understand the self and how it interacts with other people and the environment. A great deal of time and space is devoted, therefore, to the exploration of perception, intrapersonal communication, and interpersonal communication.

Because organizational members depend on one another for assistance in meeting their physical and psychological needs, and because such assistance is based on information sharing, communication at group and organizational levels is important. The manager must understand the processes by which groups develop and operate and be able to manage these processes. For these reasons, group and organizational communication are explored. Managers and organizations must engage in a variety of specific communication activities daily if they are to survive and prosper. The manager must be an effective listener, a persuasive speaker, and a capable conflict manager. The manager must understand these activities and have the necessary skills to engage in them. Thus we devote a great deal of time to the major communication activities that we feel are important to the functioning of the manager.

The ability to use language masterfully or to listen actively does not guarantee managerial success. An effective communicator is not necessarily a good manager. But it is safe to say that a poor communicator will not be an effective manager, except perhaps by chance. We developed this textbook with the sincere desire to help the reader improve his or her chances of being an effective communicator *and* an effective manager.

ACKNOWLEDGMENTS

We wish to thank the following for their support and help in the preparation of this manuscript: Pam Bennett, Janet Hill, Ann Sisemore, Doug Arnold and Susan Stephenson.

Special thanks go to Sharon Seidensticker and Beth Milligan for their outstanding assistance on the instructor's manual and the opening vignettes for each chapter.

Finally, we wish to acknowledge the reviewers who offered suggestions and comments on the early draft of the manuscript: James D. Bell, University of Texas–Austin; Norb Fernaus, Illinois Benedictine College; Thomas Fernandez, Emory University; Katherine Miller, Michigan State University; Grant T. Savage, Texas Tech University; Marvin Travis, St. Leo's College; and Peter B. Venuto, Bloomsburg University.

Dale A. Level, Jr.
William P. Galle, Jr.

Contents

Managerial

Communications

Part One

Communication

Dimensions

Chapter 1

Fundamentals of Communication

Chapter 1 Case

You are the administrative assistant to the president of a large multinational corporation. You've just left a disturbing meeting with your boss. "It seems to me," he had said, "most of our problems around here could be solved by better communication. I want you to make that your number one priority this year." Before you could begin to formulate questions, you had been dismissed. What communication problems was he talking about? Could it be technical skills—use of the language or poor reports? Has the boss noticed problems with interpersonal communications? Are you using improper media? What is communication, anyway, and where do you start diagnosing the problems the boss wants solved?

INTRODUCTION

Managerial communication has emerged as a new discipline, as illustrated by the proliferation of journal articles, books, and university courses bearing this title in recent years. Two significant trends have brought about this emergence: first, we have become an information society and that is altering the traditional approaches to management; second, tremendous technological advances demand new skills for successful communication with others.[1] Because of these changes, many organizations are realigning their communication priorities.

Managers are constantly challenged to find new ways to meet today's conditions. Wick Trujillo comments on the emergence of managerial communication: "Although the link between management and communication has been known for some time, organizational literature has only recently reaffirmed the symbolic nature of managerial communication. This is to say that managerial communication has its own identity and can stand alone in respectability."[2]

From a more general perspective Smeltzer, Glab, and Golen have advocated that managerial communication is the result of shared viewpoints of communication within the organization. The traditional domain of

3

business communication involves the structural components of correct letter writing, writing style, grammar, and report formats. The main concern of organizational communication is the system. Management views communication as a means to an end that encompasses the functional aspects of the organization. The integration of these three viewpoints has resulted in the concept of managerial communication.[3]

Traditionally, business communication emphasized skills and organizational communication emphasized knowledge or theory. Managerial communication integrates communication skill and knowledge of the entire system with the functions of the organization. Thus, the situations, skills, functions, and relationships among people in organizations are considered. Hawkins and Preston point out that "managerial communication is the process through which modification of interpersonal and organizational outcome occurs as a result of message exchange."[4]

To use their communication skills more effectively, managers need more than just a course in managerial communication. Knowing how they communicate and behave in particular situations can help managers identify their weaknesses. Volard and Davies point out that there is relatively little knowledge about the communication behaviors of managers.[5] In a study to identify communicator style behaviors that may be associated with managerial performance, David Bednar found a significant relationship in the two variables. Although the study was limited, it suggested that "such information could add clarity and precision to the notion of communication skills, and when appropriately incorporated into a manager's personal repertoire of behaviors, can be the basis of self-improvement."[6]

This chapter provides the foundation on which to develop your effectiveness as a managerial communicator. Since it is important to understand the communication process, we will first examine communication and the organization, communication and the manager, and communication as behavior. Next, some definitions and approaches to communication will illustrate the complex nature of this process.

After defining communication, several communication models are presented. The definitions and models illustrate both the communication *process* and the *behavioral interaction* necessary for effective communication. The intimate relationship between communication process and behavioral interaction is established by means of an interpersonal model.

COMMUNICATION AND ORGANIZATIONS

Common sense tells us that most of what we do is affected in some way by human interaction (i.e., some form of social behavior). Cartwright and Zander explain it this way:

> If it were possible for the overworked hypothetical man from Mars to . . . view . . . the people of Earth, he would probably be impressed by the amount

of time they spend doing things together in groups . . . . He would see that much of the work of the world is carried out by people . . . in close interdependence.[7]

In our society, we participate as members of organizations in a wide variety of activities ranging from casual socialization (attending a cocktail party) to major decision making for the majority of society's members (strategic military planning). As organizational members, we engage in a series of ongoing interpersonal relationships characterized by such terms as *works with, goes to school with,* and *talks with.*

Interaction, coordination, and communication are essential to the business organization. The typical organization is a complex pattern of interacting groups of employees, owners, and consumers. Figure 1–1 contains a more exhaustive classification of groups that constitute the business organization.

Group members supply the firm with the particular resources the firm requires and, conversely, the group members have certain needs that must be satisfied. Figure 1–2 summarizes some of the specific resources and needs of each group.

As long as group members feel that the satisfaction of their needs is equal to or greater than their resource contribution, they will continue their relationship with the firm.[8] If the firm considers the resource contribution of the individual as equal to or greater than the firm's cost, the firm will continue the relationship. This pattern of give-and-take is referred to as the **principle of reciprocity.** Bear in mind that the firm, as used here, represents all groups. For example, the employee group that desires a wage increase must negotiate with the consumer group and the stockholder group, pressuring them to accept higher prices and a lower rate of return, respectively. The employee group does not, however, deal directly with these other groups, but uses as the major coordinating agent the **manager.**

COMMUNICATION AND THE MANAGER

A manager is described as one who works through and with people to accomplish organizational objectives. The ability to work with people depends heavily on communication abilities. Peter Drucker makes this point clearly:

This means that your success as an employee . . . will depend on your ability to communicate with people and to present your own thoughts and ideas to them so they will both understand what you are driving at and be persuaded.

If you work on a machine your ability to express yourself will be of little importance. But as soon as you move one step up from the bottom, your effectiveness depends on your ability to reach others through the spoken or

---

FIGURE 1–1 Component Groups of the Corporation

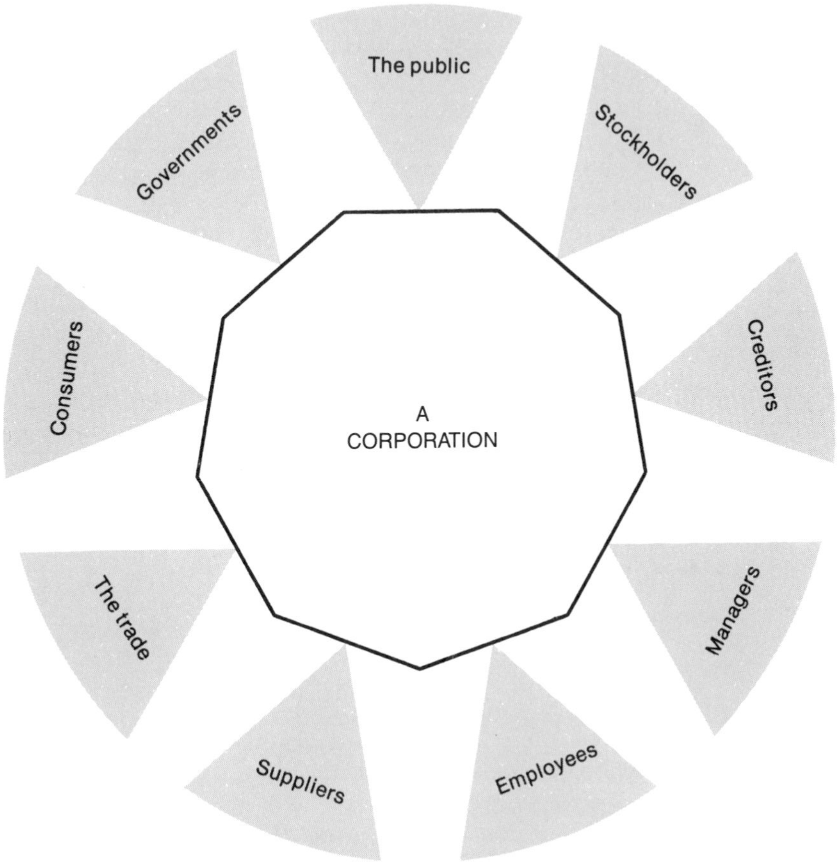

SOURCE: Richard N. Farmer and W. Dickerson Hogue, *Corporate Social Responsibility* (Chicago: Science Research Associates, Inc.), © 1973. Reprinted by permission of the publisher.

the written word. And the further away your job is from manual work, the larger the organization of which you are an employee, the more important it will be that you know how to convey your thoughts in writing or speaking . . . . This ability to express yourself is perhaps the most important of all skills you can possess.[9]

Coordination of resources and needs becomes increasingly difficult as the size and complexity of an organization increase. The ability to communicate becomes increasingly important as the manager interacts with greater numbers of people.

Considering the immense effort involved in coordinating the activities

FIGURE 1–2 Resources and Needs of Organizational Group Members

Group	Resources	Needs
Stockholders	Investment capital	Adequate rate of return
Creditors	Investment capital	Adequate rate of return
Managers	Skills, energy	Money, worth
Employees	Skills, energy	Money, worth
Suppliers	Materials, information	Sales, profits
The trade	Information, protection	Information, protection
Consumers	Money, information	Product or service
Governments	Protection, control	Tax revenues
The public	Support from community	Economic support

of a large corporation, it is no wonder that corporate executives continually complain about the inadequacies of organizational communications and communicators. Significantly, it is estimated that 60 to 80 percent of poor management decisions in business result from ineffective communications.

REQUIREMENTS FOR EFFECTIVENESS

If managers are to be effective, there must be an accurate, timely, uninterrupted, and unbiased flow of information up, down, and across the organizational structure. This requires a communication philosophy that emanates from the top of the organization. This philosophy must be accompanied by effective policy and organizational personnel who understand the communication process, the available channels and media, and their use.

Past analyses of the adequacy (or inadequacy) of organizational communication practices suggest that more emphasis is needed on establishing criteria of effectiveness. The simple act of formulating and transmitting a message cannot be equated with effectiveness. Everyone communicates; therefore, the assumption is that we are all experts. Job applicants are interviewed, tested, and evaluated for knowledge of subject matter or job content, but not for communication skills. This results in individuals who are competent within their areas of specialization but cannot interact with others because of ineffective communication skills.

To understand managerial communication you must understand the communication process and the integral part it plays in interpersonal interactions and organization relationships. Recently, many schools of business have either started or expanded their communication programs.[10] The Amos and Waters study substantiated the fact that communication skills need to be incorporated into college curricula.[11] These researchers queried practicing personnel managers concerning the achievement of re-

cent graduates who entered the job market in certain competency areas. Their findings recommended that all college courses should provide natural opportunities in the formal communication skills that are so essential to management situations.

Frequently, unskilled communicators receive insufficient assistance in improving their skills and costly and irrelevant communications go to uncomprehending receivers. This point is well made in an incident that occurred in Houston, as reported by the Associated Press.

> The parents of a Houston high school pupil received a message from the principal about a special meeting on a proposed educational program. It read: "Our school's cross-graded, multi-ethnic, individualized learning program is designed to enhance the concept of an open-ended learning program with emphasis on a continuum of multi-ethnic academically enriched learning using the identified intellectually gifted child as the agent or director of his own learning. Major emphasis is on cross-graded, multi-ethnic learning with the main objective being to learn respect for the uniqueness of a person."
>
> The parent wrote the principal: "I have a college degree, speak two foreign languages and four Indian dialects, have been to a number of county fairs and three goat ropings, but I haven't the faintest idea as to what the hell you are talking about. Do you?"[12]

Have you received messages that caused you to react as the parent did in this case? More important, have you sent messages that caused others to react in this fashion? This textbook is a starting place to develop your communication skills and to improve your ability to evaluate communications in terms of effectiveness. It is hoped that you will be able to avoid the embarrassing situation the high school principal was in by developing effective communication skills.

You can begin by recognizing that we are not experts all the time. With that in mind, we can ask: What is communication? Why doesn't it work properly all the time? How can we make it work better?

COMMUNICATION AS BEHAVIOR

Communication complicates, and is complicated by, what we do and do not do, what we know and do not know, and how we view ourselves (our self-concept) and others in our environment. This may be illustrated by way of a simple model portraying the cyclical pattern of our decision-making behavior.

In Figure 1–3 the behavior pattern consists of six different phases or states. Listed below each state are some of the major factors that influence it. In reality these states are not as clear-cut as they are represented in the figure; no model does complete justice to that part of reality it is intended to represent.

In the figure, the "present state" essentially defines who we are and

FIGURE 1–3   Decision Making—Behavior Cycle

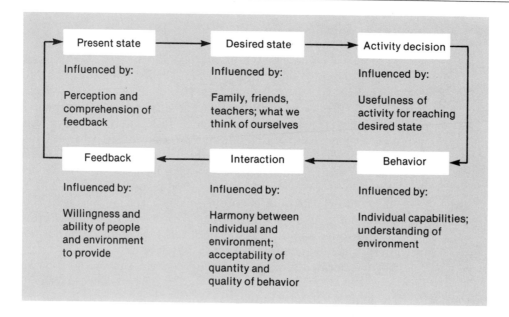

what we are. In the present state we are always developing and refining our "desired state,"—who we want to be, and what we want to be, *sometime in the future*. We must decide what is necessary to achieve the desired state; we must choose to act in some fashion. Our choices may be simple or complex, short or long range, but we must choose from the alternatives available. Once we have chosen an alternative, we engage in the behavior we believe the most appropriate to that alternative.

Interaction with people and objects in our environment usually provides us with the feedback necessary to decide whether or not we have achieved our currently desired state. If we have succeeded, we begin the cycle again by identifying a new or updated desired state. If we have not completely succeeded, we make necessary adjustments at some stage in the cycle.

It should be evident that our behavior is bounded by the extent of our interactions and that these interactions may be largely communicative in nature. Therefore, our ability to communicate affects (and is affected by) each state in a variety of ways. For example, our knowledge about the environment, our current assessment of our competencies (our self-concept), and the messages we receive from others (primarily reference groups) have an impact on our desired state and the alternatives we perceive to be available.

Our communicative interactions also affect our determination of appropriate behavior patterns and interaction with the environment. Finally, the feedback that is so important in measuring success is primarily a matter of communication.

To understand this cycle more fully, consider the decision-making behavior of Jack Hughes. Jack is about to graduate from high school, and his desired state is being reformulated and refined as he plans his future. Jack is contemplating a college career. How and why did he arrive at this decision? He has been influenced by some very important people: his family, friends, teachers, and counselors. Jack, like most of us, wants to live comfortably, assume a responsible position in life, and perhaps be a community leader. How should he achieve this desired state? He has the possibility of either working in his father's business or starting his own business. Either option could help him gain respect, maturity, and a measure of wealth. Jack could choose a college career in business. He even thought about studying medicine, but after consulting some professional people and some honest introspection, Jack decided that he has neither the interest nor the talent to become a physician.

Jack has decided to pursue a law degree. He wants to be a lawyer and feels sure he can achieve that goal. When he enters college, Jack will have to determine what is required to complete his degree. He will have to work hard to gain admission to law school. If he is successful in determining from friends, teachers, classmates, and administrators what he must do, and does it successfully, Jack will have completed a major goal which he believes will move him to his desired state. If Jack receives negative feedback (e.g., poor grades), it will be a sign that he should review the entire cycle to determine where he made a mistake. Were his goals poorly chosen? Did he err in deciding what behavior is necessary? Is he interacting improperly with his environment (teachers, classmates)? Is there something wrong with the quality of feedback?

This cyclical process should help us to understand the extensive role of communication in our lives, particularly as we move on to the task of understanding communication both as a process and as a behavioral interaction.

DEFINITIONS OF COMMUNICATION

What is communication? This question provokes a different definition from every person who answers it. Many writers define communication as the transmission of ideas. This simple definition places great emphasis on the process of communication. Adler and Rodman say that: "Communication refers to the process of human beings responding to the . . . symbolic behavior of other persons."[13] This definition recognizes both the

process and the behavioral interaction of the persons engaged in the communication act.

Himstreet and Baty define communication by saying:

> As a manager, you must be concerned with the transmission process and the flow of information. As a writer and speaker, your major concern is for the construction and delivery of an effective message. And as a sender and receiver of messages, you are obliged to be concerned with meaning. These three approaches to defining communication simply attempt to isolate aspects of the communication process for better understanding. Essentially, businesspeople who want to be known as good communicators must combine *skill* in using language, *knowledge* of management and business operations, and *skill* in human relations.[14]

Norman Sigband does what many writers probably would like to do— he avoids defining communication and justifies his position by saying:

> A comprehensive definition of communication would be helpful to you in today's business world, but such a definition really doesn't exist. Communication involves so many elements—from function to structure—that even a definition that included the motivational aspects, the organizational aspects, and the writing and speaking skills of the sender and the receiver would merely border on description.[15]

Reflecting on these differing definitions and approaches, you should begin to sense the immense complexity of communication. The definition of effective communication in this text is *a meeting of the minds for the purpose of conveying information, instilling a belief, inducing emotion, or eliciting behavior*. This definition is intended to convey the idea that effective communication is both a **process** (the written-visual-nonverbal-vocal-auditory exchange of symbols and stimuli), and a **behavioral interaction** (result of the process). A look at some communication models should help illustrate both the process and the interaction.

COMMUNICATION MODELS

Definition, Functions, Types

Models for communication research have received attention since about 1950. Before looking at some specific communication models, we will focus on the definition, functions, and types of models.

A model represents an object or process in the real world. It can be a map (to route a trip), a complicated econometric formula (to predict national or state income), a replica of an automobile or airplane (to test in a windtunnel), or a statue (to idolize). These examples give us a common definition: a model is a representation of some subject of inquiry. The subject may be an object, event, system, or process.

Descriptive models tell how things are; normative models tell how things ought to be. Models can help organize disjointed information by showing connections between the information. If you were planning a trip between New York City and San Francisco, would you just begin driving? Or would you look at a map and plan your trip according to certain criteria (the most scenic route, the fastest route, a route to include Chicago) and the highways that met your criteria?

Models also serve to predict and measure—from simple yes or no predictions to completely quantitative predictions and measurements that answer the questions of when and how much. The examples of the econometric model to predict income and the automobile windtunnel illustrate these functions.

Models also serve as heuristic devices that lead to the discovery of new information and methods. Every model has the potential to lead other model builders to new, better, greater, more efficient, or less costly models.

Models may be one of four types: iconic or physical, verbal-pictorial, analogue, or symbolic. Iconic or physical models look like the subject they represent. They may be two- or three-dimensional, and they can be scaled up or down. This type of model ranges from the two-dimensional simplicity of a snapshot to larger-than-life statues of military heroes in parks, to architectural models of planned developments.

In theory, every concept or subject of inquiry starts out as a mental picture and is translated into words or drawings. A verbal model is a statement, in words, of the subject of inquiry. A pictorial model is a drawing of the subject of inquiry. Frequently, these are used in combination to illustrate abstract subjects of inquiry. Let's look at the concept of communication—can we build an iconic model of the communication process? No. We can build statues of two people facing each other, but the statues do not represent the process of communication. How can we discuss, investigate, and learn more about this process? The best way is by developing some verbal-pictorial models. Several of these models will be presented and discussed in more detail later in this chapter.

An analog model is one that has one set of properties represented by another set of properties. For example, a topographical map uses a color code with an explanatory legend to represent elevations above sea level, and an illustration in a geology textbook might use an x, an o, or a dot to represent strata formations.

Symbolic models (much like the analogue model) give the components of what is being represented—and their relationships—in mathematical or logical form. A simple example is the formula for compound interest. Statistical or econometric models illustrate the usefulness of this model. Even a simple change in a formula (as in the case of predicting national or state income) can drastically and vividly change the final outcome. And, of course, computers can facilitate thousands of manipulations in a matter of seconds.

Advantages and Disadvantages of Models

Models provide a frame of reference for the consideration of a problem or subject of inquiry and open up the problem of abstraction (such as the subject of "communication process"). If a model is used to test or measure, and the model fails, the nature of the failure may suggest a clue to the deficiencies of the model.

Models also have inherent disadvantages. They oversimplify and make abstract the subjects of inquiry. No model of communication can adequately include and describe all the components, processes, and interactions that are a part of the communication act. No amount of time and effort in constructing a model will guarantee success in predicting or measuring a given subject of inquiry.

Some Specific Models

Dozens of models have been developed and published in the last 30 years. All of these have added to the body of knowledge and had an impact, but we will present here only a few models that we feel contribute to an understanding of and focus on both the *communication process* and *behavioral interaction* on which our definition of communication rests.

A Process Model.   Charles Osgood noted that each individual functions simultaneously as a source and destination and as a transmitter and receiver. We regularly encode, transmit, receive, and decode our own messages through an elaborate feedback mechanism that is a self-contained communication system. This self-contained system corresponds to the Shannon-Weaver model; however, Osgood has rearranged the components into what he describes as a "communication unit," equipped both to send and to receive messages. This model is shown in Figure 1–4. The unit that is illustrated represents only one person. To be a complete

FIGURE 1–4   The Shannon-Weaver Communication Model

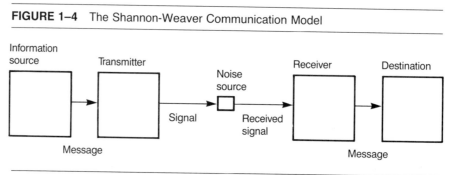

SOURCE: Claude E. Shannon and Warren Weaver, *The Mathematical Theory of Communication* (Urbana: The University of Illinois Press, 1949), p. 98.

model, it must include two or more units. Between any two or more units is the message, which connects the units into a single system.

Osgood's model focuses on the communication unit (including both encoding and decoding functions) and recognizes intrapersonal communication.

Interaction Models. The primary focus of Osgood's model was on the technical or communication process. In contrast, the following models show interest in the process, but focus on the nontechnical or interaction between the participants during the communication act.

Newcomb's model (see Figure 1–5) illustrates the communication act in its simplest form: A transmits information to B about X. Although there is an implied process, we cover this model as an interaction model because of the use (and emphasis) of the terms *orientation* and *coorientation*. This model focuses on the orientation of each party to the other and to the subject. Each arrow represents an orientation, and taken together, form coorientations that impact on the ultimate effectiveness of the interaction.

The model consists of the following four orientations: (1) A's orientation toward B, including attitude, feelings for, and opinions of B; (2) B's orientation toward A, in the same sense; (3) A's orientation toward X, including knowledge of and attitude toward the subject; and (4) B's orientation toward X, in the same sense. Thus, the stronger and more positive the orientations are, the greater the possibility of effective communication. If any one of the orientations is neutral to negative, the possible outcome of the communication interaction is likely to be neutral to negative. The more positive the orientations are between persons and subjects, the more likely the persons will choose to interact and the more alike their interests and activities tend to become.

Wilbur Schramm is credited with several variations of models and we will present here the one that depicts the interactive nature of the communication process. Figure 1–6 identifies person A as the sender-encoder

FIGURE 1–5 Newcomb's Minimal A-B-X System

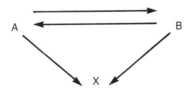

SOURCE: Theodore M. Newcomb, "An Approach to the Study of Communicative Acts," *Psychological Review* 60 (November 1953), p. 394.

FIGURE 1–6   Schramm's Communication Model

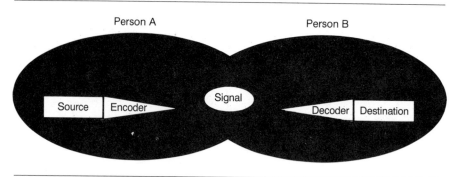

SOURCE: Wilbur Schramm, ed., "How Communication Works," in *The Process and Effects of Mass Communication* (Urbana: University of Illinois Press, 1955), pp. 4–8.

and person B as the receiver-decoder. Each person brings his or her own field of experience or frame of reference to the communication interaction. The frames of reference, shown by the oval symbol, are a composite of the person's education, background, attitudes, likes and dislikes, and all the experiences the person has had. The signal, or message, that A sends to B must fall within the "common" frame of reference area to be considered effective communication. If A speaks in German and B does not understand German, the message remains in person A's frame of reference (though the two may have overlapping frames of reference). If person A is a physician giving a diagnosis or a computer expert describing a new program, and B has limited knowledge of medical terminology or computer jargon, the signal is likely to be "on the line" or in both person A's and the common frame of reference area. The same thing can happen, in reverse, if A is talking about a subject in which B is more knowledgeable (haven't you ever wanted to tell someone, "Stop talking, I know more about this than you do"?).

The major contribution of this model is the emphasis on the individuals' frames of reference and the necessary overlapping of the two frames of reference for effective communication to occur.

Systems Model.   Thayer has proposed that communication occurs at one or more of four levels in a systems model—intrapersonal, interpersonal, organizational, or communication system. He suggests that communication involves the strategic or tactical competencies of either or both the originator or receiver. In his model one or more of the basic communication processes is/are used: acquiring, processing, generating, or disseminating. Three components—competencies, processes, and levels of analysis—are illustrated in Figure 1–7.

FIGURE 1–7 Thayer's Model

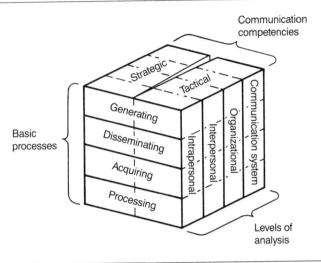

SOURCE: Lee Thayer, *Communication and Communication Systems* (Homewood, Ill.: Richard D. Irwin, 1968), p. 272.

The significant contribution of this model is stated by Thayer: "It may be apparent that the framework for organizing communication methods and techniques could be used as well to isolate problems—from the most elementary and unidimensional (one's ability to speak intelligibly, for example) to the most sophisticated and multidimensional (one to which all of the factors represented in the total matrix contribute)."[16]

Behavioral Model. Although most communication model builders would profess an interest and concern for the ultimate result of the communication act, Campbell and Level initiate the discussion of their model by saying that the sender must first determine the desired behavior of the receiver. This behavior may range from an observable activity to simply "being aware" of something. Thus, while the model (Figure 1–8) shows both a communication process and behavioral and environmental interactions, the emphasis is on the result or outcome of the process and interactions.

At first it appears to be a complex and cumbersome model, but one can follow the numbers and arrows to identify the process and interaction of the participants. Each step is crucial to the overall success of the model, but step 3 (for the encoder) and step 6 (for the decoder) deserve special comment. Symbolic interpretation refers to the idea that (1) meanings cannot be imposed on one person by any other person, and (2) each per-

FIGURE 1–8 The Campbell-Level Model

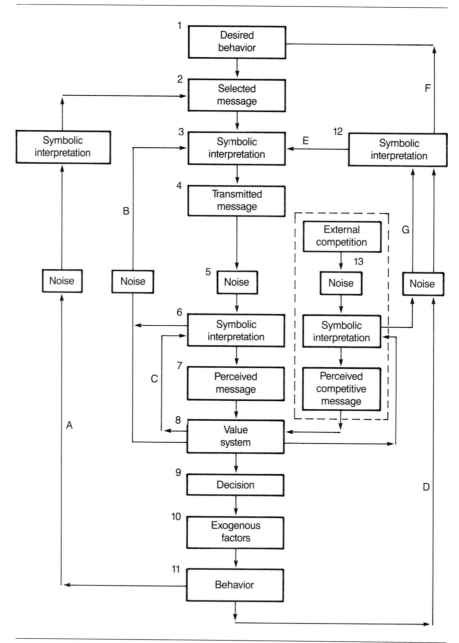

son gives his or her own interpretation to all stimuli based on that person's field of experience or frame of reference.

The focus of this model is on the desired behavior identified at the start (top of the model) by the sender, and the resultant behavior of the receiver that is observed at the bottom of the model. This is often described as a "black box" model, with something happening in each of the boxes. The model is useful because research can be directed on discrete portions of the communication process.

SUMMARY

Communication is an inevitable part of our personal and organizational lives. Management in this country has recently begun to take an increased interest in communication as a skill and necessary function and recognize it as an essential part of their responsibility.

The need for managers who can communicate effectively will increase despite computer techniques that will modify organizations and changing technology. The term *managerial communication* is a broad concept that integrates the function, skill, and knowledge of communication and management toward the achievement of organizational goals.

In this chapter we have looked at the significance of communication in organizations and have explored the complexities of the communication act exhibited in definitions and models.

We spend much of our time accomplishing objectives as group members, and this requires the coordination that is made possible by communication. The typical business organization is made up of a variety of groups (employees, consumers, and stockholders). Communication is essential to coordinate the efforts of these groups. The principal coordinator in the business firm is the manager, and since the manager gets things done through and with people, communication skills are a cardinal qualification.

Knowledge of the communication process and the resulting interactions among people is essential to effective communication. Several definitions and communication models were presented: the technical or process models emphasize communication as on ongoing process while the nontechnical or behavioral interaction models focus on the interactions.

As an interpersonal process, communication behavior requires awareness. We must be aware of messages coming to us from our environment in order to respond to them. Communication is not guaranteed by awareness alone. A message cannot be decoded if the receiver does not have language compatibility or the proper vocabulary. Thus, proper language use is underscored as an element of effective communication.

Two very important components of effective communication are the ability and skill to effectively use language and to apply behavioral principles. These topics will be developed further in Chapter 2.

DISCUSSION QUESTIONS

1. In what ways do the members of groups in a business organization supply the firm with resources? Represent needs to be satisfied? What are some of the specific resources and needs of these groups?

2. Why is the first step toward improving communication skills the recognition that we are not communication "experts"?

3. Why is communication so difficult to define?

4. Explain in detail three reasons communication skills are crucial to the effective management of a business.

5. Define the principle of reciprocity and explain why it is important for a manager to be aware of this principle.

6. How does a communication model serve as a heuristic device?

7. Give a short working definition of communication and explain two concepts of effective communication that are emphasized in the definition.

8. Why is it not possible to develop an *iconic* model of the communication process?

9. What does it mean to say that a model creates an abstraction of the subject of inquiry it represents?

10. What is the important contribution of the Osgood model of communication?

11. List three categories of communication problems that the Shannon-Weaver model illustrates.

12. What are the implications of the role of frames of reference in the Schramm model of communication?

13. Some models are concerned with the technical, or process, aspects of communication, while others focus on the nontechnical, or interactive, components of communication. Describe a model that focuses on the technical process, and contrast it with a model that focuses on the nontechnical interaction between communication participants.

14. Briefly describe the Campbell-Level model. What is the particular emphasis of the Campbell-Level communication process?

EXERCISE

1. Diagram the six phases of decision-making behavior. Briefly explain your diagram (Figure 1–3) and explain why communication is crucial in the various phases.

NOTES

[1]Larry Smeltzer, Janice Glab, and Steven Golen, "Managerial Communication: The Merging of Business Communication, Organizational Communication, and Management," *The Journal of Business Communication* 20, no. 4 (1983), pp. 71–78.

[2]Wick Trujillo, "Organizational Communication as Cultural Performance: Some Managerial Considerations," *The Southern Speech Communication Journal* 50, no. 3 (1985), p. 202.

[3]Smeltzer et al., "Managerial Communication," p. 75.

[4]Brian L. Hawkins and Paul Preston, *Managerial Communication* (Santa Monica, Calif.: Goodyear Publishing, 1981), p. 27.

[5]S. V. Volard and M. R. Davies, "Communication Patterns of Managers," *The Journal of Business Communication* 19, no. 1 (1982), pp. 41–53.

[6]David A. Bednar, "Relationships between Communicator Style and Managerial Performance in Complex Organizations: A Field Study," *The Journal of Business Communication* 19, no. 4 (1982), pp. 51–75.

[7]D. Cartwright and A. Zander, *Group Dynamics*, 3rd ed. (New York: Harper & Row, 1968), p. 3.

[8]This relationship has been simplified for purposes of discussion. A major variable—alternatives—has been omitted. If a higher level of benefits or lower level of costs can be attained elsewhere, the individual is likely to move if the effort is worthwhile.

[9]Peter Drucker, *People and Performance* (New York: Harper's College Press, 1977), p. 262. Reprinted by permission of Harper & Row.

[10]Mary Munter, "Trends in Management Communication at Graduate Schools," *The Journal of Business Communication* 20, no. 1 (1983), pp. 5–11.

[11]Nancy N. Amos and Gail R. Waters, "A Nation at Risk: The Imperative for Effective Communication," *The Journal of Business Education* 60, no. 5 (1985), pp. 184–87.

[12]*Johnson City Press Chronicle,* January 26, 1977, reported by Associated Press.

[13]Ronald B. Adler and George Rodman, *Understanding Human Communication,* 2nd ed. (New York: Holt, Rinehart & Winston, 1985), p. 4.

[14]William C. Himstreet and Wayne Murlin Baty, *Business Communications,* 7th ed. (Boston: Kent Publishing Co., 1984), pp. 6–7.

[15]Norman B. Sigband, *Communication for Management and Business,* 3rd ed. (Glenview, Ill.: Scott, Foresman, 1982), p. 23.

[16]Lee Thayer, *Communication and Communication Systems* (Homewood, Ill.: Richard D. Irwin, 1968), p. 274.

SUGGESTED READINGS

COLEMAN, LINDA J., and SUSAN RAWSON ZACUR. "Communication as a Business Skill." *Supervisory Management* 29, no. 11 (Fall 1984), pp. 38–43.

FISHER, DELBERT W. "A Model for Better Communication." *Supervisory Management* 27 (June 1982), pp. 24–29.

JOHNSON, JACK E. "Communications Exchange: A Motivational Activity." *American Business Communication Association Bulletin* 45 (December 1982), pp. 29–30.

ROUNDY, NANCY, and CHARLOTTE THRALLS. "Modeling the Communications Context." *Journal of Business Communication* 20 (Summer 1983), pp. 27–46.

SHAPIRO, IRVING S. "Managerial Communication: The View from Inside." *California Management Review* 27, no. 1 (Fall 1984), pp. 157–72.

Chapter 2

The Role of Language

Chapter 2 Case

You have recently been selected district sales manager for a textbook publishing company. Sales in one of your territories have declined noticeably in recent months. You note that the territory was taken over 18 months ago by a new salesman. His personnel file tells you that he is young, aggressive, has a degree in marketing from a major university, and was highly recommended for the job. You arrange an interview with him to get his opinions on the sales slump. During the interview, he appears calm and confident, and seems convinced that "it's a tough territory," but that he will soon be able to "turn things around." You are impressed by his positive attitude, but notice that his speech is peppered with slang, jargon, and grammatical errors. What suggestions might you make? Would your answer vary if your company sold prescription drugs? Building materials?

LANGUAGE AS REALITY

The English language is our primary means of communication and plays a significant role in our total scheme of living. Language gives us the symbols that we use to perceive and comprehend things, events, people, happenings, and relationships in our environment. A number of pyschologists and linguists believe that language is the basis for what we think, how we think, and whether we think at all. The central idea of their hypothesis is that language functions not simply as a device for reporting experiences but, more significantly, as a way of defining experience.[1] For example, when the United States began manned space missions, the astronauts repeatedly stated that there were no words adequate to describe the view from space, or to express what they were feeling. Consequently, the astronauts were unable to define and share their experiences with those of us who were earthbound.

Language is not just a communication tool. It stands between its user and reality and directly influences the user's perceptions and behavior. Language provides a basis for analyzing and organizing experience into

useful patterns and categories. Taken to extreme, this means that different languages by using different systems of categorization and organization, create distinct worlds for their respective societies—not just the same world with different labels. And just as societies create unique languages, so, in a sense, do individuals.

INDIVIDUAL DIFFERENCES

Effective use of language is not a simple task, and it becomes more difficult because of our individual uniqueness. Because we are unique, the meaning of a message can be completely different to a sender and a receiver. Misunderstandings can result because we, as communicators, reflect our own predispositions and expectations. In his article dealing with the dynamics of ambiguity in communication, H. R. Smith details the mechanisms by which we encounter and convey our perceptions of reality.

First, the information an individual brings into his information processing operation is a unique product of that particular individual. On the one hand, it is a product of his sensory equipment, which cannot be quite the same in any two people. And it is also a product of past learning—and that is even more divergent from one person to the next. Which is to say that everything we experience is a manufacture of our nervous system.

Second, not only is everything each of us holds to be reality self-manufactured; in addition, whatever we want then to communicate must be remanufactured. As this has so aptly been put, "Experience cannot be transmitted as experience." It must rather be translated into sights and sounds—to then run the gamut again of the capacities of whoever is at the other end. There can be no guarantee that this reassembly operation will produce a product closely resembling the original.

Third, to reiterate for emphasis, information and communication manufacturing must begin with the stored experiences, the memories of senders and receivers. To expand a little on a famous saying about this, every way of seeing is a multitude of ways of not seeing. Because the same happening can so dramatically mean different things to different people, everyone literally lives in his own highly personalized world. If then, communication partners do "see" things differently as they are communicating, much of the result must be miscommunication.[2]

Alfred Korzybski, noted semanticist and author, developed the notion of individual differences from a slightly different perspective.[3] He noted that we often use "maps" to help understand and discuss the features of a particular "territory" in which we are interested. The features of the territory are clearly represented on the map, but the map is *not* the territory. Unfortunately we lose sight of this difference and treat the map as if it were the territory. We confuse the symbols we use with the things

they represent. The map inside our minds is not nearly the same as the reality outside our minds, and each of us carries around in his or her mind a slightly different map of the same territory. To appreciate the impact of this problem on communication, imagine how difficult it might be for you and a friend to meet somewhere in New York City if each of you created and used your own map.

The world exists in our minds, and it is a little different for each person because we are individuals with unique experiences. We will say more about the nature of individual differences in Chapter 5, Intrapersonal Communication. Presently, you should become sensitive to the fact that individuals (as well as cultures) have their own unique language for perceiving and recording reality, and this uniqueness frequently leads to ineffective communication.

A MEETING OF MINDS

Our efforts will be more meaningful and productive if we understand others and communicate so that they understand us. *Communicating effectively is, and should be, approached as a challenge to our creative abilities.*

Imagine that you are standing on one side of a river, and you want to get an object or package to someone on the other side. In the absence of a bridge, the most appropriate solution would be to place the package on a vessel that floats and transport it to the other side. Without any disruption (e.g., collision with another vessel, rough water), the package would be lifted from the vessel in the exact form in which it was placed. Just as the package had to cross a barrier (water), our messages must cross the barriers of time and space. Since human communication involves moving messages across *space* and *time*, you must employ an appropriate vessel to transport your message across these barriers. "Vessels" used for human communication across time and space are called **codes.**

There are many different codes including music, fine art, computer languages (COBOL, FORTRAN), "body" language, the English language. Each code has two components: **elements** (e.g., words, punctuation marks) and **structure** for combining the elements (e.g., rules of grammar). Different codes vary in terms of their structural flexibility and the singularity of meaning of their elements. Compare, for example, a computer language and the English language. A highly flexible code increases the freedom of composition for the sender, but it also increases the latitude of interpretation for the receiver, and consequently the chance of miscommunication.[4]

Assume that you want to communicate with someone. The message you want to communicate is X. (X may represent any message such as information, a directive, or an expression of feelings.) After selecting an appropriate code, the next task is to **encode** the message. This is done by

carefully selecting and combining elements of the code to externally represent your message as Y. In effect, Y serves as the vehicle on which your message is conveyed physically across time and space to the receiver. The receiver will then receive the message, Y, **decode** it, and interpret it to be X, the message that you intended. This process is illustrated in Figure 2–1.

Consider the following example. Donna Drock is a new production employee who has been working hard for the two weeks she has been on the job. Her supervisor, Charlie Hardin, has the following reaction to Drock's performance. "Donna has worked very hard and has done an outstanding job since she has been here. I am proud of her, and I want to tell her what I think of her work. She would probably be pleased to know this and to hear it from me."

Hardin cannot physically lift this evaluation from his head and place it into the mind of Drock. He must instead choose the appropriate words and address them (in spoken or written form) to Drock. Hardin decides that the message would have its greatest impact if spoken face to face. So at the appropriate time Hardin approaches Drock and says, "Donna, you have done an excellent job in the two weeks you've been here, and I want you to know that I appreciate your efforts."

If Hardin's nonverbal cues are consistent with his words, if there are no external distractions, and if Drock is familiar with all the words used by Hardin, Drock will receive the message intended by Hardin. The result will be a **meeting of minds.**

Direct mind-to-mind transfer of information and ideas is not possible (excluding such phenomena as extrasensory perception and mental telepathy). Transfer of information across time and space is impossible without the use of some code. In a code such as the English language, the challenge is to select, combine, and transfer words in such a manner that they create in the mind of the receiver exactly what is in the mind of the sender.

FIGURE 2–1   A Meeting of Minds

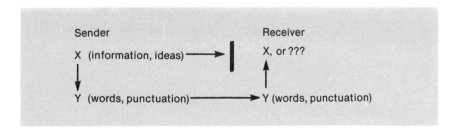

VOCABULARY

There are two essential components of a code: elements and structure. It might seem, at least on the surface, that the words (elements) and the rules of grammar (structure) that constitute the English language should be relatively fixed at any given time. For example, an unabridged dictionary should contain all the words of our language, and a basic grammar book should contain all the rules. If the language is constant at any given time, doesn't it act on all of us in the same manner? If so, why do we have so many problems communicating? We have already identified individual differences as a source of difficulty, but there is another problem we need to explore in this chapter.

The set of elements (words) we use is perhaps the less stable of the two components of language, and consequently words are a greater source of difficulty in our communication efforts. For example, Ogden and Richards reported as early as 1923 that there were some 600,000 words in the English language.[5] English is a dynamic language and this number has not decreased. In fact, due to the increase in technical and professional language, there are easily another 100,000 words that can be added to the list today.

There are more than 14,000 definitions for 500 of the most commonly used words. That is an average of 28 definitions per word. This is hard to believe but a brief examination of an unabridged dictionary confirms it. Examination of just a few pages of a popular collegiate dictionary revealed the following.

Word	Number of Meanings Reported
out	25
part	23
pass	51
pick	26
play	33
point	47

Is it any wonder that we have as much difficulty as we do in our communications? Perhaps we should feel satisfied that we communicate as well as we do.

S. I. Hayakawa pointed out that people too often "assume that the search for the meanings of words begins and ends with looking them up in a dictionary."[6] A dictionary is actually nothing more than a history book that details the various meanings assigned to words in the past. It is obvious as you look through a dictionary that some meanings are no longer useful, and other meanings have yet to be assigned and recorded.

Meanings are not in words, but rather in people as they use the lan-

guage each day. This is the most difficult principle of communication to understand and accept. Words do not possess any inherent meaning; people assign meaning to words. This point can be clearly illustrated by considering the valuation of U.S. currency. The cost of the paper, ink, and labor used to make a $1 bill, a $5 bill, and a $100 bill is far less than a dollar. While their "inherent" value is less than a dollar, each bill would buy a considerable number of pieces of paper the size (2.5 by 6 inches) of a dollar bill. What makes these bills so valuable? The cost of production of these three bills should be approximately the same, but you get five times as much with a $5 bill as with a $1 bill. One hundred times as much with a $100 bill! Why? We have assigned a certain value or meaning to these pieces of paper, and in this same way we attach meaning to words.

Several years ago, the Supreme Court ruled that portions of a recorded comedy routine on obscene words could not be broadcast by a radio station. In his reaction to the ruling, the comedian pointed out that words are harmless, and that they are what we make them in our minds. We can, and do, attach to words whatever meaning we wish.

Where do we learn meaning that we attach to words? These meanings are largely influenced by the **concept formation process.**

CONCEPT FORMATION PROCESS

If you were asked to write five statements about a samovar, could you do it? Would the statements be concise, clear, and intelligent? How about writing five statements about the Statue of Liberty? It would be easier to write five concise, clear, intelligent statements about the Statue of Liberty because you have formed a concept—a mental image or picture—of it. You probably have no concept to go with the label "samovar," and without an adequate concept of some part of reality it is difficult to communicate about it effectively. Concept quality and sophistication have an obvious and significant influence on communication quality; therefore, it is important to understand the concept formation process.

In the progression from infancy to adulthood and throughout our adult lives we are continually learning about our environment. As we are exposed to objects, events, and people, we form concepts and refine them on the basis of new information. Concept formation is the result of **generalization, discrimination,** and **transfer**—three distinct capabilities that allow us to organize our world in a variety of ways.

Essentially, generalization requires an individual to understand that objects, events, and people possess common elements or characteristics, and can be classified on the basis of those commonalities. For example, an infant who repeatedly observes a number of different human beings such as mother, father, brother, and sister will recognize certain common characteristics. When the infant learns a label, such as "dada," she will

attach this label to *all* humans she comes in contact with. The child has mentally noted the commonalities of human beings, but has not learned to differentiate between them.

Discrimination is the ability to identify and distinguish correctly between different elements or characteristics, and to respond properly to them. Returning to our previous example, the child gradually learns to distinguish between the physical and behavioral features of various adults and begins to understand what a mother is, what a father is, and so forth. As these concepts (father, mother, sister) are refined on the basis of new information, she simultaneously acquires appropriate new labels to go with them.

Research suggests that discrimination behavior is a function of language and the ability to apply it, the latter improving with age. The learning of concepts is simplified and enhanced by language because it provides additional cues for distinguishing objects, people, places, and events.

How do we "see" new concepts? Can we conceptualize something that we have not yet experienced? In order to be conceptualized and communicated about, the new experience must be fitted into the most appropriate word or words of our current vocabulary. This transfer of elements from one situation to another is facilitated by language. Since we use words to describe commonalities, we are capable of transferring and generalizing responses to new stimuli. Thus, we form new relationships and conceptualizations from old ones. One may claim never to have heard or seen the word *eclectic*. After being introduced to the word through a class lecture, after hearing the word pronounced, and after seeing several examples of eclectic theories, the person may come to class two days later and report, "I have seen and heard the word *eclectic* used several times in the past two days." Does this mean the person never heard or saw the word before? Probably not; but it does mean the person had no prior conceptualization of the letters e-c-l-e-c-t-i-c in that sequence. Thus a word has no meaning until we give it meaning, and that meaning comes from our conceptualization.

Consider another example. The letters c-a-r have no meaning or significance to a baby until exposure to numerous experiences of mother, father, brother, or sister saying "car" or "go for a ride." Only after repeated sessions does the child attach any significance to "car"—and even then it is an audible stimulus. It may take another year or two to associate the visual stimulus with the sound he has heard for some time. As we grow older and have more experiences, the same stimulus, c-a-r, may take on new and varied meanings. To the teenager it may mean a beautiful piece of metal with a fine-tuned motor; to a parent who has lost a child in an accident it may mean death; and to someone on vacation it may mean freedom and the ability to get away. All of these are conceptualizations—meanings that someone attaches to a given word. Thus the letters c-a-r have no more and no less meaning than we have learned to give

---

FIGURE 2–2 Population Subdivision by Concepts

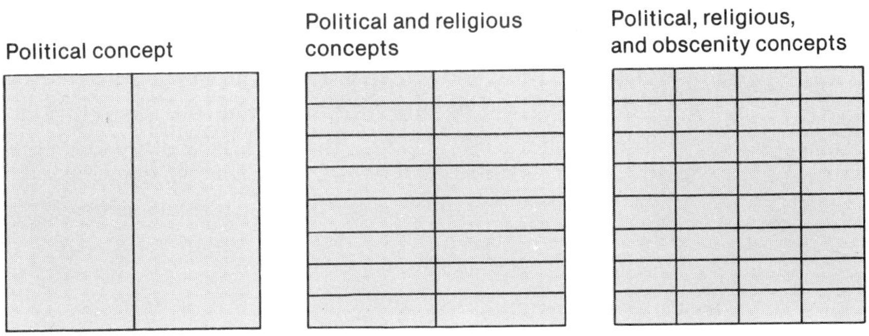

| Political concept | Political and religious concepts | Political, religious, and obscenity concepts |

them from our parents, our teachers, our peers, and our own experience. Once we learn and give some meaning to c-a-r, we can add new and different words and expand our total number of conceptualizations: new car, antique car, race car, toy car, black car, wrecked car, my car, car motor, car insurance, and on and on.

Concept formation can be used to partially explain the uniqueness of every individual. Consider the concept of government, for example. In the United States we have two major political parties, each with a different concept of government. We could divide the people of this country into two groups on the basis of a political concept. Then assume that we have eight major religious denominations, each with a different concept of God. Within each of the two major political groups we would probably find one or more individuals who hold each of the eight religious concepts. Thus, we would have 16 separate groups (see Figure 2–2).

Assume that there were only two concepts of obscenity and further subdivide the 16 political-religious groups into 32 groups. Using other concepts we could derive thousands of groups. As we add concepts, the size of each group diminishes. Eventually, if we used enough concepts to differentiate individuals, we would arrive at 235 million unique groups of one. Thus, you can begin to realize the significant role of concept formation as both an influence and a source of difficulty in communication.

FACTS, INFERENCES, VALUE JUDGMENTS

To further complicate matters, what we store in our memories as reality is not always objective and verifiable. Rather, as Smith's earlier comments indicated, it is our interpretation of reality. Reality for each of us consists of a collection of **facts, inferences,** and **value judgments.**

A fact can usually be verified. For example, the room temperature is a fact and it can easily be verified or measured.

An inference is a conclusion reached after consideration of the facts in evidence. An inference is not itself a fact. For example, if the room temperature has been stable day after day at 68 degrees, you might say that the room temperature tomorrow will be 68 degrees. This is not a fact, but a conclusion reached after considering the facts in evidence (i.e., the daily temperature readings). It is always preferable to act on factual information. However we often find ourselves in situations where sufficient facts are not available and there is no time to gather them. Consequently, we draw inferences and act on them. We are often disappointed to learn that our inferences were incorrect. We say or do the wrong thing, and then have to take corrective action or suffer the consequences, or sometimes both.

We must be aware of the consequences when we act on inferences. The risks of saying or doing the wrong thing must be consciously considered. We should let others know that we, or they, are acting on inferences that carry certain risks. Alternatively, we could postpone our communications and other actions until we have time to collect sufficient information.

A value judgment is just that, a personal judgment based on an individual's value system and not on supportable fact. Because we mistakenly treat value judgments as supportable facts, communication encounters frequently have a negative outcome. For example, suppose two individuals walked into a room where the temperature was 68 degrees. One might say that the room is cold; the other states that it is too hot. Who is correct? Is there any objective measure that can be used to settle the discrepancy? Probably not, because the individuals' reactions to the temperature are based on their personal chemical and psychological makeup. If they cannot realize the true basis of their disagreement, they may never get beyond arguing whether the room is too hot or too cold.

The same problem occurs when two individuals observe a work of art, and one adores it while the other abhors it. This is an example of the time-worn cliche, "Beauty is in the eyes of the beholder." Reality for the individuals in both of these situations is based solely on what is inside them and not on any externally objective standard. Our egocentricity keeps us from seeing the distinction between what is factual and what is not, and frequently precludes the development of more productive relationships.

We will not refrain from making value judgments. But we need to be aware of our abundant use of them, and the risks involved therein. We must label value judgments as such for the benefit of our listeners or readers, and for ourselves. Perhaps then communications and relationships would improve.

IMPROVING COMMUNICATION THROUGH EFFECTIVE LANGUAGE USAGE

We have described the communication process as a rather difficult one, possessed of many pitfalls. The process is dependent on the use of a code that is vague, imprecise, and full of pitfalls. Yet our language is all that we have—there is no feasible alternative. The best approach to effective communication, therefore, is to become sensitive to the many weaknesses, as well as the strengths, of our language, and to use it as best we can. The remainder of the chapter is devoted to that goal.

One of the difficult and consistent challenges of effective communication is adapting to a given receiver. Webster states that to adapt is to "make suitable to," and two central issues of adaptability are *what* is said and *how* it is said.

Selection of Information

An appropriate starting place for a discussion of adaptability is the selection of information to be included in the message. With the contemporary phenomenon of information overload, the task of selecting only the most appropriate information is more important than ever before. The complexities of an ever-increasing rate of change increase the amount of available knowledge; consequently, information management and selection become crucial.

Pick and choose information that is significant before beginning your message. A piece of information that seems significant under one set of circumstances may seem just the opposite under other circumstances. Many individuals are tempted to communicate without giving adequate consideration to information selection, and they create messages filled with irrelevancies, ambiguities, and omissions. A better approach is to evaluate the contextual variables and select information within that framework. Some of the most important contextual variables are discussed next.

The Objective of the Communication. It is essential to clearly specify the exact purpose of a message before beginning any communication. What is it that you intend to accomplish? Do you simply want to convey information? Do you want to influence an individual's beliefs or behavior? Do you want to describe your emotions? The purpose of a communication will influence the content of the message. Not knowing that purpose, or having too many purposes for any given message, is likely to spell failure.

The Quality of the Sender/Receiver Relationship. Another obvious factor that affects the content of a given message is the specific relation-

ship quality (e.g., formal-informal, trustful-distrustful, supportive-defensive, hostile-friendly). Relationship quality will dictate what information should be included or excluded, and the limits of acceptable language. You might be more willing to disclose your feelings and problems in a trustful, supportive relationship than in one characterized as distrustful and defensive. Consider the difference between a husband-wife relationship and a superior-subordinate relationship. The very nature of these relationships will have an impact on what is shared and how it is shared. The husband and wife will probably have a more intimate and open sharing of their perceptions and feelings, while the superior and subordinate will share information more formally because of the relationship imposed by the organization.

The Needs of the Sender. It is safe to say that all communicative behavior serves some purpose. Assuming that all behavior is directed toward need satisfaction, you should be able to identify the specific personal need that you are trying to satisfy in any communication situation. The nature and intensity of that need will probably help determine what you will or will not include in a message. If you are desperate to get a job or to persuade someone to do something for you, you may be tempted to exaggerate, modify, or even falsify information. You may also be tempted to resort to more violent or aggressive language. If you are conscious of your needs and how they affect communication, it will help you control and clarify the tone, content, and intensity of your message.

The Needs of the Receiver. Your receiver also has certain needs to be met in each situation. You should attempt to verify or estimate these needs in order to address them satisfactorily. Communication may fail if you do not satisfy the needs of the receiver. It may be necessary to include or exclude certain information, or couch information in certain terms to make it more acceptable to the receiver. If you were presenting a proposal to top management for a project costing $1 million, you would have to satisfy some need of top management to gain acceptance of your project. You would want to emphasize the advantages to top management (e.g., cost savings, return on investment) rather than detailing the project specifications.

The Knowledge Level of Sender and Receiver. The importance of knowledge to effective communication has already been established. The level of knowledge of both sender and receiver will have an impact on what is included in a message. If, as a sender, you do not possess knowledge, you obviously cannot include it in the message, and this diminishes the likelihood of accomplishing the objective of the communication. Take the time and effort to become adequately informed.

Sensitivity to the receiver's awareness and knowledge level is imperative. If certain information is already known or unnecessary to the receiver, it should not be included. If information is needed by the receiver, you certainly would want to include it. Classroom teachers must constantly make on-the-spot assessments of their students' knowledge to determine whether to elaborate or be brief on a given topic. If the teacher is not thorough enough, the students do not learn adequately; if the teacher is too thorough, the students become unattentive.

The Level of Sender/Receiver Interest in the Subject. If you have ever listened to someone speak about a pet topic, you know how intense and lengthy a message can get. What if that person is talking to someone who has little or no interest in the subject? Can you imagine the impact on the receiver's attention level? Students who have been forced to sit and listen to an instructor's complaints about the ineptitude of university administrators can readily appreciate this problem.

Imagine how frustrated a receiver might be if he had an intense interest in a topic, and you, having little or no interest, sent an abbreviated or incomplete message. Government employees are often perceived as uncaring or incompetent because although their work may seem routine to them, the service they provide may be monumentally important to a client. As a result their communications tend to be brief and insufficient, and the client goes away dissatisfied.

Be sensitive to the level of interest in the topic held by you and the receiver. Although your enthusiasm (or lack thereof) about a subject tends to dictate what you say, the receiver's interest should be the controlling factor.

The Sender's Attitudes toward Self and Receiver. In many communication situations individuals tend to feel quite confident and good about themselves. This usually results in more aggressive, confident language that is clearer and more direct. In other situations, individuals tend to feel uncertain about themselves and lack the necessary confidence to communicate effectively. They include more tentative, apologetic, and self-effacing message content, and this diminishes the clarity and overall quality of communication.

Likewise the sender's attitude toward *a receiver* will influence the content of a specific message. If a sender has *positive* feelings toward a receiver, the message may be more complete, informative, and sensitive. A *negative* attitude toward the receiver may result in incomplete, abrasive, perhaps even antagonistic, messages. For example, a co-worker who works hard and receives a promotion may be praised in glowing terms as "deserving," or abruptly condemned as an "apple-polisher." A well-developed sense of awareness of attitudes and their impact on communications is, therefore, essential.

The Attitudes of the Receiver toward Self and Sender. Just as a sender's attitudes toward self and receiver influence message content, the *receiver's attitude* toward the self can also influence message content. If a receiver's attitude toward herself is negative and *if the relationship is important,* the sender might devote some portion of a message to neutralizing the negativity and reinforcing positive qualities of the receiver or the relationship. In those situations where a receiver's attitude toward herself is *positive,* the sender, at his discretion, may or may not address the receiver's attitude. Consider, for example, the case of a child who lacks the necessary confidence to complete a task. Before assigning the task, the parent or teacher might address the child's interest and ability to complete the task, possibly complimenting certain necessary qualities which the child possesses. If, on the other hand, the child had the necessary confidence, the parent or teacher might simply make a brief positive reference to the child's abilities.

A receiver's attitude *toward a sender* may also influence message content. To the extent that a receiver's attitude toward a sender is negative *and the relationship is important,* the sender may devote some portion of the message to neutralizing the negativity and improving the relationship. If the receiver's attitude is negative and the relationship is *not* important, less time is spent on improving the relationship. For example, if you were communicating with someone who intensely disliked you, you would have a tendency to maintain a rather formal tone, limit your message to substantive content, and avoid emotional references (especially if the relationship was relatively unimportant). The more important the relationship becomes, the more likely you are to try to include some pleasant statements in your messages in an attempt to overcome the receiver's attitude.

When a receiver's attitude is *favorable,* a sender may want to devote some portion of the message content to reinforcing this attitude. However, in the case of a well-established, highly favorable receiver attitude, it may be unnecessary to devote much message content specifically to the relationship. This is most typically true in the case of close friends or working associates.

The Receiver's Time Span of Attention. Some receivers have a great deal of time to read and listen; others have precious little time for such activity. You should carefully estimate the amount of time a given receiver can or will devote to your message. If a receiver will allow only 3 minutes for what you consider a 10-minute message, you obviously have some editing to do. Whenever possible, determine the amount of time you will have before you begin planning your message.

The Relevant Socio-Cultural System. Our last contextual variable is based on Berlo's notion that senders communicate with receivers within a specific socio-cultural system, and there are many different systems.[7] The

sender must determine the particular system in which he or she is communicating at any time in order to be aware of the "norms" of that system. For example, as a student, you probably would not openly and directly criticize your instructor's lectures, but you might criticize a clerk's performance in a department store. Even if you did criticize your instructor, you would not use the same tone that you would use with the clerk. The reason for the differential treatment of the instructor and the clerk lies in the unwritten norms of acceptable behavior. Be aware of those norms to avoid conveying an improper message in improper terms. You must be aware of the relevant socio-cultural system and its norms to be effective.

Tone

In addition to selecting information (*what* is to be communicated), a second major decision concerning adaptability is *how* that information should be constructed. This very important issue is generally referred to as **message tone.**

Everyone can recall a situation where a message was judged not by what was said, but by *how* it was said (tone of voice). Likewise, we have all "read between the lines" of a written message. There was an unexpressed message created by the sender in these situations. These additional messages are referred to as **metacommunication.** Metacommunication as it relates to oral communication will be fully introduced and discussed in Chapter 3, Nonverbal Communication. In the present section we wish to address some of the sources of metacommunication directly related to language.

One researcher sought to determine which aspects of language were most likely to cause metacommunication.[8] Figure 2–3 lists and ranks techniques in terms of their likelihood of provoking metacommunication. These factors fall into two main categories: word choice and grammatical structure.

Word Choice. A natural outgrowth of a discussion on tone is a concern for word choice. A well-chosen, well-placed word or phrase frequently can be the difference between a successful and an unsuccessful message. For example, two college buddies, Melvin and Jack, were looking at some of Melvin's vacation photos. Jack pointed to an obese female in one of the photos and queried, "Who's that fat broad?" Melvin angrily replied, "That's my mother!" Imagine how Jack felt. The relationship between these two individuals was a bit uncomfortable, at least for a while.

The following word-choice considerations are presented to heighten your sensitivity to the power of words and their influence on tone. In turn, this should improve your effectiveness as a communicator and keep you from doing what Jack did in the previous example.

FIGURE 2–3 Techniques Most Likely to Cause Metacommunication

Writing technique	Rank
Grammatical usage	1
Euphemism	2
Split infinitive	3
Superlative	4
Spelling	5
Vocabulary	6
Phatic communication	7
Trite expression	8
Exclamation point	9

SOURCE: Marlin C. Young, "A Study of Four Problems Relating to Awareness of Metacommunication in Business Correspondence" (unpublished Ed.D. dissertation. Arizona State University, 1974), p. 37.

Functionalism (zero-base communication). Take the time to examine various objects commonly found in our environment (e.g., automobiles, trees, typewriters) and notice that there are no "extra" parts attached to these objects. While there are obviously some exceptions, most objects, whether manmade or natural, consist only of parts that serve some purpose. Likewise, your messages should be examined carefully to be sure that each word is proper, functional, and adds something of value to the message.

One way to achieve greater functionalism is to extract deadwood from your messages. Deadwood is defined as a word, phrase, or sentence that adds absolutely nothing of value to a message. We are quite abusive in our use of deadwood, as shown in the following examples. From a daily newspaper:

Original	**Corrected**
Genuine beef liver	Beef liver
(What other kind is there?)	
Semiboneless meat	?
(Do you give this to a semidog?)	
Video movies	Movies
(Perhaps this should be videotape?)	

From various television programs:

Original	**Corrected**
A complete sellout	A sellout
(Isn't a sellout a sellout?)	
A viable alternative	An alternative
(Is it an alternative if it isn't viable?)	

Original	**Corrected**
Fundamental basics	Basics
(Aren't basics fundamental?)	
Before a live audience	Before an audience
(Would you use a dead audience?)	

With commitment and practice you can eliminate meaningless words or phrases without altering the impact of your messages. The examples that follow are offered to help you recognize deadwood in some common phrases. Unnecessary words are lined out and substitute words are suggested in parentheses.

at this ~~point in~~ time (now)
in the near future (soon)
in the event that (if)
with regard to (concerning)
five ~~in number~~
make an adjustment on (adjust)
until ~~such time~~ (when)
during the period (while)
due to the fact that (because)
in ~~the state of~~ California
long ~~period of~~ time
we are ~~involved in~~ writing
one area of concern is ~~that of~~ training

Examine the following sentences and the alternatives.

Original: Robert and Joseph were conducting an intense conversation regarding whether canines or felines are the most covetable members of the animal kingdom.

Alternative: Bob and Joe were arguing whether cats or dogs were better pets.

Original: You cannot possess the finer confections within your grasp and simultaneously derive the delectation resulting from the actual consumption of those confections.

Alternative: You can't have your cake and eat it, too.

Many words and expressions are used as a matter of habit. Others are used to impress rather than to express a thought. These are incorrect reasons for choosing words; they imply a lack of deliberation and concern, and are an outright abuse of the receiver by the sender. Discipline will extinguish "choice-by-habit" behavior and reduce the temptation to impress. Take the necessary time to examine your messages and evaluate the appropriateness of each word you use. If a word serves no purpose, eliminate it! Words are not cheap; it takes time, effort, and money to prepare and convey a message.

Concrete versus abstract language. One characteristic of language highly relevant to adaptability and tone is the degree of abstraction possible through word choice. Just about any subject can be discussed using abstract or concrete words. Abstract words usually are associated with intangible ideas rather than concrete things. Concrete words, on the other hand, typically represent tangible things. We could discuss the meaning and advantages of freedom as an intangible privilege. Alternatively, we could discuss the right to vote, which is a concrete reality of freedom. We could talk about gross national product, or we could talk about tractors and loaves of bread. We could talk about living things or we could talk about cats and dogs.

The English language allows us to prepare messages at varying levels of abstraction or concreteness. Consider the following sequence of words: transportation, surface transportation, road transportation, automobiles, station wagons, Chevrolet station wagons, your blue 1985 Chevrolet station wagon. Whether we talk about the general notion of transportation, about automobiles as a means of transportation, or about your personal means of transportation is determined by the specific situation.

Choosing the wrong level of abstraction can significantly detract from the effectiveness of your messages. If you communicate at too high a level of abstraction for your receivers, they will not understand you and you risk frustrating, embarrassing, or offending them. For example, a plant manager who calls a meeting of supervisors and discusses the virtues of corporate excellence rather than how to solve the immediate inventory problems facing the supervisors succeeds only in turning off his audience.

If you communicate at a level too simple or concrete, your receivers may feel you are communicating "below their level." They may become bored or alienated. The executive who calls a meeting to discuss strategic planning and then insists on talking only about the specific problems in inventory control is likely to bore everyone except the inventory manager.

Another danger of abstract messages is that your receivers are, to some extent, invited to infer whatever concrete message they desire. If it is not the one you intended, you have miscommunicated. This often happens when a political candidate makes campaign promises in abstract terms to a broad constituency, and ultimately disappoints constituents by not meeting their specific expectations.

In summary, consider the situation and the receiver when you choose the level of abstraction or concreteness in your communications.

Jargon and technical language. Jargon is the technical language of a specialist group, and is usually meaningless or confusing to outsiders. The following examples are from a dictionary of terms used in coal mining.[9]

Blossom: the decomposed outcrop of a coal bed.
Bone: slaty coal found in the coal seam.

Creep: the forcing of pillars into soft bottom by the weight of a strong roof.

Horseback: a sharp rise in a coal seam.

Loblolly: huge mudhole in mine.

There is nothing inherently incorrect about the use of jargon; in fact, it is often necessary and practical. Such language is designed as a form of shorthand and makes intragroup communication highly effective. If a specialist is preparing a message for consumption by another specialist, jargon can be used to achieve greater clarity and to save time. It must be used with caution, however, when communicating with nonspecialists. Members of the legal profession, for example, have been criticized because their messages are so cryptic that no one but another member of the profession can understand them. For the nonspecialist user of legal documents, such "legalese" may be worthless at best, antagonizing at worst.

Some critics of jargon claim that jargon users abuse their specialized language by using it as a social device rather than as a communication tool. They say that jargon is often used to intimidate or embarrass nonspecialists, and make them aware of their outsider status. This temptation is present, but must be resisted at all costs. Jargon is a tool for more effective communication, but should be used deliberately with the receiver's identity and background in mind.

Denotative and connotative meaning.   When we look up a word in the dictionary, we may find two different types of meaning: denotative and connotative. The *denotative* meaning is the specific, direct meaning that serves functionally to point to or identify a thing or characteristic. The word *car* refers to a specific type of object that you could point at and say, "There is a car." Denotative meaning is objective and literally refers to or points to the thing or characteristic being discussed. It provides a kind of generic label for any instance of the thing we want to communicate about.

The *connotative* meaning, by contrast, is evaluative in nature. It is often ulterior, implied by the context in which the word is used and by the individual using it. Most words in the English language are used to convey several different meanings, and a thing or characteristic can be referred to or described using any one of several words. The denotative meanings of these words may be similar enough to identify the same thing or characteristic, but the connotative meanings may be quite different. Compare the words *cheap* and *inexpensive, house* and *home, female* and *broad, male* and *jock.*

The evaluative character of connotative meanings is extremely pertinent to word choice. For example, an individual who spends his or her income sparingly and frequently takes advantage of sales may be variously called *tight, cheap, thrifty, frugal,* or *wise.* All five words describe the be-

havior in question, but each represents a different evaluative reaction to such behavior. Which is accurate or appropriate? Any of the five labels may be correct or appropriate, *depending on the situation.* The meaning we convey is a result of our word choice, not the nature of the behavior.

Connotative meaning is a reflection of our individual values and perceptions, and we must carefully select words in view of each situation. A word that suitably conveys denotative meaning may convey a connotative message that is unintentional, offensive, and possibly even contradictory to receiver expectations.

Euphemisms and dysphemisms.

Frequently when composing a message, we are reluctant to use certain words or phrases (e.g., die, failure, incompetent, lie) because of the offensive associations and responses they elicit. Instead we choose a word or phrase that is more acceptable in its impact; die becomes *passed away,* failure becomes *nonfulfillment,* and garbage collector becomes *sanitation engineer.* These substitute words evoke a less offensive, or even positive, response and are called *euphemisms.*

On other occasions we use certain words to amplify a negative feeling and heighten emotions. For example, those who oppose the practice of abortion may label pro-abortionists as "killers," "murderers," or "baby butchers." Business executives refer to government regulation as "creeping socialism." Participative management is frequently labeled by its detractors as "communism." These substitute words which evoke a heightened negative response are called *dysphemisms.*

The skill required for euphemistic communication is highly marketable in our society. Government workers spend much of their time properly massaging facts to make them more acceptable. Instead of cutting the budget, for example, they would *modify monetary expenditures.* During the Vietnam War, a military campaign across international borders was called a *limited protective incursion.* Such communicators can command high salaries in advertising and public relations by enhancing the image of a company and its products through the use of euphemistic language.

Some language experts feel that the English language is in trouble. They observe that direct communication, has given way to communications that "sound good," even though they convey nothing. The epitome of this criticism is the Doublespeak Award given annually by the National Council of Teachers of English, which is intended to call attention to "dishonest and inhumane use of language." Candidates for the award include: "unlawful or arbitrary deprivation of life" (killing), "permanent prehostility" (peace), and "violence processing" (combat).

There is a danger of becoming insensitive to such abuses and dismissing them as amusing examples of bureaucratic ineptitude. Meanwhile, they may conceal morally questionable behavior and blunt our perceptions of a reality that is too painful to deal with.

The habitual use of such words is a blatant violation of effective com-

munication. Euphemisms are often pretentious and ornate. Dysphemisms tend to be too obvious in their negative character and are, therefore, distasteful. Consequently, both are ineffective and should be used sparingly. The use of euphemisms or dysphemisms should be intentional, based solely on situational factors.

Negative language.   Our final word-choice consideration concerns the negative and positive capabilities of our language. Whenever we communicate with others, we usually have some particular expectation in mind regarding the receiver's response. Stated in simple behavioral terms, we present a stimulus and expect a fairly specific response. The nature of the response generally is influenced by the nature of the stimulus. It is reasonable to assume that if we present a negative stimulus, we will get a negative response; likewise, a positive stimulus usually elicits a positive response.

The positive or negative manner in which we express our thoughts influences the tone of the message; the tone influences how a receiver perceives the message and responds to it. Use positive language whenever possible. Admittedly, positive messages are sometimes harder to compose than negative ones, but the benefits of a positive response are worth the effort. Don't say what you cannot do for an employee or customer; say what you can do. Don't tell a subordinate how not to do something; tell that subordinate how to do it correctly. Examine the examples that follow.

> I cannot have the salary figures ready by tomorrow morning.
> I can have the salary figures ready by tomorrow afternoon.
> You shouldn't use form A for nonskilled employees.
> You should use form C for nonskilled employees.
> Our customer representative cannot see you before next Monday.
> Our customer representative can see you next Monday.

In these examples the impact of negative information is minimized by expressing positive statements. By virtue of *expressing* the positive we are *implying* the negative. This can be quite effective; however, there are two unintended outcomes to be aware of.

First, the receiver may consider this approach deceitful, and may be offended. If so, you have compounded the negative; the individual responds negatively to the message *and* to the way it was presented. The receiver's emotional response in this case is, "Quit beating around the bush and get to the point! Who do you think you are talking to?" If such a response is likely, it is best to express the negative thought as simply and clearly as possible.

The second unintended outcome of the implied negative involves clarity of meaning. The receiver may not infer the negative as you intended. If not, you may evoke an incorrect response and place yourself

in the position of having to clarify the negative aspect of your original message. This could intensify the negative response by the receiver. For example, Bob Townes submitted a proposal for an equipment change in his department. After reading the proposal, Bob's boss decided that the proposal had merit but would be impossible to implement because of the cost. She called Bob into her office and explained, "Bob, your proposal has merit; however, you should concentrate on the other projects we discussed. Perhaps we can take a closer look at this proposal later." Because this was a project in which Bob was intensely interested, he was back in the boss's office one week later with the same proposal.

The effectiveness of implied negatives frequently depends on the awareness level or social perceptiveness of the receiver. You must be able to judge accurately the ability of the receiver to comprehend the meaning implied. Bob, apparently quite naive regarding the boss's method of refusal, believes the message meant what it said and goes back a week later. Eventually the boss will have to state her refusal in simple, clear terms. This may seem like a big buildup to a big letdown to Bob. If a negative cannot be implied clearly, with little or no chance of misinterpretation, it is best to express it simply and clearly.

Some critics feel that the easiest way to create a negative tone is to use negative words such as: unfortunate, sorry, regret, problem, difficulty. There is nothing inherent in these words that guarantees a negative response. What usually makes the difference between a positive and negative response is the context in which such words are used. Suppose, for example, that a customer service representative is responding to a claim concerning a defective product. In her message to the customer she states, "I am sorry this happened to you." The effect of this statement may be extremely positive because it is empathetic and shows the customer that the representative cares. In fact, if the statement were not included, the message might have a negative impact. Thus, contextual variables (receiver expectations) must be considered.

When words or expressions have a negative impact, it is frequently because they are unintentionally offensive or antagonistic. They give the impression that the sender is condescending or preaching, and have the effect of diminishing the importance or integrity of the receiver. Some examples are:

> Your company has not lived up to its claim.
> You don't know . . .
> You made a mistake . . .
> You failed to . . .

There are occasions where such words and phrases are appropriate; we suggest only that they be used prudently. The tone of a message is not usually set by one or two words; however, persistent and frequent use of negative words and expressions can generate a negative tone.

In summary, our recommendation is to state your messages positively. However, if contextual variables indicate that a negative word or expression is the clearest alternative for the intended effect, then use it.

Grammatical Structure. Since the word is the basic unit of communication you must give proper attention to word choice. With words you have the power to help or harm people, to make them feel good or feel bad. By speaking or writing the "right" thing in a given context you can bring people closer together or drive them apart. Since relationships are so vital in an organizational setting, saying the right thing and using the right words should be a never-ending challenge.

It is not enough to select words that are effective. You must be able to combine them properly for optimal impact on the receiver, and this requires a solid understanding of language and the capacity to use it. If you do not know and understand the basic rules of processing information, you will be at a definite disadvantage.

Social observers and researchers feel that our ability to use the English language properly is decaying. Because of this, we underscore the necessity for a solid foundation in grammar. Your exposure to language began as an infant and has been amplified through formal education beginning at about age six, and it is assumed that you have received adequate training in grammar. We will not review the basics of grammar in this text, but we feel it is appropriate to review some of the most frequently cited weaknesses and problems of grammatical usage in business communications.

Active versus passive voice. The *active voice* uses more action language and places emphasis on people or actors, whereas the *passive voice* emphasizes action or actor qualities. The active voice is more dynamic and certainly much clearer in most cases. There is less discretion in the receiver's interpretation because what is done and who does it are more clearly stated. Consider the following examples.

Passive Voice: The files were removed from the cabinet.
Active Voice: Mr. Brown removed the files from the cabinet.
Passive Voice: Fewer young people are being employed in favor of older workers.
Active Voice: Employers are hiring older workers rather than young workers.

The active voice places the people responsible for the action in the spotlight. There is no interpretation or guessing required as to who did what. In the first example, the receiver has no idea who removed the files. This invites the receiver to guess, investigate, become frustrated, or remain

ignorant. In addition, critics point out that the passive voice is a boring construction. The active voice generates more human interest because it calls attention to the actors. The obvious rule of thumb is to use the active voice as much as possible.

There are two exceptions to this rule. The first exception is when the action, rather than the actors, is more important. The accomplishment of a particular goal may merit more attention than the people who did it (hotel reservations have been made for vacation; physical inventory has been completed; inclement weather has ended). In such instances, the passive voice is appropriate.

The second exception occurs in situations where we prefer to avoid calling attention to the individual responsible for certain actions. For example, a trainee in a printing office applies too much lubricant to a machine, it malfunctions, and the office is delayed in delivering some of its clients' orders. The trainee is embarrassed and apologetic, and nothing is to be gained by identifying him and his mistake. The printing office manager could respond to inquiries regarding delays, by passively stating that the machine is down.

Subject-verb agreement.   A number of distracting grammatical constructions are the result of poor habits of grammar. One such construction is disagreement between the subject and verb of a sentence. The verb must agree in number with the subject: when the subject is singular the verb must be singular; when the subject is plural the verb must be plural. Compare the following incorrect constructions with the corrected versions.

> *Incorrect:* The union members wants the bargaining committee to push for higher wages.
> *Correct:* The union members want the bargaining committee to push for higher wages.
> *Incorrect:* The results shows a positive relationship.
> *Correct:* The results show a positive relationship.
> *Incorrect:* The criteria for promotion was explained to the workers.
> *Correct:* The criteria for promotion were explained to the workers.

Pronoun-antecedent agreement.   Pronouns reduce the repetition of nouns and allow greater freedom in sentence construction. There are, however, some recurring problems in the use of pronouns.

One distracting problem is disagreement between a pronoun and its antecedent—the noun it replaces. If the antecedent is singular, a singular pronoun must be used; if the antecedent is plural, the pronoun must be plural.

Antecedents and pronouns must also agree in gender. If an anteced-

ent is male or female, then the pronoun must be male or female. If the antecedent is neuter, the pronoun must also be neuter. Examine the following incorrect and corrected illustrations.

Incorrect: The committee forced their will on the organization.

Correct: The committee forced its will on the organization.

Incorrect: Each of the workers is entitled to their benefits.

Correct: Each of the workers is entitled to his or her benefits.

Incorrect: If anyone in the class is interested in what the professor had to say, they should let me know immediately.

Correct: If anyone in the class is interested in what the professor had to say, he/she should let me know immediately.

The pronoun must be carefully placed so that its antecedent is clear. This is particularly true when the pronoun could refer to either the subject or object in a sentence. The following example illustrates this problem.

Unclear: After the dean advised the student, he was upset. (Who was upset?)

Clear: The student was upset after being advised by the dean.

Consider another awkward construction.

Unclear: The employees exhibited a positive attitude toward the supervisors because they are fair. (Who is fair?)

Clear: The employees feel the supervisors are fair. As a result they exhibited a positive attitude toward the supervisors.

Modifiers. Another part of speech that deserves a warning label is the modifier. The use of modifying and conditional clauses is natural in communication. However, we sometimes go to extremes and instead of simplifying or clarifying an idea, we muddle it even more. Examples of this problem are common in legal and financial documents. Consider the following passage from a medical insurance policy.

For a pregnancy which exists when employment terminates and which would have been eligible for maternity benefits if employment had continued, coverage will be extended as follows, provided termination was for a reason other than termination of the coverage or for an amendment which would terminate this coverage for the person's present classification.

Did you understand the message? Consider one more example. When a school board refused to bargain with a local teachers union, the latter filed suit to force the school board to come to the bargaining table. The following is the formal ruling of the judge.

It is clear that under the federal statutory scheme upon which the state structure is in no small part based in the same areas of conduct to which the

Congress and the General Assembly have both addressed themselves, refusal of the defendants to bargain with certified union until disposition of the de-certification petitions would, at least under the National Labor Relations Act, constitute an unfair labor practice.

Did you understand the judge? How many times did you have to read his ruling? Could these examples have been stated more clearly? Trying to include too many conditions that bear on a thought tends to overload the thought and make it difficult, if not impossible, to understand. The result is a lack of communication.

There is another danger when using modifiers and modifying clauses. A modifier must be properly placed within a sentence so that the reader clearly knows what is being modified. An improperly placed modifier may result in frustration and confusion on the part of the receiver. Consider the following statements.

After baking in the oven for 30 minutes, I removed the mixture. (Who or what is baking?)

With a few corrections you should be in a position to complete your report. (Who or what needs to be corrected?)

No handbooks will be distributed to faculty members that are out of date. (Who or what is out of date?)

The questions that follow the above examples can be answered only by assumption on the part of the receiver. To remove any doubt in the mind of the receiver, and to eliminate the need to make assumptions, the statements could be rephrased as follows:

After the mixture baked for 30 minutes, I removed it from the oven.

With a few corrections to your report, you should be in a position to complete it.

No outdated handbooks will be distributed to faculty members.

Misuse of modifiers typically results from the violation of a basic principle of communication: create messages for your receivers, *not for yourself.* What is crystal clear in your mind may be muddy water in the mind of your receiver.

Parallel construction. Often a letter, report, or speech will contain a listing of several items such as findings, conclusions, or recommendations. To achieve greater message clarity, these items should be stated using a consistent or *parallel construction*. Consider the following examples.

Nonparallel: Feedback is advantageous because it allows greater clarity, you can be more precise, readability is enhanced, misunderstandings are minimized, and you can use it to greatly reduce conflict.

Parallel: Feedback is advantageous because it increases clarity and pre-

cision, enhances readability, minimizes misunderstandings, and reduces conflict.

The construction in the first statement is inconsistent, using the terms *you, it, readability,* and *misunderstanding* as the subjects. This inconsistency is conducive to confusion and miscommunication. In the second statement, the same construction is used consistently, and it clearly identifies *feedback* as the subject. It is easier to comprehend the list of advantages when parallel construction is used.

Sentence fragments. The final aspect of grammatical structure that merits special attention is the sentence fragment. A fragment is simply a partial sentence that conveys only a partial thought. The omission of part of a complete throught may leave the reader in a state of confusion, and the reader may fill in the blanks with incorrect content.

There are only limited situations in which the fragment, or "telegraphic message," can be successfully utilized. It can be used when the sender is absolutely sure that the omitted portion of the complete message will be understood by the receiver. This depends in large measure on the nature of the relationship between the sender and receiver. For example, close friends can often communicate successfully using telegraphic messages.

The fragment also may be appropriate when the context makes the omitted portion of a message clear. Consider the following passage from the earlier section in this chapter on Vocabulary:

You get five times as much with a $5 bill as with a $1 bill.
One hundred times as much with a $100 bill.

Note that the last statement is a fragment. The first two words of the previous sentence, "You get," are clearly implied by the context, and we can reasonably expect that this would be understood by the receiver. Consequently, the fragment is permissible.

Except under these special circumstances, the safest approach to effective communication is to use complete and coherent sentences.

Unity, Coherence, Transition, and Idea Arrangement

The emphasis thus far has been on word selection and grammatical construction. Yet it is necessary that all of the words and sentences fit together to produce a coherent, unified message. To create such a final product it is important to understand the notions of unity, coherence, transition, and idea arrangement.

Unity. *Unity* is combining or ordering parts into a whole to achieve a singleness of effect. A message should be unified in order to have pre-

---

FIGURE 2–4 Illustration of Unity

---

cisely the effect intended. All of the parts must be shaped and molded to appear to the receiver as a whole with an overall purpose. Speeches, reports, or letters that do not possess unity will appear incoherent and disjointed, just as surely as if they were missing some words. Figure 2–4 illustrates this point.

Figure 2–4A contains 10 randomly arranged asterisks that seem to be unrelated because they lack organization. As a result, they do not appear as a whole. In Figure 2–4B the 10 asterisks appear as two rows of 5 or, alternatively, as five columns of 2 asterisks. In this instance organization is enhanced by spatial arrangement. In similar fashion we should arrange words or ideas into a pattern to facilitate organization in the minds of our receivers. (In Chapter 5 we will have more to say about perceiving things in a unified manner under the topics of perceptual organization and closure.)

Coherence. To achieve unity, *coherence* is essential. Coherence is a systematic connection that ensures that the pieces blend together effectively. Think of how distorted and disconnected a completed jigsaw puzzle would look if the edges did not match and colors did not blend from piece to piece. You would perceive a number of separate pieces rather than a smooth, flowing picture. This is how your messages will appear without adequate coherence. All words, sentences, and paragraphs must stick together to form a unified message that will elicit the response you desire from your receiver. The key to coherence is effective *transition.*

Transition. Imagine yourself on a vacation, traveling by automobile from Washington, D.C., to Dallas, Texas. You would have to travel on a number of different highways. Suppose all of the signs showing the highway numbers, including those marking the junctions, were suddenly removed. Would you feel lost? Confused? Frustrated? How would you get to Dallas? How long would it take? Would you have enough time?

Verbal transition may be thought of as those junctions in the highway system, or the edges of the pieces of a jigsaw puzzle. Losing your reader or listener is especially easy when moving from one idea to the next. If a part of your message seems disjointed from or unrelated to that which

preceded it, the receiver may be left with a sense of confusion. Consequently, the reader is forced to determine the direction of the message. The direction taken by the receiver may not be the same one you intended, and miscommunication may be the result.

To prevent this, some transitional cue or sign must be provided to alert the receiver to expect what is coming. You must mentally take the receiver by the hand and lead him or her through the entire message. As your message moves from one idea to the next, there should be a smooth flow so that the reader does not get lost, confused, or frustrated.

The more unrelated or dissimilar the ideas are in a message, the greater is the necessity for good transition. Conversely, the more closely related the ideas are, the less hazard there is of losing or confusing the receiver. The more effective the transition is, the more the receiver will perceive your message as unified and logical.

Transition may be accomplished in a number of ways. A transitional cue is a word, phrase, or sentence that introduces or relates one idea to another. One approach is to use an explicit reference to ideas presented in a preceding or following section of your message. For example:

> The *preceding arguments* clearly establish the superiority of our product.
>
> The *following facts* can be used as a basis for implementing the new procedure.

Transition can also be effected by careful use of certain key words or phrases that tie parts of a message together. For example:

> First, . . . Second, . . . Third, . . .
>
> Free enterprise is based on certain responses . . . . One response is . . . . Entrepreneurship is another response . . . .

Another suggested means of transition is the use of conjunctions or "bridge" words. These are words that indicate a connection between parts of a message. Some examples are:

> *And*—signifies an addition.
> *But*—signifies a contrast.
> *However*—signifies a contrast.
> *Therefore*—signifies one idea logically follows another.
> *Consequently*—signifies one idea is the result of another.
> *Meanwhile*—signifies a shift or change in time orientation.

Idea Arrangement.   An integral part of unity and effectiveness is idea arrangement. The impact of your messages is greater if the flow of ideas is suited to both the receiver and the given context and purpose. Consider the logical flow of ideas. Is one point dependent on another? Will the

receiver understand and accept one point better if it is preceded by others? Which ideas should follow which for maximum clarity? Such questions must be answered from the receiver's perspective, *not from yours*! There are three common bases for idea arrangement: deductive, inductive, and chronological.

The *deductive* approach to arrangement involves movement from general to specific, or from main ideas to subordinate ideas. Using this approach, you begin by stating your most important information or idea at the beginning of your message. The main point then is followed by any necessary subordinate or supportive statements. Consider the following message.

> Thank you for submitting your paper to be considered for inclusion in the Academic Affairs track for the upcoming Fall Conference.
>
> You should be hearing from me around October 15 regarding the outcome of the reviewing process. If your paper is selected for the program, I will see that you receive instructions for preparing the Proceedings copy. If yours is a multi-authored paper, I will be communicating only with you in an effort to reduce the correspondence load connected with the conference.
>
> Again, thank you for your desire to participate in the conference. I look forward to meeting you in December.

The main point in this letter is to acknowledge the receipt of a research paper and to thank the receiver for the efforts. This is expressed in the beginning of the message and is followed by a number of explanatory or supportive comments. Information regarding what may happen in the future *as a result of receiving the paper* (subordinate idea) is included to make the message complete. This additional information is provided *in anticipation of the informational needs of the receiver.*

Additionally, it is worth noting that the supportive points all relate to the main purpose of the message. Any ideas that are totally unrelated may thoroughly confuse the receiver. If you must include an idea or piece of information totally unrelated to the purpose of the message, include a qualifying phrase indicating to the receiver the unrelated nature of that portion of the message. Otherwise, the receiver, after due consideration, may still be confused.

To summarize the deductive approach, the receiver is given the main idea first, followed by any necessary supporting information.

The *inductive* approach moves from specific to general, or from supportive points to the main point of a message. Thus, you begin by enumerating one or more specific subordinate ideas and moving eventually to the most important idea. This approach is especially applicable when it is useful or necessary for the receiver to digest the supporting ideas *before* getting to the main point of the message. The following text illustrates the inductive approach.

This morning we received your Form AB, listing the officers of your organization. Five of the individuals listed do not appear on our records as being members.

According to our records the chapter held initiation on December 10. We have not, however, received the initiation fees or membership forms for these initiates. Apparently, several of them are now officers in the organization.

We cannot recognize these individuals as officers or as members until their initiation records are complete. Please submit the required forms and fees at once so that we may add these people to our roll.

You will no doubt identify the main point in the last paragraph. The writer is in need of some specific information (and money) regarding new members of the organization. In order to request the desired response, the sender felt it necessary to offer the reader some supportive background information. The sender takes the receiver through a number of clarifying points to get to the main point. Only after these supportive explanatory ideas are expressed can the sender logically present the request.

To contrast the effect of the deductive and inductive approaches more clearly, examine the following paragraphs which contain essentially the same information. The only difference is the order in which that information is presented.

DEDUCTIVE

For the following reasons, I request that you dismiss the citation issued to me for illegally parking in a fire lane. I was not teaching during the summer term and had no particular reason to arrive early on campus. I was busy working at home, preparing for the fall semester, when I realized I needed a number of books from my office. Being an energetic and enterprising individual, I decided to drive to campus and get the books I needed. Since I arrived on campus after 10 AM, it was, as you well know, impossible to find a parking space. Considering that I had to haul many heavy textbooks from my office to my car, and that I would be only a few minutes, I felt it would be OK to park in the fire lane, especially since everyone else does so when loading and unloading. While in my office, I received an important phone call from my superior. Obviously I could not refuse the call, which took 10 minutes. By the time I returned to my car, there was a citation on it. Had it not been for the call from my boss, I would not have been in the fire lane.

INDUCTIVE

I was not teaching during the summer term so I had no reason to arrive early on campus. I was working at home, preparing for the fall semester, when I realized that I needed a number of books from my office. Being an energetic and enterprising individual, I decided to drive to campus to get the books. Since I arrived after 10 AM, it was, as you well known, impossible to find a parking space. Considering that I had to haul many heavy textbooks

from my office to my car, and considering that I would be only a few minutes, I felt it would be OK to park in the fire lane, especially since everyone else does so when loading and unloading. While in my office I received an important phone call from my superior. Obviously I could not refuse the call, which took 10 minutes. By the time I returned to my car there was a citation on it. Had it not been for the lengthy call from my boss, I obviously would not have been parked in the fire lane, and would not have received a citation. I therefore request that you dismiss the citation issued to me for parking in a fire lane.

A third possible arrangement is chronological, which is the arrangement of ideas in a time sequence. In many instances, a message deals with information concerning the occurrence of events past, present, and future, and the most appropriate arrangement for these events may be chronological. The following text illustrates the chronological approach.

> Our records indicate that on April 23 you ordered two films from us. On August 1 these films were sent to you for a three-day evaluation period. During our September inventory check we were unable to locate the films or any indication of their return to our office.
>
> Would you take a few minutes now to tell us if you have returned the films, the date on which they were shipped, and the method of shipment used. If you have not returned the films, would you please place them in the mail and drop us a note indicating the shipping date.
>
> We appreciate your attention and cooperation in this matter. It will help us to meet the needs of your colleagues who desire to preview the films. Thank you.

In this situation a chronology of events is traced and spelled out for the receiver in an easy-to-follow manner. What was done in the past is developed first, followed by what is now being done, so that plans for the future may be carried out. In many instances chronology is the best approach because it allows for a clearer presentation of ideas.

Idea arrangement can involve a combination approach in many cases. It is not uncommon to encounter a message that uses two approaches simultaneously. For example, go back and look at the illustration of the chronological approach. Note that it builds from a number of specifics to the main point of returning the films.

SUMMARY

We started this chapter with a statement about the importance of language. Because we use language to interpret, label, and communicate about reality, it is critical to understand its functions and limitations. The richer our appreciation of the role of language, the richer our communications and, therefore, our lives will be.

A significant part of language is words. English is a dynamic lan-

guage; words are constantly being added and deleted. Many words are used to convey multiple meanings. The 500 most frequently used words in the language have approximately 28 meanings each.

Even though we all have at our disposal the same words and rules of grammar, we continually experience communication failures. These failures stem from the dynamics of language, from individual differences between people, and from the manner in which these differences affect language usage.

As we progress from infancy to adulthood, we see and remember the world a little differently. Consequently, when we talk about it, we are each talking about something a little different.

The differences that make each of us unique are partially a function of concept formation, a process by which we form mental pictures or images of the people, places, objects, and events in our world. Concept formation involves generalization (observing commonalities), discrimination (observing differences), and transfer (moving observed differences and similarities from one situation to another). As we experience our environment we gradually develop and refine our concepts of the people, places, objects, and events we encounter. Simultaneously, we learn and attach labels or words to these concepts. These concepts and labels help us to structure our environment and bring order out of chaos. Without these concepts and labels it would be difficult, if not impossible, for us to communicate. What is critical and must be remembered, however, is that each of us develops a unique set of concepts and labels based on our unique background and experiences.

A prerequisite to effective communication is sensitivity to contextual variables, especially the receiver. Contextual variables include, but are not limited to, the objective of the message, sender-receiver relations, the needs of the sender and receiver, the knowledge level of the sender and receiver, the attitudes of the sender and receiver, the receiver's time span of attention, and the relevant socio-cultural system. The major challenge is to select the appropriate information and present it to the receiver within the context of the situation so as to achieve a meeting of minds.

A significant influence on receiver response is tone. Tone refers to how you express yourself, and it may be extremely formal, extremely informal, or any place in between. In written communication the exact tone you convey is manifested primarily by word choice and grammatical structure. The words you choose and the way in which you combine them are largely responsible for the impact of a message. Because words carry both denotative and connotative meaning, the appropriate words in any situation must be chosen very carefully and deliberately.

In addition to word choice, the construction of a message can influence the receiver's perception of the message and of the sender. To communicate effectively is to avoid some frequently cited weaknesses of con-

struction including overuse of the passive voice, frequent use of sentence fragments, improper use of modifiers, pronoun-antecedent disagreement, and subject-verb disagreement.

Beyond appropriate word choice and grammar, attention must be given to the overall structure of a message. Messages that are overloaded with too many ideas are difficult to read and comprehend. They are, consequently, potentially confusing and dangerous. Additionally, the parts of each message should be blended into a single unified whole. To achieve unity, coherence is necessary so that all words and ideas fit systematically together. Two ways to achieve coherence are transition and idea arrangement.

Verbal transition involves the use of a word, phrase, or sentence to mentally guide the receiver from one idea to another. Idea arrangement helps to order ideas for the greatest impact on a particular receiver. Three common arrangements are deduction, induction, and chronology.

The complexities of communication should be obvious from our discussion of the limitations of language and the complications created by individual differences. Effective messages do not come naturally; you must work hard, exercise discipline, and remain sensitive to the ideas and guidelines presented in this chapter. These guidelines are intended to help you develop the necessary sensitivity; the discipline and hard work are up to you.

DISCUSSION QUESTIONS

1. Discuss the various functions of language and their importance to the communication process.
2. Discuss H. R. Smith's treatment of the way individuals encounter reality and convey their perceptions. Emphasize Smith's ideas concerning the emergence of ambiguity in the communication process.
3. What point is H. R. Smith making when he declares, "Experience cannot be transmitted as experience"?
4. How are "maps" employed in language usage? Give some examples. What are some of the benefits and problems with the use of maps in language?
5. Define codes. Explain the significance of codes to language. Identify three codes other than the English language. Compare the elements and rules for combining them.
6. Distinguish between encoding and decoding. Use an example to illustrate the distinction.
7. Discuss whether or not the English language is relatively fixed in terms of its major elements, words, and rules of grammar.
8. Discuss in detail the three distinct conceptual capabilities that allow us to organize our world in a variety of ways.

9. Define generalization, discrimination, and transfer. Discuss their role and significance in the concept formation process.

10. Reflect on your initial weeks and months as a college student. What concepts did you have to seriously alter or refine? Compare your responses with those of your classmates? Were there any similarities? Why?

11. Define and distinguish facts, inferences, and value judgments. What role do they play in communication and miscommunication?

12. Describe four factors of effective communication that should be considered in adapting messages to a specific receiver.

13. How do sender and receiver attitudes affect communication?

14. Define abstract and concrete as they apply to word selection. What factors influence the level of abstraction in word selection?

15. What is the difference between the denotative and connotative meanings of words? Give several examples of each.

16. What are euphemisms and dysphemisms? Give examples of each. When, if ever, should they be used?

17. "An integral part of unity and effectiveness is idea arrangement." Compare and contrast the three common bases for idea arrangement.

EXERCISES

1. Draw a diagram illustrating the communication of a message through the coding process. Briefly explain your diagram.

2. List five concepts on a sheet of paper while a classmate does the same. Switch lists and see how many examples of each concept you can identify. Reverse the process by listing five or six examples of a concept and ask your classmate to identify the concept you had in mind.

3. Assume you are a new worker arriving on the job. List five concepts that would require some modification as a result of performing a new job for a new company. As a supervisor, explain how you could assist a new worker in this concept formation task.

4. Consult the books of *Exodus* or *Deuteronomy* in the *Bible*. Note that some of the 10 commandments are stated negatively. How would you restate them positively to be consistent with the others?

5. Record a television commercial and evaluate the message in terms of how well it was adapted to purpose, target consumer group, and context.

6. Compare the message from exercise 5 with an advertising message from a print medium. Note the differences, if any, in word usage. Why would the different media possibly require different words?

7. Write a 15-second commercial message for television with the purpose of selling:
   a. A snack food.
   b. A personal hygiene product.
   c. A compact car.

8. Write a coherent set of instructions for the following tasks, assuming that the reader has never seen these objects or performed these tasks before:
   a. Tying a shoestring.
   b. Putting on a coat.

NOTES

[1] Harry Hoiler, *Language in Culture* (Chicago: University of Chicago Press, 1954), p. 93; Edwin Hollander, *Principles and Methods of Social Psychology* (New York: Oxford University Press, 1967), chap. 9.

[2] H. R. Smith, "Communication by Ambiguity," *Readings in Interpersonal and Organizational Communication* (Boston: Holbrook Press, 1973), pp. 173–74.

[3] A. Korzybski, *Science and Sanity*, 3rd ed. (Lakeville, Conn.: The International Non-Aristotelian Publishing Company, 1948), p. 11.

[4] For a more extensive treatment of codes, see D. K. Berlo, *The Process of Communication* (New York: Holt, Rinehart & Winston, 1960), pp. 54–62.

[5] C. K. Ogden and I. A. Richards, *The Meaning of Meaning* (New York: Harcourt Brace Jovanovich, 1923).

[6] S. I. Hayakawa, "How Words Change Our Lives," *Saturday Evening Post*, December 27, 1958, pp. 22, 72–74.

[7] Berlo, *Process of Communication.*

[8] M. C. Young, "A Study of Four Problems Relating to Awareness of Metacommunication in Business Correspondence." Unpublished Ed.D. dissertation, Arizona State University, 1974.

[9] W. J. Roden, *Coal Miners' Jargon* (Big Stone Gap, Va.: Mountain Empire Community College, 1972).

SUGGESTED READINGS

Booher, Diana. "Writing More but Enjoying It Less?" *Training and Development Journal* 38, no. 11 (November 1984), pp 48–51.

Danesi, Marcel. "Visual Metaphors: Psycho-Linguistic Aspects." *Interfaces* 15 (March 1985), pp. 20–29.

Fielden, John S., and Ronald E. Dulek. "How to Use Bottom Line Writing in Corporate Communications." *Business Horizons* 27, no. 4 (July–August 1984), pp. 14–30.

MAX, ROBERT R. "Wording It Right (Correctly)." *Training and Development Journal* 39, no. 3 (March 1985), pp. 50–51.

PICKENS, JUDY E. "Language for All: How to Write and Speak without Bias." *Management World* 13, no. 10 (November 1984), pp. 34–35.

REEP, DIANA C. "Stop Writing the Wrongs." *Personnel Journal* 63, no. 9 (September 1984), pp. 68–72.

VARDAMAN, GEORGE T; CARROLL C. HALTERMAN; and PATRICIA BLACK VARDAMAN. *Cutting Communications Costs and Increasing Impacts: Diagnosing and Improving the Company's Written Documents.* New York: John Wiley & Sons, 1970.

Chapter 3

Nonverbal Language

Chapter 3 Case

You are a supervisor in the headquarters office of an international charity organization. Your division is responsible for the personnel activities for the organization's employees worldwide. You have spent a busy morning on the telephone averting crises. You've just loosened your tie, put your feet on the desk, and settled back in your chair to read the final report on the big campaign when one of the payroll clerks knocks on your door. "Come in," you say, "my door is always open. What can I do for you, Marge?" Marge takes a seat and begins droning on and on about her latest complaint. You've heard it all before, so you continue reading the report, making margin notes, nodding and murmuring all the appropriate phrases to Marge. The phone rings twice; each time you ask Marge to excuse you while you take the call. Just as you reach the final pages of the report, Marge's voice breaks into your thoughts. "You're right. A formal grievance is the only answer." She's out the door before you can get your feet on the floor to follow her. Where did you go wrong? You said all the right things, didn't you?

INTRODUCTION

"It's not what he said, but how he said it that upset me."
"I couldn't talk if I couldn't use my hands."
"It was written all over her face."
"He had laughing eyes."

You have probably heard most of these statements, and know their meaning. Interpreted literally, most of them sound silly, but each illustrates a different aspect of the increasingly important subject of nonverbal communication. We have discussed the role of language and how it influences our thinking and behavior. From earliest infancy we are impressed by parents, relatives, and other adults with the task of learning the mother tongue and honing our language skills. Our vocabulary is expanded, and

the rules of grammar are drilled into us each day for much of our first two decades of life, lest we suffer the woes of illiteracy later.

Most of us emerge from this process with some competence in language skills; we can speak, and we can write. Nonverbal communication is a fascinating area of interpersonal relations in which we receive no formal training. We learn it, painfully or joyfully, from everyday living. This lack of training and awareness is one of the major distinctions between verbal and nonverbal communication. If we are to be optimally effective in a managerial setting, we need to complement our language skills with a grasp of what nonverbal communication is and how to use it.

In this chapter we will identify the functions of nonverbal language and examine various ways in which it has been classified. We will also illustrate how a manager can use knowledge of nonverbal communication to create a healthier, more productive organizational climate.

THE SIGNIFICANCE OF NONVERBAL COMMUNICATION

Communication has been defined as sending and receiving messages. Most people consider communication in terms of the words they speak or write, but this ignores the very important role of its nonverbal aspects. In fact, nonverbal communication can often be of equal or greater importance than the actual words communicated. In a classic study, Mehrabian estimated that the total impact of a message may be represented by the equation:

$$\text{Total impact} = 0.07 \text{ verbal} + 0.38 \text{ vocal} + 0.55 \text{ facial/body.}[1]$$

In other words, the verbal message may contain as little as 7 percent of the effect of a message, while vocal qualities and facial and body movements make up the remaining 93 percent.

The impact of nonverbal communication depends on the channels and media being used. The Mehrabian formula applies in face-to-face situations. When communicating by telephone, the 55 percent for facial body is redistributed to verbal and voice; in writing a letter, the total impact is distributed between the verbal message and the tone created by the writer.

THE FUNCTIONS OF NONVERBAL COMMUNICATION

While verbal language can be used to communicate almost anything, nonverbal language is more limited and primarily reflects a sender's feelings, likes, and preferences. Brown and Keller have stated that nonverbal communication supplements the verbal so as to answer several questions that are aroused by verbal interaction.[2] Among these questions are:

How should I go about translating the statement?

How can I evaluate the person speaking to me?

What kind of relationship between us is being developed by this conversation?

The scope of these questions suggests the significance of the nonverbal portion of a message: nonverbal communication is the key to understanding the meaning of verbal communication. Consequently, as Knapp has stated[3]:

> Nonverbal communication should not be studied as an isolated unit, but as an inseparable part of the total communication process. Nonverbal communication may serve to repeat, contradict, substitute, complement, accent, or regulate verbal communication. [See Figure 3–1]

Let us take a closer look at some of the specific functions identified by Knapp.

Accenting

Paul Watzlawick and his colleagues tell us that messages contain meaning at two levels: factual content and information about the relationship between the sender and receiver.[4] A simple command to a subordinate not only informs the subordinate of the specific behavior the superior expects, but also defines the nature of the relationship by virtue of the superior giving the command to the subordinate and not the reverse. This relationship information is emotional and serves to support or underscore the verbal message.

When we communicate factual information, we often have an emotional response to the information that we feel compelled to communicate. We may think the information is good or bad, we may be pleased or displeased with it, but we fail to verbalize our emotions because language seems inadequate or incomplete for such disclosure. Consider the executive who is angry with a subordinate manager for making a serious mistake (e.g., grossly exceeding his budget). The executive could communicate his feelings by clearly and rationally stating that he is angry. He could say to the subordinate, "On a scale of 1 to 10, 10 being the angriest I can

---

FIGURE 3–1   Functions of Nonverbal Communication

Accenting:	Adding emphasis to the verbal message.
Contradicting:	Signaling the opposite of the verbal message.
Substituting:	Replacing the verbal message.
Complementing:	Sending the same message nonverbally.
Regulating:	Controlling the flow of the verbal message.

get, I am at 10!" But that may not be sufficient to indicate the intensity of his anger; it would not convey how the executive feels. Instead, he slams a door or pounds his fist on a table while screaming at the manager. Figure 3–2 illustrates one method of accenting a communication.

Contradicting

Some people are not in touch with their emotions and, therefore, cannot express them. Others have not learned how to express their emotions, or are embarrassed to do so. Some experts believe that as we are socialized, we learn certain roles that are indigenous to our age, race, gender, or socio-economic status. These roles prohibit public expression of certain emotions. The result is that verbal expressions of emotions are insincere and inaccurate descriptions of how we really feel, and they contradict the messages that are communicated nonverbally. See Figure 3–3 for an example of these contradictions.

If the nonverbal cues are compatible with the verbal message, we take the message as honest, straightforward, and sincere. If the nonverbal cues contradict what is said, we don't know what to believe about the message—we may disregard it altogether. Keltner has noted that:

> when information communicated through the nonverbal channels contradicts information communicated through the verbal channels, the nonverbally communicated information seems to predominate in the interpretation of the person receiving the two sets of information.[5]

FIGURE 3–2   Accenting

"I'm upset with you,
young man!"

FIGURE 3–3 Contradicting

"...and Horace is
signaling his delight at
your dinner invitation."

SOURCE: *Reader's Digest*, September 1985, p. 109.

Substituting

It appears from research that nonverbal language is much more widely used than previously believed, perhaps even more than verbal language. It is used in social settings (e.g., parties, bars, restaurants) to convey image, mood, or need. People are becoming more sensitive to it in business situations—in meetings, interviews, superior-subordinate relations. We are discovering that our dress, posture, and body language all affect our success in life. Some enlightened, enterprising individuals in the legal profession are using videotape to improve their ability to interpret and send nonverbal signals in the courtroom.[6] According to Dr. Elisabeth Kubler-Ross, a Chicago psychiatrist, even terminally ill patients communicate nonverbally that death is imminent.[7]

Considering the growing recognition and use of nonverbal language, it is fitting that it should function as a substitute for verbal messages on occasion. Figure 3–4 shows some everyday substitutes. Certain nonverbal cues have distinct meanings so widely known and agreed on that they have become an accepted part of our culture and our language. These cues, because of their distinct meaning and common usage, act as substitutes, conveying messages without any necessary verbal content. Objects and gestures, while not the only types, are excellent substitutes. A tongue-in-cheek account in the *Kansas City Star* illustrates how extensively we have developed substitutes.

FIGURE 3–4 Substitutes

As Americans lose the ability to speak coherently to each other in words, they speak increasingly in clothing, jewelry, gimcracks, and hair. Just the other night I met a woman whose finger told me she was divorced. The finger bore the latest thing in talking jewelry—a divorce ring. A divorce ring looks like a wedding band with a crack in it and costs between $300 and $350.

An expensive way, you may say, of notifying strangers that you have been in and out of marriage, and so it is, but in the age of talking costumes it is a commonplace sum to pay for the pleasure of avoiding conversation.

In Henry James's day, this woman and I might have had a subtle conversational encounter from which I might have ingeniously extracted her story. These days it is no longer necessary. Her Florentine purse instantly told me everything I needed to know of her reckless disregard for money, which had doubtless led to the divorce. Moreover, my Brooks Brothers suit and my naked ring finger told her everything she needed to know about me; to wit, that I was not an adventurer, that I was married, and that I was devious.

All this was announced by the suit which said, "Married, but not adventuresome," and the absence of a wedding ring on my marital-status communication finger, which said, "He is trying to conceal his married state." After my dreary old button-down collar had assured her that I had no eye whatever for chic, we moved apart, having communicated everything without having spoken a word.[8]

Complementing

To complement means to add that which is lacking or deficient to make a thing complete, to add something that is mutual or compatible. Body language is frequently used as a nonverbal complement for verbal messages. For example, most people, when giving directions, will support their verbal message with hand gestures. The directions could be given without the complementary gestures, but they are more complete and possibly more accurate with the gestures. We recognize the hand gestures in Figure 3–5 without any verbal message.

Other examples are a child who smiles and hugs her parents while pronouncing her love for them, or a new employee who stutters when reporting that she made an error.

Regulating

The political debate is popular spectacle during political campaigns in the United States. These debates occur in a carefully prescribed format with strict rules for controlling the agenda and opportunities for each person to speak. There is usually a moderator or regulator who controls the actions of the candidates.

In everyday interpersonal encounters there are no moderators or regulators to indicate when and for how long an individual may speak. Somehow this is worked out between individuals, usually without the use of any verbal messages. Instead, it is done with nonverbal language. We can convey our distaste for a particular subject and have it taken off the agenda. We can nonverbally tell an individual when we want to interrupt and say

---

FIGURE 3–5 Complementing

"Just a little bit!"   "Right on!"

something. We can signal when we want an individual to keep talking because we are interested in what she is saying. We can tell an individual when we want to end a conversation without uttering a word. This regulation is achieved with nonverbal cues. "Quiet, please" is the unspoken message in Figure 3–6.

For example, if John is conversing with Sue and needs to break off the conversation, he can continuously look at his watch, give very abbreviated responses to Sue, and discontinue eye contact. These cues act as signals to Sue that John wants to stop talking. At some convenient point, one of them will then break off the encounter.

TYPES OF NONVERBAL COMMUNICATION

We all send and receive nonverbal messages, but few of us have formally studied the complexities of nonverbal communication. Those who have studied it have developed several categories to help us understand and use nonverbal communication. Ruesch and Kees divided nonverbal communication into three areas: sign language, action language, and object language.[9] Hayes also places nonverbal communication into three categories: kinesics, paralanguage, and proxemics.[10] Goldhaber has devised three slightly different categories: body, voice, and environment.[11] A more exhaustive grouping offered by Emmert and Brooks utilizes 18 categories.[12] There are numerous other systems of classification that are

---

FIGURE 3–6 Regulating

Shhh!

even more specialized, depending on the researcher's interests. These classification schemes can be sorted into three commonly accepted major categories, as shown in Figure 3–7.

Kinesics: The Body

Within Ruesch and Kees' "action" category, Goldhaber's "body" category, and Hayes' "kinesics," we find the body. Kinesics is the study of communication through body motions, and there are numerous ways of describing and studying those motions. Birdwhistell, a pioneer in the field, classified the study of body motion into prekinesics (those motions the body is capable of), microkinesics (those motions capable of expression) and social kinesics (the specific meaning of specific motions in a given culture).[13]

Ekman and Friesen classified body language using five categories.[14] *Emblems* are intentional gestures with generally understood meaning: a sign language. Our culture is rich with emblems: the "V" sign for victory, the hitchhiker's thumb, or the index finger meeting the thumb in a circle for "ok!" Figure 3–8 gives a few examples of common emblems.

Illustrators are body movements that accompany or help to illustrate the verbal message. The movements are tied directly to the verbal message and serve to support or underscore it. For example, an individual could verbally describe an object and simultaneously form the shape or dimensions of the object with his hands or fingers, as in Figure 3–9.

Affect displays are movements, especially facial, which supplement the verbal message and show the emotional condition of the speaker. A wide, beaming smile denotes happiness of an employee who has just been promoted. Wide eyes and pursed lips indicate excitement and anxiety when a child visits Santa Claus for the first time. Affect displays are difficult to consciously control because they reflect our emotions. They are more accurate statements of how we truly feel and may contradict our verbal expressions. Figure 3–10 is an example of an affect display.

Regulators are head movements, eye movements, and vocalizations used to regulate conversation. For example, slow periodic head nods tell a speaker that the listener understands the message and to continue. A

FIGURE 3–7 Types of Nonverbal Communication

Ruesch and Kees	Hayes	Goldhaber
Sign	—	—
Action	Kinesics	Body
Object	Proxemics	Environment
—	Paralanguage	Voice

FIGURE 3–8 Emblems

series of quick nods, on the other hand, accompanied by an upheld open palm can signal the speaker to pause so that the listener can respond.

Adaptors are subconscious movements that allow us to adjust emotionally to the interpersonal climate in a given situation. These movements are frequently learned during early socialization as ways to respond to

---

FIGURE 3–9 Illustrators

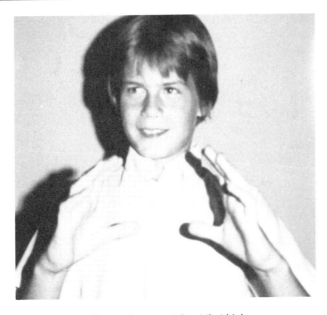

That sucker was at least that big!

FIGURE 3–10 Affect Display

situational pressures. We may experience tension, anger, joy, or other emotions which, for a variety of reasons, we cannot or will not address verbally. Instead, we deal with them by engaging in various gestures or behaviors which often appear as nervous tics. Examples might include smoothing the hair, drumming the fingers, jiggling a foot or leg, or fondling an object.

Body Size and Shape.   Many features of the body are capable of communicating messages instantaneously. For example, body size and shape have always been associated with various stereotypical traits and behaviors. In one of the earlier trait theories of personality, Sheldon identified three basic body types and accompanying behavioral characteristics.[15] Figure 3–11 shows these basic body types.

Endomorphs have short, fat, round physiques. They are typically assumed to be warm, sympathetic, soft-hearted, content, affable, and sociable.

Ectomorphs have thin, tall physiques. These individuals are characterized as shy, cautious, tense, serious, and self-conscious.

FIGURE 3–11 Body Shapes

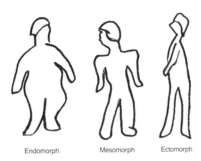

Endomorph   Mesomorph   Ectomorph

Mesomorphs have muscular, well-proportioned physiques. They are characterized as active, dominant, cheerful, energetic, courageous, and hot-tempered.

In addition to physique, other body features can generate nonverbal cues. These include, but are not limited to, skin color or complexion (e.g., black, white, fair, olive), gender, physical handicaps or blemishes, hair color or length, and body odor.

Posture and Gestures. Posture and gestures are frequently learned responses which tend to be culture-bound. They are one of the most revealing categories of body language and can be open and expansive or defensive and close to the body. Posture can yield clues about interpersonal feelings; leaning toward a speaker indicates liking and interest, while leaning away signifies dislike or disinterest.

People of higher status will typically assume a much more open, expansive, and relaxed posture in the presence of lower status individuals, who may assume a very rigid posture when with those of higher status. The executive who calls a subordinate into his office and proceeds to put his feet up on his desk may be sending, intentionally or unintentionally, a message of superiority to the subordinate. The subordinate may feel intimidated or resentful, and therefore demotivated, hostile, and uncooperative (see Figure 3–12).

Postural differences exist on the basis of gender as well as on the basis of status. A rigid posture from a man usually signals dislike, whereas from a woman it may signal liking. Women respond more consistently than men when confronting someone they dislike by constantly looking away from the person.

Congruent postures, or postural echoes, are mirror images of another's posture. For example, if one person shifts weight or direction, the other shifts. A posture echo typically signifies rapport, agreement, or identification, and is more likely between people of relatively equal power

FIGURE 3–12   The Effects of Posture on Behavior

© Gary Hovland

and status. Noncongruent posture between two individuals may be a signal of difference or dislike.

The Face and Head.   The face is probably the most complex of the nonverbal communication modes because it can express an extraordinary range of emotions. Facial expressions communicate the most personal types of information because the face is highly visible and makes intimate self-disclosures regularly and with ease. Dittman has stated that the face is a rich and reliable source of information about how the person behind the face is feeling.[16] Look at the facial expressions in Figure 3–13.

Many nonverbal signals emanate from the orientation of the head. A bowed head usually conveys shyness or withdrawal, while an upright head conveys confidence, alertness, and interest. A cocked head usually signifies curiosity, suspicion, or rejection. Cocking the head back slowly indicates disbelief or doubt.

Head nods are a positive sign, while lateral head shakes are a sign of negative feeling. Both can have a profound impact on the behavior of the person to whom they are directed.

Eye Movement.   As part of the richness of the face, eye contact provides a set of cues that we can use to help interpret a message and to understand the person sending the message. There is a great deal of justification for referring to the eyes as the "windows of the soul." For example, narrow, squinty eyes imply caution, thoughtfulness, or confusion. Wide-open eyes signify interest and attentiveness. Staring often is a sign of aggression and/or hostility.

FIGURE 3–13 The Face Is Capable of a Wide Range of Messages

In a conversation, the listener's eyes can be read to elicit his response. They can be used to regulate or control the speaker, or to express interest and involvement.

Seeking eye contact is a means of indicating a desire to open a conversation. The reverse is also true; if we want to avoid a relationship, or if we want to discontinue a relationship, we break eye contact. For example, students who are unprepared for class discussion or reluctant to participate in discussion will avoid eye contact with the professor.

Monitoring eye contact is helpful in detecting the listener's level of interest and openness. A noticeable lack of eye contact may be the cue that our message is not being received positively. An individual tends to increase eye contact with another when there is some positive response being received, and to avoid eye contact when there is some negative communication.

Proxemics: The Environment

Within Goldhaber's "environment" and Hayes' "proxemics," we find many cultural cues. These cues can be revealed in our use of space and our choices and habits of dress.

Space. We learn early in life what our culture considers appropriate in the management of space. It is axiomatic that most animals and humans tend to mark off specific territories for different activities such as mating, working, playing, and eating.

Edward Hall, who has written extensively on the subject, has identified three types of space: feature-fixed (permanently arranged space such as a building interior), semifixed-feature (space rearrangeable by moving objects such as furniture), and informal space.[17] In his discussion of in-

formal space, Hall has identified certain space "zones" that most Americans observe. These zones describe the physical distance people maintain in different situations:

Intimate—0 to 18 inches.
Personal—1½ to 4 feet.
Social—4 to 12 feet.
Public—more than 12 feet.

Hall's Space Zones are demonstrated in Figure 3–14.

As long as we maintain these proper distances, communication moves freely. When these distances are violated, we become nervous and uncomfortable, and communication is hampered. For example, the next time you dine with a casual acquaintance or a stranger, note carefully how you and your companion mutually agree, *without a word being spoken* to divide the table into equal shares. If you trespass by placing your possessions on your companion's side of the table, your action probably will provoke some defensive behavior from your companion. Defensive behavior may take the form of noticeable uneasiness or nervousness, pushing your possessions back to your side of the table, backing away from the table, or, ultimately, leaving the table. The net result in such situations is that we become concerned with protecting our territory rather than concentrating on the topic of discussion, and communication suffers.

Dress. In nonverbal communications dress is one of the most fascinating and consistent ways to send a message. According to dress expert and

---

FIGURE 3–14 Hall's Space Zones

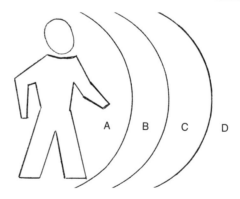

A (intimate) = 0–18 inches.
B (personal) = 18 inches to 4 feet.
C (social)   = 4 to 12 feet.
D (public)   = Beyond 12 feet.

author John Molloy, there are basically three reasons why man puts on clothing:

1. To protect himself from the elements.
2. To obey whatever his laws of modesty happen to be.
3. To "look" good to the people around him, or to the people he's going to meet, or to the world in general.[18]

Clothing can vary as much as the people who wear it, as shown in Figure 3–15.

With dress we can reflect image, mood, identity, power, wealth, or authority. M. L. Rosencranz studied the relationship between dress and work habits, values, and personality. She found a significantly high positive correlation between women's awareness of clothing and their socioeconomic status, education, and intelligence.[19]

It is easier to command respect when dressed formally (e.g., business suit) than casually (e.g., jeans and sweatshirt). M. Lefkowitz and his colleagues demonstrated the power of dress by showing that pedestrians will violate traffic lights more when led by a well-dressed individual than when led by a poorly dressed individual.[20] This is one of the important reasons people in positions of authority often wear specialized, easily identifiable uniforms (e.g., police officers, fire fighters, physicians).

Dress can also be used to convey such qualities as consistency, confidence, and comfort. For example, a visit to most fast-food or hotel chains will show that the employees who deal with the public are in some kind of dress uniform. This uniform signals to the consumer such desirable qualities as neatness, orderliness, and consistency. Galle and Patrick found that students confronted with constantly changing nonverbal signals from their professors' dress could not accurately assess the social climate in the classroom.[21]

FIGURE 3–15   Dress: Clothing and Its Messages Are as Diverse as the People Wearing It

We all wear our own personal uniform. It is our means of communicating to others who we are, what we are, and how important we are to the world. We hope that by revealing these things to those around us, we will elicit the kind of treatment we desire. This is especially true in the business organization.

Dressing for success in business is very big business. According to Molloy,

> Successful dress is really no more than achieving good taste and the look of the upper-middle class, or whatever is perceived by the greatest number of people to reflect these qualities.[22]

In the introduction to *Dress for Success*, Molloy advised his readers that dressing for success could help open doors to the executive suite, facilitate movement up the social ladder, and make selling easier.[23]

By developing an awareness of clothing and its impact, managers can communicate more accurately and completely with others in their environment. They can send more consistent cues to create and maintain the proper social climate, and possibly help their careers along at the same time.

Paralanguage: The Voice

Hayes's "paralanguage" and Goldhaber's "voice" constitute another area of nonverbal analysis. Paralanguage, or paralinguistics, deals with *how* something is said rather than *what* is said. Essentially it involves classifying characteristics of the voice. A popular scheme is that developed by G. L. Trager, who divided paralanguage into the four categories in Figure 3–16.[24]

Voice qualities refer to the voice itself and include pitch, rhythm, tempo, and volume. Voice qualities can make a great deal of difference in the interpretation of a verbal message. According to Davitz, a soft, low-pitched voice and a slow rate of speech indicate liking, whereas a high-pitched voice indicates anger. Moderate rate, pitch, and volume indicate boredom.[25]

Vocal characterizers include such vocalizations as clearing the throat, coughing, yawning, laughing, grunting, and crying.

FIGURE 3–16 Categories of Paralanguage

Voice qualities:	Pitch, rhythm, volume.
Vocal characterizers:	Grunts, coughs.
Vocal qualifiers:	Variations in volume, tone.
Vocal segregates:	Pauses, nonfluencies.

Vocal qualifiers refer to variations in tone or intensity of speech. A temporary increase in rate or volume, for example, shows impatience or anger, respectively. Nonverbal meaning from qualifiers is clearly illustrated by repeating the sentence, "I didn't say he stole your car," seven times, stressing a different word each time.

Vocal segregates are simply pauses or periods of silence between utterances, but may include "ah's," "um's," and other nonfluencies. Vocal segregates attest to the statement that silence can speak as loudly as words. Sterett, for example, found that job applicants that took longer than the average three seconds to respond to interviewer questions were rated less confident, less organized, and less ambitious than those who responded more quickly.[26]

To be unaware of the richness of paralanguage may be likened to listening without having your ears on. Many messages are communicated to us solely through these various facets of voice. Communication is more profitable to those who are able to sort and classify the nonverbal cues of paralanguage. In an argument, an individual may use volume (i.e., shouting) to convey certain emotional cues that the individual cannot or chooses not to verbalize. Regional dialects quickly communicate information to a listener about a speaker's background. We frequently infer as much from how a person speaks as from what is being said, and a knowledge of paralanguage allows us to do so more accurately.

MANAGERIAL APPLICATIONS

There is a growing body of literature attempting to relate nonverbal communication to various aspects of management. In this section we will identify a few major examples of this trend.

Motivation

One of the most significant areas of management research and development is motivation. Numerous studies have been, and continue to be conducted in an attempt to uncover the complexities of what motivates individuals, especially in the workplace.

One group of researchers investigating the concept of the "self-fulfilling prophecy" believes that how an individual behaves is a function of how he is treated.[27] According to Hill, motivation "is not so much a personal characteristic as it is a product of the interaction between an executive and an individual staff member."[28] A great deal of that interaction involves the use of nonverbal language to communicate managerial confidence and expectations clearly.

Baird and Wieting conclude that nonverbal cues can be used to communicate high expectations. These researchers draw on the literature to

identify desirable characteristics of a good superior-subordinate relationship. Among those characteristics identified are warmth, respect, concern, equality, and a willingness to listen.[29] Baird and Wieting observed that messages occur at two levels and set forth a number of ways in which nonverbal messages can reflect some of those desirable leadership qualities.

First, they recognize certain temporal features that can be instrumental in improving superior-subordinate relationships—the superior should be punctual, limit the duration of the meeting, and focus the agenda to suit the superior *and the subordinate.*

Second, the setting is important; it must be comfortable and nonthreatening, warm and inviting, not cold and formal. The physical distance between the superior and subordinate should be minimal, and the body orientation should be open and toward one another.

Posture should be open and relaxed; unfolded arms and legs can be used to show liking, interest, and attention. Gestures should be minimized, especially those that are distracting and negative (such as twiddling the thumbs or drumming the fingers). Touching is acceptable to convey trust and sensitivity.

Finally, the superior can enhance the interaction by conveying positive vocal cues. High pitch and volume will signify anger while soft pitch, low volume, and regular rhythm convey affection.

According the Baird and Wieting three conclusions are in order:[30]

1. Supervisors motivate or demotivate subordinates by communicating high or low expectations to them.
2. Much of that communication is accomplished nonverbally, so that environmental, physical, and vocal cues convey information to the employee.
3. By carefully using these nonverbal factors, supervisors can deliberately eliminate low-expectation cues and substitute behavior indicating high expectations.

Leadership

A variety of theories of leadership have developed over the past 50 years, but most agree that there is the need to display some regard and respect for the followers. This regard and respect can be clearly and accurately conveyed nonverbally.

M. Remland provides such evidence using social exchange theory. He first observes that, according to social exchange theory, "a superior gains influence over subordinates by exchanging behavior in a trade that is regarded as 'equitable' by the subordinates."[31] For example, a superior provides guidance and expertise (cost) to subordinates in exchange for esteem and status (benefit). The subordinate gives up a certain amount of

esteem (cost) to get the help needed to do her job (benefit). As long as the manager can maintain a reasonable balance between his costs and benefits and those of the subordinate, the relationship will continue satisfactorily. If the relationship becomes too costly for either member, it will be adjusted or ended.

According to Goldhaber, superiors (as higher status members) have more control over the environment than lower status members. Specifically he has stated three principles indicating that the higher up a person is in an organization:

1. The more and better space she has.
2. The better protected her territory is.
3. The easier it is to invade the territory of lower status people.[32]

Goldhaber's principles make it clear that superiors have control of the environment. Consequently, they have an excellent opportunity to convey their consideration for subordinates.

Remland describes considerate leadership behavior as that which "communicates high esteem or regard for subordinates by reducing the status discrepancy they perceive."[33] He goes on to point out that "the superior would be seen as more considerate to the extent that he or she is *given credit* for reducing the esteem cost incurred by subordinates."[34] Superiors can accomplish this by trading nonverbal displays of status for greater interpersonal influence.

Remland says we can accomplish this by respecting temporal norms of frequency, punctuality, content, and duration when communicating with subordinates. What typically happens in superior-subordinate contacts is that temporal norms are suited to the needs of the superior at the expense of the subordinate. According to Remland, managers can change this and benefit greatly.

The frequency of contact should not be unilaterally determined by the superior. If subordinates have an agenda, they should be able to initiate contact. The time of both superior and subordinate is important, and this message can be communicated by superiors who are as punctual as their subordinates.

Remland agrees with Baird and Wieting on the proper use of environmental factors. Figure 3–17 illustrates a very definite message from the environment. Furniture choice and arrangement can be used to establish a cold, formal, authoritative setting, or a warm, informal, cooperative setting. Improper spatial behavior may convey to subordinates the message that the superior's space is more important, and, therefore, the superior is more important. Remland agrees with Baird and Wieting that executive space is more expansive and better protected. This territoriality usually creates negative attitudes and messages (e.g., I'm better than you), and inhibits open, positive interaction.

In the area of kinesics Remland, like Baird and Wieting, feels that postures and gestures send strong nonverbal messages that could convey

FIGURE 3–17   Messages from the Environment

superior status and feelings toward subordinates. An open, relaxed posture conveys a lack of threat, while a closed posture signals a negative feeling.

Remland concludes that effective leadership depends on effective communication and a part of that communication is nonverbal By learning to encode and decode nonverbal language, managers can create better interpersonal relationships and function as more effective leaders.

Coordinating Words and Actions

Do actions speak louder than words? Yes, and managers should be acutely aware of this fact. Managers frequently confuse words with the objects they represent. Saying that something will happen is not the same thing as making it happen. Communicating words must be followed up with consistent actions. It is vital that managers get their actions in line with their words.

According to Tracy, actions serve two basic purposes:

1. They get the attention of an audience.
2. They reinforce a verbal message.[35]

Sometimes we use actions to get the attention of employees, but the action is mistaken for the message because the latter is either nonexistent or unclear. Tracy warns that to avoid misunderstandings of our actions we must carefully plan our actions so they will convey the same message as our words. Managers should consider the viewpoints of the employees by asking and answering such questions as:

How are they likely to interpret our actions?
What are they looking for?
What are they expecting?[36]

If the words of management build expectations and there are no consistent actions, rumors will exist in the absence of solid information and employee attitudes and productivity will be negatively affected. These consequences can easily be avoided using Tracy's commonsense approach:

> For good communication, words and action should be planned together. Plan your employee communications to coordinate with words. Be aware that action is easily misinterpreted, but also be aware that words without appropriate action lack force and are often unconvincing. Don't promise action and then fail to deliver.[37]

LIMITATIONS

The study of nonverbal communication is not an exact science. The use of language is limited by our inability to interpret and apply it consis-

tently. In the case of nonverbal language, there are many reasons why individuals demonstrate the vast number of cues they do, and not all of them "make sense." Before leaving the subject, we will identify a few of the shortcomings of nonverbal communication.

Culture

Nonverbal signals vary from culture to culture, from subculture to subculture, and even from individual to individual. Hall's space taxonomy can be applied nicely in our culture, but not necessarily in other cultures where the zones are quite different. In Spain, the manager of an apartment building where one of the authors lived onced backed the author completely around a dining table. The building manager was unknowingly and unintentionally violating the author's intimate zone.

Gestures and postures, temporal norms, and vocal cues also vary from culture to culture. This is why the peoples of certain nations and cultures have earned reputations for stereotypic traits and behaviors. According to one study, Jewish people exhibit short, choppy gestures and nervous energy. Italians use bold, sweeping gestures, while the French use elegance and grace, and the Germans use gestures more sparingly.[38]

Changing Roles

Roles and role behaviors created by various cultures prohibit certain kinds of emotional responses. Crying has been traditionally acceptable behavior for females, while viewed as a sign of weakness in males. If we cannot express our emotions verbally or nonverbally, we are not fully communicating with our receivers. Perhaps with changing roles (e.g., more androgynous behavior) in the latter part of the 20th century, we all will learn more about our emotions and how to express them.

Language Dynamics

We must learn to encode our emotions with new behaviors when we express them. These new behaviors require us to learn new nonverbal cues and negate some that we are already familiar with. We said in Chapter 2 that the English language is dynamic; so is nonverbal language. It is constantly changing, and that makes it difficult to understand and apply.

Signs, body language, and voice characteristics do not consistently mean the same thing. A person who continuously blinks his eyes and breaks eye contact may not be communicating anything whatsoever. The blinking may be simply the result of a physical condition, poor-fitting contact lenses, or a bad habit. In a cold room, folded arms could signal defensiveness or arrogance—or simply that the person is cold. Great care must be taken in decoding and interpreting nonverbal signals, but these

signals are an important dimension of our knowledge of communication and contribute to maintaining interpersonal relationships.

SUMMARY

We have described nonverbal language—the second major language of communication. Nonverbal language complements verbal language and often provides a means of accurately interpreting it. An understanding of nonverbal language is a necessary part of the manager's communication tool kit.

Nonverbal communication is vital and it is complex. There are at least five functions of nonverbal communication: accenting, substituting, complementing, contradicting, and regulating. There are three major categories of nonverbal language: kinesics or body cues; proxemics or use of the environment; and paralanguage or characteristics of the voice.

Managers who can accurately encode and decode nonverbal cues will be more effective in such important functions as motivation, leadership, and introducing change. The manager who ignores these cues or fails to develop the proper encoding and decoding skills might just as well attempt to communicate without a sense of hearing or the ability to speak. Consequently, much of the communication required for effective information sharing and relationship building will not happen. Therefore, the effective manager is one who is fluent verbally and nonverbally.

DISCUSSION QUESTIONS

1. Compare and contrast verbal and nonverbal communication. Explain how the two interact.
2. Knapp identified five specific functions of nonverbal communication. List these functions and explain three of them in detail.
3. Describe the three commonly accepted major categories of nonverbal communication.
4. Ekman and Friesen classified body language using five categories. Describe three of those categories and give examples for each.
5. Explain kinesics and describe the main areas studied in kinesics.
6. How do posture and gestures contribute to communication? Give specific examples for each.
7. How do the face and head play a role in communication? Give specific examples.
8. How does eye contact affect communication? Give specific examples.
9. What is proxemics? Discuss the various aspects of proxemics.
10. What is paralanguage? Describe the G. L. Trager classification scheme.

11. Discuss how dress affects communication.

12. Why is it important for a manager to be aware of the impacts of nonverbal communication? Discuss the interaction of motivation and nonverbal communication.

13. How are leadership and nonverbal communication related? What implications should a manager draw from this relationship?

14. Remland describes considerate leadership. Discuss his ideas in detail and explain why being considerate might be an important factor in leadership.

15. There are pitfalls for a manager when his actions and words conflict. Give some examples of conflicting managerial statements and actions. Indicate some practical steps that managers can take to remedy these conflicts.

16. Discuss some of the shortcomings of nonverbal communication. How can misinterpretation of a message be traced to the shortcomings?

17. Read the following statement aloud seven times, stressing a different word each time: I didn't say he stole your car. What differences in meaning are communicated by stressing the different words? Why is there an apparent difference when we stress different words?

EXERCISES

1. Stand at the doorway to a classroom, restaurant, or other public facility that seats a large number of people. Describe the pattern as individuals choose a seat. Can you offer an explanation for this pattern based on the concepts presented in the chapter?

2. Take frequent walks around your campus or city. When you encounter an individual walking in the opposite direction try to maintain eye contact until you pass. Note how many individuals are willing to maintain eye contact. As you maintain eye contact, vary your facial expression from a smile to a frown and note whether that increases or decreases the amount of eye contact. Also note any physical characteristics that differentiate those who maintain contact and those who do not.

3. Visit your university cafeteria or a city restaurant and take along some books or other possessions. Find an individual who is seated alone at a table, and ask the individual if you may joint him/her. Once you are seated, gradually, almost imperceptibly, push your belongings in the direction of your table mate. As you begin to take up more and more of the table, note carefully how he or she responds.

4. Study "The Attorney's Office" carefully. Identify and explain the numerous nonverbal errors made by the attorney.

The Attorney's Office

Recently, I scheduled an appointment at 2:00 P.M. with an attorney to discuss a civil case. He hadn't arrived at 2:10 P.M., and I asked his secretary if he was out for lunch. She smiled cunningly and said, "He'll prob-

ably be a few minutes late, as usual." I became resentful and was convinced that he was having a few drinks while I waited. Finally, at 2:25 P.M. he entered the office, walked over to me, and introduced himself. I expected to be taken into his office, but instead he excused himself to visit "briefly" with one of his partners. I remained standing for five more minutes (feeling rather awkward) until he returned and led me into his office. I sat down and noticed that he had left the door open. As I discussed the details of the case, he listened to me and signed 8 to 10 papers on his desk. After 10 minutes, the phone rang, he answered it, and said, "I'm sorry, I can't talk to you now, I'm with a client." As soon as he hung up, it rang again. This time he turned in his swivel chair so that his back faced me. He spoke with his caller, a woman, for about 10 minutes. I gave him a dirty look when he resumed eye contact with me. He promptly buzzed his secretary and asked her to "hold all calls." He then got up and shut the door. Just as I thought he was settling down to give me the attention I was paying for (at $40 per hour), he placed both feet on his desk, removed a brush from his desk drawer, and began to shine his shoes!

In this episode, much more was communicated than the words used as we discussed the case. In fact, the legal advice given to me by the attorney was quite sound. Yet, I left his office ready to file a complaint with the Bar.

SOURCE: Gerald H. Goldhaber, *Organizational Communication* (Dubuque, Iowa: William C. Brown, 1974) pp. 131–33. Used with permission.

NOTES

[1]Albert Mehrabian, *Nonverbal Communication* (New York: Aldine and Atherton, 1972), pp. 21–23.

[2]Charles Brown and P. Keller, *Monologue to Dialogue* (Englewood Cliffs, N.J.: Prentice-Hall, 1973), p. 97.

[3]Mark Knapp, *Nonverbal Communication in Human Interaction* (New York: Holt, Rinehart & Winston, 1972), p. 21.

[4]Paul Watzlawick, J. Beavin, and D. Jackson, *Pragmatics of Human Communication* (New York: W. W. Norton, 1967).

[5]John Keltner, *Interpersonal Speech—Communication* (Belmont, Calif.: Wadsworth Publishing, 1970), p. 112.

[6]Associated Press, "Nonverbal Communication Being Used to Help Judges," *Tulsa World*, February 1, 1981.

[7]"Expert Says Patients Signal Needs at Death's Approach," *The New York Times*, April 4, 1981.

[8]Russell Baker, "Attire All Too Revealing," *Kansas City Star* (*New York Times* News Service), December 1975.

[9]J. Ruesch and W. Kees, *Nonverbal Communication* (Los Angeles: University of California Press, 1956).

[10]M. Hayes, "Nonverbal Communication: Expression without Words," in *Readings in Interpersonal and Organizational Communication*, ed. R. Huseman, C. Logue, and D. Freshley (Boston: Holbrook Press, 1973), pp. 25–39.

[11]G. Goldhaber, *Organizational Communications* (Dubuque, Iowa: William C. Brown, 1974).

[12]P. Emmert and W. Brooks, *Methods of Research in Communication* (Boston: Houghton Mifflin, 1970).

[13]R. Birdwhistell, *Kinesics and Context: Essays on Body Motion* (Philadelphia: University of Pennsylvania Press, 1970).

[14]Paul Ekman and W. Friesen, "The Repertoire of Nonverbal Behavior: Categories, Origins, Usage and Coding," *Semiotics* 1 (1969), pp. 63–92.

[15]William Sheldon, *Atlas of Men: A Guide for Somatyping the Adult Male at All Ages* (New York: Harper & Row, 1954).

[16]Allen Dittman, *Interpersonal Messages of Emotion* (New York: Springer Co. 1973), pp. 113–14.

[17]Edward Hall, *The Hidden Dimension* (Garden City, N.Y.: Doubleday Publishing, 1966).

[18]John Molloy, *Dress for Success* (New York: Warner Books, 1978), p. 12.

[19]M. L. Rosencranz, "Clothing Symbolism," *Journal of Home Economics* 54, no. 12 (1962).

[20]M. Lefkowitz, R. Blake, and J. Mouton, "Status of Actors in Pedestrian Violations of Traffic Signals," *Journal of Abnormal and Social Psychology* 51 (1955), pp. 704–6.

[21]W. Galle and S. Patrick, "The Effects of Professors' Mode of Dress on Student Perceptions," Proceedings of the American Business Communication Association, Southeast, April 1982.

[22]Molloy, *Dress for Success*, p. 8.

[23]Ibid., p. 9.

[24]G. L. Trager, "Paralanguage: A First Approximation," *Studies in Linguistics* 13 (1958), pp. 1–12.

[25]J. R. Davitz and L. Davitz, "Nonverbal Vocal Communication of Feeling," *Journal of Communication* 11 no. 1 (1961), pp. 81–86.

[26]J. Sterrett, "Body Language and Job Interviews," *Journal of Business Education* 53 (1977), pp. 122–23.

[27]See, for example, D. McGregor, *The Human Side of Enterprise* (New York: McGraw-Hill, 1960); R. Rosenthal and L. Jacobsen, *Pygmalion in the Classroom* (New York: Holt, Rinehart & Winston, 1968); D. Eden, "Self-Fulfilling Prophecy as a Management Tool: Harnessing Pygmalion," *Academy of Management Review* 9, no. 1 (1984), pp. 64–73.

[28]N. Hill, "Staff Members Do Better When You Set High Standards," *Association Management* 9, no. 2 (1977), pp. 75–77.

[29]J. E. Baird and G. Wieting, "Nonverbal Communication Can Be a Motivational Tool," *Personnel Journal* 58, no. 9 (1979), pp. 607–10.

[30]Ibid.

[31]M. Remland, "Developing Leadership Skills in Nonverbal Communication: A Situational Perspective," *Journal of Business Communication* 18, no. 3 (1981), pp. 17–29.

[32]Goldhaber, *Organizational Communications*, pp. 150–52.

[33]Remland, "Developing Leadership Skills," p. 19.

[34]Ibid., p. 21.

[35]L. Tracey, "Do Actions Speak Louder than Words?" *Personnel Journal*, December 1982, pp. 882–83.

[36]Ibid., p. 882.

[37]Ibid., p. 883.

[38]F. Davis, *Inside Intuition* (New York: New American Library, 1973).

SUGGESTED READINGS

BULL, PETER. *Body Movement and Interpersonal Communication*. New York: John Wiley & Sons, 1983.

DEAL, TERRENCE E., and ALLEN A. KENNEDY. "Rites and Rituals: Culture in Action." *Modern Office Procedures* 28 (January 1983), p. 12.

HALL, JUDITH A. *Nonverbal Sex Differences: Communication Accuracy and Expressive Style.* Baltimore: Johns Hopkins University Press, 1984.

HILLISON, JOHN, and LORENZA LYONS. "Speaking without Words." *Journal of Extension* 20 (September–October 1982), pp. 14–17.

KATZ, ALBERT M., and VIRGINIA T. KATZ, eds. *Foundations of Nonverbal Communication.* Carbondale: Southern Illinois University Press, 1983.

REMLAND, MARTIN S. "Leadership Impressions and Nonverbal Communication in a Superior Subordinate Interaction" *Communication Quarterly* 31, no. 1 (Winter 1984), pp. 41–48.

THOMAS, ANDREW P., and PETER BULL. "The Role of Pre-Speech Posture Change in Dyadic Interaction." *The British Journal of Social Psychology* 20, no. 2 (June 1981), pp. 105–11.

Chapter 4

Channels, Media, and

Sociotechnical Systems

Chapter 4 Case

You are the CEO of a major manufacturing firm with plants located in 18 cities around the country. During the course of a typical day's work, situations such as those that follow will occur. What form of communication is best suited for each and why?

1. A new safety regulation has been mandated by OSHA.
2. A supplier in a remote overseas location has missed a critical shipment. You must determine when the shipment can be expected, notify the production departments affected, and find out how the delay will affect each one.
3. The cafeteria in the headquarters building must be closed for 10 days to replace asbestos insulation.
4. The dollar amount of all employee's paychecks will be less next month because Social Security withholding has been increased.
5. You have received an anonymous letter from a customer alleging that one of your sales representatives is receiving kickbacks.

INTRODUCTION

A frequent communication problem results from lack of careful attention to media selection. Despite the fact that business organizations have all the communications tools they need to communicate with great efficiency, company executives complain about the inadequacies of organizational communications and communicators. One factor that is often overlooked or not given proper attention is the selection of channels and media.

Assume that your management group has been given the responsibility to develop and implement a new company program. To do this, you must communicate with many people. What is to be communicated? To whom? By whom? When? What channels and media should be utilized?

The answer to any one of these questions may affect the total outcome and effectiveness of the new program. To be effective, there must be complete, accurate information communicated up, down, and across the organizational structure. The information must be communicated to the right people at the right time, and it must be transmitted using the most effective channels and media.

The organizational setting, including a company philosophy that is accompanied by policy and supported by top management, is essential to the success of a communications program. Also, the success of a communication may stem from the communicator and his or her effectiveness in choosing the right word at the right time. The relationship between the communicators, and the amount of trust that has developed between them, is a crucial factor in determining the success of communication. Finally, if the communicators knew what media were available, how to use them, and the advantages of each in different situations, it would aid in the proper selection of media and contribute to more effective communication within the organization.

DEFINITIONS

Some authors make a distinction between channels and media, but we prefer to think about and use these concepts together. The medium is the hardware of communication (e.g., letter, telephone, television, newspaper), and the channels are the *relationships* or communication *links* between two or more persons.

Another way of differentiating between these two concepts is to think of channels as oral, written, nonverbal, and multiple. The media associated with these are listed in Figure 4–1. Our concern in this chapter will be with selected media as defined and illustrated here.

CRITERIA FOR ANALYZING COMMUNICATION MEDIA

In many organizations, office communications have "grown up" with the business. Letters, reports, interoffice memos, bulletin boards, and the telephone are the most common forms of communication media. Today there are many media and forms of communication by which messages may be transmitted. The growing complexity of communication requires that an organization plan and organize its communication activities in order to select the proper media for each need.

Keeling, Kallaus, and Neuner suggest the following conditions as essential to all organizations that desire effective communications:

1. Information must be transmitted quickly enough to be current.
2. Information must be accessible, that is, easily retrieved for use.

FIGURE 4–1 Channels and Media of Communication

Oral	Written	Nonverbal	Multiple
Speeches	Letters	Touch	Television
Radio	Memos	Wink	Films
Telephone	Newspapers	Physical proximity	
	Bulletin boards		

3. Information must be provided on an economical basis, bearing in mind the volume of messages sent and the urgency with which each must be sent.
4. Information should be accurate and should be received in a usable condition.[1]

These conditions suggest the possibility of grouping communication needs by the urgency, the frequency, the speed and accessibility, and the cost of the message.

Other considerations that deserve attention in analyzing a communication system are:

1. The quantity and type of information to be provided.
2. The effect of peak load periods.
3. Message intensity.

Message intensity concerns the impact of the communication on the receiver, and individual needs must be considered. For example, some people perform better when orders and requests are transmitted verbally— others need written messages.

The best media for use by an organization can be determined by the effectiveness of the media. The most commonly accepted hierarchy of effectiveness of communications is as follows:

Level 1: The most effective communication is a two-way, face-to-face situation where *(a)* the verbal (the *meaning* of the words), *(b)* the vocalization (rate, pitch, force), and *(c)* the nonverbal (facial expressions, gestures, posture) all combine to give one intended message. Each person has the opportunity to see, hear, interpret, *and* both give and receive feedback.

Level 2: The next most effective communication is also two-way, but not in a face-to-face situation. Nonverbal aids are not available in this situation, and the intended message must be conveyed through verbal symbols and vocal emphasis only. Each party may hear, interpret, and have the opportunity for feedback, but the lack of any nonverbal communication severely limits the effectiveness of the communication.

Level 3: The least effective communication is a one-way situation. In the case of a letter, the receiver must rely on the meaning of the words (verbal), supplemented in a limited way by nonverbal aids such as the quality of the paper and the format of the letter. Immediate feedback is

not possible. In the case of a recorded telephone message or a television advertisement, vocal and/or nonverbal symbols may add to the intent of the message, but again, immediate feedback is not possible.

A summary of the criteria for selecting the most appropriate and effective channels and media is given in the next section. These include: availability, cost, speed, impact, purpose, interaction, and receiver capabilities.

Summary of Criteria

Availability.   The first step in the choice of media is to assess the current resources. What methods currently are available within the organization? Is there a newspaper or magazine? Does the organization have printing equipment? Are there bulletin boards, loudspeaker systems, or opportunities for face-to-face contact? When managers know what they have available, they can proceed to look at some of the other criteria for proper media selection and finally determine what new methods are desirable.

Cost.   As the availability of media is determined, the cost of using a given medium should be calculated. The cost must be weighed against the speed of transmission and the total effectiveness of the medium. For example, when speed is the most important consideration in communicating, a telephone call may be the most effective medium, even though it might be more expensive than a letter. If speed is not a factor, but interaction between the parties is necessary, the telephone might still be used. But if speed or interaction is not required, the cost factor might prevail, and the letter is judged equally effective and less costly.

Speed.   The urgency of a communication and the speed of using a given medium are other factors in the proper selection of media. If there is a necessity to communicate immediately, the choice of sending a letter could be disastrous. Urgency of communicating may also be tied to the choice of informal or formal channels. Informal channels of communication are faster than normal ones. If an informal channel is used, it should be reinforced by sending the same message through the formal channels. An informal channel (regardless of media) may meet the need for communicating quickly, but follow-up through a formal change gives additional credibility and authority. Of course, adequate planning may help to reduce much of the need for speed of transmission.

Impact.   Although an important or urgent message *may* require a medium that is fast, speed is sometimes a secondary consideration. The first consideration may be the impact of the communication on the receiver.

If an employee receives only written messages from the supervisor, a personal visit by the supervisor may have a greater impact on the employee than any combination of written messages. Also, since some channels and media that ordinarily carry a certain type of message may carry other types of messages less effectively, one should consider the use of several channels and media for maximum impact.

Purpose.   What channels and media are most adaptable to the purpose of the communication? Are you trying to inform? In communicating a quantity of technical information, a written report, supplemented by charts and figures, may have the greatest long-term effectiveness. If you are trying to stimulate, convince, or motivate, then a two-way, face-to-face mode of communication may be the most effective. This allows the meaning of the words to be enhanced by both the vocalizations and the nonverbal behavior of the sender and gives added intensity to the intended purpose of the communication.

Interaction.   Feedback and response may, on occasion, be the most important consideration in media selection. If the message is intended to teach a new employee to perform a complex task, it is best accomplished by a two-way, face-to-face interaction in which the employee has the opportunity to respond to the supervisor, and vice versa. A progress review of an employee may use a written document, but a face-to-face interaction is crucial to the interpretation, understanding, and acceptance of this written evaluation. The face-to-face method allows for a complete circuit, whereas a written medium typically provides for only one-way transmission of information.

Capabilities.   The capabilities of the receiver may be a crucial factor in determining the media selection. Is the person receiving the communication well educated? If the receiver's ability to read and understand is limited, an office memo explaining a new and complex method of purchasing supplies may go unheeded. A verbal message that is broken into small parts and is easy to comprehend may better explain the new method.

In applying these criteria, it is clear that the communication needs may be met by one form or the other. Written communications are more specific and provide documentation for the future. However, they are usually one-way and do not allow for immediate feedback. Oral, face-to-face communications allow for personal interaction—including immediate feedback—but can be forgotten later.

In a study reported in the *ABCA Journal*, Level suggests that communication methods are "situation effective"; that is, some situations call for oral, some for written, some for oral followed by written, and some

for written followed by oral. Ten business situations were identified as being communicated best by the following methods:

Written

1. Information requiring some future employee action.
2. Information of a general nature.

Oral

1. Employee reprimands for work deficiency.
2. Dispute settlement among employees concerning a work problem.

Oral/Written

1. Information requiring immediate employee action.
2. Information concerning an important change in company policy.
3. Communication of a company directive (order).
4. Information to (your) supervisor concerning work progress.
5. Promotion of a safety campaign.
6. Employee commendation for noteworthy work.

Written/Oral. This was not chosen as a most effective method by a majority of the respondents in the survey for any of the situations identified.[2]

A 10-year follow-up study by Goebel, Morton, and Level indicated that although managers *believe* that a combination of oral and written communication is most effective in all 13 sample situations studied, in practice they use methods much like those found in the first study.[3]

WRITTEN COMMUNICATION MEDIA

To decide what form of written communication to use, the media available should be outlined and examined for their particular advantages and disadvantages (see Figure 4–2). The media included here are: letters, mailgrams, computer electronic mail, interoffice memos and reports, facsimile reproductions, teletype messages, telegrams, electronic longhand transmission, newspaper and magazine publications, handbooks and manuals, bulletins and posters, and inserts and enclosures.

One advantage common to all forms of written communication is message documentation for future reference: the sender or receiver can check on the message sent. The disadvantage of written communication is the absence of nonverbal signals and immediate feedback integral to face-to-face communication.[4]

FIGURE 4–2 Written Communication Media

Medium	Most Frequent Use	Advantages	Disadvantages
Letter	External communication	Relative low cost; unlimited length; convenient for receiver and sender	Slow; reaches only one person at a time
Mailgram	External communication	Speed; relative low cost	Limited length for cost
Computer electronic mail	External communication	Speed; convenience	Equipment cost, receivers limited to those who own equipment
Telegram	External communication (global)	Available to any part of the world	Relatively high cost limits length
Facsimile reproductions	External and internal communications	Speed; accuracy	Cost
Teletypewriter	Interoffice or interplant	Printed record of a two-way conversation	
Electronic longhand	Interoffice or interplant	Speed; accuracy; security	Initial cost
Memoranda and reports	Internal	Unlimited length; low cost; convenient for sender and receiver	Delivery may be costly; excessive use may result in inattention on the part of receivers
Newspapers and magazines	Internal—company news or employee news	Reach a wide audience; can serve as a motivator for employees to participate in company activities; style reflects company philosophy	Limited to informal matters
Handbooks and manuals	Internal communication	Good reference for company policies, rules and regulations, benefits, etc.	May need frequent updating as policies and procedures change
Bulletin boards	Internal communications	Low cost; wide exposure	Improper positioning may result in inadequate exposure
Inserts and enclosures in pay envelopes	Internal communications	Wide exposure; low cost; high impact if sparingly used	Overuse may result in inattention by employees

ORAL COMMUNICATION MEDIA

The selection of written, oral, or some combination of communication media ultimately is left to the senders and their assessment of what will best accomplish a given purpose. Generally, oral communication is considered effective in more situations than written because of the opportunity

for immediate feedback. Private face-to-face communication, telephone conversations, conferences, and even speeches before large audiences allow for immediate interaction between sender and receiver(s). In addition, oral communication can reach many people at one time. When the speaker's status, prestige, or personality is viewed as highly positive, the "personal" touch of oral communication can aid in the immediate acceptance of a message by a receiver.

Figure 4–3 summarizes some of the advantages and disadvantages of various types of oral communication. Those included are: telephone, intercommunication and paging systems, closed-circuit television, conferences and meetings, and speeches.

SOCIO-TECHNICAL SYSTEMS

Alvin Toffler's book *Future Shock*[5] warned of a myriad of changes that have been predicted for the next few decades. He emphasized that many organizations would not be prepared to cope with these changes. Any change in an organization poses a challenge to managers for more effective communication, but those that involve the communication system require both human and technological adaptation.

The knowledge explosion, rapid product obsolescence, the changing composition of the labor force, an increasing internationalization of business, and newer and more sophisticated technological advancements are issues crucial to all organizations.

Information will have to be processed more quickly and accurately to aid in decision making. Interpersonal communications will have to be adapted to the needs of a changing labor force. Organizational communication systems must be developed to handle the massive information influx. Communications of the future will have to encompass both the human and technological aspects. This combination of human interaction and technological advancements is what we call a **sociotechnical communication system.**

Wilson Dizard comments in *The Coming Information Age* that the next stage of the new information economy is emerging. It involves industries and organizations, both private and public, that will be the primary users of the new high-technology network. Dizard says:

> Some of the most extensive changes will take place in business offices. The trend toward automated office operations is already running strong in large organizations. In the next decade, it will encompass even the smallest firms, making them essentially computer-based communication centers. The automation of office procedures will probably account for the largest dollar-volume share of the expanded information sector in the next few years.[6]

FIGURE 4–3   Oral Communication Media

Medium	Advantages	Disadvantages
Telephone	Relative low cost; wide variety of services (WATS, conference calls, answering machines, etc.), speed; immediate feedback	No face-to-face communication possible
Intercommunication (intercom) and paging systems	Low maintenance costs; convenience	Initial installation costs
Speaker type	Convenient for general announcements or locating persons within buildings	No privacy, little or no discrimination in transmission or sending between stations
Phone type	More privacy, selection in transmission	
"Bellboy" signaling device (beeper)	Good for keeping up with employees or other persons traveling within a limited geographic area.	
Closed circuit television		
For security	Most complete visual and auditory coverage	Cost limits use to large organizations
For announcements and to introduce new products within the company	Novelty; can reach many people at one time; provides at least one-way visual stimulus	Cost; time to produce materials; interruptions of regular work schedules
For training, welcome, and orientation	All employees receive the same information, information is complete	May be perceived as impersonal or boring, should be used in conjunction with other media
For evaluation of interviewing techniques or product presentations	Sales or interviewing personnel can receive feedback on their verbal and nonverbal styles	
Conferences and meetings (complete coverage in Chapter 7)	Two-way communication available, immediate feedback	If poorly planned and executed, they may be time-wasters
Speeches and oral reports (covered in detail in Chapter 11)	Permit interaction	If poorly planned or delivered, they may be boring and waste time

Two issues, telecommunications and information overload, are now of vital concern to the organizational communicator. Telecommunications will have a great impact on the nature of work when and as it becomes more computer mediated. Keen uses the term *compunication* to describe the linkage between computer and communication.[7] This linkage has be-

gun but is progressing slowly. This slow development does not mean, however, that it will be many years before dramatic changes occur.

One innovation that is in existence in Great Britain is an information network called Prestel. It supplies thousands of homes and offices with a full range of computerized information services. Dizard describes the system as follows:

> It is based on the telephone, the TV set, and a "black box" attachment that costs less than $200. The service is linked to hundreds of databases, providing hundreds of thousands of pages of information which can be ordered up on the television screen by dialing the appropriate computer through the telephone system. The data ranges from the frivolous to the practical to the profound. What is my horoscope for today? Who won the fifth race at Ascot this afternoon? Which library provides the best bibliographic information on the combinatorial mathematics of scheduling? Prestel tells all, for a fee that is added to one's telephone bill at the end of the month. It is a working system that is being replicated in a half-dozen other European countries.[8]

In Sweden, firefighters have an ingenious telecommunications system for ensuring efficient responses to fire alarms. Records are kept on each building, including construction features, number of occupants, and any special characteristics. Also, the quickest route from the nearest fire station to each building is calculated and stored in the data bank. When a fire breaks out, all of this information can be instantly retrieved on a computer terminal. This is an imaginative application of computer power, but Dizard points out its interest for another reason.

> The computer containing the data is located in Cleveland, Ohio. The 8,000-mile electronic round trip involved in the transmittal of information to and from the Cleveland computer was not a deterrent in awarding the data bank contract to an American bidder, the GE Company. . . . These networks are, in a very real sense, indifferent to time, place, and distance.[9]

New and complex technologies require a learning curve with long lead times before they are used to any great extent. On a graph, adaptation to the acceptance of change related to technologies may begin horizontally. After a period of incubation and acceptance, the learning curve takes off straight up the graph until it begins to level off.

Many businesses will not be able to keep pace with this rapid advance of technology. However, if business is to survive, two changes must be made: first, the organization should be designed around telecommunications; and, second, the basic managerial functions must be restructured.[10] A first step toward readiness for these changes would be to begin developing a training thrust toward careers in telecommunication to meet the needs of the future.

All organizational communicators currently face the crucial issue of information overload. One author claims this is evidenced by the fact that workers handle more information than they do material goods.[11] Al-

though information has increased, man's capacity for learning and adjustment to it has not, and our society has a mass of unprocessed information—an information overload or lag.

Two kinds of information are involved in the lag. First, there is additive, digital, or analytical information that is easily counted or categorized. Second, there is information that is a result of thinking and understanding—processed information. Calculated information, the first type, continues to accumulate quickly, while thought-processed information develops more slowly.

Several conditions lead to processing information more slowly. The human brain quickly becomes overloaded, and this creates a bottleneck. Some information is irrelevant to us, but we must process it before we realize it is of no use. Traditional meanings are rapidly being altered, and a variety of codes makes decoding difficult.

Most managers are frustrated by the inability to process information quickly and accurately. Data of all sorts are available, but it must be interpreted or sorted out, and that is difficult.

Communication overload has not always been a problem. If history had taken a different turn, we probably would not face this challenge today. Consider a fable about some 15th century citizens faced with evaluating a new technology.

> In the city of Mainz, Germany, Master Johann Gutenberg has just developed a machine that can reproduce manuscript-like pages in many copies. News of his work has reached the local ruler, the Elector of the Rhineland Palatinate. In the spirit of Renaissance inquiry, the Elector asks a group of scholars and businessmen to assess the new machine's impact on the local economy and culture. Since bureaucracy is just beginning to assert itself as an organizational force, the group is designated the Select Committee to Evaluate Multiple Manuscript Production.
>
> The committee visits Gutenberg's workshop, where the proud inventor demonstrates his machine. The committee is impressed, but skeptical. After considerable debate, the group submits its report to the Elector. The machine is undoubtedly a technological advance, the report concludes, but it has only limited application to Palatinate needs. The committee recommends that the government not invest research and development funds in the project. Its reasons are direct and cogent: (1) a large work force of monks copying manuscripts would lose their jobs if the Gutenberg machine were encouraged; (2) there is no heavy demand for multiple copies of manuscripts; and (3) the long-term market for printed books is doubtful due to the low literacy rate.[12]

If the decision of the committee in the fable had really been made, we would never face the problem or challenge of communication overload. But that challenge, and the challenge of telecommunications, is real. How do we come to grips with these issues? Calvin Pava urges management to foster the organizational learning and change that are needed to

extract maximum advantage from new equipment. He continues by saying:

> Management should formulate a general policy that leads others to explore opportunities for organizational learning and change. This policy should address not only operator training and procedural enhancements, but broader issues, namely, the structural and cultural variables that new information technology will inevitably affect (for example, the company's mission, strategy, human resource policies, and competitive advantages). While management should sanction organizational innovation in its statement of policy, it should not specify precise alternatives. This mixture of suggestion and ambiguity will cue members of the enterprise to the priority of organizational learning and change while leaving room for their own inquiry and subsequent contribution.[13]

Managers can encourage employees to learn more about the computer by rewarding them for their achievements. "You have to recognize strides," says Peter Pastor, associate product manager for Tang, in the beverage division of General Foods Corporation. "By rewarding the people who excel at computing in their jobs with plum assignments or promotion, you tell other people that the way to get ahead is by becoming more advanced—it's that and peer pressure."[14]

Interpersonal Relationships, Communication, and Socio-Technical Systems

When the term *cottage industry* was coined, home computers were the dream of only a few forward-looking engineers. Cottage industry originated with rural housewives in Vermont who worked at home—primarily during the winter months—making sweaters, scarfs, and caps. They worked at their own speed, on their own time, and sold their wares to local and regional clothing stores. The AFL–CIO felt that this activity violated federal laws prohibiting piecework and "sweatshops." The cottage industry has spread to *telecommuters*. A growing number of telecommuters work at home, at their own speed, on their own time, and sell their wares (the output of computers, word processors, terminals, printers) to the public.

Few would question the rapid increase in the use of computer technology in our society. Computers have gone beyond the office and now permeate elementary schools, colleges, and universities—even the home. The manuscript for this text was prepared on a home computer.

Projections for the future of the computer and the rapid growth in its number and importance is almost beyond comprehension. Most users of computers have extolled only the virtues of the computer and its effects. Recently there is a growing concern to some that computer technology will drastically affect the interpersonal relationships and communication behaviors among people. Renfro, for example, has said:

Sociologists . . . should be sending up warning flares about the sociological disaster the home office could bring. One of the principal functions of work in America, author Studs Terkel claims, is "schmoozing"—achieving a sense of companionship and togetherness among workers as they chat about their lives and gripe about common problems.[15]

These concerns are not limited to the telecommuter in an office or the home. They also affect the secretary who sits at a word processor much of the day, the supervisor who communicates with a terminal, and the student who spends much of his or her time in the computer lab at a college or university. Communication, sociology, and anthropology journals are giving more and more space to the avoidance of oral communication and interpersonal anxieties that may become the diseases of computer technology. Gratz and Salem have commented, "the promise of a new generation reared on Pac-Man, Space Invaders, and Computer Assisted Instruction, with *inadequate skills in relationship-building and manifest anxiety* when confronted with a quasi-open system poses a new hazard on this otherwise idyllic horizon."[16]

The lack of interpersonal stimulation and communication for those who spend several hours a day at a home computer or office terminal may become the overriding concern of future managers.

SUMMARY

Marshall McLuhan popularized the phrase "the medium is the message." This may exaggerate the importance of the medium to the total communication process, but many writers agree that "it is clearly no overstatement to say the right medium for the right message improves the chances of gaining a desired response from a receiver."[18]

Written communication provides records of messages that can be read (or studied in the case of a lengthy report) at the convenience of the receiver. It can also serve as documentation at some future time. The biggest disadvantage of written communication is the lack (or delay) of interaction and feedback. Written media discussed in this chapter, with advantages and disadvantages of each, included: letters, interoffice memos and reports, facsimile reproductions, teletype messages, telegrams, electronic longhand transmission, newspapers and magazine publications, handbooks and manuals, bulletins and posters, and inserts and enclosures.

Oral communication provides the advantage of interaction and feedback. It does not, however, provide documentation (except in the cases of recording equipment and CCTV). Oral communication media discussed in this chapter, and their advantages and disadvantages, included: telephone, intercommunication and paging systems, closed-circuit television, conferences and meetings, speeches, and oral reports.

In addition to each of the media meeting or not meeting (minimally or effectively) each of the criteria discussed, each medium must be evaluated in relation to the purpose of the communication and the capabilities of the receiver(s). These two items are "situation specific." In other words, each message is different, the purpose varies, and the receivers vary in their ability to comprehend the message. Thus, the sender must evaluate correctly the alternatives and determine priorities in order to achieve maximum effectiveness. The proper choice of a medium (or some combination of media) is crucial to the overall effectiveness of the communication.

Finally, the concept of a sociotechnical communication system was introduced. This is the blending of human interaction and technological advancements. Two of the most pressing problems that face managers today are telecommunications and information overload. These are challenges that must be adapted to and overcome. Management must redefine its goals and functions and continue to make positive use of technological advancements. In the words of Dizard, "In considering strategies for the information age, we must be aware of the psychic forces that have created the new environment. The most important of these is the American technological myth, the search for a new Eden through the melding of (human) nature and the machine."[19]

DISCUSSION QUESTIONS

1. Discuss three important factors that should be considered in selecting the best media for an organization.

2. List the various levels in the hierarchy of effectiveness of communication. Describe each level and explain why one level is more effective than another.

3. Discuss the conditions that Keeling, Kallaus, and Neuner recommend as essential to effective organizational communication.

4. List four of the criteria that are important in the selection of appropriate media and explain why each is important.

5. What does it mean to state that communication methods are "situation effective"? Give four examples of business situations that call for a specific form of communication.

6. List three written media commonly available to a business organization and discuss the advantages and disadvantages of each medium.

7. List three oral communication media and discuss the advantages and disadvantages of each medium, given a business setting.

8. Discuss the pros and cons regarding the use of oral versus written communication in the business setting.

9. Discuss the problems and the benefits associated with the sophisticated tech-

nological advancements of communication media in business organizations.

10. Define telecommunication and information overload. Explain their importance to the business firm and its management.

NOTES

[1]B. Lewis Keeling, Norman F. Kallas, and John J. W. Neuner, *Administrative Office Management*, 7th ed. (Cincinnati: South-Western Publishing, 1978), p. 162.

[2]Dale Level, "Communication Effectiveness: Methods and Situation," *ABCA Journal* 10, no. 19 (Fall 1972), pp. 19–25.

[3]Brad Goebel, Shelby Morton, and Dale Level, "Communication in Business: Situational Effectiveness & Usage," *National ABCA Convention*, New Orleans, November 1982.

[4]Keeling, Kallas, and Neuner, *Administrative Office Management*, p. 202.

[5]Alvin Toffler, *Future Shock* (New York: Random House, 1970).

[6]Wilson P. Dizard, Jr., *The Coming Information Age* (New York: Longman, 1982), p. 6.

[7]Peter G. W. Keen, "Communications in the 21st Century: Telecommunications and Business Policy," *Organizational Dynamics* (New York: AMACOM, 1981), pp. 54–67.

[8]Dizard, *The Coming Information Age*, pp. 7–8.

[9]Ibid., pp. 148–49.

[10]Keen, *Organizational Dynamics*, pp. 54–67.

[11]Orrin E. Klapp, "Meaning Lag in the Information Society," *Journal of Communication* 32, no 2 (Spring 1982), pp. 56–66.

[12]Dizard, *The Coming Information Age*, pp. 44–45.

[13]Calvin H. P. Pava, *Managing New Office Technology: An Organizational Strategy* (New York: Free Press, 1983), pp. 8–9.

[14]Henry Fersko-Weiss, "Managing Your Employees to Level 3," *Personal Computing*, June 1986, p. 98.

[15]W. L. Renfro, "Second Thoughts on Moving the Home Office," *The Futurist*, June 1982, p. 44.

[16]Robert D. Gratz and Phillip J. Salem, "Technology and the Crisis of Self," *Communication Quarterly* 32, no. 2 (Spring 1984), p. 102 [Emphasis added].

[17]John F. Magee, "What Information Technology Has in Store for Managers," *Sloan Management Review* 26, no. 2 (Winter 1985), p. 46.

[18]Walter St. John, "In-House Communications Guidelines," *Personnel Journal* 60, no. 11 (November 1981), p. 872.

[19]Dizard, *The Coming Information Age*, p. 22.

SUGGESTED READINGS

GREEN, DAVID, and KATHLEEN J. HANSELL. "Videoconferencing." *Business Horizons 27*, no. 6 (November-December 1984), pp. 57-61.

MILLER, MARC. "Electronic Mail: Can It Become a Corporate Alternative to the Post Office?" *Management Review 73*, no. 12 (December 1984), pp. 15–18.

PATKAR, VIVEK. "Vanishing Skills: A Need for Revival." *Human Systems Management 5* (Spring 1985), pp. 74–75.

PENROSE, JOHN. "Telecommunications, Teleconferencing, and Business Communications." *The Journal of Business Communications* 21, no. 1 (Winter 1984), pp. 93–111.

REINSCH N. L., JR., and PHILLIP V. LEWIS. "Communication Apprehension as a Determinant of Channel Preferences." *The Journal of Business Communications* 21, no. 3 (Summer 1984), pp. 53–61.

Communication Strata

Chapter 5

Intrapersonal Communication

Chapter 5 Case

You are a midlevel manager in a large urban bank. You have just come from your weekly head-knocking session where you and your fellow mid-levels, both men and women, have tried to get the older execs to see the wisdom in your plans for participative management and expansion. They ask for your ideas, and you give them. Then you all sit around the table and play a game of "yes, but." If this bank doesn't move into the 20th century, you think, none of you will have jobs. Such conservatism! From the way those guys talk, you'd think we were in another depression, and everybody knows that can't happen again.

What's the problem here?

INTRODUCTION

Language plays an extraordinary role in communication. Much of our thinking about, reaction to, and control over our environment is a direct consequence of our facility with language. We have explored the reality of individual differences and their impact on communication. In this chapter we will expand the notion of individual differences, focusing on those attributes that tend to influence the communication abilities of the individual.

PERCEPTION

We constantly take into account various aspects of our environment and store them for future use. This "taking into account" is called *perception*. Webster defines perception as an "awareness of the elements of the environment through physical sensation, interpreted in light of experience."[1] There are at least two noteworthy points about this definition. First, awareness comes through physical sensation. We frequently think of perception as seeing, but perception occurs through all five senses. We often

perceive with more than one sense, using each sense to substantiate or refine what is detected and interpreted by the others. For example, a cup of dark brown liquid perceived only by sight could be interpreted to be paint, coffee, soda, or tea. If we felt the cup and noted that it was hot, this would suggest that it contained coffee or tea, but we still could not be certain. If we smelled or tasted the liquid we could determine what it is.

The second point to note is that interpretation is an essential part of perception, and it occurs within the context of our past. Our present perceptions are a combination of what we are currently perceiving and what we have already perceived. In the example above, we would define the dark liquid (reality in this case) in terms of those possibilities we are familiar with—paint, coffee, soda, or tea. If the dark brown liquid was a foreign substance, we would have to learn a new concept to accompany the new part of reality we "discovered."

Based on our definition we can identify three distinct steps in the perceptual process: *access, awareness, and interpretation.* Look for a moment at Figure 5–1.

Access

You cannot attend to any stimulus in the environment unless you somehow have access to it. This requirement sounds rather elementary; however, it is often overlooked. For example, if a manager does not maintain proper contact with subordinates, he cannot personally or directly become aware of one subordinate's pleas for direction, or the need to reinforce the outstanding performance of another. Another example would be when a manager prepares a letter, memo, or other announcement regarding the work environment, but fails to distribute the message effectively. If the message is not accessible, employees cannot possibly become aware of it, much less interpret and respond to it.

Awareness

Guaranteeing access to environmental stimuli does not, of course, guarantee perception. We do not pay attention to all of the stimuli that constantly bombard us, but we selectively detect and attend to only certain ones. This behavior is referred to as **perceptual selectivity.** Take a moment and focus on each of your senses. Listen to the sounds you were not

FIGURE 5–1 The Perception Process

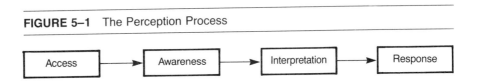

aware of a moment ago. Notice the details around you that you had not seen earlier. It should not take you long to note something "new." This is because you have been highly selective in your previous perceptual behavior.

We engage in selective perception for two basic reasons: *self-interest* and *physical limitations.* We usually attend to those aspects of the environment that are consistent with our past experiences and support our current view of reality. Study your environment carefully for a few minutes and closely note the colors, textures, and detailed features of the objects and people around you. As you do so you will begin to realize just how much detail you had not previously paid attention to.

The number of details in the environment in which you are *not* interested is overwhelmingly greater than the number of things in which you are interested. When you do pay attention to something new in your environment, it is probably because it has become important to you. Think about some part of your environment that has recently come to your attention for the first time. Why has it come to your attention?

We also engage in selective perception because we do not have the time or energy to attend to everything in the environment. Think for a moment about all the books you would have to read, all the trees, birds, and flowers you would have to become aware of, all the laws of nature you would have to understand. Think about how little you actually know about many of the people in your environment. How long would it take you to learn all these details? There is no way that you can attend to every detail in the environment. Fortunately, you don't want to. But if you do choose to focus your attention on an environmental stimulus, you must subsequently interpret the stimulation.

Interpretation

Interpretation provides us with an understanding of our encounters with environmental stimuli and allows us to decide how to react to those stimuli. A key process that facilitates interpretation is **perceptual organization.**

Imagine how confusing it would be if you awoke to discover that someone had moved all of the familiar objects (furniture, buildings) in your environment to a different location and had changed all the familiar markings. What if each day you had to reassess and designate the people you considered friends and enemies? Such frequent changes would make life most difficult. To increase the predictability in our lives (and, therefore, our ability to cope with life), we organize and store information about things and people in previously defined categories for quick and easy reference the next time we encounter them.

When you meet an individual for the first time, you begin collecting information about that person—age, place of residence, occupation, reli-

gious preference, education, gender, and attitudes. Based on this information, the individual is placed into certain predetermined, predefined categories such as old, young, black, white, friendly, egotistical, threatening, lives in my neighborhood, good person to study math with, or a person to avoid. This determines what the person means to you, if anything, and how you want to respond to him or her.

The next time you encounter the individual or discuss him or her with someone else (assuming you choose to do so), you will recall the information you already have stored. The information or, more precisely, the *categories in which you stored the information* will provide the cues for your responses. Further encounters will also afford the opportunity to collect additional information and, if necessary, reclassify the individual.

Stop and reflect on some of your recent experiences with new foods, new places, new activities, and new people. Did you categorize them? How? How did you respond to them? How will you respond to them in the future? What do they mean to you?

We interpret and attach meaning to our new experiences by comparing them with those stored in our memories, noting similarities and dissimilarities. If the stimulus is consistent with stimulus-related information and experiences we already have stored, we will accept and assimilate it into one or more storage categories (e.g., a good place to eat, a trustworthy individual). If the stimulus is inconsistent with our current information, or if we cannot use our stored experiences to explain the inconsistency satisfactorily, we will reject it. Alternatively, we may place it in a new temporary or tentative storage category until we assimilate it into memory or make a judgment to reject it. The stored information will be used in the future to help us cope with the environment. (Review the section on concept formation in Chapter 2 for further explanation of how we assimilate new experiences into our current view of reality.)

We structure our perceptions by two methods: figure-ground and gestalt. In the figure-ground approach, the individual focuses on one object while the remainder of the environment acts as a backdrop. This approach emphasizes the importance of context in perception; what we see depends on what is available for comparison in the environment. For example, a piece of gray paper will look much lighter when compared to black paper than when compared to white paper. An atmospheric temperature of 65 degrees would seem cooler in June than in January. Figure 5–2 contains some examples of figure-ground patterns.

In the gestalt approach, we see relationships between the parts of the environment that result in a pattern. Rather than focusing on just one object at a time we group everything into an explainable whole. Look at Figure 5–3A. Do you see a series of unrelated spots or a picture of a dog? In each example, organization is enhanced by spatial arrangement.

Basic to the gestalt approach is the principle of **closure:** the tendency to mentally fill in "gaps" in existing information. Closure allows us to in-

FIGURE 5–2   Figure-Ground Patterns

A.

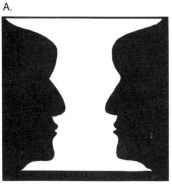

B.

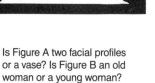

Is Figure A two facial profiles or a vase? Is Figure B an old woman or a young woman?

terpret incomplete information and formulate a response based on that information. There is a danger that we will fill in the blanks with inappropriate information and, consequently, make an inappropriate response.

Attribution, the tendency to impute causality, is another basic principle of the gestalt approach. Not only do we see a complete picture but we "make up" an explanation for what we see. We impute relationships between objects, people, or sequences of events. We may even attribute motives to the people in our perceptions.[2]

FIGURE 5–3   Gestalt Patterns

For example, a plant manager arrives at work one morning and finds a group of union organizers in the parking lot handing out union literature. He sees a group of employees huddled together, one of whom has been known to be sympathetic to unionization. The manager perceives that the sympathizer is a part of the organizing effort and is trying to persuade the other employees to actively support the union.

The employees could be talking about last night's football game, how to solve a long-standing production problem, or any of a number of things unrelated to unionization. The manager has chosen to see a relationship between all of the individuals and activities in the parking lot. His interpretation of what he sees will further reinforce his view of and responses to the sympathizer.

According to H. H. Kelley, individuals attribute behavior to other individuals on the basis on three primary factors:[3]

1. *Consensus*—How others would handle the same situation as the perceived individual. For example, when a manager has to deal with a problem employee, would other managers handle the situation in similar fashion?
2. *Consistency*—How the perceived individual behaves when the same situation recurs. For example, when a manager must reprimand employees, does he always do it the same way?
3. *Distinctiveness*—How consistently the perceived individual behaves across a variety of situations. For example, is a manager inept just at reprimanding employees, or does he botch everything?

SITUATIONAL INFLUENCES ON PERCEPTION AND COMMUNICATION

Why do we attend to certain specific details of the environment? Why do we interpret the objects and people in our environment the way we do? Why do we respond to them as we do? We can answer these questions by identifying some of the major factors that account for individual differences in perception and communication.

Look at Figure 5–4. Is the circle round or lopsided? Focus your attention on the circle long enough and you will see that it appears to be lopsided. In a sense, the circle represents the world around us, which exists in some purely objective and measurable state. We could analyze the air around us and define it in terms of temperature, humidity, and barometric pressure. We could measure and define this book in terms of its weight and thickness, or in terms of its chemical composition. We could describe a person biologically or chemically using objective, scientific measures and principles. Alternatively we could describe the air as hot or

cold, the book as interesting or boring, and the person as short or tall, fat or skinny, attractive or ugly.

Our personal characterizations of reality do not always coincide with the objective version. Our view of reality is distorted much as the circle in Figure 5–4 seems distorted. What causes us to see a distorted circle? It is the lines that are superimposed over the circle. Each of us superimposes a uniquely individual set of lines over the objective environment and we all have our own unique set of lines.

Those lines constitute our **perceptual set,** the "window" through which we view the world at any given moment. Because we each have a different perceptual set, we see and communicate about a slightly different world. There is an old joke that illustrates this. If you ask a mathematician how much 2 + 2 equals, he will answer 4. If you ask a statistician, she will say, "Something between 3 and 5 with a high probability of 4." If you ask a politician, he will say "Whatever you want it to be." Imagine how complex and challenging it must be for a group of representatives from such diverse areas as marketing, production, personnel, engineering, and finance to arrive at a decision concerning a companywide problem.

The perceptual set is composed of all the factors that influence us as we perceive and communicate about our environment. These factors are many and varied: some are constant, others are fleeting; some are intense, others are quite weak. During an important meeting you may have a headache or feel some hunger pangs because you did not eat breakfast. These temporary distractions could keep you from being an effective listener or from participating in an important decision.

There are three influences that impact on the perceptual process:

FIGURE 5–4   Perceptual Distortion

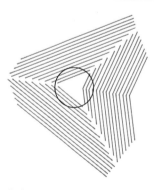

Is the circle round or lopsided?

characteristics of the perceiver, characteristics of the perceptual target, and contextual characteristics (shown in Figure 5–5). These mental and psychological characteristics can have a continuous and cumulative effect on the individual's perceptual behavior. The inherent features of the objects and people being perceived and the contextual variables operating in the environment are also important in their impact.

Characteristics of the Perceiver

Our perceptions are consistent with our self-interest and our current view of reality, and certain factors within the perceiver dictate that current view. Knowledge of those factors could give us insight into an individual's perceptual behavior and, therefore, allow us to be more effective communicators.

FIGURE 5–5   Influences on Perception and Communication

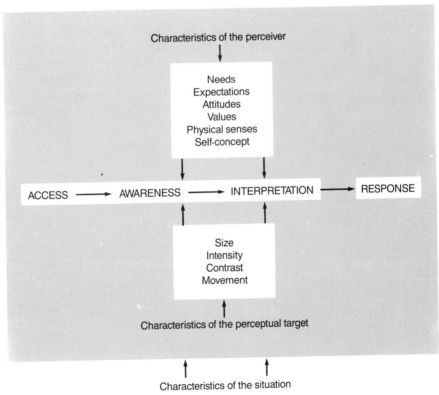

Needs. One of the most temporal and changing perceiver characteristics is the set of needs operating within the individual. There are many different theories explaining how our needs affect our behavior. Maslow's theory of a need hierarchy suggests that the search for satisfaction of our needs is what compels us to behave as we do. Maslow separates human needs into five different classes: physiological, security, social, esteem, and self-actualization.[4] Herzberg's controversial duality theory identifies many needs which are separated into two major categories: motivators and hygiene factors.[5]

These and other theories separate needs into two general categories: physical and psychological. Physical needs affect the body and include food and protection from the elements. Psychological needs affect the mind and include protection from arbitrary action by others, membership in organized society, and self-development. The type and intensity of needs will vary from individual to individual. Consequently the goals individuals set for themselves and how they choose to accomplish those goals differ immensely.

Our needs have an immediate and profound effect on what we perceive and how we perceive. Assume you are on vacation and have been driving all morning. As lunchtime approaches, your stomach begins to growl, and you may stop noticing the sights along the highway and watch for only one thing: restaurant signs. Your perception of a police officer who gave you a speeding ticket would be different than your perception of a policeman who helped you when your were mugged.

Consider an example in the workplace. Jerry Simmons, a conscientious worker, is being considered for a promotion. He has heard no news about the decision, is growing anxious, and begins to focus more and more on everything his boss says or does. If Jerry's need for information is acute enough, it will heighten his attention to his boss's words and actions, perhaps even to the point of misinterpretation.

Because needs influence perception, they are also a primary influence on our communicative responses to environmental stimulation (i.e., what we say and how we say it). In the example above concerning the police officer, imagine the language used by an individual who is about to receive a speeding ticket. Compare that to the language used by the individual who is assisted by a police officer after being mugged. Imagine Jerry's response if he doesn't get the promotion he is hoping for. He may become verbally abusive with his superiors, his co-workers—even his family. Our communicative behavior is frequently an outward reflection of our needs.

Our needs influence our perceptions, and what we perceive has an impact on our present and future needs. What we learn about the environment helps us to develop and shape our needs. Much of the racial strife of the 1960s in the United States and the continuing strife in many Third World countries can be attributed to the experience of the "have-nots" discovering the affluence of the "haves." As the former group hears

and reads about a better standard of life, they gradually establish a new pattern of needs. This new pattern of needs subsequently influences their response to the environment. Physical violence (including revolution) may be the only response deemed effective by the have-nots. Gradually, as needs are reformulated they influence perceptions. This reciprocal influence continues to shape not only who and what we are, but also who and what we expect to be.

Expectations.   Another powerful influence on perception is the set of expectations we carry into a situation. Frequently a situation possesses characteristics similar to past situations. Those characteristics (which we have organized and stored for future use) will be recalled and will mentally prompt us to "see" similar features in the current situation. This happens when we enter our homes, offices, and other places. It also happens when we encounter friends, neighbors, or co-workers. This tendency to see things the same way as before is referred to as **perceptual constancy.** When we enter a relatively new situation, we review in our minds whatever knowledge we possess regarding the situation (e.g., experience from similar situations, what we have been told) and create a set of expectations about the way things should be or the way we would like them to be. Once we develop these expectations in our minds, we perceive reality as we expect to perceive it. It is very difficult to proofread something you have written; you see on paper what you are mentally set to see.

Expectations are particularly powerful because we like a certain amount of predictability in our lives. We like to anticipate outcomes accurately and tend to respond to situations in a way that will guarantee that we are right. In effect, we behave in accordance with our expectations. A widely accepted concept in management literature is the *self-fulfilling prophecy.*[6] According to this concept a person will take appropriate actions to guarantee a particular outcome that is consistent with his or her perceptions and expectations. Consider the following example.

A manager who perceives an employee as marginally productive and expects the employee to fail will respond in a way that guarantees that outcome—regardless of the employee's actual potential. A major part of the manager's response in this instance will be her communications with the employee. Nonverbal communications, which constitute the relationship climate, will tend to be either nonexistent or of poor quality, and encouragement to perform at higher levels will tend to be minimal. Thus, while expectations are basic to what we perceive, they are also a key to how we respond.

Knowledge, Feelings, and Behavior.   In Chapter 2 we said that concepts are learned "mental pictures" of objects, people, and events. As we

develop a new concept, we often attach some emotional value to that concept (e.g., good, bad, love, hate). Such value-laden concepts are called **attitudes.** Attitudes have motivational qualities that predispose us to respond in a particular way toward objects, people, and events in our environment.

Attitudes are learned through *socialization,* the continuous process by which we learn to function as social beings. With assistance and pressure from the family, the school, the church, peer groups, and other socially valued individuals, we are taught what to believe or disbelieve and what to like or dislike. The resultant system of beliefs and disbeliefs, likes and dislikes, ultimately directs our behavior. We can dissect an attitude into its three components to illustrate this influence:

1. *Cognitive*—reflects the knowledge we possess relative to a particular subject. It predisposes us to certain beliefs and disbeliefs.
2. *Affective*—reflects our basic emotions relative to a particular subject. It indicates our basic likes or dislikes.
3. *Action tendency*—identifies our basic behavioral readiness or possible response to a particular subject.

To understand these components and their relationship clearly, consider the attitude of most people toward one of nature's least understood animals, the snake. Because most people know little about snakes, they have reasoned or been taught (i.e., they believe) that all snakes are harmful. This, of course, is not true.

On the basis of limited knowledge and negative beliefs, most people dislike snakes (i.e., their emotional response is negative). Consequently, most people behave predictably by withdrawing from or attempting to destroy snakes. Even more predictable are the verbal and nonverbal responses of most people when discussing snakes.

An individual's response to an object or person is influenced by likes and dislikes, and those in turn are influenced by the quality and quantity of knowledge a person possesses. What we believe and how we feel can have a definite impact on what we say and how we say it. This is frequently made clear by the open conflicts between management and labor during contract negotiations. Basic disagreements can make communication difficult, and at times even impossible. The more we understand an individual's attitude toward a subject, the more effective we can be in our communication encounters.

A word of caution is in order regarding attitudes and emotional behavior. Just as our height, weight, and hair color are a part of our physical makeup, our emotions are a part of our psychological makeup. It is difficult (if not impossible at times) to turn them on or off at will, and this sometimes makes it difficult to be an effective communicator.

Any stimulus, under the right conditions, might cause a loss of emotional control. It could be a person's looks, the length of his hair, the

language he uses, or an idea he expresses. A sender may unknowingly "with a phrase or two, show utter disregard for an idea you hold dear . . . and instead of thinking constructively . . . you let your emotions get away from you."[7] When this happens, productive communication ceases and argument and counterargument replace useful dialog. Each person tunes out the other person and starts a mental debate, and there is little possibility of awareness and understanding. Consider this example:

Husband (after a rough day at the office):   Dear, where did you hide the bottle opener?

Wife (who has also had a rough day):   What's the matter with you, are you blind? It's where it always is!

According to Harris,[8] such a transaction would end any search for the bottle opener while the husband and wife debate each other's organizational abilities, "blindness," and stupidity. The bottle remains unopened, and an argument is well under way. In the next chapter, Interpersonal Communication, we will examine several models that suggest ways of understanding and controlling our emotions as we interact with others.

One final point must be made before we leave attitudes. To the extent that our concept formation and attitude development abilities continue to mature, our needs become more sophisticated. In essence, the more we learn, the more we need. The flow of influence is obviously reciprocal. As our needs change and grow, they tend to influence the extent to which we learn new and more sophisticated concepts and attitudes. A college student, for example, who feels the need for personal and professional growth, must learn new concepts and develop new attitudes consistent with that need. Consequently, there is a "snowballing" effect as these factors continually interact and influence each other.

Values. Values are ideals or "ways of life" that reflect the qualities of living we have determined to be important. These qualities are learned through the socialization process, and are taught initially by the "moralizers" in our environment (parents, preachers, teachers, employers, politicians, doctors). These individuals try to persuade us to subscribe to certain concepts of right and wrong behavior that serve as the foundation for our values. As we mature, if we have been encouraged to think independently, we will begin to assess and clarify the values that will lead us through our adult lives. Values, like attitudes, are important because they have a profound and lasting influence on our perceptions of, and responses to, the environment. Consequently we do not change our values frequently or abruptly.

As we expand our social environment and interact with individuals with different values, we seldom modify or change our values. Change, when it occurs, is the result of a powerful influence by an extraordinary individual or some traumatic experience. We may encounter an individ-

ual (teacher, employer, political leader, future spouse) who will inspire us to change the way we view important parts of life. You may recall a teacher or other individual in your past who caused you to change certain fundamental aspects of your view of life. Historical examples might include Ghandi, Lenin, Hitler, John Kennedy, and Martin Luther King.

Also on rare occasions we may go through an experience (the death of a loved one, war, economic depression, sexual maturity or decline) that profoundly alters our evaluation of what is important about ourselves or our environment. Such reevaluation prompts us to change one or more of our basic values and, consequently, our response to the environment. Recently, there have been numerous books, articles, and movies about individuals who suffered the horrors of the Vietnam War and how the experience changed their basic approach to life. Individuals who have lost a loved one to drunk driving or experienced a catastrophic illness tell how the experience changed their evaluation of what life is fundamentally all about.

Values are developed for various segments of life (e.g., religion, government, nature, work, relationships, life itself) and collectively constitute our **value system.** We may develop basic religious values that govern our belief in God, life, death, or life after death. These values guide our thoughts and actions on such issues as capital punishment and abortion. Certain political or economic values could govern our beliefs regarding the use of power and the distribution of wealth. Such values influence the way we respond to issues like medical care for the indigent or social security for the elderly.

Just as our values can influence our perceptions, our perceptions can influence our values. The result is an intense reciprocal relationship whereby values and perceptions simultaneously influence each other. Because environmental change constantly challenges the validity of our values, it is natural and essential that we continually seek information in order to clarify these values.

As independent adults, we seek information to maintain the integrity of our value system. If we have not been encouraged to think independently during our formative years, we may rely on others (moralizers, heroes) to maintain the integrity of our value system. Consequently, our ability to perceive and respond to the environment will be severely limited by the preferences and influences of others.

Physical Development of Senses.   Of course, the physical development of an individual's five senses will have an impact on certain perceptual abilities. A blind person cannot become aware of, or respond to, visual cues. A person whose olfactory nerve was destroyed by a virus cannot attend, or respond, to the fragrance of a flower or the danger of smoke. When trying to understand the factors that account for individual differences in perception and communication, we should maintain a sensitivity

to any physical shortcomings that prohibit or hinder others from being able to react totally to their environment. Certain individuals compensate with one sense for that which they lack in another. Be ready to provide additional or different messages for those who cannot respond to more traditional cues.

Characteristics of the Perceptual Target

While we have clearly established the role of individual characteristics in perception, they are not the sole influences on what we perceive. Another set of factors concerns the thing, place, or person being perceived. By varying certain characteristics of an object we can enhance the likelihood of that object being perceived. Such characteristics include *intensity, motion, size, location, repetition, contrast, proximity in time, and proximity in space.*

Intensity. Intensity refers to the strength or magnitude of an environmental stimulus. A loud sound, for example, will be attended to more quickly and more frequently than a low humming sound. A bright light will catch your attention quicker than a dim light. An organizational maxim that clearly suggests the importance of intensity is "the squeaking wheel gets the grease." If you want to call attention to an object, intensify some particular qualities of the object or messages about the object.

Motion. Motion is a well-known and frequently used way to call attention to a stimulus. Note the number of commercial signs that simulate motion in an attempt to get your attention and your business. Commercial signs are not the only things that move, of course. Individuals who work at a fast pace and keep their activities and careers moving at a rapid tempo are more easily and frequently noticed.

Size. The physical magnitude of an object often enhances the likelihood that the object will be perceived. We notice tall and obese individuals in a crowd first. Our attention seems automatically drawn to things that are large, whether they are people, cars, diamonds, houses, or whatever. In our society, we frequently subscribe to the notion that "bigger is better." This is not always true, but when we want to call attention to ourselves and our achievements, we believe that the way to do so is through bigness or exaggeration.

Location. Certain objects are more "visible" in certain places than in others. For example, as you walk through a supermarket or department store, notice that the products placed at eye-level on the shelves, seem much more visible. When you travel on interstate highways, notice how

high the signs for service stations are placed. When objects are placed outside this "zone of visibility" the probability of perceiving the object is dramatically decreased.

Repetition.   Because there are so many stimuli in the environment at any given time, many of them go unnoticed. This may be because the stimulus was not accessible, or there may not be an awareness of the stimulus. To be sure that a stimulus is noticed, it may be necessary to repeat it several times. It is hoped the stimulus will be accessed and attended to during those repetitions. Advertisers are aware of this; consequently, their messages can be seen or heard quite frequently.

Contrast.   One of the ways in which we organize our perceptions is to place certain features of the environment in focus, while all other features serve as a backdrop. This is the figure-ground pattern; it allows us to use contrasts as a convenient means of calling attention to a stimulus. When certain features of the environment do not fit our expectations, we tend to notice them quite easily.

Advertisers use the "principle of white space" in newspapers and magazines. Essentially this consists of surrounding a printed message with a large white or blank border to direct the reader's attention to the printed message. As another example, individuals attempt to call attention to themselves by dressing in unusual, more noticeable clothing.

Proximity in Time.   We can enhance the likelihood that some feature of the environment will be noticed by timing. As creatures of habit, we develop certain patterns of behavior and we learn to expect certain sequences of events. We can use this knowledge to increase the probability of awareness and response. Using advertising again as an example, it might be more effective to run a restaurant commercial just before people are preparing to eat, rather than just after they have eaten. It would be bad timing to place a work-related announcement inside a pay envelope on a Friday afternoon.

Proximity in Space.   Just as we can enhance perception by relating stimuli on a time dimension, we can also use the space dimension. By placing objects close to other things we can increase access and awareness. A message board placed close to a water cooler or coffee machine may help to get something noticed. Department stores and supermarkets are highly skilled at the use of proximity of space for enhancing awareness and sales. Notice how carefully various related items are arranged in proximity to one another (e.g., coffee filters next to coffee instead of paper products).

Contextual Characteristics

Culture. The effects of culture on perception have been well noted in the field of social psychology. The unique characteristics of a culture are thoroughly ingrained in its members and influence what those members see and how they see it. Consider the following unusual account of a football game played in England, and reported by a British journalist.

> "All those people out there with big shoulders just running into each other and hiding the ball under them while they run," said Bernard Lockhurst, traffic coordinator at the game. "The clock stops, they huddle, shout out numbers, clap hands, and then they start hitting each other all over gain. I mean, is that all football is about?"[9]

The culturally induced perceptual set of the British reporter is obviously quite different from that of most knowledgeable U.S. football fans, who would find this description amusing.

Cultural differences, according to Tajfel, fall basically into three categories: *functional, familiarity,* and *communication systems.*[10] Functional differences concern our ability to perceive certain differences in parts of the environment which are useful in coping (e.g., discrimination between acceptable foods and nonedible foods).

Familiarity concerns our ability to perceive and discern differences between various objects that are an important part of the culture (e.g., automobiles and rock groups in the United States). Communication systems concern the language of the culture as a means of categorizing and labeling reality. This was discussed in great detail in Chapter 2.

Social Systems. We have discussed the importance of social systems as a determinant of language usage. As a part of the contextual fabric, the relevant social system can have an impact on what and how we perceive. Social systems consist of a set of roles, relationships, behavioral norms, and status assignments. These factors can influence perception directly or indirectly through our expectations, attitudes and needs.

If, for example, we witness a professor critically evaluating the performance of a group of students in a classroom setting, we perceive this as necessary and correct. That is the professor's role; it is acceptable behavior; and, of course, the status assignment allows her to do so. If the same professor, serving as a member of a Chamber of Commerce committee, criticized the committee members, it might be perceived as uncalled for, out of place, or unacceptable.

Physical Conditions. The contextual characteristics we have discussed thus far have been psycho-social in nature. There are also certain physical conditions that might influence what we perceive and how we perceive it. If you visited the Bahamas and it rained for the duration of your stay,

you would have a less positive perception than if the sun shone during the entire visit. If you were in a movie theater and a screaming infant were seated next to you, your perceptions of the movie (and the theater) might be quite negative. Don't certain objects in our environment seem more romantic or frightening after dark than they do in daylight?

THE SELF-CONCEPT

We previously introduced the notion of concepts and concept formation (Chapter 2). We defined a concept as a mental picture of something in the environment. Earlier in this chapter we discussed attitudes and defined them as concepts with an emotional load or valuation. The most important and emotion-laden concept for any individual is **self-concept**— the way we view ourselves.

Self-concept is a relatively stable set of perceptions about the self and how it differs from others in the environment (see Figure 5–6). It reflects our attitudes, values, skills, goals, and perceptions. Self-concept is immensely important because it is the key to adjustment and social relationships.

People behave in order to maintain their self-concept. Most of our behavior is an act of confirming the self-concept, and is therefore intrinsically rewarding. If we know how an individual perceives himself and his environment we can understand and predict his behavior more effectively.

We join groups or seek out experiences that will confirm the self-concept. We also attempt to influence the environment or people in the environment in order to create outcomes that enhance the self-concept.

FIGURE 5–6   The Self-Concept

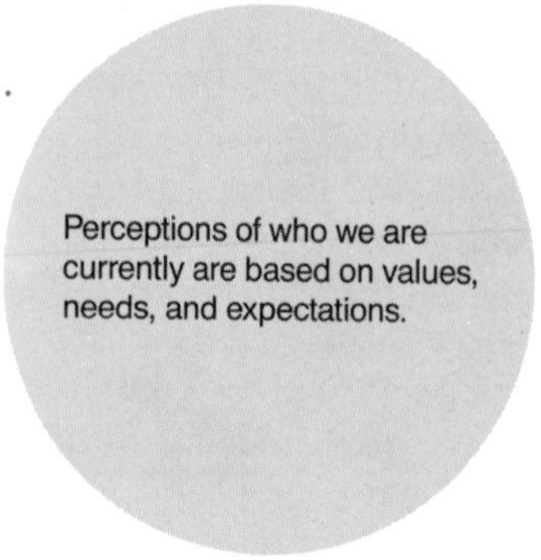

Perceptions of who we are currently are based on values, needs, and expectations.

We often go to extremes to confirm the self-concept, and information that threatens the self-concept will elicit defensive responses.

We deal with relationships between the self and the environment through **roles.** Roles guide our behavior and serve to strengthen or weaken the self-concept. For example, an individual's self-concept may include a goal for becoming an executive, awareness of certain extraordinary competencies, and the belief that he or she is a leader. This person will probably respond to the environment by seeking out roles that confirm the belief in leadership qualities, support the goal of becoming an executive, and encourage those special competencies.

Roles provide order and constancy in our lives. We see ourselves as being consistent with certain long-term roles (father, professional educator). We may see other roles as temporary or short term (cook at a Kiwanis barbecue, scout leader).

If the self-concept is congruent with the roles we assume, we will experience high levels of performance, satisfaction, and motivation. The opposite outcome may occur as a result of incongruence between roles and the self-concept. Our self-concept is built on socially acceptable role behaviors, but there are occasions when these roles may be incongruent with the self-concept. When this is the case the roles do not lead to personal growth, but instead may detract from the self-concept and force the individual to take some action to protect the self-concept.

For example, a new manager may be hired to revitalize a sagging department within an organization. Part of this revitalization requires getting rid of the nonproducers, but the new manager may not see this as consistent with his easy-going character. Such role behavior may make the individual uncomfortable to the point of giving up the management position.

There are situations in which pressure to conform conflicts with the self-concept. For example, a group of workers may pressure a co-worker to join them for a few drinks after work. If such social activity is not consistent with the co-worker's self-concept, the individual may refuse to go along. This unwillingness to conform may result in isolation for such unsociable behavior. However, if the co-worker sees himself as becoming or needing to become more outgoing and gregarious, he will join the group for drinks; he will go along with the group and alter the self-concept accordingly.

We build our lives around roles that enhance our competencies so that we may have a greater sense of adequacy or self-esteem. Some experts believe that the notion of self-esteem is at the heart of the self-concept because it is a basic statement of our self-worth. According to Murphy, "the individual perceives himself as figure in the figure-ground pattern that is each social group."[11]

Our self-perception and its influence on the self-concept are critical to communication and affect our receptivity to social influence. Individu-

als with low self esteem are often shy and anxiety-ridden in their inter-personal efforts, while individuals with high self-esteem are confident and complete in their communications.

Whether we are influenced by messages from others depends, to some extent, on the strength of the self-concept. With a strong self-concept we are likely to be confident and self-assured, and thus less suscep-tible to external influences. Individuals with a weak self-concept may be more externally directed, and therefore more susceptible to direction from others. When our esteem is low, we are more receptive to people who offer affection than when our esteem is high.

The self-concept is not fixed; it is flexible and can be modified. Part of social adjustment is the modification of the self-concept to fit new sit-uations. While we maintain a fairly consistent self-concept at any given time, we also strive to develop a better self. This "ideal" self is what we would truly like to be under ideal circumstances (see Figure 5–7).

Achieving the ideal self requires more energy, skill, and persistence than we possess. It also requires change, and that often conflicts with the current self. The greater the conflict, the slower and more difficult the change. Consequently, achieving that ideal state seems elusive to most of us.

The formation of the self-concept is a transactional process of give and take in which the self-concept affects, and is affected by, perception and communication. It is the result of constant socialization. The self-concept is influenced by the environment, social conditions, and other individuals in the environment. Occasionally we get new insights into why or what we are through such interaction. These insights change how we see ourselves and how we respond to the environment.

According to Schein we are a "set of social selves," and we use these selves to respond to differing environments. Schein states, "Each of us

FIGURE 5–7   The Ideal Self

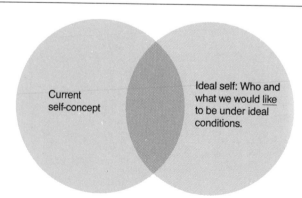

learns to construct somewhat different selves for the different kinds of situations in which we are called on to perform, and for the different kinds of roles we are expected to take."[12] The President of the United States, for example, may see himself as two distinct individuals according to the role he takes. When he is on the working floors of the White House he assumes a different role than when he is upstairs in the family quarters. Our social selves change with changing roles and environmental demands.

According to Schein, our underlying values, needs, and personality are not always consistent with our social selves. In such instances we may respond in ways that are seemingly "out of character" or inconsistent. This can be seen when a person experiences some real or perceived deficiency in a competency or value and attempts to compensate for it. The result is that outward behavior does not equal inner feelings.

For example, an individual may experience fear in a crisis, but because he is with friends, he assumes a heroic role in an attempt to end the crisis. Often, as a result of the transactional nature of self-concept development, we respond to something called the "other" self (see Figure 5–8). This is a concept of ourselves as we believe others see us. According to Cooley:

> As we see our face, figure, and dress in the glass, and are interested in them because they are ours, and pleased or otherwise with them according as they do or do not answer to what we would like them to be; so in imagination we perceive in another's mind some thought of our appearance, manners, aims, deeds, character, friends, and so on, and are variously affected by it. A self-

FIGURE 5–8   The Other Self

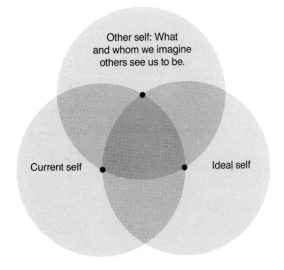

idea of this sort seems to have three principal elements: the imagination of our appearance to the other person, the imagination of his judgment of that appearance, and some sort of self-feeling, such as pride or mortification.[13]

We cannot get inside a person and see her motives, attitudes and values; we can only infer that person's qualities and characteristics from outward behavior. Some students of behavior feel that this is also true for the self. We can know ourselves only by our outward behavior. Whether this is true or not, it should be obvious that the self-concept has a major role in the explanation of individual differences. By understanding the self-concept we can better understand the communicative nature of the individual.

INDIVIDUAL DISTORTIONS

Thus far we have focused on a description of the how's and why's of individual differences in perception and communication. From that description we can identify some perceptual and communicative distortions that we should avoid.

Stereotyping

In our discussion of perceptual organization we noted that as we perceive objects and people we categorize them to help us cope with a complex world. A hasty or sloppy categorization leads to **stereotyping.** Stereotyping occurs when we *prematurely* place something or someone into one of our categories based on incomplete or incorrect information. On the basis of such improper classification, we then attribute qualities to the thing or person that are incorrect.

We have a multitude of stereotypes in our society: "old people," who are cranky, weak and nonproductive; "young people," who are nonproductive and rebellious; "college students," who are over-confident, underworked, and do nothing but party; "professors," who are aloof, intellectual, and otherwise nonproductive.

The danger is using stereotypes is that we fail to discriminate between different objects or people. In our haste we do not see the important differences between similar things and we say or do the wrong thing.

As a result of the "old people" stereotype, we often overlook or fail to acknowledge outstanding talent. Those of us not in the same category fail to trust and utilize the outstanding minds and skills of "young people" or "college student" stereotypes. We often confine our thinking and our relationships because of our stereotypes.

We must become more sensitive to individual differences and appreciate those differences for what they are to overcome stereotyping. Realize that stereotyping influences our responses to the environment and can

lead to irrational, prejudicial behavior. This can have embarrassing and damaging effects on our lives and the lives of those improperly categorized. Everyone who is old or young, male or female, is not the same and should not be treated the same. The differences are important: take the time and make the effort to learn what they are.

Halo Effect

When we initially encounter a person we immediately interpret and evaluate him or her. That first encounter often yields a positive or negative first impression based on some outstanding quality. When the individual is encountered later in other situations, that quality will be unduly influential in our perception of that individual. Such over-reliance on one quality is referred to as the **halo effect.**

In effect, the person has a halo around his or her head, and can do no wrong (or right, in the case of a negative impression). For example, John is an outstanding student in Professor Smith's Economics I class. Because of his highly positive initial impression of John, Professor Smith treats John in a highly complimentary fashion and ignores John's deficient performance while he is enrolled in Economics II.

The halo effect gives us a rigid and perhaps inaccurate evaluation of the individual. We fail to see the whole person and ignore differences in the individual under varying circumstances and at different times. We need to become more sensitive to the whole person and recognize that people behave differently over time and under varying conditions. John in Economics I is not necessarily John in Economics II.

Polarization

When we perceive, interpret, and evaluate the objects in our environment we essentially identify the qualities of those objects. Frequently we note those qualities by using words that denote extremes (e.g., hot-cold, good-bad). Our language is constructed in two-value terms, so it is convenient to structure our thinking this way. Unfortunately, when we describe things in black and white terms we tend to ignore the gray areas that are often rich with information.

It is easier to label objects using extremes. We don't have to work as hard to gather the information necessary to differentiate between shades of gray. We are in a hurry, too lazy, or not motivated to discover the differences.

This lack of discovery has a cost. By shoving everything into one extreme category or another we cannot enjoy or appreciate the various shades of gray. We cannot even respond in appropriate ways because we are unaware of differences. People are neither all good nor all bad. There

are some highly productive employees who need help with problems. There are some not-so-productive employees who can be encouraged to become more productive.

We must first become sensitive to our tendency to categorize and talk about eveything in polar terms. Then, we need to learn to specify degrees of difference in a quality or characteristic possessed by an individual. Simultaneously, we need to use more categories and words to represent the gray areas. This would result in more diversity and richness in the messages that we receive from the environment. Subsequently, we would be able to develop more differentiated and appropriate responses.

Perceptual Defense

Earlier we introduced the idea of a perceptual set. We said it was "all the factors which influence us as we perceive and communicate about our environment." As this set becomes increasingly complex and sophisticated, we become more reliant on it and, therefore, more comfortable with it. After all, it is our view of the world and we use it to cope with life.

If someone says or does something that challenges our perceptual set, we will engage in yet another form of perceptual behavior: **perceptual defense.** There are several characteristic defensive reactions: denial, avoidance, projection, and rationalization. These reactions can be seen in the following example.

John is told that his close friend Fred was caught cheating on an exam. John's initial response may be to defend his perception of Fred by simply denying the report, labeling it as untrue, and offering information about Fred's honesty and integrity. John might also respond by avoiding the individual who told him about Fred. (This is typical of the smoker who gets so tired of reading about the harmful effects of cigarette smoke that he quits reading.) Another possibility for John is to project the blame or fault onto another student, the teacher, or possibly the individual reporting on Fred's behavior. A final possibility would be for John to find some rationalization to explain Fred's behavior (i.e., stress, a vindictive teacher) and thereby account for the "inconsistent" report he received about Fred.

Perceptual defense is a major factor in resistance to change. Organizations frequently experience major problems when introducing change because they overlook and underestimate the power and significance of perceptual defense. If we want to understand fully an individual's perceptions and behavior, we must have a full appreciation for the influence of the perceptual set on behavior.

SUMMARY

Situational factors that influence how individuals respond to stimuli can help us understand the differences in how individuals cope with life.

One of the primary determinants of how we cope is perception, the act of taking the world into account. What we take into account and how we do so directly affect what we know and don't know, what we are and are not. There are three necessary stages in perception: access, awareness, and interpretation. After going through these stages, we can decide on a response.

Several individual characteristics influence our perceptual abilities: needs, expectations, knowledge, feelings, behavior, values, and physical development of the senses. While all of these factors influence the individual's perception, what the individual perceives may influence these factors.

In addition to the characteristics internal to the individual, other factors can influence perception. Certain characteristics of the thing being perceived can play a role in perception. Such qualities as intensity, motion, size, location, repetition, contrast, proximity in time, and proximity in space may determine whether an object is perceived or not.

Several contextual factors may influence an individual's perception. The culture in which we function can influence our perceptions—it trains us in how to look and what to look for. The social system we are in can dictate what and how we perceive as a result of role behaviors, relationships, and status distribution. The physical conditions of the context can have an immense influence on what we perceive and how we perceive it.

Self-concept is one of the most important influences on individual perception and behavior. We say and do things to maintain the self-concept or to help transform it into what we want it to be. We often assume various professional and social roles that afford us the opportunity to become what we want to be.

As a result of our individuality we are motivated to see things as we want to see them. Because of a lack of motivation or competence, we often do not see things as they really are. We engage in various kinds of perceptual distortion such as stereotyping, the halo effect, polarization, and perceptual defense. Overcoming these distortions may require more effort or better social skills, and often the ability and willingness to change the way we see ourselves and others. These requirements will be addressed in Chapter 6, Interpersonal Communication.

The importance of our intrapersonal abilities and skills—all those issues discussed in this chapter—cannot be overemphasized. They form the basis on which we build our interpersonal relationships, our small group interactions, and our communications within the organizational setting. Our perceptual abilities, needs, expectations, values, and self-concept

must be addressed and resolved to our satisfaction before we can hope to be effective communicators in higher level communication situations.

DISCUSSION QUESTIONS

1. Define perception. Why would perception and communication be impossible without all three steps in the perceptual process? Why is it important for a manager to have an understanding of the perception process?

2. What is meant by perceptual set? Why is an understanding of the perceptual set important in communication?

3. Compare and contrast the figure-ground and gestalt approaches to structuring perception.

4. A stereotype is defined as an oversimplified, standardized mental picture based on uncritical judgment. List some words, phrases, or statements used to stereotype people. What does each mean? Why do we stereotype people? Is there an alternative to stereotyping? Explain.

5. Differentiate between stereotyping and the halo effect. Explain how each would influence our behavior (negatively or positively) toward the targets of such behavior.

6. How are attitudes formed? Discuss the three components of attitudes in your answer. How do attitudes affect communication?

7. Discuss the impact of needs and expectations on communication, and vice versa.

8. How do characteristics of the perceptual target influence perception? How can a communicator influence these characteristics to improve communication?

9. Give some examples of the four defensive behaviors:
   a. Denial.
   b. Avoidance.
   c. Projection.
   d. Rationalization

10. There are three basic categories of cultural differences according to Tajfel. List them and explain why the business communicator needs to be aware of cultural differences.

11. Define self-concept. Explain how it develops and why understanding this concept is important to a business communicator.

12. Identify a situation in which an individual or group of individuals demonstrates consistently strong (positive or negative) reaction patterns toward another individual or group. Using the three-component model of an attitude, explain how such patterns might have developed.

13. Explain how needs might influence perceptions, and how perceptions might influence needs. Demonstrate your understanding of the relationship between these two factors by citing examples.

EXERCISES

There are two extremes of perceptual inaccuracy. One is when we see things that are not there, and the other is when we do not see things that are right before us. Complete the following exercises. After each, compare your responses with those of your classmates and give reasons for responding as you did. What perceptual errors did you commit? Compare the nature of the first two exercises. How are they different?

1. Read the following story.* Assume that all the information presented in it is definitely accurate and true. Read it carefully because it has ambiguous parts designed to lead you astray. You can refer back to it whenever you wish.

   Next read the statements about the story and check each to indicate whether you consider it *true, false,* or *questionable.* "T" means that the statement is definitely true on the basis of the information presented in the story. "F" means it is definitely false. "?" means that it may be either true or false and that you cannot be certain on the basis of the information presented in the story. If any part of a statement is doubtful, mark it "?". Answer each statement in turn, do not go back to change any answer later, and do not reread any statements after you have answered them. Correct answers are given at the end of the exercises for this chapter.

The Story

A business man had just turned off the lights in the store when a man appeared and demanded money. The owner opened a cash register. The contents of the cash register were scooped up, and the man sped away. A member of the police force was notified promptly.

Statements about the story

1.	A man appeared after the owner had turned off his store lights.	T	F	?
2.	The robber was a man.	T	F	?
3.	The man appeared did not demand money.	T	F	?
4.	The man who opened the cash register was the owner.	T	F	?
5.	The store owner scooped up the contents of the cash register and ran away.	T	F	?
6.	Someone opened a cash register.	T	F	?
7.	After the man who demanded the money scooped up the contents of the cash register, he ran away.	T	F	?
8.	While the cash register contained money, the story does not state how much.	T	F	?

*The story and statements are a portion of the "Uncritical Inference Test," © 1955, 1964, 1979, and 1986 by William V. Haney. Reprinted from William Haney, *Communication and Interpersonal Relations: Text and Cases,* 5th ed. (Homewood, Ill.: Richard D. Irwin, 1986), pp. 213–14. Used with permission.

9.   The robber demanded money of the owner.   T   F   ?
10. A businessman had just turned off the lights when a man appeared in the store.   T   F   ?
11. It was broad daylight when the man appeared.   T   F   ?
12. The man who appeared opened the cash register.   T   F   ?
13. No one demanded money.   T   F   ?
14. The story concerns a series of events in which only three persons are referred to: the owner of the store, a man who demanded money, and a member of the police force.   T   F   ?
15. The following events occurred: someone demanded money; a cash register was opened; its contents were scooped up; and a man dashed out of the store.   T   F   ?

2. Study the following illustration and count the total number of squares you see. Compare your answer with those of your classmates.

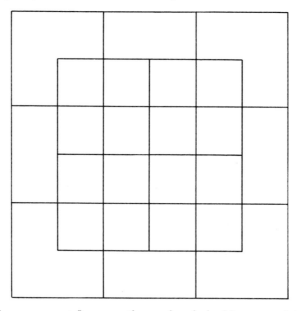

3. The U.S. government for more than a decade had been supplying economic and military advisory aid to the government of South Vietnam. In the mid-1960s, the U.S. government became militarily involved in the conflict in that nation by furnishing combat personnel, expecting a quick victory based on superior military power and training. Much to the dismay of government leaders and citizens, the conflict lingered on.

Because of increasing American combat deaths, there was much internal dissension in the United States, with a wide spectrum of emotions concerning the conflict and the official position of the U.S. government. In the latter part of 1969, news reached the American people of a "massacre" committed by

U.S. Army personnel in which more than 100 harmless Vietnamese citizens were murdered for no apparent reason. Screams of resentment were numerous and loud in the United States. Military leaders were under attack because of this much criticized event.

On one occasion when another hamlet was burned down, the orders that led to the burning were retraced. Those orders were as follows:

> From the division headquarters to the brigade headquarters: On no occasion must hamlets be burned down.
>
> From brigade to battalion headquarters: Do not burn down any hamlets unless you are absolutely convinced that the Viet Cong are in them.
>
> From battalion headquarters to the infantry leader: If you think there are any Viet Cong in the hamlet, burn it down.
>
> From the company commander to the infantry: Burn down that hamlet.

Reflect the knowledge, needs, attitudes, and experiences of the various individuals involved in this situation. Speculate as to why and how the original order was completely reversed after only three transmissions.

4. Select a topic or subject toward which you have a strong attitude (either positive or negative). Prepare a 10- to 15-minute talk supporting the opposite position. This talk should be convincing enough to persuade your classmates to adopt your position. You should be prepared to answer all questions and defend your position against any criticism. After the presentation, describe and analyze the feelings you experienced before and after the presentation. Describe the procedure and rationale you used to prepare for your talk.

5. Assume that you are about to be introduced to an individual who is a close personal friend of (name to be provided by instructor). How would you characterize this individual on the following factors?

Political affiliation	Position on church activism
Religious affiliation	Position on ERA
Position on gun control	Position on social services programs
Position on gay rights	Position on free enterprise
Position on equal housing	Position on the importance of education
Position on labor unions	Position on capital punishment

Compare your responses with those of your classmates. How were you able to respond as you did with such limited information about the individual? Do we respond in this fashion frequently? Why? Discuss the consequences of such behavior.

Answers to Exercise 1

1. ?   Do you know that the businessman and the owner are one and the same?

2. ?   Was there necessarily a robbery?

3. F   The man did demand money.
4. ?   Was the owner a man?
5. ?   May seem unlikely, but the story does not preclude it.
6. T   Story says the owner opened the cash register.
7. ?   We don't know who scooped up the contents.
8. ?   The dependent clause is doubtful—the cash register may or may not have contained money.
9. ?   Again, a robber?
10. ?   Could the man merely have appeared at a door or window but did not actually enter the store?
11. ?   Stores generally keep lights on during the day.
12. ?   The man who appeared could have been the owner.
13. F   Story says the man who appeared demanded money.
14. ?   Are the businessman and the owner one and the same—or two different people? Same goes for the owner and the man who appeared.
15. ?   "Dashed?" Could he not have sped away? We don't even know if he entered the store.

NOTES

[1] *Webster's Seventh New Collegiate Dictionary* (Springfield, Mass.: G & C Merriam Company, 1961), p. 626.

[2] H. H. Kelley, "The Process of Causal Attribution," *American Psychologist* 28 (1973), pp. 107–28; also see H. Harvey and G. Weary, "Current Issues in Attribution Theory and Research," *Annual Review of Psychology* 35 (1984), p. 428.

[3] Kelley, "Process of Causal Attribution."

[4] Abraham H. Maslow, *Motivation and Personality* (New York: Harper & Row, 1954).

[5] Frederick Herzberg, Bernard Mauser, and Barbara Snyderman, *The Motivation to Work* (New York: John Wiley & Sons, 1959).

[6] See, for example, Douglas McGregor, *The Human Side of Enterprise* (New York: McGraw-Hill, 1960); and Allen Cohen, S. Fink, H. Gadon, and R. Willits, *Effective Behavior in Organizations* (Homewood, Ill.: Richard D. Irwin, 1984).

[7] J. Campbell Connelly, *A Manager's Guide to Speaking and Listening* (New York: Ronald Press, 1967), p. 57.

[8] Thomas Harris, *I'm OK–You're OK* (New York, Avon Books, 1969), chap. 5.

[9] United Press International, "British on NFL," *The Boston Globe*, August 7, 1983.

[10] H. Tajfel, "Social and Cultural Factors in Perception," in *Handbook of Social Psychology*, ed. G. Lindzey and E. Aronson (Reading, Mass.: Addison-Wesley Publishing, 1967).

[11] G. Murphy, *Personality: A Biosocial Approach to Origin and Structure* (New York: Harper & Row, 1947), p. 766.

[12] Edgar Schein, "The Individual, the Organization and the Career," in *Organizational Psychology*, ed. D. Kold, I. Rubin, and J. McIntyre (Englewood Cliffs, N.J.: Prentice-Hall, 1979), p. 504.

[13] C. H. Colley, *Human Nature and the Social Order* (New York: Charles Scribner's Sons, 1922), p. 184.

SUGGESTED READINGS

CUSHMAN, DONALD P., and DUDLEY D. CAHN, JR. *Communication in Interpersonal Relationships*. Albany: State University of New York Press, 1985.

DAVIS, DEBORAH, and THOMAS HOLTGRAVES. "Perceptions of Unresponsive Others: Attributions, Attractions, Understandability, and Memory of Their Utterances." *Journal of Experimental Social Psychology* 20 (September 1984), pp. 383–408.

DUNCAN, STARKEY, JR., and DONALD W. FISHE. *Interaction Structure and Strategy*. New York: Cambridge University Press, 1985.

GODDARD, ROBERT W. "The Pygmalion Effect." *Personnel Journal*, 64, no. 6 (June 1985), p. 10ff.

GRATZ, ROBERT D., and PHILIP J. SALEM. "Technology and the Crisis of Self." *Communication Quarterly* 32, no. 2 (Spring 1984), pp. 98–103.

HANEY, WILLIAM V. *Communication and Interpersonal Relations: Text and Cases*. Homewood, Ill.: Richard D. Irwin, 1979.

HUMPHREY, RONALD. "How Work Roles Influence Perceptions: Structural-Cognitive Processes and Organizational Behavior." *American Sociological Review* 50 (April 1985), pp. 242–52.

REARDON, KATHLEEN K. "It's the Thought that Counts." *Harvard Business Review* 62, no. 5 (September–October 1984), p. 136ff.

RIGGS, JANET M., and NANCY CANTOR. "Getting Acquainted: The Roles of the Self-Concept and Preconception." *Personality and Social Psychology*, Bulletin 10 (September 1984), pp. 432–45.

SPITZBERG, BRIAN H., and WILLIAM R. CUPACH. *Interpersonal Communication Competence*. Beverly Hills, Calif.: Sage Publications, 1984.

STAINTON, R. S. "Challenging Conformity: Reality Is in the Eye of the Beholder." *The Business Quarterly* 49, no. 2 (Summer 1984), pp. 80–84.

Chapter 6

Interpersonal Communication

Chapter 6 Case

"I don't understand how this could have happened. At least twice a week since I gave you this assignment, I've stopped by to ask you if you had any problems. Each time, you said no. Now, here we are, less than a week before this order is due at the customer's shop, and it's all wrong. How could you do this?"

"Gee, boss, I can't tell you how sorry I am, but our unit got off on the wrong foot on this thing. It must have happened at the original briefing session."

"But you kept saying there weren't any problems."

"Well, I didn't think there were. Everything was going along according to schedule . . . at least the schedule we thought was right."

What happened here?

INTRODUCTION

All of us find interaction with others both necessary and desirable. Life is a continuing series of interactions in which we share information about ourselves and our environment, and communication is usually necessary to cope with the mundane affairs of everyday life or to engage in new and uncertain endeavors. This is especially true in a business organization where information is its lifeblood, and interpersonal relationships constitute the underlying superstructure.

In this chapter we will examine several models of interpersonal communication to demonstrate effective methods of sharing information and building relationships. We begin with a look at how two individuals share information.

THE INTERACTIVE COMMUNICATION PROCESS

Several distinct stages are involved as Person and Other engage in interpersonal communication. These stages collectively constitute the **interactive communication process** as illustrated in Figure 6–1.

Stimulus, Attention, and Stimulation

Starting at the top center of Figure 6–1, assume that Person has conveyed to Other an encoded message. This encoded message becomes a stimulus for Other and is intended to have a very specific effect on Other's behavior. However, the stimulus will go unnoticed unless Other is aware of it.

The importance of awareness to interpersonal communication is well illustrated by the question: Is there a noise in the forest when a tree falls if no one is there to hear it? The answer obviously is that there is a stimulus, but no stimulation. No message can have an effect, intended or otherwise, if no one is paying attention to it.[1] Receiver attention is fundamental, yet managers often overlook this critical requirement. They write memos or letters that are unread, or they conduct meetings and deliver speeches that are unheard. Sending messages cannot be equated with re-

FIGURE 6–1 The Interactive Communication Process

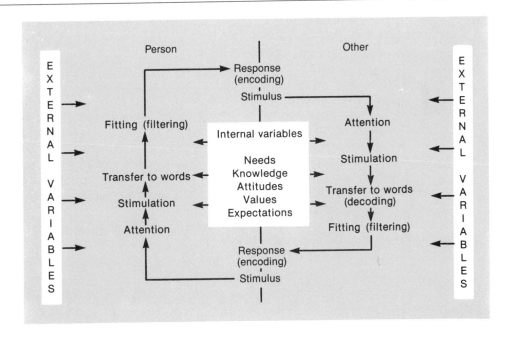

ceiving and understanding—this fallacy is at the root of many ineffective attempts to communicate.

If Other is paying attention, she will be sensually stimulated; yet there is no guarantee that the stimulation will be that which was intended. The message may be distorted because of **external noise**—an unintended stimulus external to Person and Other that interferes with the reception of the original stimulus. Machine noise in a factory, street noise, a defective typewriter, or a telephone call during a meeting could all be examples of external noise. External noise should be eliminated if communication is to be totally effective. No matter how carefully a message is composed, once it is distorted, it will not elicit the intended response, except by accident.

External variables are often beyond our control: all we can do is identify them and adjust to them to avoid as much negative impact as possible. If the maintenance department of a university decides to operate a lawnmower or other equipment just outside a classroom, communication in the classroom is next to impossible. That activity may be beyond the immediate control of the instructor or the students. The obvious action to minimize its effects is to close the windows to the room or move to another location.

Decoding

As stimulation occurs, the externally received message must be decoded or transferred into meaningful terms by Other. To decode successfully, Other must have at her command the necessary terms and concepts into which the stimulus can be transferred. Appropriate word choice is exceedingly important at this stage. If Other does not have the necessary vocabulary into which to decode the message, the communication process will break down. Once the message is decoded successfully, it is subjected to **filtering.**

Filtering

Inside each individual is that lengthy set of stored information we earlier labeled the perceptual set—the beliefs, emotions, and programmed behaviors that we use to function each day (See Internal Variables in Figure 6–1). As a message is received, it is compared with the receiver's thoughts, feelings, and behavioral propensities. This filtering process frequently produces a message different from the one initially decoded.

Filtering can be intentional or unintentional. Intentional filtering is a calculated, deliberate response based on formal reasoning. Unintentional filtering is an unpremeditated response that occurs as a result of emotional reactions or mechanical failures (e.g., typographical error). A major difference between these two types of filtering is the clarity of the rela-

tionship between the filtering behavior and its purpose. Since unintentional filtering often occurs at a subconsciousness level, the individual may not realize that filtering has occurred or why it has occurred. For example, Janet's secretary tells her that a particular letter has been filed. This is unimportant to Janet; she is preoccupied with an urgent matter, and so she blocks it out. Three hours later she asks the secretary where the letter is.

Intentional filtering is often associated with "gatekeepers" and "opinion leaders." These individuals receive information from one source and then select, edit, and transmit it to other sources. The supervisor receives information from higher levels of management and then decides what to pass on to the employees. Corporate promoters and spokesmen say only those things that enhance the image of their products and corporations while avoiding even factual statements that may be harmful. According to Miller there are three types of filtering: **leveling, sharpening,** and **assimilating.**[2]

Leveling.   As a receiver processes a decoded message, parts of the message may be incompatible with the individual's thoughts, feelings, or behavioral tendencies. Consequently those parts are rejected or simply ignored. This is leveling, and it produces a message different from that which the sender intended. As the receiver "remanufactures" the message, she may communicate a somewhat different message.

For example, the chairperson of a university department is told that a retiring faculty member will not be replaced. The reason for this decision is declining enrollments in the department—largely the result of a lack of student recruitment by the chairperson. At the next departmental meeting, the chairperson announces to the faculty that the university administration has canceled a position due to declining enrollments. Because of the inconsistency between the administration's reason and what the chairperson believes, the chairperson simply omits the portion of the message referring to the lack of recruitment. The original message is distorted as a result of the leveling, and the faculty does not get the complete and accurate message.

Sharpening.   Another variation of message filtering is sharpening. In some instances portions of a message are extremely compatible with an individual's beliefs and feelings. It may be, for example, something highly important to the individual's self concept. Because of its importance, that portion of the message is magnified and perhaps blown completely out of proportion. For instance, a new supervisor is told that her performance is excellent, and that if she continues at her present rate of development, she *may be considered* for a promotion. The supervisor then begins telling people that she is about *to receive* a promotion and salary increase.

Assimilating. A receiver may attach particular meaning or interpretation to portions of a message not intended by the sender. Some particular preconditioning may cause an individual to read into a message something that simply is not there, even by implication. This phenomenon is referred to as assimilation and occurs as a result of unclear and misleading messages. A political candidate, for example, might state that, if elected, he will do what he can for farmers. After the candidate is elected to office, farmers begin making specific demands based on their needs. When they present their demands, they state that the candidate promised these things, which of course he did not. A commercial advertisement, as another example, might state that a product can help to improve an individual's personal appearance. After using the product, the consumer complains because he is not more personally attractive to others.

It is difficult to qualify all filtering as good or bad. Recall that a major topic in Chapter 2 was adapting. Part of adapting is the selection of information suitable to a given set of circumstances. This is a form of intentional filtering that is basic to effective communication. Filtering is dangerous when it increases the probability of misunderstanding or when it threatens the quality of a relationship.

Completing the Interaction

Once the message has been filtered, Other encodes a response which could be a simple spoken or written message, or a complex series of verbal and nonverbal cues. This response then becomes a stimulus for Person. At this point we could go through the same stages for Person, completing one cycle of the interactive process.

INTERPERSONAL PERCEPTION

As indicated in Figure 6–1, the interactive process is influenced by those variables that constitute the perceptual set. This influence is referred to as **internal noise**—intended or unintended stimuli generated within Person or Other that interfere with message composition and reception. We have focused on the *intrapersonal* influences that account for individual differences in perception and communication. Here we will look at the ways in which perception affects interaction between Person and Other. We can see the effects in Figure 6–2, which illustrates the model of interpersonal perception developed by Nord.[3]

In the lower portion of the model, two circles represent the inner world of two individuals—Person and Other. You should recognize these components of the perceptual set from our discussion in Chapter 5. The perceptions of Person and Other (i.e., what they see, hear, etc.) are de-

FIGURE 6–2   Interpersonal Perception

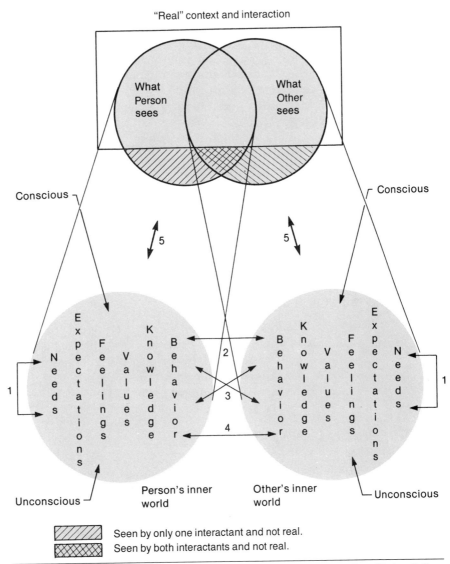

SOURCE: Walter Nord, *Concepts and Controversy in Organizational Behavior* (Santa Monica, Calif.: Goodyear Publishing, 1976), p. 24.

picted in the upper portion of the model. Close examination of that portion provides some interesting findings.

The rectangular box represents the real world in which interaction occurs. As you look at the rectangle, observe that neither of the two individuals perceives the entire real world. This is due to the phenomenon of selective perception discussed in Chapter 5. Neither Person nor Other has the time or the inclination to perceive all there is to perceive.

A second observation is that Person and Other do not see exactly the same portions of reality. Large proportions of the circles of Person and Other are unique. Again, the perceptions of each individual are selective, based on their perceptual sets which, of course, are not the same.

A third observation is that there are certain commonalities in the perceptions of Person and Other, represented by the overlapping of the two circles. This overlapping represents a shared perceptual set and the basis for shared information. As Walter Nord has noted, "Fortunately, there is enough shared experience concerning a sufficiently large number of objects to permit social organization to exist."[4] As the perceptual sets of Person and Other become more similar, communication becomes easier and more effective.

Consider the perceptual sets of two strangers from different nations and cultures. Similarities would be almost nonexistent and communication would be difficult at first. But if these individuals live and work close to one another and become intimate friends, the similarities in their perceptual sets and perceptions will grow to the point where interpersonal understanding and communication will flow with ease. A certain look, sigh, or grunt can replace sentences and paragraphs. This ease of communication is evident on television shows where a team of individuals work together intimately (i.e., "Star Trek," "The Tonight Show," and "Cagney and Lacey"). This is why communication experts repeatedly exhort us to consider our receivers carefully before we attempt to communicate. If we can identify commonalities of perception, we have a better basis on which to share information and maintain interpersonal relationships.

Observe that portion of each circle that rests outside the rectangle. This area represents things that are not part of the real world, yet are very real to Person and Other. As Person and Other interact *with their environment,* part of their response is the internal creation of their own private version of reality. They literally see what is not there, at least not for others to see.

Consider the example of Person and Other sitting in a classroom. Person observes that the room is too dark. Other states that it is too bright. Who is right? We could observe the illumination level by measuring it with a light meter, but that would not alter Person's or Other's reaction to the brightness of the room. The difference in responses is a result of the individuals' physical makeup, visual acuity, and so forth.

This can present some serious communication problems. The part of the world in which Person lives is created out of public view and is not available to Other unless Person chooses to share it. Information sharing is critical to the development of effective interpersonal relationships.

Finally, in Figure 6–2 there are five different flows of communication. Channel 1 is internal to the individual and represents information flows between the individual's conscious level and subconscious level. These communication flows are continuous, and they directly influence the individual's behavior, both overt and covert, present and future. It is also through this channel that the perceptual set is constantly being updated and refined.

Channel 2 carries communications at a conscious level between Person and Other. Because Channel 2 communications occur at a conscious level, they are the most frequently used types and are conveyed through conventional oral and written channels. These channels and the messages that flow through them historically have received the greatest amount of attention from researchers and practitioners. Barriers to channel 2 communications were discussed earlier in this chapter and in Chapter 4.

Channel 3 carries mainly nonverbal messages between the conscious mind of Person and the subconscious mind of Other, and vice versa. Person may be consciously sending information to Other which Other is not consciously aware of receiving. An example of this is subliminal advertising, which became popular in the late 1950s. More recently Wilson Key has suggested that various advertisers are effectively using subliminal messages that are sexually seductive.[5] Proponents of subliminal communication contend that a message can be received at the subconscious level without being received at the conscious level. An individual receiving such a message may inexplicably engage in behavior without really understanding why.

A second type of communication occurs in Channel 3 when Person receives information at a conscious level from Other which Other is not aware of sending. For example, a mother who wants to reassure a child tells the child, "I love you." If the mother's tone is irritable, it communicates an entirely different message to the child. This confusing double meaning is referred to as a **double bind,** because the receiver is actually receiving two different and conflicting messages. The double bind is a serious source of difficulty in communication because the receiver is put in the position of having to choose the message to which she will respond.

Channel 4 carries exchanges at a subconscious level, and neither individual may be aware that any communication is taking place. Such messages are not sent or received at a conscious level; therefore, they tend to be incidental and most frequently nonverbal. In a superior-subordinate encounter, for example, the superior, without any conscious effort, may assume a dominating posture or a condescending tone of voice that

clearly conveys his superior status. The subordinate may respond subconsciously by assuming a sheepish look or a meek tone of voice.

Channel 5 carries information between the individual and the environment. We have previously noted that while the individual's perceptual set colors the world as he or she sees it, the world also influences the individual's perceptual set. It is through this channel that such influence occurs.

The five channels described in Nord's model make it clear that information sharing can be an extraordinarily complex process. Nord clearly suggests the need to develop a sensitivity to all channels and the messages coming through them. Such sensitivity is critical to improving interpersonal skills, but does not guarantee success.

FEEDBACK

The nature of the interaction process, coupled with the effects of individual differences in interpersonal perception, suggests the need for a proactive approach to information sharing. The foundation of such an approach is feedback.

The Function of Feedback

"I know you believe you understand what you think I said, but I am not sure you realize that what you heard is not what I meant." This not-so-easy-to-remember but highly substantive caveat is more than adequate justification for soliciting and using feedback. To the extent that we do not mean what we say or we do not understand what we hear and read, feedback should be a vital part of our communication effort. Feedback is information that signals whether or not we have been understood. It tells us what the other person has received, interpreted, and understood our message to be, and how successful we have been in the role of sender/encoder.

Possible Consequences of Feedback

In some instances we are afraid of feedback; in other instances we don't think we need it. In either case, when we don't receive feedback, we don't receive its beneficial and constructive effects. Look closely at Figure 6–3, which shows the possible responses when feedback is provided.

When feedback is provided (stage 1), there are three possible outcomes (stage 2). If there is no attention or response to the feedback, no energy is generated and there is no improvement in individual behavior or in the quality of relationships. If no energy has been generated, nothing can or will happen except by accident.

FIGURE 6–3 Responses to Feedback

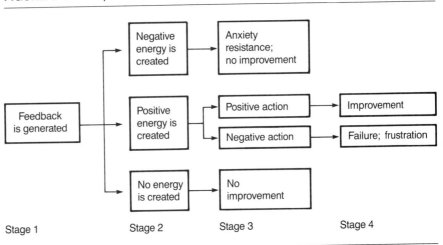

SOURCE: Adapted with permission from David A. Nadler, *Feedback and Organizational Development: Using Data-Based Methods* (Reading, Mass.: Addison-Wesley Publishing, 1977), p. 146.

If energy is created, it can be directed in one of two ways. A work climate that fosters anxiety and defensive attitudes will usually result in the creation of negative energy. If the energy is directed negatively, it will be used to deny or fight the reality of the feedback. The result is increased anxiety, resistance, and no improvement on the part of the recipient. If, for example, an employee who works in a defensive environment is confronted with the fact of his declining productivity, he may resist that reality by claiming that the data, the data collector, or the feedback provider are wrong. The outcome is no improvement in employee performance.

In a constructive and supportive work climate, the energy generated in stage 2 will be directed positively to identify problems and generate solutions. In this case the employee who is confronted with his declining productivity chooses to respond positively by identifying reasons for the decline and developing solutions to overcome it.

If positive energy is created, stage 3 suggests that there must be an outlet or means for applying the positive energy to create positive or negative action. When an employee responds positively to feedback, there must be resources and a supportive managerial climate that allow for the constructive use of the energy. Assume, for example, that an employee responds positively to feedback and wants to work to improve his performance. To improve, the employee needs training, but the organization does not provide or encourage employee training. (It may seem unreasonable and irrational for the organization to take such a position, but it can and does happen due to financial difficulties, a lack of under-

standing of employee development, or a lack of managerial expertise.)

The result (stage 4) is likely to be frustration, failure, and no improvement! If, on the other hand, the training, resources, and encouragement are provided, the outcome is likely to be improved performance.

In stages 2 and 3, there is the potential for defensive behavior such as the classic mechanisms we discussed in Chapter 5 (denial, avoidance, projection, rationalization). A person is likely to engage in these defense mechanisms if subjected to a climate that elicits and reinforces such behavior. If the proper support is provided, the individual has the opportunity to utilize feedback to improve.

SUPPORTIVE-DEFENSIVE CLIMATES

The importance of the environment in precipitating either resistance or change is suggested in the following passage from an article on management style in *AT&T Magazine:* "How do you build a frog? Do you study the croak, the prodigious leap, the hyperbolic eyes? No, . . . you study the pond."[6]

The role of the work climate is specifically demonstrated in Jack Gibb's model of supportive-defensive climates.[7] After several years of research into the small group communication network, Gibb concluded that to improve communications within organizations, we must examine interpersonal relationships and make any changes in these relationships that will lead to a reduction in defensiveness.

He observed that individuals in groups characterized by low or high defensiveness behaved in characteristically different ways, which he labeled *supportive* and *defensive*. Gibb contrasts the behavior characteristics of supportive and defensive climates in Figure 6–4. A more detailed explanation of these categories is given in Figure 6–5.

While defensive behaviors generally arouse defensiveness and sup-

---

FIGURE 6–4 Categories of Behavior Characteristics of Supportive and Defensive Climates in Small Groups

Defensive Climates	*Supportive Climates*
Evaluation	Description
Control	Problem orientation
Strategy	Spontaneity
Neutrality	Empathy
Superiority	Equality
Certainty	Provisionalism

SOURCE: J. R. Gibb, "Defensive Communication," *Journal of Communication* 2, no. 3 (September 1961), p. 143. Reprinted by permission of the International Communication Association.

FIGURE 6–5   Characteristic Categories of Behavior

Defensive climates	*Supportive climates*
Evaluation: To pass judgment on another; to blame or praise; to make moral assessments of another; to question his standards, values, and motives and the effect loadings of his communications.	*Description:* Nonjudgmental; to ask questions that are perceived as genuine requests for information; to present "feelings, events, perceptions, or processes that do not ask or imply that the receiver change behavior or attitude."
Control: To try to do something to another, to attempt to change an attitude or the behavior of another—to try to restrict his field of activity; "implicit in all attempts to alter another person is the assumption of the change agent that the person to be altered is inadequate."	*Problem orientation:* The antithesis of persuasion; to communicate "a desire to collaborate in defining a mutual problem orientation in the other"; to imply that he has no preconceived solution, attitude, or method to impose upon the other; to allow "the receiver to set his own goals, make his own decisions, and evaluate his own progress—or to share with the sender in doing so."
Strategy: To manipulate others; to use tricks to "involve" another, to make him think he was making his own decisions, and to make him feel that the speaker had genuine interest in him; to engage in a stratagem involving ambiguous and multiple motivation.	*Spontaneity:* To express guilelessness; natural simplicity; free of deception; having a "clean id"; having unhidden, uncomplicated motives; straightforwardness and honesty.
Neutrality: To express lack of concern for the welfare of another; "the clinical, detached, person-is-an-object-of-study attitude."	*Empathy:* To express respect for the worth of the listener; to identify with his problems, share his feelings, and accept his emotional values at face value.
Superiority: To communicate the attitude that one is "superior in position, power, wealth, intellectual ability, physical characteristics, or other ways to another; to tend to arouse feelings of inadequacy in the other; to impress the other that the speaker is not willing to enter into a shared problem-solving relationship, that he probably does not require help, and/or that he will be likely to try to reduce the power, the status, or the worth of the receiver."	*Equality:* To be willing to enter into participative planning with mutual trust and respect; to attach little importance to differences in talent, ability, worth, appearance, status, and power.
Certainty: To appear dogmatic; "to seem to know the answers, to require no additional data"; and to regard self as teacher rather than as co-worker; to manifest inferiority by *needing to be right,* wanting to win an argument rather than solve a problem, seeing one's ideas as truths to be defended.	*Provisionalism:* To be willing to experiment with one's own behavior, attitudes, and ideas; to investigate issues rather than taking sides on them, to problem solve rather than debate, to communicate that the other person may have some control over the shared quest or the investigation of ideas. "If a person is genuinely searching for information and data, he does not resent help or company along the way."

SOURCE: J. R. Gibb, "Defensive Communication," *Journal of Communication* 2, no. 3 (September 1961), p. 143. Reprinted by permission of the International Communication Association.

portive behaviors ordinarily generate defense reduction, the degree to which these responses occur depends on the individual's previous level of defensiveness as well as the general climate at the time.

In a superior-subordinate relationship, if the subordinate perceives the superior as having any of the defensive characteristics, the chances increase that the subordinate will become defensive. However, if the subordinate perceives that the superior possesses the supportive characteristics, defensive behavior will be minimal or nonexistent.

A supportive style results in improved organizational effectiveness by enhancing the subordinate's feeling of personal worth and importance, creating a feeling of esteem, and generating an atmosphere of trust. This leads to more open communication between the subordinate and the superior.

"Equality" is one of the characteristics of the supportive climate and it may have special significance in interpersonal influence. If the leader views herself as being equal to subordinates and is open to influence by subordinates, the subordinates may then feel that communication is worthwhile. Lee Thayer indicates that successful leadership in most democratic situations is just as much a function of the leader being influenced by the subordinate as it is the subordinates being influenced by the leader.[8]

Power, authority, and status incongruities between two individuals in an organization can impede the proper flow of information. Subordinates tend to filter out "bad news" that should be communicated to superiors. The frequency and seriousness of the filtering of upward communication tend to increase as the climate in the organization becomes more defensive.

Gibb's findings imply that people clearly respond to the environment in which they must function. If we want to encourage certain behaviors in an individual, we must develop an environment conducive to such behavior. Therefore, the manager who wants to encourage distrust, anxiety, and dependence should maintain a defensive environment. On the other hand, the manager who wants to enhance open communication, individual growth, and strong interpersonal relationships should maintain an open, supportive climate.

THE JOHARI WINDOW

A model that clearly suggests the benefits of such a climate is the Johari Window.[9] This useful tool for understanding and improving interpersonal relationships is basically an information-sharing model (shown in Figure 6–6). You can construct a Johari window for all interpersonal relationships and the other person in these relationships can construct his

FIGURE 6–6   The Johari Window

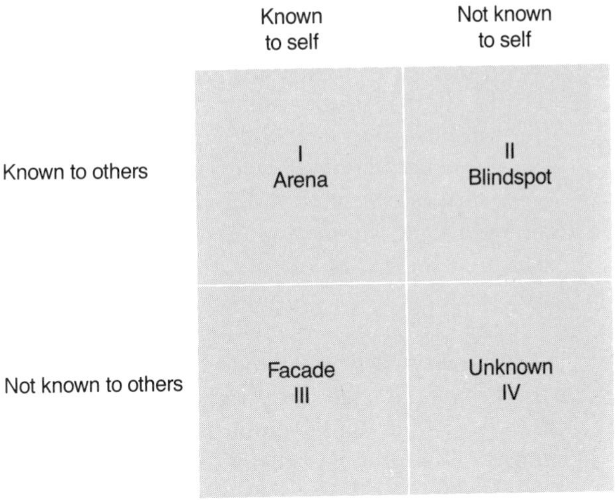

Known   Not known
to self   to self

Known to others

I Arena	II Blindspot

Not known to others

Facade III	Unknown IV

SOURCE: Adapted from *Group Processes: An Introduction to Group Dynamics* by Joseph Luft by permission of Mayfield Publishing Company (formerly National Press Books). Copyright © 1963, 1970, by Joseph Luft.

or her own window. The window is divided into four quadrants, each representing a different information-sharing posture between Self and Other.

The Arena

Quadrant 1 contains information that is known both to Self and Other. Because such information is "public," this quadrant is referred to as the **Arena,** the open area of a relationship. The Arena corresponds to the area of overlap in Nord's interpersonal perception model shown in Figure 6–2, and serves as the basis of the relationship between Self and Other. The size of the Arena indicates the quality of a relationship. When two individuals enjoy openness and share information, their communication, and therefore their relationship, strengthens and grows.

The Blind Spot

Quadrant 2 contains information known to Other but unknown to Self. For example, Other might possess information about Self's chances for a promotion, Self's effect on other people, and how others feel about Self. These things are not known to Self because Other has not volunteered

the information or Self has not requested or paid attention to it. Because of Self's lack of awareness of information held by Other, quadrant 2 is referred to as the **Blind Spot.**

The Facade

Quadrant 3 contains information known by Self but unknown by Other. This is information that Self has decided to withhold. Such information includes Self's true emotional state, career plans, ideas, talents, and responses to others. In an effort to protect ourselves or build a power base, we are often unwilling to disclose such information, so we put on a "front" and hide behind it. Therefore, quadrant 3 is referred to as the **Facade.**

The Unknown

Quadrant 4 contains information unknown to both Self and Other. For that reason it is called the **Unknown.** Information in this area may concern an infinite variety of matters such as untapped feelings, skills, abilities, and needs. Such information is highly valuable to the continued growth of Self and Other; unfortunately, it is hidden to both individuals. It can be discovered and unlocked by open interaction.

Through interpersonal synergism both individuals discover unknown qualities and dimensions of information. The key is to encourage and intensify interaction so that the synergy can generate the information lying in this region. As interaction and synergy occur, more information is moved from the Unknown region to the Arena.

We are challenged by the creators of the Johari Window to expand information sharing (the Arena) to some optimal level. This is accomplished through two mechanisms: **exposure** and **feedback solicitation.**

Exposure and Feedback

Exposure is the act of sharing information in a relationship. It requires Self to expose to Other her feelings, opinions, knowledge, and preferences that are relevant to the relationship. This can be difficult because many individuals have had little experience with open, candid communication and may feel uncomfortable or simply not know how to begin the process.

Exposure can also be risky for Self. Self may be reluctant to let Other know what her feelings are because Other might use such information against her. Individuals often refrain from letting others know how they feel because they fear the information may be used against them. If successful, exposure causes the Arena to expand vertically at the expense of

the Facade and the Unknown. (Realize that exposure by Other is feedback for Self, and vice versa.)

Feedback for Self is generated by seeking the feelings, opinions, knowledge, and preferences of Other. By asking, and then carefully listening, the Arena can be expanded horizontally at the expense of the Blind Spot and the Unknown. Soliciting feedback requires a certain amount of credibility and trust. Self must devote time and effort to building the proper base before feedback is forthcoming. Feedback solicitation usually fails if Self is not serious, and instead conveys a lack of interest in the information Other contributes to the relationship.

Communication Styles

The key to successful use of the Johari Window is a willingness of both individuals to seek feedback, to listen, and to disclose information openly. If either party is unwilling to do any of these things, then attempts at more fruitful relationships may turn out to be frustrating and unsuccessful. Individuals who favor one communication mechanism to the exclusion of the other tend to develop a distinctly unbalanced interpersonal style.

The Over-Exposer. The individual who is always exposing, talking, giving his opinion, and not listening to anyone but himself is probably incapable of understanding others. Such a person tends to have a very large Blind Spot and, consequently, his interpersonal relationships will suffer (see Figure 6–7).

Individuals who find their relationships lopsided in this fashion

---

FIGURE 6–7 The Result of Too Little Feedback and Too Much Exposure

Arena   Blind spot

Facade   Unknown

should make a special effort to be better information collectors. They need not diminish their exposure level, but should spend more time asking questions and listening to the people around them. By continuing to share their feelings and ideas *and* soliciting more feedback, such individuals can enjoy much more balanced and productive relationships.

The Under-Exposer.   The individual who never discloses his feelings, but always seeks the information or position of others places those others in an uncomfortable position. Others never know where such a person stands; consequently, they are unsure, uncomfortable, and even frustrated around such a person. As a result, they will be cautious or suspicious, never fully trusting or disclosing. This person usually is ineffective interpersonally because of a large Facade (see Figure 6–8).

An individual who is willing to engage in exposure may encourage others to be more open and honest. Feedback should also be solicited, but individuals need to be open and prepared to share their feelings and ideas. Others will respond and relationships will be richer and more productive.

The Organizational Hermit.   Some individuals engage in neither feedback nor exposure and have no basis at all for a relationship. These social hermits know very little about themselves or others. Likewise, others know little about them. The social hermit suffers from a large Blind Spot, Facade, and Unknown (see Figure 6–9).

Individuals whose relationships are depicted in Figure 6–9 must come out from behind their unwillingness to interact and experiment with some exposure. If they share their feelings and ideas, others may be able to reciprocate and share in a relationship.

FIGURE 6–8   The Result of Too Little Exposure and Too Much Feedback

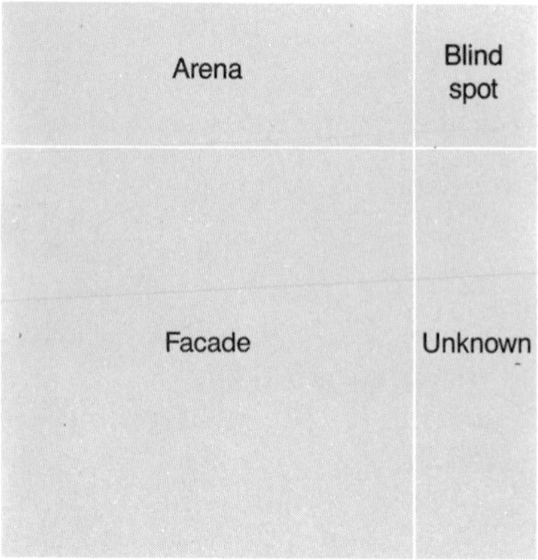

FIGURE 6–9 The Result of Too Little Exposure and Too Little Feedback

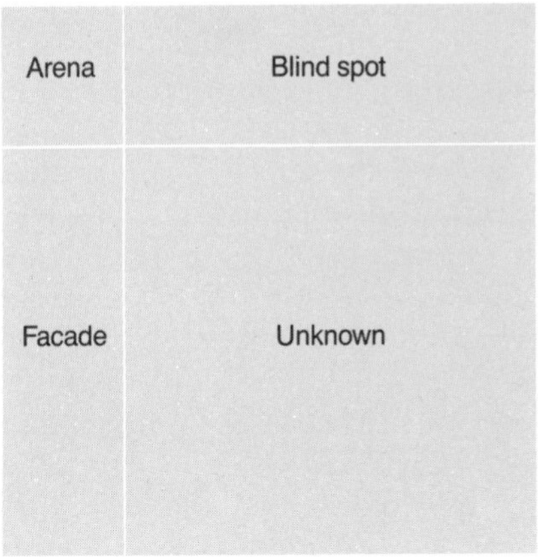

Arena	Blind spot
Facade	Unknown

The hermit must also be willing to discover how others feel through feedback solicitation. Gradually, as the hermit receives feedback from others and responds to it, he will send out a signal that he wants to participate in meaningful relationships. It is unlikely that others will share, however, until the hermit demonstrates his willingness to be a party to a relationship.

Johari Dynamics

The Johari Window has a dynamic nature that can help you understand the "living" quality of relationships. It clearly depicts the life of a relationship in terms of information flows. Consider, for example, what happens to marital partners, business partners, or parents and their children. When two individuals first form a relationship, there is a high level of information sharing. Information is pouring into the Arena from the other three quadrants (see Figure 6–10). Individuals who successfully maintain a strong relationship do so by growing individually, sharing their experiences, and simultaneously growing as a couple. The Arena continues to grow and remains large at the expense of the other quadrants.

If the individuals do not grow individually, or if they choose not to share their experiences, they will not continue to grow as partners in a relationship. The size of the Arena will shrink, and the relationship will suffer (see Figure 6–11).

Later in the life of a relationship, the participants (husbands and wives, parents and children) may realize what has happened and may want to revive a diminished relationship. Consequently, the individuals may begin to intensify their contact and sharing. As new and greater lev-

FIGURE 6–10   Expanding the Arena: The Growth of a Relationship

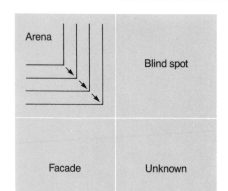

els of information are poured into the Arena, the relationship can be restored and expanded (see Figure 6–12). This is often the case as people move in and out of relationships, letting them contract and then attempting to rebuild them.

Keep your exposure and feedback solicitation balanced as you increase the size of the Arena. Increase the use of each mechanism only to the point where you and the other person are comfortable and effective with each other. Obviously, the appropriate balance and level of development differs for each relationship. For example, a manager, by virtue

FIGURE 6–11   Contracting the Arena: The Decline of a Relationship

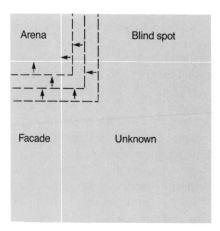

FIGURE 6–12   Restoring the Arena: The Renewal of a Relationship

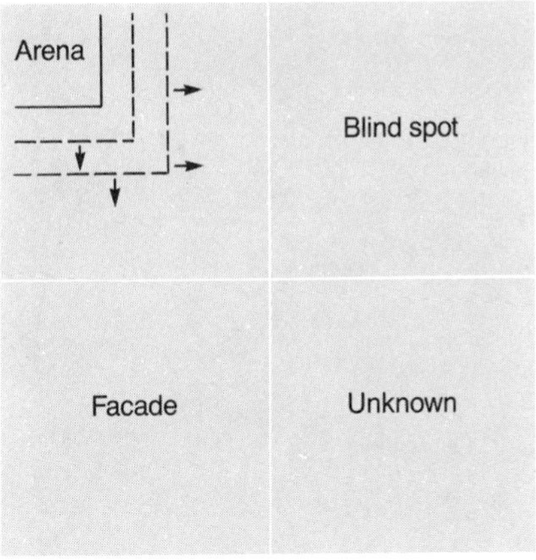

---

of her leadership position, may use slightly more exposure than feedback solicitation.

Keep appropriate information in the relationship and inappropriate information out of the relationship. For example, the subject of a manager's health and marital problems is appropriate between family members or close friends, but is inappropriate for a superior-subordinate relationship.

Once you begin to reap the benefits of open interaction, clearer information sharing, and more effective relationships, you may be reluctant to settle for anything less.

TRANSACTIONAL ANALYSIS

In Figure 6–1 we illustrated the interactive process whereby Person provides a stimulus, and Other responds. This stimulus-response pattern is the basic unit of **transactional analysis.** Transactional analysis (TA) was developed by Eric Berne[10] and popularized by such individuals as Thomas Harris[11] and Muriel James and Dorothy Jongeward.[12]

The Ego States of TA

TA assumes that we exist as three different people by moving in and out of three distinctly different states of being called **ego states.**

Parent Ego State: This state contains attitudes and behaviors incorporated from external sources—primarily our parents. All the actions and expressions of the young child's parents and other relevant adults are recorded and managed by the Parent within us. To be "in one's Parent"

means that the individual is in the same state of mind as her parents. Inwardly the Parent directs the individual to act as his parents instructed: "Always clean your plate, brush your teeth, and shine your shoes." "Never talk to a stranger." "Children should be seen and not heard."

The Parent ego state is expressed in either critical or nurturing behavior. The "Critical Parent" is evaluative and disapproving, frequently expressing our greatest fears and prejudices. "I always said you never could trust those people." "They're all alike." "Why doesn't he get a job!" "She ought to stay at home with her children!"

The "Nurturing Parent" expresses concern for others, but usually from a position of superiority. This nurturing is condescending and paternalistic in nature, indicating that the nurtured person is incapable of caring for himself. Consider the following expressions. "Come here, poor dear, let me take care of you (since you can't)." "Let me do that for you (since you can't do it yourself)." "Now, now, don't fret, I'll make it better (since you can't)." These responses come not only from our biological parents, but from the Nurturing Parent within our teachers, bosses, secretaries, spouses, and so forth. Frequently the nurtured person feels even more dependent and inadequate as a result.

The Parent is troublesome in interpersonal relations because the expressions associated with it have little relevance to current conditions, are unpremeditated, and are automatic. For example, the admonition that "She ought to stay at home with the kids" doesn't consider the fact that she is a widow and can't afford to stay home with the kids. If "she" did stay at home and existed on welfare payments, the Parent would most likely respond with, "Ain't it awful! She ought to get a job."

Child Ego State: The Child contains all the impulses that come naturally to an infant: a sense of curiosity, creativity, and a desire to explore and experience the environment. It also contains the recordings of the child's early experiences, how he responded to them, and how he feels about himself and others. Because of his state of helplessness and dependency, the young child repeatedly experiences feelings of inadequacy. Simultaneously, he feels that the adult helpers in his world are terrific, superior people.

The natural feelings of growth and inadequacy are what influence the behavior of the Child in each of us. Too frequently, expressions of natural feelings (e.g., screaming, giggling, laughing, questioning) are suppressed, and feelings of inadequacy overcome us. As biological adults, the Child in us expresses those feelings in various ways. "I wish I could . . . (but I know I never will)." "Mine's bigger than yours (*you* feel inferior for a while)." "Just wait 'til tomorrow! (I'll show you who's bigger, better, more important)."

Adult Ego State: The Adult is oriented toward current reality and the objective gathering of information. The information-seeking Adult is expressed by such interrogatives as who, why, when, how, or where. The

Adult is highly organized and functions by objectively testing reality, estimating probabilities, and computing responses. For example, if the Adult admonished a mother to "stay at home with her children," it would be on the basis of a logical analysis of the situation, not on the basis of some emotion-charged, archaic role model.

The adult has analytical and reality-testing capabilities and should be our controlling state. The Adult should be sensitive to the Child and Parent ego states, and allow both to function. The Adult should screen and control the destructive emotional expressions of the Child and the archaic expressions of the Parent, and help us become more in touch with our environment and ourselves. The result will be more open, honest, and relevant expressions of how we really feel.

Transactions: The Basic Unit of TA

Understanding the role of the ego states in interpersonal relations and increasing the control of the Adult can be accomplished by improving one's ability to analyze transactions. The basic unit of TA is the transaction, and there are three basic types: **complementary, crossed,** and **ulterior.**

Complementary transactions. A complementary transaction occurs when Person, while in a given ego state, creates a stimulus-message that is addressed to one of Other's three ego states. This stimulus then elicits an appropriate response from the ego state in Other that was addressed by Person.

With reference to Figure 6–13, assume that Person and Other have been working hard all day (mostly in their Adult ego state) and now want to relax, play, and have fun. Person (who has slipped into his Child ego state) then says to (the Child in) Other, "Let's go have a beer." Other (who has also slipped into his Child ego state) says to Person, "Great. Let's go."

FIGURE 6–13 A Complementary Transaction

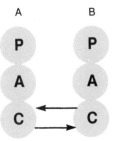

Person got the desired response, which was complementary to the stimulus. The transaction was a success; communication continues and so does the relationship.

Crossed Transactions.   Suppose that in response to Person's invitation to go have a beer, Other (who refuses to shift from the Adult to the Child ego state) said, "No, we've got three more reports to complete. Maybe later." This is a crossed transaction, and it is illustrated in Figure 6–14. Person was communicating from the Child ego state to Other's Child, but Other was responding from the Adult ego state to Person's Adult ego state. In this case Person did not get the desired response and may be offended by Other's response, perhaps even to the point of becoming defensive or angry. The result could be a breakdown in communication and in the relationship.

Ulterior Transactions.   There is a third possible outcome to Person's invitation to go have a beer. Person might say, "Let's go have a beer." Other could respond with, "No, we've got three more reports to complete." Person could reply, "Boy, you sure are a hard worker!" (See Figure 6–15.)

At one level Person (mainly through the spoken words) is ostensibly commending Other's devotion to completing the task. At another level (mainly through tone of voice) Person may be saying, "Gee, you're an old stick-in-the-mud, and I don't like you that way!" This is an example of an ulterior transaction—Person is actually communicating two different messages simultaneously, one on the surface and another below the surface. The ulterior message says something about the relationship and is the message that Other will respond to. Ulterior transactions, like crossed transactions, are problematic and often result in interpersonal conflict.

To the extent that we understand where other people are "coming from" (i.e., in which ego state they are operating), we can better "transact" with them. If we can identify a person's current ego state, we can better understand the message and provide more meaningful responses. TA

FIGURE 6–14 A Crossed Transaction

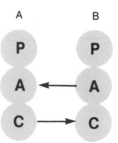

FIGURE 6–15 An Ulterior Transaction

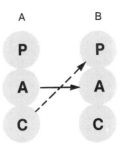

provides a useful framework for analyzing and understanding the content and the context of transactions.

We have only described TA here; proper knowledge and training are required to apply TA. We strongly recommend the references cited as a place to begin building your knowledge of this highly useful approach to improving interpersonal relationships.

INTEGRATING THE MODELS

As you look back at the various models of interpersonal sharing presented in this chapter, you will see that they overlap and reinforce one another. For example, Smith demonstrated how the characteristic behaviors of the ego states of TA correspond with the characteristic behaviors of Gibb's supportive-defensive climates.[14]

Consider the "Critical Parent" of TA. Individuals operating from this ego state tend to send evaluative and controlling messages ("You're over budget. From now on you'll have to get my approval for expenditures"). This message could create a defensive climate.

The Adult tends to send descriptive, problem-solving, empathic messages ("Let's review your budget and see what we might be able to do about the shortage").

Messages sent by the Child often have a tendency to convey disinterest ("I don't care"), disapproval ("That's not so terrific"), or superiority ("I've done better than that"). On other occasions the Child might engage in more expansive ("Gee, that's great") and exploratory ("How come. . . .") messages.

There are many other combinations of ego states and climate characteristics. A thorough understanding of these combinations can be helpful in analyzing communication situations and choosing the most appropriate response.

SUMMARY

The quality of a relationship is directly related to the quantity and quality of information sharing.

The Johari Window illustrates the vital role of information sharing in the development and maintenance of interpersonal relations. To the extent that parties to a relationship can continuously channel useful information from the Blind Spot, the Facade, and the Unknown into the Arena, the relationship will remain open and productive. Channeling information into the Arena is directly related to the abilities and willingness of the parties to disclose their feelings, opinions, and ideas, and to elicit feedback regarding the feelings, opinions, and ideas of others.

Feedback lets us know how well we are doing and offers us an opportunity to improve our efforts. A manager can create a climate that is conducive to the generation and constructive use of feedback, or she can create an environment with little or no feedback and improvement. According to Gibb, the climate created by a manager is a function of certain characteristic behaviors. Supportive, constructive climates are created by managers who are descriptive, empathic, egalitarian, and problem-oriented in their treatment of subordinates. Defensive, destructive climates are created by managers who are evaluative, controlling, condescending, and dogmatic.

According to Transactional Analysis, information sharing is complicated by the fact that an individual can shift ego states to become any one of three different senders or receivers. An individual can be in her Parent, Adult, or Child state while sending a message to a receiver who may also be in any of the three states. If the sender or receiver attempts to relate to the other from an inappropriate ego state, communication will cease. If communications are to remain open and effective, the parties to the relationship must understand the need to communicate *from* and *to* the appropriate ego state.

Each of us must assume the responsibility for improvement and make an effort to be a better communicator in order to enjoy meaningful and productive relationships. The models presented in this chapter are an attempt to help the reader understand that responsibility, and to suggest some ways to improve on the effort.

DISCUSSION QUESTIONS

1. Distinguish between the different types of filtering. Explain the impact of filtering on the communication process.

2. Distinguish between internal and external noise and explain the impact of each on the communication process. Identify five sources of external noise. Suggest ways to reduce or eliminate noise.

3. The Nord model of interpersonal perception is illustrated and discussed in Chapter 6. The model emphasizes the importance of differences and similarities in the way Person and Other view reality. Explain those differences and similarities and their importance for understanding how communication takes place.

4. Briefly explain the five different flows or channels of communication depicted in the Nord model.

5. In the upper portion of the Nord model, part of what Person and Other see lies outside the reality rectangle. What does this portion of the circles represent? Why is it so problematic? How does it contribute to communication breakdowns?

6. Discuss the importance of feedback and its relationship to individual and organizational change. Include a discussion of positive and negative response to feedback and the kind of organizational climate conducive to positive responses.

7. Compare and contrast supportive and defensive organizational climates and their impact on communication.

8. Explain the four quadrants on the Johari Window. How is the Johari Window used to improve interpersonal relationships?

9. In accordance with Johari dynamics, explain how the Arena can be expanded and how this expansion affects interpersonal behavior.

10. Identify the various communication styles depicted in the Johari Window. What can a manager do to improve his communication style in accordance with the Johari Window?

11. Define the three ego states of transactional analysis. What are some typical cues that help to identify each ego state?

12. Explain the three different types of transactions that can occur. How can an understanding of transactional analysis be helpful in a business communication situation?

13. Why is an understanding of the dynamics of interpersonal behavior crucial for a manager? Discuss two models the manager might use to organize his or her approach to interpersonal business communication.

14. Assume you are placed in a room with one other person that you have never met. Describe in detail what would probably take place.

EXERCISES

1. Draw a diagram illustrating the interactive communication process. Using the diagram as the basis, explain the interactive process. As you explain the process, identify the specific sources of communication breakdown.

2. After reading the following articles, ask one of your instructors to allow you to come into the classroom for 15 to 30 minutes. Using the designs described in

the articles (or one of your own), replicate the experiments described. Discuss the results.

H. J. Leavitt and R. A. Mueller, "Some Effects of Feedback on Communication," *Human Relations* 4 (1951), pp. 401–10.

William Haney, "A Comparative Study of Unilateral and Bilateral Communication," *Academy of Management Journal* 7 (June 1964), pp. 128–36.

3. Select a topic or subject toward which you have a strong attitude (either positive or negative). Prepare a 15-minute talk supporting the opposite position. This talk should be convincing enough to persuade your classmates to adopt your position. Be prepared to answer all questions and defend your position against any criticism. After the presentation, describe and analyze your feelings before and during the presentation. Describe the procedure and rationale you used to prepare your talk.

4. Each of the statements below reflects behavioral characteristics of Gibb's defensive-supportive climates and the three ego states of transactional analysis.* See if you can identify the characteristics and ego states in each.

   a. (1) _____ "Your petty cash account is short again. You'll have to get my approval for all petty cash expenditures in the future."

   (2) _____ "Let's go over your petty cash procedures and see what we can do about these shortages."

   b. (1) _____ "My proposal is based on some sophisticated concepts you may not understand."

   (2) _____ "Please let me know if I'm communicating my proposal to you in an effective way."

   c. (1) _____ "John, you did a fine job on this report. As soon as these minor errors are corrected, it will be ready to go."

   (2) _____ "I'm disappointed to see your poor proofreading habits are resulting in errors in your reports."

   d. (1) _____ "This project must be finished by Friday, no matter what!"

   (2) _____ "Joe, how's your schedule look this week? Our reputation with the Morton Company depends on finishing their project by Friday."

   e. (1) _____ "These are my instructions, and I expect you to follow them precisely."

   (2) _____ "I've worked out some instructions for this job. Let me know if you have any questions or suggestions."

   f. (1) _____ "Well, Joan, I'll have to think about your request; I have a lot of other things to consider before I make my decision, you know."

   (2) _____ "Joan, as soon as I get the new production schedule, I can let you know about taking next Friday off."

---

*SOURCE: Norma Carr-Smith, "Overcoming Defensive Barriers to Communication: A Transactional Analysis Approach," *The ABCA Bulletin* 41, no. 1 (March 1978), p. 15. Used with permission.

NOTES

[1]For an expanded discussion of this point, see Lee Thayer, *Communication and Communication Systems* (Homewood, Ill: Richard D. Irwin, 1968), chap. 4.

[2]George Miller, *Language and Communication* (New York: McGraw-Hill, 1951), p. 249.

[3]Walter Nord, *Concepts and Controversies in Organizational Behavior* (Santa Monica, Calif: Goodyear Publishing, 1976), p. 24.

[4]Ibid, p. 23.

[5]Wilson B. Key, *Subliminal Seduction* (New York: New American Library, 1974); *Media Sexploitation* (Englewood Cliffs, N.J.: Prentice-Hall, 1976).

[6]Len Moran, "Inside the New AT&T Manager," *AT&T Magazine* 1, no. 2, p. 3.

[7]Jack R. Gibb, "Defensive Communication," *Journal of Communication*, September 1961, p 143.

[8]Lee Thayer, *Communication and Communication Systems*, p. 229.

[9]Joseph Luft, *Group Processes: An Introduction to Group Dynamics* (Palo Alto, Calif.: Mayfield Publishing Company, 1963).

[10]Eric Berne, *Games People Play* (New York: Grove Press, 1964).

[11]Thomas Harris, *I'm Okay You're Okay* (New York: Harper & Row, 1967).

[12]Murial James and Dorothy Jongeward, *Born to Win* (Reading, Mass: Addison-Wesley Publishing, 1971).

[13]Ibid.

[14]Norma Smith, "Overcoming Defensive Barriers to Communication: A Transactional Analysis Approach," *The ABCA Bulletin* 41, no. 1 (March 1978), p. 12.

SUGGESTED READINGS

BAXTER, CAROL, and THOMAS CLARK. "My Favorite Assignments: Putting Organizational and Interpersonal Communication Theory into Practice: Classroom Committees." *ABCA Bulletin* 45 (September 1982), pp. 38–41.

DENNY, RITA. "Marking the Interactional Order: The Social Constitution of Turn Exchange and Speaking Turns." *Language in Society* 14, no. 2 (March 1985), pp. 41–62.

DOBBINS, GREGORY H. "Effects of Gender on Leaders: Responses to Poor Performers: An Attributional Interpretation." *Academy of Management Journal* 28, no. 3 (September 1985), pp. 587–98.

ZAHRA, SHAKER A. "A Comparative Study of the Effects of Role Ambiguity and Conflict on Employee Attitudes and Performance." *Akron Business and Economic Review* 16, no. 1 (Spring 1985), pp. 37–42.

Chapter 7

Group Communication

Chapter 7 Case

You are the assistant manager of a major retail establishment, looking forward to promotion to a manager's job. You feel the next vacancy is yours if only you can successfully implement the new incentive plan handed down from headquarters. It won't be easy: your sales force is made up of people who have become friends, and the new plan will force them to compete with one another. While it has always been customary for the sporting goods department to compete with the cosmetics department, and for ladieswear to compete with menswear, the new plan calls for competition within departments. You are to present the new plan next week at the monthly staff meeting. How will you do it? What preliminary work, if any, will you do?

INTRODUCTION

We have observed that people spend much of their lives in groups. Individuals bring their values and perceptions into these groups hoping to satisfy some of their needs and wants. Their interpersonal skills and abilities dictate how effectively they will function as group members and, therefore, how successful the groups will be.

Groups are extremely useful and necessary, and we will examine their various functions and features in this chapter. We will define what a group is and provide insights into why groups are so pervasive and necessary in our lives. We will then outline the group development process and describe the behavior and communication that characterizes each phase of the process.

We will identify the major features which ultimately determine the nature of a group and how it will function. Finally, we will see how these features and functions apply in two critical areas for the manager: small group meetings and group decision making.

WHAT IS A GROUP?

Many people think of groups simply as a collection of people, but we are more precise than that and divide these collections of people into two parts. An **aggregation** is a collection of people who happen to be in the same place at the same time, perhaps even doing the same thing, but not necessarily for the same reasons, and certainly not collectively. A **functional group** is two or more people intentionally interacting with each other in an attempt to accomplish a common objective. The fundamental distinction is the lack of interaction and common purpose.

John Brilhart, in an effort to differentiate these two groups, lists the following five characteristics of a functional group:

1. A small enough number of people so that each is aware of and has some reaction to the other(s).
2. A mutually interdependent purpose—the success of each is contingent on the success of the others in achieving its goals.
3. A sense of belonging or membership, where each person identifies with other members of the group.
4. Oral interaction between group members.
5. Behavior based on norms, values, and procedures accepted by all members.[1]

These characteristics constitute what might be called "groupness," or what is traditionally called togetherness, camaraderie, or esprit de corps. It is a property that groups possess and aggregations do not.

An effective manager should be aware of these characteristics and how they govern group outcomes. For example, the size of a group can have an overwhelming effect on its members and its ability to function. Determining the optimum size is not always easy or obvious—too few or too many people can have equally devastating effects on a group.

Members of an aggregation (e.g., people at an airline terminal, bus station, restaurant, or cocktail lounge) may all be found in one location, possibly doing the same thing, but *not together*, and *not for the same reason*. There could be 25 individual reasons for 25 people to be in a cocktail lounge. Members of an aggregation operate independently, and there is no need for them to interact.

By contrast, interdependence, interaction, and communication are vital to the members of a functional group. For members to determine their common mission and accomplish it, there must be a discussion of what they will do and how they will do it. The members of a functional group would be at a cocktail lounge for a common purpose—perhaps an informal meeting or a party, celebrating a special occasion for one of the members, or just relaxing. The very act of being together helps to strengthen the interpersonal bonds and maintain the group.

The level of interaction and how it occurs depend on various group features: structure (i.e., relationship patterns), cohesiveness (i.e., what makes a group come together and stay together), conformity (i.e., achieving consensus, agreeing to and enforcing behavioral norms), size (how many members is enough), composition (member background, goals, and interest), and status. Managers need to understand these features because as they vary, so will group communication patterns and member behavior. Before we discuss these features more thoroughly, let's digress long enough to recognize the importance of studying groups, and outline their development process.

THE SIGNIFICANCE OF GROUPS

Individuals are influenced by society, and can emerge as its "victims" or its "products." However, it is difficult to point to society and say, "there it is, and this is how it created its victims." If we cannot specifically identify or locate it, how can we understand or control society's influence?

In Chapter 2 we introduced the abstraction ladder, which depicts the ability of our language to represent reality in either concrete or abstract fashion. Society happens to be one of those abstractions of reality; however, we can make it concrete by identifying the groups in a society.

Groups act as intermediaries between individuals and society, and influence the individual through the accepted values and behavioral standards of the groups to which he or she belongs. For example, a college student who belongs to a fraternity will be strongly influenced by the collective beliefs, feelings, and behavioral tendencies of the fraternity members. The individual members of a religious group are influenced by its creed and social standards. Members of recreational, ethnic, professional, geographic, and, ultimately, nation groups are influenced by the perceptions, emotions, and behavioral expectations embraced by each group. This influence process and its effects on individual behavior make the study of groups important.

WHY BELONG TO A GROUP?

Each individual is drawn to a group by individual circumstances and reasons, but we can identify some common reasons for group membership.

Enhanced Productivity

The most pervasive reason for joining groups, especially work groups, is **enhanced productivity**—the ability to accomplish goals that an individual

could not accomplish alone. It would take an individual most of a lifetime to single-handedly secure the necessary resources to build an automobile or a home, and then to actually build these things. A quick glance around at our many material possessions makes it clear why we join forces to physically generate the output that constitutes our standard of living. Through division of labor, specialization, and combination of our physical, financial, political, or informational resources, we can have what would otherwise be impossible.

Aside from the overwhelming need to pool resources and work together to be more productive, there are some social-psychological reasons why we join groups.[2]

Social Reality

Think of a place (e.g., a city, state, nation) that you have never visited. You have never been there, but you feel secure in your belief that it exists. This belief is based on photographs, maps, film, or descriptions from friends who have been there. These pieces of evidence provide you with a physical reality, which allows you to be aware of and deal with these places when the need arises. In a similar fashion **social reality** concerns the social landscape.

To feel secure and cope with parts of the environment that we have not previously experienced, we need information regarding the social fabric. We often get this information by joining various groups. For example, in the workplace a new employee might join formal and informal groups in an effort to learn more about the philosophy and style of management, the employees, and the work climate. When an individual relocates to a new city, she may join several groups in an effort to learn more about the social, economic, and political makeup of the community.

Social Identity

A second reason for seeking group membership is **social identity.** Individuals often seek to reinforce their self-concept and esteem by joining groups. Based on their announced beliefs and goals and the public behavior exhibited by their members, groups generate a particular image or identity. Consider the U.S. Marines, the Ku Klux Klan, the Moral Majority, the PLO, the Teamsters, Sears, IBM, and McDonald's. A member of these groups assumes, at least to some extent, the identity of the group. The group helps us to learn and reinforce who we are, what we believe, and how we should behave. We have opportunities to achieve our goals and receive recognition and praise for our efforts. If we want to communicate to others a certain image, or self-concept, we can do so through group membership.

Social Support

A final reason for joining groups is **social support.** As we grow and learn, we continually update the list of goals we wish to accomplish. Frequently an individual will formulate a goal that can be achieved only with the influence and power of other individuals. Their backing, in the form of economic, legal, or moral support, increases the individual's credibility.

Just as it is easier for an individual to accomplish more with physical support, it is also easier to accomplish some goals with social support. This point is clearly enunciated in the historical adage, "We must surely hang together or we shall all hang separately." Consequently, the founders of various groups (e.g., AFL–CIO, NAACP, MADD, Sierra Club) have found it easier to confront financial or political might or public apathy because others stand in support and increase their credibility.

HOW DO WE CHOOSE A GROUP?

What factors cause a person to choose a particular group? Here, again, there are some common reasons.

Proximity and Convenience

There are a variety of organized groups to turn to for our physical, social, and psychological goals. We frequently choose a specific organization because of its physical closeness and convenient access. The choice of a financial institution, church, country club, or civic group may ultimately be based on its proximity to home or work, the hours it is open, or the time of day when meetings are held. For example, employees who work on each floor or wing of a building will often congregate and form groups.

Special Interests

In the pursuit of work and leisure we develop special interests (e.g., computing, accounting, teaching, skydiving, auto racing, riflery, bird watching). As these interests become sufficiently widespread, organizations emerge to serve the needs of those who share the interests (e.g., AICPA, NEA, American Rifle Association, American Hot Rod Association, Audubon Society). Our society is rich in diversity with a wide array of professional, ethnic, regional, political, and recreational groups. The groups we choose to join are a reflection of our special interests.

Special Issues

Individuals sometimes encounter a troublesome set of circumstances or consequences created by changing environmental forces. Our environment is always changing, and this creates new problems and issues. Some issues (e.g., industrial pollution, hazardous waste, public education, employment-at-will) affect large numbers of people. Others (abortion, AIDS, capital punishment, farm subsidy programs) affect fewer individuals but are acute in their impact. Dealing with these issues requires a joint effort and elicits the creation of a group. The number and seriousness of the issues we are confronted with and how we choose to respond to those issues will affect our propensity to join particular groups.

We join groups for different reasons, and we choose specific groups based on several different criteria. Regardless of which groups we join, they all share a common development process.

THE GROUP DEVELOPMENT PROCESS

How does a group get started? A model developed by Tuckman proposes four stages: **forming, storming, norming,** and **performing.**[3]

Forming

This stage constitutes the period in the life of a group when the members first come together for basic orientation. The members of the group are introduced, given their charge, and told what the basic format of the group will be. A formal leader (e.g., chairperson, president) may be identified.

Forming can be brief or lengthy. If a committee is coming together to solve a problem, the organization is small, and the individuals all know one another, not much time is spent allowing members to get to know each other. On the other hand, if a multinational corporation is bringing together members of a project team from all over the world, it may take more time for these individuals to become acquainted and feel comfortable together. There may be formal meetings, cocktail parties, and dinners scheduled to promote the group development so that members can subsequently work together.

In the forming stage, behavior is relatively formal, cautious, impersonal, and perfunctory. Communication is also likely to be formal, impersonal, polite, and staged, lacking commitment and emotion. Once the members know each other's names, backgrounds, and so forth, this stage is essentially completed and they can move into stage two, storming.

Storming

Storming is a fascinating stage because here the group members begin groping for an accurate understanding of who wants to get what done. They want to learn the "nitty gritty" of what hidden or personal agenda items exist and how they might affect the formal group goals. Here the group members begin posturing and struggling for power. Determination of the power of other members is crucial to future loyalties, the development of power bases, and the ultimate power structure of the group.

Based on their assessment of the power structure, group members will begin influence efforts to get support for their personal position and goals, and to establish power blocs. This is commonly seen at national political conventions where various individuals and interest groups campaign and caucus to establish their power position.

This stage may contain a high level of conflict because individuals are explaining their position and trying to influence each other. In our discussion of the Johari Window, we indicated the need for a balance between disclosure and feedback solicitation. As group members attempt to persuade one another of the importance of their position, disclosure will probably exceed feedback solicitation. When two group members "discuss" who should use the group's limited resources or how some task should be accomplished, each will insist on convincing the other how much greater his need or his way is, and not listen carefully to how important the other's need is.

Effective information sharing is obviously crucial but does not typically take place in the storming stage. Individuals become egocentric and want to elevate the importance of their position. Conflict, anger, frustration, and hostility are natural in this stage. Communication is not forced; it flows easily. Each group member is trying to convince others of the validity of his or her position, and this makes communication highly charged with emotions, very personal, persuasive, and even argumentative.

Unless group members realize what is happening, they will remain stalled in the storming stage indefinitely until an outside force either moves the group out of that stage or accomplishes the task. When group members recognize the interpersonal conflicts and resolve them, they can move into the next stage.

Groups usually move out of storming with a recognition of the need to decide how the group is to move forward and perform its work. To do so, group members need to develop behavioral standards and decision rules. This is the substance of the next stage, norming.

Norming

After the storming activities, the group is ready to make some decisions about how to proceed to accomplish its objectives. These decisions result

in a set of norms regarding acceptable procedure. A norm is defined as "an authoritative standard; a principle of right action binding upon the members of a group and serving to guide, control, or regulate proper and acceptable behavior."[4]

Norms may be written or unwritten depending on the level of formality within the group. As an organization grows in size, its level of formality and need for written standards also grows. However, even in the largest and most formal organizations many group norms may not be written, especially those dealing with status and status recognition. You would be hard-pressed to find anything written in corporate manuals and handbooks regarding the deferential treatment (larger space, rigid posture) accorded executives. Nonetheless, the subordinate who does not extend such treatment to those above him may be in for a short career.

In most functional groups there are specific tasks to be completed, and many of the norms will address how these tasks are to be accomplished. Norms may concern group membership, relationships among group members, relationships with outsiders, procedures for starting and completing tasks, accountability, and so forth. Common formats for stipulating formal written group norms include statements of philosophy, policies, operating procedures, job descriptions, by-laws and constitutions, and rules and regulations.

Groups that are part of a larger organization (e.g., committees, project teams, subsidiaries) are furnished with certain norms—policies, procedures, rules, regulations—already established by the larger organization. The group may have to create norms for its specific task, membership, and environment, but it will be constrained by the norms of the organization. The group cannot exceed the minimum (or maximum in some cases) behavior standards permitted by the larger organization.

Norms created within the group are derived from the nature of the group's objectives and the perceptions, values, and needs of the members. To the extent that group members are interested in satisfying social-psychological purposes, they will develop norms to make these purposes easily identifiable and intentionally distinguish them from the rest of the world. For example, to belong to a VFW club, an individual must have served in the armed forces. To become a CPA, you must pass a rigorous examination demonstrating extensive knowledge of accounting.

Performing

With the objectives of the group established and the means of accomplishment stipulated, members can now get on with the task for which they were brought together. In the performing stage the group becomes productive and the results of the three earlier stages will be tested. If the membership was properly constituted, the charge clearly drafted and

communicated, and the norms derived in an acceptable fashion, the group should be capable of performing.

Errors in those earlier stages, will make the group nonproductive. Group members then have to return to the beginning to work through the stages again and adapt the necessary changes.

Beyond Performing

In response to a dynamic environment, groups frequently have to accomplish specific tasks within a specific time frame. For example, the new president of a university learns that travel policies and practices are inconsistent from college to college. Because of tighter budgets and greater fiscal accountability, travel practices must be clarified and adhered to. She appoints a university-wide committee to develop a comprehensive set of travel policies and procedures and report to her within two months. When such groups complete their task they will have no further need to exist and will be *dissolved*.

Some groups are given a specific, open-ended charge that is accomplished sporadically as a function of the actions of individuals or changes in the environment. A grievance committee, for example, has a specific charge, but does not meet on any kind of regular basis. Instead, members wait for certain conditions to occur and then perform their task. Such groups are not dissolved after handling a grievance; they simply *adjourn* until conditions warrant a meeting.

Many groups are given a general, open-ended task to perform and must meet on a regular basis. For example, members of a board of directors, city council, or faculty senate meet regularly because their task is ongoing. Frequently, because of changes in membership, task, or organizational policies and regulations, such groups must *reform*. The group will return to the forming stage and work through the development process. The duration and difficulty of the reforming depends on the seriousness of the changes that caused the reforming.

GROUP CHARACTERISTICS

How well a group performs will depend on the level of groupness it achieves. Groupness is a function of several group characteristics. How do these characteristics influence the communication, behavior, and ultimate performance of the group?

Structure

As individuals join a group, they seek activities and relationships that are productive and satisfying. The ultimate pattern of organized relationships

that results is the group structure. Structure is important because it affects the tasks an individual is responsible for, the quality of member relationships, member satisfaction, and, ultimately, the group's effectiveness.

Some of the most important research on stucture has focused on the design and outcomes of communication networks.[5] There are many network possibilities, some of which are shown in Figure 7–1. These are rather simplistic, but they adequately represent the basic set of superior-subordinate and peer relationships that characterize most organizations. The central and peripheral roles of leader and follower are indicated by L and M, respectively.

The structures vary in degree of centralization and amount of possi-

FIGURE 7–1 Communication Networks

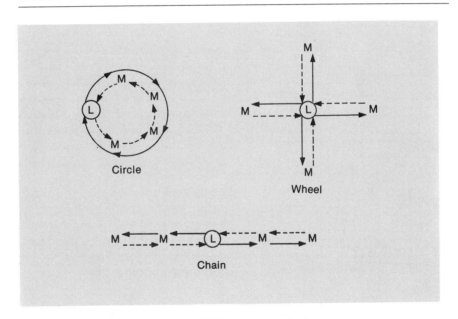

	Circle	Chain	Wheel
Task speed	Slow	Fast	Fast
Task time	High	Low	Low
Task efficiency	Poor	Good	Good
Organizational development	Extremely slow	Slow, stable	Quick, stable
Error rate	High	Low	Low
Feedback	High	Low	Low
Peripheral satisfaction	High	Low	Low
Central satisfaction	High	High	High

ble member contact. The wheel is the most centralized, while the circle allows for the greatest number of contacts. Variables measured in different studies include speed of task accomplishment, accuracy of task accomplishment, frequency of communication, errors committed, and member satisfaction.

As we illustrated in the section on group development, before a group can begin performing it must first organize. The wheel is the quickest to organize and the most accurate at task performance. Because of the immense number of contacts possible in the circle, the amount of communication and confusion is appreciable. As a result, it is the slowest to organize and, therefore, the most inefficient at task accomplishment. Circle members send more messages and make the greatest number of errors. While the central individual (L) in each of the networks experiences greater satisfaction than the peripherals (M), circle members registered the highest overall satisfaction. These findings must be used carefully because they are applicable only when simple problems or tasks are involved.

The wheel network is the most efficient for solving simple problems because simple tasks require limited processing of information. Complex tasks require more and different information, and more intense sharing and processing; consequently, greater interaction is necessary.

For solving difficult problems, the decentralized (circle) pattern is the better arrangement. These findings clearly suggest that the most effective communication structure will be determined, at least partially, by the nature of the work done by a group.

Cohesiveness

Cohesiveness is the extent to which group members are attracted to each other and the group. Cohesiveness is a function of interpersonal attractiveness, external threat or competition, group size, group status, severity of initiation, and the group's reputation for effectiveness.

Interpersonal Attractiveness. Increased opportunities for interaction result in increased interpersonal attractiveness and cohesiveness. Cohen and his colleagues make this point with the following observations:

1. The greater the opportunity/requirements for interaction, the greater the likelihood of interaction occurring.
2. The more frequent the interaction among people, the greater the likelihood of their developing positive feelings for one another.
3. The greater the positive feelings among people, the more frequently they will interact.[6]

Interpersonal attractiveness is also enhanced by similarity of member attitudes and values. Individuals who come from the same or similar so-

cio-economic background, who share the same outlook, values, and interests, will find each other attractive. People who live in the same neighborhood, attend the same schools, and get excited about the same sports find one another desirable and pleasing.

External Threat or Competition. Intergroup competition and outside threats generally have the effect of bringing group members closer together. Often group members will compete with one another until there is an external threat, but unite to defeat the threat. An example is the process the two major U.S. political parties go through every four years to identify their nominees for the presidency. Various factions within each party fight to secure votes and nominations. However, once the parties choose their candidates, the members cooperate to defeat the other party's candidate. This unity induces greater group interaction and increases cohesiveness.

Group Size. Group size and cohesiveness tend to be inversely related. As a group gets larger it becomes more difficult to maintain the intimacy required for group attractiveness.[7] The joint tasks of communication and coordination of effort are more formidable in a bigger group. Specialization becomes more attractive or necessary, and it becomes increasingly difficult for all members to interact and get to know one another. It is also more difficult to identify and satisfy the needs of each member. As communication and group member satisfaction decrease, splinter groups form in an attempt to satisfy those needs. Thus larger groups generally report less satisfaction and cohesiveness than smaller groups.

Group Status. Status is defined as the hierarchical positioning or "pecking order" of individuals within a group. Status is accorded to an individual on the basis of such factors as personal characteristics, title, visibility, influence, security, and accomplishments. Those who possess more status can direct the behavior of those with less status. For example, J. Horowitz and his colleagues found that generally higher-status members attract other high-status members and low-status members.[8] Thus status affords the individual greater opportunities for influence.

Severity of Initiation. In the introduction to his work on the concept of cognitive dissonance, L. Festinger noted that "the individual strives toward consistency within himself . . . consistency between what a person knows or believes and what he does."[9] Marketing experts understand the value of providing consumers with postpurchase satisfaction. Consumers seek consistency between their actions (purchases) and their feelings and beliefs about those actions. If they feel good after a purchase they will: (1) be more satisfied, (2) recommend the product to others, and (3) repeat the purchase. Astute marketers help consumers deal with dissonance by providing messages that make them feel good about the purchase.

The same is true with group memberships and initiation. Festinger's observation is reflected in research evidence which indicates that a severe initiation promotes greater liking and cohesiveness.[10] The more effort and time an individual puts into *joining a group,* the more he will like it as a justification for investing the time and effort. This is necessary for internal consistency. Those who voluntarily join groups with relatively severe initiation (e.g., fraternity, professional, or military) tend to develop and maintain a strong liking for the group.

Group Reputation for Effectiveness.   A final factor bearing on interpersonal attractiveness and cohesiveness is the group's reputation for effectiveness. If a group can attract resources to do its work, it will diminish intragroup competition and increase interpersonal attractiveness. If a group has the proper resources it can accomplish more, and this success makes a group attractive to its members as well as outsiders.

With adequate resources, a group can concentrate on other things, including the maintenance of strong member relationships. The less intragroup conflict a group experiences, the more successful, attractive, and cohesive it is likely to be. According to research findings by Raven and Rietsema, increased cooperation and clarity of goals are both a cause and an effect of members feeling good about their successes and themselves.[11]

Conformity

Cohesiveness increases the ability of a group to influence its members to conform to group norms. As groups achieve a greater level of cohesiveness, they achieve greater conformity. Cohen and his colleagues distilled the following principles about this relationship:

1. The more cohesive a group, the more similar will be member output.
2. The more cohesive a group, the more it will enforce compliance with norms.
3. The more an individual fails to conform to the group, the more frequently negative sentiments will be expressed toward him or her by the group.[12]

When a member fails to conform, the group will communicate at an increasing rate in an attempt to get the deviant member to conform.[13] At some point, however, the group will decide to give up on the deviant, decrease communication at a rapid rate, and possibly ostracize the member.

Increasing cohesiveness facilitates increased communication which, reciprocally, increases cohesiveness. Group members share perceptions, needs, and values; thus information sharing is easier. Interdependence is higher; thus influence is greater. Accordingly, group members will routinely expect to direct each other's behavior to achieve greater conformity.

FIGURE 7–2 The Relationship between Group Composition, Task Type, and Performance

Group Composition	Task Type	Performance
Homogeneous	Simple	High
Homogeneous	Complex	Low
Heterogeneous	Simple	Low
Heterogeneous	Complex	High

Group Composition

Group composition has a powerful impact on the quantity and nature of communication within a group. A convenient scheme for categorizing group members for purposes of discussion is a bipolar continuum ranging from homogeneous to heterogeneous.

Homogeneous members have similar backgrounds, education, values and need, and this generally diminishes conflict and improves cooperation and communication between group members. The major drawback of homogeneity is the quality of sameness. This sameness is not a problem when dealing with simple tasks, because they require the limited perspectives and great efficiency of a homogeneous group. But homogeneous members are less likely to develop new perspectives, and their ability to add to a creative solution is limited.

When a task or problem requires diverse perspectives, a variety of information, and new ideas, heterogeneity, or dissimilarity of members, is more effective.[14] Complex problems require greater creativity in piecing together unrelated information. If heterogeneous individuals can come together and share, a better decision will result. The relationship between group composition and task complexity for successful performance is depicted in Figure 7–2.

Group Size

Group size is also important as it relates to intragroup cooperation and productivity. For example, if a group gets too large, it requires more communication and coordinating efforts, and sharing information adequately becomes difficult. However, large groups are able to divide a task and get more accomplished. Small groups allow for more intimacy and information sharing. Szilagyi and Wallace sum up the effects of group size with the following principles:

1. Very small groups show more tension, agreement, and asking of opinions, while large groups show more tension release and giving of information.

2. Groups with an even number of members have greater difficulty obtaining a majority, resulting in more tension.
3. Members of smaller groups report greater satisfaction than those in larger groups.
4. The relationship between group size and performance is somewhat inconclusive, depending on task type.
5. Increased group size leads to job specialization, less effective communication and diminished satisfaction.[15]

Groups composed of four members or less are usually too small to accomplish group tasks. An even number of members may be ineffective because of the possibility of standoffs. When group size is larger than eight, the development of factions or cliques is a distinct possibility. Conventional wisdom and group size research suggests that a group size of five to seven seems to be most effective.[16]

Group Roles

We have previously discussed the function of roles in identifying and supporting the self-concept and know that a role is a set of activities or behavioral expectations inherent in a position. Organizations formalize role expectations in the creation of job descriptions, policies, procedures, and rules and regulations.

Within the framework of those formal behavior expectations, each individual customizes his position by adapting his or her personality to the formal role expectations. The outcome of this process is often referred to as the **enacted role,** the individual's actual behavior based on his perception of the role.

If an individual successfully adapts his personality to the formal role, he will be happy and will remain on the job. If the organization disagrees with the adaptation and insists on something different, the individual may be unhappy and ultimately leave the job.

When individuals join a group, they often assume a number of different roles that can facilitate group performance. These roles fall into three categories: task-oriented, relations-oriented, or self-oriented.[17]

Task-oriented roles are geared to getting the work done. Specific task roles include:

1. Initiator—Sets the group in motion by providing direction and identifying the task or problem.
2. Information seeker—Solicits ideas and opinions; collects factual information of value to the group.
3. Information provider—Offers ideas, opinions, information, relevant experiences, and suggestions.
4. Clarifier—Keeps group discussion on track by clarifying or inter-

preting information, coordinating group efforts, and clearing up confusion.

5. Summarizer—Provides closure by evaluating the group's efforts and bringing together points of discussion; offers conclusions and recommendations.

Relations-oriented roles are geared to maintaining the proper social atmosphere. Specific relations roles include:

1. Harmonizer—Mediates conflict and reduces tension.
2. Supporter—Gives praise and acknowledges the contributions of others; generates friendliness and interpersonal warmth.
3. Gatekeeper—Facilitates participation by keeping channels open and encouraging sharing.
4. Standards monitor—Keeps the group aware of objectives and standards of performance; makes sure group members adhere to those standards.
5. Compromiser—Keeps discussion from bogging down by compromising ideas or suggestions.

Self-oriented roles are geared to protecting the interests, needs, and objectives of the individual. Specific self-oriented roles include:

1. Dominator—Asserts superiority and manipulates group members with authoritativeness, flattery, and so forth.
2. Bragger—Calls attention to himself by boasting and reporting on accomplishments.
3. Blocker—Acts like a "wet blanket"; resists group efforts by being blatantly negative.
4. Avoider—Protects self by maintaining social distance and refusing to become an active participant.

Group members can and frequently do assume more than one role simultaneously. The success of the group depends on the roles chosen and if those roles complement each other.

Because they are self-serving, self-oriented roles are generally distracting and detrimental to the group process. If everyone is trying to protect his personal interests, no one will be looking out for the interests of the group.

If a group is too relations oriented, too little work gets done. If, on the other hand, the group is only task oriented, group members may begin to feel alienated and drop out. A balance of task and relations roles is most appropriate for maximum performance.

We have looked at some of the major variables that influence a group's constitution and performance. Now let's look at two of the most important and time-consuming functions of groups: meetings and decision making.

GROUP MEETINGS

Group meetings can be divided into two categories: those that emphasize the sharing of information and those that focus on the decision-making process. Two distinguishing characteristics that separate these are the direction of the communication flow, and the end result of the meeting.

In the meeting situation that emphasizes dissemination of information (often called a briefing session) the flow of communication is primarily downward from superior to subordinate. A decision has already been made (e.g., a new policy or procedure has been formulated) and must now be communicated to those who will need the information to function properly. Although questions may be entertained by the speaker or manager, the decision has occurred prior to the meeting.

Other situations that emphasize information sharing, with the implication of two-way or multidirectional communication, are the workshop and the study group. These focus on information exchange among the participants with the end result being a greater awareness or knowledge of a given subject. The information that is exchanged may be material specifically researched for the meeting, or the experience of those participating.

Other meetings that share information include panel discussions (several persons drawn together for information sharing on a specialized topic, usually for a specialized audience), symposiums (prepared speeches on some aspect of a specialized topic followed by discussion), and public forums (a public presentation frequently before a nonspecialized audience with a question and answer session).

The purpose of the decision-making meeting is the recommendation or approval of some action. It may require a great deal of time, energy, and information sharing to reach a decision. Committees, commmissions, councils, and other highly structured decision-making groups employ parliamentary assembly and formal rules of order.

The conventional staff meeting may be formal or informal and may have a combination function. Information may be shared in the form of announcements, and participants may be called on to report on activities in which they are engaged. The meeting may also involve decision making.

Planning the Meeting

The success of meetings and conferences is directly proportional to the amount of planning that has been done. Was the agenda prepared and distributed to the attendees? Were any special assignments or requests for reports made to those expected to present them? Was the meeting time communicated far enough in advance so that everyone could reserve the time?

Adequate facilities are a very important part of any meeting. The meeting leader should verify that the meeting place is large enough so that participants do not feel crowded, but not so large that there is too much extra space. Routine issues also need attention prior to the meeting: restrooms; smoking policy; availability, portability, and comfort of chairs and tables; adequacy of lighting; support for audiovisual aids (e.g., screens, extra bulbs for projectors, extension cords); and a sound system. All materials (e.g., chalk, paper, pencils, instructions, chalkboard, projectors) should be readily available to those who need them.

The meeting leader must anticipate and overcome many problems in advance. The following list provides some suggestions and help for planning the meeting.

1. Prepare and send out notices of the meeting. Three to 10 days in advance is appropriate timing. Avoid giving too much time (participants may forget) or too little notice (participants may already be booked with other appointments).

2. Be specific about the time of the meeting, both the start and finish. This ensures that everyone is there on time. Discourage latecomers by not allowing any backtracking to subjects already covered. End the meeting at the scheduled time.

3. Plan and distribute an agenda to encourage participants to be prepared to discuss the subject matter intelligently. Make sure anyone who is scheduled to give a report is aware of that fact, and specify the approximate time limit.

4. Study. Be familiar with announcements so it does not appear that you are reading them for the first time. Know the subjects that will be discussed so you can cut off discussion and move on or ask for more detail at the appropriate times.

5. Announce the purpose of the meeting. If the purpose is to give information, do not ask for opinions or advice. This could cause participants to feel ignored and resent future meetings. If the meeting is to result in a decision, make sure everyone is aware of that and has the necessary facts. Invite thorough discussion before the goup commits itself.

Conducting the Meeting

Assuming you have done all you can to prepare for the meeting, the next step is to carry out the meeting. While each meeting varies according to its purpose, location, and participants, the following are some common points to be aware of.

1. Develop a good opening. Choose words and examples carefully to fit the location and the group. Welcome the group, then identify the topic and objectives of the meeting. If there are an-

nouncements or reports to be given, get them out of the way quickly so the focus of attention is on the main topic(s).

2. Guide the discussion to accomplish the objectives. In each session there are goals and objectives to be obtained. As the leader you must keep the discussion on the subject and direct it toward the attainment of objectives. An effective leader quickly develops the ability to ask good questions—avoid questions that can be answered by a simple yes or no. Thought-provoking questions and negatively phrased questions are sometimes effective in arousing discussion. Make sure that all members of the group have an equal opportunity to participate in the discussion.

3. Maintain control of the discussion without being autocratic or domineering. The amount of control, and the manner in which it is handled, should be directed toward getting sound, unbiased opinions that represent the thinking of the entire group. Side conversations and long-winded speeches should be discouraged. At times, it may be necessary to interrupt a participant to get the conversation back on the track. You can tactfully inject an internal or progress summary to aid the participants in collecting their thoughts. Make certain that all members understand and appreciate the fact that each participant is entitled to his or her own opinion. Healthy discussion can lead to disagreements; if these disagreements lead to a better understanding of the topic, they should not be avoided. Encourage members to weigh and evaluate each argument on its own merit. It is your responsibility to develop and maintain a spirit of cooperation throughout the meeting.

4. Conclude the meeting on schedule. Never prolong a meeting just to fill in time; the costs of a conference are too great to waste the time and energies of the participants. No healthy result can come from a discussion if it ends with disagreement and ill feelings among the members. Conclude with a summary of all points agreed on and, if appropriate, a statement of how a decision is to be implemented, when, and by whom. All participants should know what is expected of them *after the meeting has been concluded.*

Dealing with Problem Individuals

Some "problem people" may need special attention on the part of the leader. The following suggestions may help to handle such individuals and maintain the spirit of cooperation necessary for an effective group meeting.

1. The *argumentative participant* argues about even the most insignificant detail and may attempt to impose his opinion on the entire

group. The leader should encourage other participants to react to this person freely, pointing out how absurd, foolish, or far-fetched some of his statements really are. Above all, this individual should not be allowed to impose on or intimidate the others in the group.

2. The *nontalkative participant* is reluctant to offer his opinion. This may be due to his superior's inclusion in the group, or he may be shy by nature. The leader can address this individual by name and ask for information or an opinion. Occasionally, praise from the meeting leader or the individual's superior is good support. Additional encouragement can be provided by asking this person to research a subject and give a report at a later meeting.

3. The *indifferent participant* does not participate within the group. The group leader may need to determine this individual's likes, dislikes, and special interests and bring up these subjects. Often a direct question affecting work or tactfully sought-out advice can bring this individual back into the group. Care must be taken, however, not to seem patronizing, because this could encourage indifferent behavior in others as a way of getting attention.

4. The *over-talkative participant* frustrates and inhibits the group. The leader can tactfully interrupt this individual and ask others to comment, or fail to recognize this person either by not calling on him or by not looking at him. If these methods fail, the leader may need to talk with this individual privately.

5. The *obstinate participant* uses the phrases "it won't work," "we've tried that before," or "it's just another passing fad." The leader should draw this person out and try to find the reasons for the obstinance. Also, the leader can call on others to counter these arguments, show how the current situation may be different from previous ones, or tactfully bring the discussion to a close.

6. The *resentful participant* often feels that she knows all there is to know about the subject, or at least more than anyone else, and resents being at the meeting or her role. The leader should get this individual to share her knowledge and experiences with others in the group to alleviate some of her resentment. If the meeting is called to discuss change, the leader can explain how it will benefit her.

Focusing Attention

Frequently problems are not created by individuals or the situation, but by interaction of the two. Some examples follow.

1. The leader can establish and hold the attention of the group with appropriate audiovisual aids: slides, chalkboard, flipcharts, films,

records, and experiential exercises such as role playing, case studies, and small task groups. Citing specific cases can provoke discussion, or the leader can call for actual cases from group members.

2. The leader should attempt to anticipate controversial and sensitive topics and have a plan for handling them. If caught off guard, the leader should be courteous, tactful, and diplomatic. If the subject has little or nothing to do with the group task, the leader should point out why this topic should not be discussed now, but at a later date or by another group. If there is a request for confidential information, there should be an explanation why the leader cannot be the source of that information.

3. Problems and discussions that are not of interest to the entire group should be avoided. The leader should restate the problem or solutions, summarize frequently, and question members to determine whether there are other parts of the discussion that need to be included. If members tend to ramble, the leader can avoid calling on them or quickly get them back into the main issue. A direct question can often get the group thinking about the subject under discussion.

4. Two or more participants carrying on a side discussion can be annoying and may upset the entire group. The leader should quickly direct a question to one of the members involved and ask them to address their comments to the entire group. Or, the leader could stop the main discussion and call the attention of the entire group to the side conversation. This will generally discourage and stop side conversations. Side discussions can be productive when two members are comparing notes and reinforcing one another regarding some issue they think should be brought before the group. Calling attention to these individuals will then bring the issue before the group.

After the Meeting

What goes on after the meeting can be equally as important or more important than the meeting itself. This is the time for action! This is the time for follow-up!

1. Distribute a written record (memorandum, minutes) of the meeting to all who participated and others who need to be informed of what went on during the meeting. This should include any special assignments, reports, or responsibilities that were accepted by any of the participants.

2. Follow up on any implementation. Was someone to do something? When? Where? How? See that it is done, and when it is

completed, offer some praise or commendation. This will encourage more high-quality participation at future meetings.

3. Do not criticize members outside of the meeting, telling others how someone did not contribute or wanted to take over the meeting. This should be done after the meeting in private with the individual responsible.

4. Learn from your mistakes. Plan to do a better job next time, including weeding out any participants who consistently show an inability to contribute or to get anything out of the meeting.

GROUP DECISION MAKING

In *The Human Organization,* Rensis Likert describes the different effects that two extreme styles of leadership can have on the operating characteristics of an organization. Likert's exploitive-authoritative style has many similarities to Gibb's defensive climate discussed in Chapter 6. In Figure 7–3 you can see how the two opposite styles of leadership affect the communication process. Free, open, and more accurate communication is facilitated more by the participative, supportive style than by the exploitive-authoritative.

Thus, if open, free, and accurate communication is to take place within an organization, work unit, or group meeting, there must be a supportive relationship among the participants. The subordinates must feel free to speak their minds without fear of reprisals from their superiors. The subordinate must perceive the superior as a source of help.

With increasing focus on Japanese management in the 1970s and 1980s, and books popularizing the theory Z management style, there has been a trend toward more participative management in many business organizations.[18] Participative management redistributes authority for problem solving and decision making to various organizational levels and is designed to provide for greater member interaction, representation, and involvement. If people participate in organizational programs, they are more likely to support those programs.

Another trend in some organizations is what some writers call the **plural executive.** Since a chief executive cannot possess all the knowledge and skills necessary to manage effectively at all levels and can't find the time to deal with all the problems of a given position, a "management team" aids in decision making.

In the past, the president or plant manager had little difficulty in keeping up and dealing with all the demands of the office. But with the increased sophistication of contemporary businesses, advances in technology, greater quantity of communication, more complex operations, larger work groups, and more pressures from external groups, group decision making has gained greater respectability.

FIGURE 7–3 Comparative Organizational and Communication Characteristics of Different Leadership Styles

Operating characteristic	Exploitive-authoritative	Participative-group
Character of communication process.		
1. Amount of interaction and communication aimed at achieving objectives.	Very little.	Much with both individuals and groups.
2. Direction of information flow.	Downward.	Down, up, and with peers.
3. Downward communication.		
a. Where initiated.	At top of organization or to implement directives.	Initiated at all levels.
b. Extent to which communications accepted by subordinates.	Viewed with great suspicion.	Generally accepted, but if not, openly and candidly questioned.
4. Upward communication.		
a. Adequacy of upward communication via line organization.	Very little.	A great deal.
b. Subordinates' feeling of responsibility for initiating accurate upward communication.	None.	Considerable responsibility felt and much initiative.
c. Forces leading to accurate or distorted information.	Powerful forces to distort information and deceive superiors.	Virtually no forces to distort and powerful forces to communicate accurately.
d. Accuracy of upward communication via line.	Tends to be inaccurate.	Accurate.
e. Need for supplementary upward communication system.	Need to supplement upward system by spy, suggestion, or some similar devices.	No need for any supplementary system.
5. Sideward communication, its adequacy and accuracy.	Usually poor because of competition between peers and corresponding hostility.	Good to excellent.
6. Psychological closeness of superiors to subordinates.		
a. Accuracy of perceptions by superiors.	Often in error.	Usually quite accurate.

SOURCE: Rensis Likert, *The Human Organization: Its Management and Value* (New York: McGraw-Hill, 1967), pp. 16–18.

Models of Sharing Authority

Models have been developed which suggest that the manager may be more effective by sharing her decision-making authority. L. Greiner, for example, has suggested the sharing of power for more effective change management.[19] Using three levels of power—unilateral, shared, and delegated—he identified seven different sharing strategies ranging from the issuance of decrees to the use of sensitivity training.

Unilateral Power
Decree approach—issue unilateral announcement.
Replacement approach—replace individuals in a change role.
Structural approach—change roles and relationships.

Shared Power
Group decision approach—decision based on group discussion.
Group problem-solving approach—group identification of problem and solution.

Delegated Power
Data discussion approach—focus on information analysis and sharing by group members.
Sensitivity training approach—change flows from greater interpersonal sensitivity and awareness.

While Greiner's model relates specifically to the introduction of change, Tannenbaum and Schmidt's classic work on leadership patterns deals more directly with approaches to shared decision making. According to Tannenbaum and Schmidt, the research findings of the post–World War II era have presented the contemporary manager with a dilemma:

> Often he is not quite sure how to behave; there are times when he is torn between exerting "strong" leadership and "permissive" leadership.[20]

To help managers deal with this problem Tannenbaum and Schmidt provide a model that depicts decision-making options along a continuum (see Figure 7–4). Although there are an infinite number of combinations of shared authority, they have identified seven discrete points that represent uniquely different approaches to making a decision.

At the boss-centered extreme, the manager can simply call on his subordinates and *tell* them what the decision is. If a manager is self-assured and his subordinates are not at all concerned about the decision-making process, this approach might work. If the manager feels as though some amount of persuasion is in order, he may attempt to *sell* the decision to the subordinates. This approach carries with it at least some sensitivity for subordinates, but does not signify any concern or need for input from them.

The third approach signifies an even greater concern for subordi-

FIGURE 7–4 Continuum of Leadership Behavior

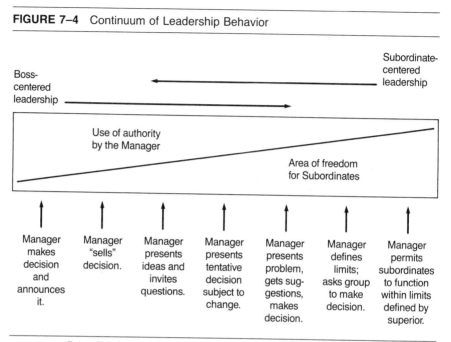

SOURCE: Robert Tannenbaum and Warren Schmidt, "How to Choose a Leadership Pattern," *Harvard Business Review,* March–April 1958, pp. 95–101.

nates, but still does not reflect a need to seek information from them. The manager calls on subordinates and discusses the decision *after it is made.* The decision has been made in the first three approaches and it will not be changed, regardless of subordinate questions or comments.

The fourth approach begins to hint at some recognition of the importance of subordinate input. Up to this point the only concern of the manager has been a sensitivity to subordinate understanding and acceptance. With this approach the manager's decision is *tentative and subject to change based on serious objection or input.*

The manager makes a tentative decision and, if warranted, he will change it. This approach recognizes the value of subordinates, but if it is used too frequently subordinates may view the manager as indecisive or weak.

The fifth approach truly recognizes the informational value of shared decision making. In this approach there is discussion *before the decision is made.* This allows the manager to utilize often valuable information possessed by subordinates, and it gives the subordinates a message regarding their worth. The obvious drawbacks are the time consumed and the admission by the manager that he does not know everything.

In the first five approaches, the manager ultimately makes the deci-

sion. Under the sixth approach *the group makes the decision within limits.* The manager describes the problem and prescribes constraints on the decision the group can make. This approach recognizes not only the informational value of participation, but taps more fully into the motivational aspects of group decision making. Of course, there must be competence and interest on the part of subordinates. If they do not have the necessary skills to identify and evaluate solutions, or if they simply do not care to get involved, this approach could easily backfire, and result in poor decisions.

The final approach occurs at the employee-centered end of the continuum. According to Tannenbaum and Schmidt it is only occasionally encountered in formal organizations. Here the group members are allowed to identify the solution to a problem *and formulate the problem.* Additionally, the constraints imposed are likely to be fewer and much broader. To participate at this extreme, group members would have to fully meet all of Tannenbaum and Schmidt's criteria for participation:

1. A high level of independence.
2. A willingness to assume responsibility.
3. A tolerance for ambiguity.
4. Identification with organizational goals.
5. A demonstrated interest in decision making.
6. The competence with which to participate.
7. An expectation of participation.

Consequently this approach would be utilized most frequently among high-level managers and other professionals.

When a manager is contemplating group decision making, he must carefully consider the advantages and disadvantages.

Advantages

Advocates of group decision making have identified a number of advantages which fall into two basic categories: better information quality and increased motivation (see Figure 7–5).

There are several advantages regarding information quality. First, participation will generally create a better pool of information. We have established that we are each unique with different learning experiences and knowledge. As we approach a decision, we can each draw on our background to contribute unique and useful information to help the group make a more informed decision.

Second, we each bring a unique perspective to the situation. The greater the diversity of backgrounds, the greater the diversity of perceptions. This diversity can help a group to see all of the facets of a problem. For example, a group consisting of nothing but accountants would not bring as much diversity of perspectives as a group representing the accounting, marketing, finance, personnel, and production functions.

FIGURE 7–5 Advantages of Group Decision Making

Improved information quality
   Better pool of information
   Increased number of perspectives
   Greater relevancy of information and values

Improved motivation
   Greater preparation of input and ideas
   Greater understanding of decisions
   Greater acceptance of decisions
   Greater commitment to decisions

Third, the group would be better able to identify the relevant information and values needed to make a decision. An individual making a decision would be forced to use his own values and criteria, which may be totally inappropriate. A group, however, has the ability to scrutinize and reject information or values that are unjustified. For example, a manager who is independently choosing candidates for a layoff might select employees on the basis of friendship, hair color, nationality, personality, and personal compatibility instead of attendance, needed skills, and productivity. A group would have the opportunity to demand a justification for using such criteria and, if not inappropriate, could reject them.

The second group of advantages relates to member motivation. Group decision making can lead to greater understanding of and tolerance for others' ideas. Participation requires group members to be informed. This will encourage them to listen and respond to each other's thoughts and contributions. In addition to being better prepared for decisions, this helps to teach members a certain amount of patience, tolerance, and respect for other people and ideas.

Second, participation can contribute to an understanding of the decision itself. If group members are present to participate in a statement of the problem, the creation of alternatives and decision criteria, and a discussion of relevant information, they are better informed and will have a better understanding of the decision.

Third, participation leads to greater acceptance of a decision. If individual group members are present and become ego-involved through their contributions in the making of a decision, they will support that decision.

Fourth, participation creates much better commitment. People who contribute to a decision become ego-involved; part of them is in the decision, and they will defend it (recall our decision of perceptual defense) with their words and actions.

If a decision is made at a distant corporate office with no input from a local group, the local members may be reluctant to accept or support

the decision, especially if they disagree with it. If they had participated in the decision, they would probably work much harder to make it a success.

Disadvantages

Group decision making has its drawbacks, and managers should be aware of them. These disadvantages are shown in Figure 7–6.

The time and cost involved before a meeting can take place are two major disadvantages. In addition, there is the usual logistical problem of where and when to meet, scheduling a convenient time that fits into every group member's schedule, and communicating an agenda to all involved. Then the group must meet and the decision must be made. A manager can make a decision independently in a matter of minutes or hours. To call a group together and deliberate before arriving at a decision may involve hours, days—even weeks.

The cost of many meetings is often elusive or never calculated, and may be either an advantage or a disadvantage (relative to the criteria being used). Because more and more organizations are using the group format, it seems especially important to comment on this factor. Figure 7–7 gives some examples of how to determine the costs of a meeting using different figures.

A third disadvantage of group decision making is compromise, and it can be particularly problematic in larger groups where factions are likely to develop. If the individuals cannot arrive at a consensus, they will often use compromise as a means of making a decision. Unfortunately, in many cases the decision is suboptimal.

For example, consider the following account of an executive screening committee. After reviewing the qualifications of many applicants, the committee narrowed the field to three finalists who were then brought in for extensive plant visits and interviews. When the committee met afterwards to choose the new executive, one faction preferred candidate A while another faction preferred candidate C. Neither faction would yield to the other's choice, and to end the standoff the group chose candidate B.

FIGURE 7–6   Disadvantages of Group Decision Making

Time

Cost
Compromise
Domination
Loser alienation
Groupthink

FIGURE 7–7   Costs of Meetings (nearest dollar per hour)

Average Pay	Number of Participants				
	10	8	6	5	3
$60,000	576	264	344	288	176
$30,000	288	232	172	144	88
$15,000	144	116	86	72	44
$ 7,500	72	58	43	36	22

A fourth disadvantage stems from the makeup of the group. Some individuals are hesitant to offer their feelings and convictions in front of others because they feel intimidated. This is especially true when an individual's superior is part of the group. If the composition of personalities, status, and power is unbalanced, domination may be a serious problem and may negate any positive effects of participation.

A fifth disadvantage concerns the possible repercussions of group members who feel like losers. If a group member takes a position that is rejected by a majority of group members, the individual may experience resentment and alienation. If these feelings are severe the individual may consider leaving the group or sabotaging its efforts.

Assume, for example, that an executive planning group decides to launch a new product program, but the production manager vehemently opposes the program because he feels that it is premature. The production manager may attempt to slow down the project and cause it to fail, or if he feels strongly enough, he may simply resign.

Groupthink

A final danger of group decision making is what I. Janis has labeled **groupthink.**

> Groupthink involves nondeliberate suppression of critical thoughts as a result of internalization of the group's norms, which is quite different from deliberate suppression on the basis of external threats of social punishment.[21]

Symptoms of Groupthink.   Groupthink is the result of extreme cohesiveness. According to Janis, the main principle is that the more amiable the group, and the more esprit de corps there is, the greater the danger is that independent critical thought will be replaced by groupthink. To help groups and group leaders recognize and deal with groupthink Janis has identified eight symptoms that indicate its presence (see Figure 7–8).

1. Illusion of invulnerability: A condition of overoptimism that causes the group to fail to respond to clear and present threats.

FIGURE 7–8 Symptoms of Groupthink

Illusion of invulnerability
Rationality
Inherent morality
Stereotyping
Pressure to conform
Self-censorship
Illusion of unanimity
Mindguards

2. Rationality: Constructing rationalization to discount warnings or other negative feedback.
3. Inherent morality: Group members feel so strongly about their inherent correctness that they do not question the ethical or moral implications of their decisions.
4. Stereotyping: Group members begin to stereotype those outside the group as weak or stupid.
5. Pressure to conform: Members apply direct pressure to those who question the validity of the group's position.
6. Self-censorship: Group members impose their own censorship which suppresses their doubts and misgivings about the group's position.
7. Illusion of unanimity: As a result of their silence, group members believe there is unanimous support for positions and decisions of the group.
8. Mindguards: Group members protect the group from information that is inconsistent with the present position or past judgments of the group.

Groupthink violates any semblance of a rational process and results in ineffective decision making. Figure 7–9 contains a list of the harmful effects of groupthink.

Solutions to Groupthink. Although groupthink can become a major obstacle to effective group decision making, there are ways a group can overcome it. Figure 7–10 contains a partial list of techniques.

One obvious way to overcome groupthink is to scrupulously adhere to the scientific process. Such practice should come as a result of proper training in the process, but more importantly, from proper group leadership. The group leader should encourage and reinforce critical analysis. When groupthink develops, the group leader *unintentionally* discourages or punishes critical individual thinking.

FIGURE 7–9 Effects of Groupthink on Decision Making

Problems are not well defined
Inadequate information is collected
Information is not critically analyzed
Alternatives are not artificially limited
Alternatives are not scrutinized
Implementation is not carefully planned

In addition to fostering a climate of critical analysis, there are other group management techniques and precautions that the group leader can use. One technique is to appoint some member or members the role of devil's advocate—to question and criticize the work of the group. This role can be passed around among group members so that no one individual runs the risk of being permanently ostracized.

Another technique is to require group members to consult with outsiders regarding the issues or problems of the group, or to invite outsiders, especially experts, to group meetings. Their presence at the group meetings will ensure that group members are exposed to additional points of view and information.

If the group is large enough, it is effective to have subgroups or subcommittees working on different parts of the overall topic or problem. Alternatively, more than one group could be used to work on the same issue or problem simultaneously. This increases the amount of information and the number of perspectives considered by the group, and also generates additional alternatives.

"What if" scenarios force group members to think through the impact of their decision before it's too late. By developing alternate outcomes of a decision, the group has an opportunity to see any serious flaws that would otherwise be overlooked.

FIGURE 7–10 Solutions to Groupthink

Adhere to scientific process
Encourage critical analysis
Use a devil's advocate
Consult with outside experts
Utilize subgroups to make decisions
Use multiple groups to make decisions
Develop "what if" scenarios

Decision Styles

Having described the advantages and disadvantages of group decision making helps us decide when to use a group approach. It is not always simple to distinguish between group decision situations and individual situations.

B. Fisher offers a general rule of thumb that may be helpful: for tasks that require high-quality expertise and for which there is one "correct" or "best" answer, individuals can do as well or better than the group. For those tasks in which there is no single "best" answer and there are many alternatives, the group process can prove beneficial.[22]

If a problem requires a variety of knowledge and skills and the group reflects the needed mixture, then groups will do better. Complementarity is vital. For example, assume an executive group is considering a merger decision. The production skills and knowledge that the marketing representative lacks will be provided by the production engineer. The personnel skills lacking in the accounting representative are provided by the personnel director.

We cannot overlook the implications of Likert and other proponents of participatory decision making—some valid motivational advantages stem from group decision making. Of course, these advantages are not evident in every decision-making situation. Thus, the manager must be able to discern when he can or cannot enhance motivation through group decision making. We can summarize our discussion with the following basic guidelines:

1. If the quality of a decision is more important than employee acceptance and commitment, and if the manager, rather than the group, has the necessary information, then an individual decision is in order (e.g., a promotion decision).
2. If the quality of a decision is relatively unimportant and employee acceptance and commitment are irrelevant, then an individual decision is in order (e.g., what brand of hand soap to use in the restrooms).
3. If employee acceptance and commitment are more important than the quality of a decision, then a group consensus decision is in order (e.g., setting a new group productivity goal).
4. If decision quality and employee acceptance and commitment are equally important, then a group consultative decision is in order. Group members should be consulted individually (e.g., implementing a new budgetary process).

As problem sharing increases, information sharing and the need for participative decision making are likely to increase and appropriate communication skills and information-sharing mechanisms are required. If the group members do not have the skills, commitment, or technology for

sharing, the group may be inferior to the individual. It may be in the best interest for the manager, the group, and the organization to ensure that group members have the needed skills.

Techniques for Group Decision Making

Once you have chosen to use the group decision making approach, there are several formats available. The final section of this chapter provides a brief description of four popular techniques: **brainstorming, nominal grouping, Delphi** and **synectics.**

Brainstorming, developed by A. Osborn in the 1950s, is still a popular method for generating ideas and solving problems.[23] Brainstorming requires an open environment that encourages the free flow of ideas *while deferring judgment of those ideas.* Group members are brought together for 15 to 90 minutes and encouraged to continuously produce different and unusual ideas, regardless of how far-fetched they may seem. There is no judgment; group members need not fear criticism. As ideas are generated someone records them.

Aside from the motivational benefits of participation, the basic idea is to capitalize on the free-flowing interaction of the group members' ideas. By responding to one another's ideas spontaneously, ideas flow off of other ideas. Osborn states that "the average person can think up twice as many ideas when working with a group than working alone."[24] A critical exchange of ideas within a group can be highly synergistic and lead to more and better decisions.

Taylor and his colleagues are not impressed with the results of brainstorming. They compared the productivity of individuals in group brainstorming and individual brainstorming. Their research showed that a group of individuals working alone can develop more and better ideas than when brainstorming as a group.[25] Group brainstorming is still widely used despite these findings.

An alternative to brainstorming is the nominal group technique (NGT).[26] Individuals are brought together and asked to write down as many ideas or solutions to a problem as they can *independently.* It is essentially a modification of brainstorming with the vocal interaction removed.

At the end of some specified time period, the leader goes from member to member in round-robin fashion asking for ideas one at a time. This movement continues until all ideas have been publicly recorded. The primary advantage of nominal grouping is that the lack of interaction minimizes inhibitions, thus allowing individuals to generate more and better ideas.

Group members are given an opportunity to clarify their ideas and express their opinions. Then the group members will be asked individually to rank or vote on the ideas generated. Typically the ranking or voting will be limited to the top 5 to 10 ideas agreed on by the group.

The Delphi technique differs from the first two techniques because the group members are not assembled in one location. Individuals can be contacted at a variety of locations and asked to provide their ideas or solutions to a particular problem. The ideas are tabulated, duplicated, and shared with all group members. The members are then asked to evaluate the list of ideas and rank them or vote on them. The results are then collected, tabulated, duplicated, and redistributed. Again the group memers are asked to respond to the new list of ideas. This procedure is continued until some degree of convergence is attained.[27]

Our final technique is synectics, known as the Gordon technique.[28] In synectics the group goal is to generate one solution rather than a limitless list of possibilities.

Typically the leader will not reveal the exact nature of the problem, but will ask the assembled group to discuss the general area in which the problem exists. The leader will continue to guide the discussion in the direction of a solution by focusing and probing to get the group members to generate new perspectives and combinations of information.

The basic idea is to focus the information and backgrounds of the group members without inhibiting them, and this is accomplished by withholding the exact nature of the problem. So, for example, if an organization was trying to create a new dry cereal, the group might begin by talking about food groups, food tastes, or dining habits.

SUMMARY

In this chapter we have examined the vital role of groups in our society. They are ubiquitous, and we simply could not do without them. Consequently, the enlightened manager should understand some essential features of groups. We have identified the major reasons why people join groups and the criteria used for selecting particular groups.

We outlined the group development process as consisting of four stages—forming, storming, norming, and performing. To help the practicing manager effectively manage groups we examined a number of group features showing their effects on communication, behavior, and performance. Understanding such features as cohesiveness, conformity, and structure are basic to the manager who works with groups.

We also offered some guidance on two major areas of group activity: group meetings and group decision making. Conducting a group meeting is an involved process requiring certain steps before, during, and after the meeting. If group meetings are to be an effective means of information sharing, these steps must be carried out correctly.

The last subject of the chapter was decision making. Better information and higher motivation are two good reasons for considering group decision making. Using group participation isn't an all-or-nothing proposition. The models presented show that groups can be used in varying

degrees, but that the manager must understand the consequences of each. Group decisions are particularly good when a variety of skills are needed and the group members have those skills. Group decision making is also beneficial when it is important to group members that they participate. A key to the use of groups is careful consideration of the kind of work and the kind of workers involved.

DISCUSSION QUESTIONS

1. Distinguish between an aggregation and a functional group. Use Brilhart's five characteristics of a functional group to differentiate a group from an aggregation.

2. Individuals join groups for a variety of reasons. Discuss three common reasons for group membership and explain why managers need to be aware of these reasons.

3. Explain in detail how groups act as intermediaries between individuals and society.

4. Discuss three different factors that may cause an individual to choose a *particular* group.

5. Describe the group development process using the four-stage Tuckman model. Comment on why managers need to be aware of the group development process.

6. Compare and contrast in detail the forming and storming stages of group development. Explain why each is important for group development.

7. What are some of the problems that can be encountered in the performing stage of a group's development? Indicate why the problems develop. Suggest ways to cope with these problems.

8. Define five basic group characteristics that affect group communication, behavior, and performance. Discuss the impact of any two of these characteristics on group communication.

9. Use the "wheel" and the "circle" to describe two different designs for organizational communication networks. Under what circumstances would each be appropriate in solving organizational problems?

10. How are group cohesiveness and conformity related? Be sure to include a discussion of Cohen's principles regarding group cohesiveness and conformity.

11. Discuss how group size affects group effectiveness. What principles did Szilagyi and Wallace develop regarding group size?

12. Discuss the distinguishing characteristics of group meetings held for the purpose of sharing information and those that focus on decision making.

13. Planning for a meeting is often a key to that meeting's success. Discuss five key tasks that a meeting leader must carry out in order to plan effectively for a meeting.

14. What are the basic responsibilities of the leader in conducting a meeting?

15. Define four "problem people" types that discussion leaders frequently encounter. Give specific strategies for dealing with these individuals.

16. Why can it be said that what goes on after a meeting can be equally or more important than the meeting itself? What would you include in the normal follow-up activities?

17. Contrast the authoritative style of management with the participative style. What are some factors that have contributed to increased interest in the participative management style?

18. Discuss Likert's description of management styles and their effects on organizational communication.

19. Describe in detail the Tannenbaum and Schmidt model that depicts decision making options along a continuum.

20. Compare and contrast the first five points on the Tannenbaum-Schmidt leadership continuum with the last two points.

21. Discuss the advantages and disadvantages of group decision making.

22. When can groupthink occur? What are four characteristics of this phenomenon?

23. Discuss factors that are significant in determining whether group or individual decision making is appropriate.

EXERCISE

1. Assemble a group of six individuals, and assign a role to each. Each individual should read the general situation information below and the segment which describes his or her role. The exercise should be initiated by the individual assuming the role of Phil.

Giant Food Company*

General situation.   You are a sales representative for Giant Food Company, a wholesale supplier of packaged food products. Most of your customers are large grocery chains, but you deal with the stores on an individual basis, depending on their inventory needs. You also supply smaller independent grocery stores and some restaurants. You have a territory assigned to you in the Los Angeles area, and it is your responsibility to generate as much business as possible. You are compensated on a commission basis, and you must pay your own expenses.

You are responsible to check the stock in your customers' stores and to take orders to replace sold items. You also make recommendations to the store manager about marketing and display of your products, and you

---

*Reprinted by permission from *Organization and People*, 2/e, by J. B. Ritchie and Paul Thompson. © 1980 by West Publishing Company, St. Paul, Minn. All rights reserved.

must compete with other distributors and products for shelf and display space. Your relationship with the store manager affects how your products will be displayed and stocked, and display and stocking greatly affect the sales volume.

Your sales manager has an office in the main warehouse. He is responsible for the allocation of company property that you may use in your work. A new car has been ordered and will soon be available to one of the sales representatives in your division.

The sales representatives pride themselves on the appearance and running condition of their cars and on their economy, as they must pay all of their automobile expenses. The sales representatives often entertain their customers as part of their sales program; they feel that the car plays a vital part in the impression they make and therefore that it affects subsequent sales.

Some facts about the sales manager and the sales representatives and their cars are the following:

Phil: 14 years with the company, male, white, sales manager.
Tom: 19 years with the company, male, white, 2-year-old Toyota sedan.
José: 9 years with the company, male, Chicano, 5-year-old Chevrolet full-size sedan.
Henry: 5 years with the company, male, white, 4-year-old Ford mid-size sedan.
Susan: 3 years with the company, female, white, 4-year-old Datsun station wagon.
Paul: 6 months with the company, male, white, 6-year-old Plymouth midsize sedan.

Individual roles.   *Phil:* You are the sales manager of the five sales representatives. Every year or two you get a new car for one of them and are faced with the problem of whom to give it to and how the other vehicles should be reallocated. Often there are hard feelings about your decision, because each person has reasons for feeling that he or she is entitled to the new car. In the past, no matter what you have decided, most of them consider it wrong. You are now faced with the problem of who is to receive the new car, a Ford subcompact station wagon, next week. This year you have decided to allow the group to solve the problem, and you will make them live with their decision. They can decide what is the most fair way to redistribute the cars that are now available. You don't want to take a position because you want to do what they think is most fair.

Tom: You have a two-year-old Toyota, which runs well and has been an economical little car. You have been with the company in this position for 19 years, however, and the Toyota is just not large enough to handle the promotion and display material you must take to your many custom-

ers. Sometimes you are forced to use your family station wagon. You have the greatest dollar volume of sales of all the sales representatives, and often you can't service your customers adequately or economically because you must make several trips to an area when you begin a new promotional campaign. You think the extra room in the Ford station wagon will be adequate, and you like the economy of the subcompact. You also feel that your seniority (longer service than the sales manager) and the volume of business entitles you to the new car.

José: You have a five-year-old Chevrolet sedan, which in its day was a very nice car. You enjoy the roomy interior, because you have developed a good volume of business over the last nine years. The car is something of a gas hog and is getting very expensive to run the distances you must go to reach your area, which is mostly in the suburbs. You also feel that you need a newer car to take your customers to lunch. The Chevrolet is getting somewhat shabby. You feel that one of the reasons why you still have this old car, when newer representatives have better cars, may be that you are a Chicano.

Henry: You have been with the company five years and have a four-year-old Ford sedan. It is in fairly good shape, except for the right door, which is sprung and doesn't close tightly. That door has been an irritation since Susan backed into it two years ago in the parking lot. You feel that you deserve either the new car or her car, because she damaged yours. You don't think she should be trusted with the new car; she would probably just wreck it anyway. And she doesn't have enough business to justify it. You feel that you should receive the new car because it will help you build up your business.

Susan: You are the only woman in this position in a virtually all-male company. You feel that you are seen as an intruder and a radical, although you make every attempt to avoid that image. You expect to be treated as an equal. You have shown that your salesmanship is equal to or better than the men's. You have a four-year-old Datsun wagon. The body is OK, but the engine and the transmission, which were treated badly by the last person to use the car, are constantly giving you trouble. The Datsun has often been in the shop when you needed it, and the engine needs to be rebuilt or replaced. You need the new car so that you can be more reliable in the eyes of your customers. You think the men in the department would like to see you fail and have given you the old Datsun as a handicap. You have a good driving record, except for the time when Henry opened the door of his car just as you were backing up to the building to load display materials. He still blames you for his door, although it was really his fault.

Paul: You have been with the company only six months. You have taken over the area and the car of a former sales representative who retired and who for the past few years had been coasting and doing little to build up the business. In the past six months you have shown the company what can be done to turn around such a stagnant area. You have

doubled your business and have begun to generate a group of prospective customers, whom you must win away from the competitors. You have the oldest car and feel that it is a definite hindrance to your work. It is also uneconomical, and it needs repair. You feel that you have shown what you can do and should be rewarded with the new car, as a shot in the arm to help you build up momentum.

Exercise Questions

1. Compare your progress as a group with the Tuckman model of group development. Did you move through the various stages successfully? Did you stall at any point?

2. Was there any attempt by a group member to dominate the discussion and problem solution?

3. How did you attempt to solve the problem? What decision model did your group develop?

4. Was there any effort to discriminate on an ethnic or sexual basis?

5. Was Phil a participative or authoritarian leader?

6. Did the backgrounds of the various group members facilitate or block decision-making efforts?

NOTES

[1]John Brilhart, *Effective Group Discussion* (Dubuque, Iowa: William C. Brown, 1978), pp. 20–21.

[2]E. Hollander, *Principles and Methods of Social Psychology* (New York: Oxford University Press, 1967), chap. 13.

[3]B. Tuckman, "Developmental Sequences in Small Groups," *Psychological Bulletin* 63 (1965), pp. 384–99; S. L. Obert, "Developmental Patterns of Organizational Task Groups: A Preliminary Study," *Human Relations* 36 (1983), pp. 37–52.

[4]*Webster's Seventh New Collegiate Dictionary* (Springfield, Mass.: G. and C. Merriam Co., 1963), p. 575.

[5]This section is based on findings from several sources, including: M. Shaw, "Communication Networks," in *Advances in Experimental Social Psychology*, ed. L. Berkowitz (New York: Academic Press, 1964), pp. 111–47; H. Kelley, "Communication in Experimentally Created Hierarchies," *Human Relations* 4 (1951), pp. 39–56; M. Shaw, "Some Effects of Unequal Distribution of Information upon Group Performance in Various Cmmunication Nets," *Journal of Abnormal and Social Psychology* 49 (1954), pp. 547–53; A. Bavelas, "Communication Patterns in Task-Oriented Groups," *Journal of the Acoustical Society of America* 22 (1950), pp. 725–30; and H. Leavitt, "Some Effects of Certain Communication Patterns on Group Performance," *Journal of Abnormal and Social Psychology* 46 (1951), pp. 38–50.

[6]A. Cohen, S. Fink, H. Gadon, and R. Willits, *Effective Behavior in Organizations*, 3rd ed. (Homewood, Ill.: Richard D. Irwin, 1984), p. 86.

[7]E. Thomas and C. Fink, "Effects of Group Size," *Psychological Bulletin* 60 (1963), pp. 371–84.

[8]J. Horowitz, H. Zander, and B. Hymovitch, "Some Effects of Power on the Relations among Group Members," in *Group Dynamics*, 2nd ed., D. Cartwright and A. Zander (Evanston, Ill.: Row, Peterson, 1960), pp. 800–809; also see J. Thibaut and H. Kelley, *The Social Psychology of Groups* (New York: John Wiley & Sons, 1959).

[9]L. Festinger, *A Theory of Cognitive Dissonance* (Stanford, Calif.: Stanford University Press, 1957).

[10]Hollander, *Principles and Methods of Social Psychology.*

[11]B. Raven and J. Rietsema, "The Effects of Varied Clarity of Group Goal and Group Path upon the Individual and His Relationship to His Group," *Human Relations* 10 (1957), pp. 29–45.

[12]Cohen et al., *Effective Behavior in Organizations,* p. 92.

[13]S. Schachter, "Deviation, Rejection and Communication," *Journal of Abnormal and Social Psychology* 46 (1951), pp. 190–207.

[14]C. Smith, "Scientific Performance and the Composition of Research Teams," *Administrative Science Quarterly,* December 1971, pp. 486–95; and A. Hare, *Handbook of Small Group Research* (New York: Free Press, 1962), p. 201.

[15]A. Szilagyi and M. Wallace, *Organizational Behavior and Performance,* 4th ed. (Glenview, Ill.: Scott, Foresman, 1983), p. 176.

[16]Thomas and Fink, "Effects of Group Size."

[17]K. Benne and P. Sheats, "Functional Roles of Group Members," *Journal of Social Issues* 4, no. 2 (1948), pp. 41–49; and L. R. Hoffman, "Applying Experimental Research on Group Problem Solving to Organizations," *Journal of Applied Behavioral Science* 15 (1979), pp. 373–91.

[18]W. Ouchi, *Theory Z* (New York: Avon Books, 1983); and R. Pascale and A. Athos, *The Art of Japanese Management* (New York: Warner Books, 1981).

[19]L. Greiner, "Patterns of Organization Change," *Harvard Business Review,* May–June 1967, pp. 119–30.

[20]R. Tannenbaum and W. Schmidt, "How to Choose a Leadership Pattern," *Harvard Business Review,* March–April 1958, pp. 95–101.

[21]I. Janis, *Victims of Groupthink* (Boston: Houghton Mifflin, 1972).

[22]B. Fisher, *Small Group Decision Making: Communication and the Group Process* (New York: McGraw-Hill, 1974), p. 41.

[23]A. Osborn, *Applied Imagination* (New York: Charles Scribner's Sons, 1953); R. Kerwin, "Brainstorming as a Flexible Management Tool," *Personnel Journal,* May 1983, pp. 414ff; and S. R. Grossman, "Brainstorming Updated," *Training and Development Journal,* February 1984, pp. 84–87.

[24]Osborn, *Applied Imagination,* p. 228.

[25]D. W. Taylor, P. Berry, and C. Block, "Does Group Participation When Using Brainstorming Techniques Facilitate or Inhibit Creative Thinking?" *Administrative Science Quarterly* 3, no. 1 (June 1958), pp. 23–47.

[26]A. L. Delbecq, A. Van de Ven, and D. Gustafson, *Group Techniques for Program Planning: A Guide to Nominal and Delphi Processes* (Glenview, Ill.: Scott, Foresman, 1975); B. Stevenson, L. Michaelsen, and S. Franklin, "An Empirical Test of the Nominal Group Technique in State Solar Energy Planning," *Group and Organizational Studies* 7, no. 3 (September 1982), pp. 320–34; and J. M. Bartunek and J. Murninghan, "The Nominal Group Technique: Expanding the Basic Procedure and Underlying Assumptions," *Group and Organizational Studies* 9, no. 3 (September 1984), pp. 417–32.

[27]H. Lyons, "The Delphi Technique for Problem Solving," *Personnel Management,* January 1982, pp. 42–45; also see Delbecq et al., *Group Techniques for Program Planning.*

[28]W. J. Gordon, *Synectics* (New York: Collier Books, 1968).

SUGGESTED READINGS

ADAMS, JEFFREY B.; JEROME ADAMS; ROBERT W. RICE; and DEBRA INSTONE. "Effects of Perceived Group Effectiveness and Group Role on Attributions of Group Performance." *Journal of Applied Psychology* 15 (1985), pp. 397–98.

BARKER, LARRY L.; KATHY J. WAHLERO; DONALD J. CEGALA; and ROBERT J. KIB-
LER. *Groups in Process: An Introduction to Small Group Communication.* Englewood Cliffs, N.J.: Prentice-Hall, 1983.

BEEBE, STEVEN A., and JOHN T. MASTERSON. *Communication in Small Groups.* Glenview, Ill.: Scott, Foresman, 1982.

BETTENHAUSEN, KENNETH, and J. KEITH MURNIGHAM. "The Emergence of
Norms in Competitive Decision Making Groups." *Administrative Science Quarterly,* September 1985, p. 350ff.

BRADSTATTER, HERMANN; JAMES H. DAVIS; and HEINZ SCHULER, eds. *Dynamics of
Group Decision Making.* Beverly Hills, Calif.: Sage Publications, 1978.

CRAGAN, JOHN F., and DAVID W. WRIGHT. *Communication in Small Group Discussion:
A Case Study Approach.* St. Paul, Minn.: West Publishing, 1980.

FAIRFIELD-SONN, JAMES W. "Work Group Reaction to New Members: Tool or
Trap in Making Selection Decisions?" *Public Personnel Management* 13, no. 4
(Winter 1984), pp. 485–93.

FISHER, B. AUBREY. *Small Group Decision Making.* New York: McGraw-Hill, 1980.

KRANTZ, JAMES. "Group Process under Conditions of Organization Decline." *The
Journal of Applied Behavioral Science* 21, no. 1 (1985), pp. 1–17.

LEANA, CARRIE R. "A Partial Test of Janis' Groupthink Model: Effects of Group
Cohesiveness and Leader Behavior on Defective Decision Making." *Journal of
Management* 11, no. 1 (Spring, 1985), pp. 5–17.

LEDERMAN, LINDA COSTIGAN. "Suffering in Silence: The Effects of Fear of Talking on Small Group Participation."*Group and Organization Studies* 7 (September
1982), pp. 279–94.

MORELAND, RICHARD I. "Social Categorization and the Assimilation of 'New'
Group Members." *Journal of Personality and Social Psychology* 48, no. 5 (May
1985), pp. 1173–90.

Chapter 8

Organizational Communication

Chapter 8 Case

You are the founder and president of an advertising company, and proud of the fact that in the eight years since its inception, your company has emerged as a major force in the regional market. The company has grown from 3 employees to more than 40. Today, however, 30 minutes after the close of a meeting with your department heads, you are just now unclenching your fists. Mandy, head of accounting, and Jan, head of marketing, both of whom were there with you when you started this business from nothing, have been at each other's throats for months. Jan, a graduate of the state's most prestigious business college, has just presented her monthly "grandiose scheme" for cornering the market; Mandy has once again provided the "gloom and doom" reasons it won't work. Jack, the new kid on the block, a finance major from State University, can't get a word in. What can you do? Why has a three-person operation that succeeded beyond anyone's expectations become unwieldy?

INTRODUCTION

In this chapter we will look at the macro-level communication requirements of an organization and offer some possible strategies for achieving optimum resource coordination. We begin our coverage with an introduction to the basic systems model.

THE BASIC SYSTEMS MODEL

We often hear references to systems such as the ecosystem, biosystem, or life support system. Many textbook authors view their disciplines as systems, and we read about management information systems, personnel systems, accounting systems, distribution systems, and so forth. It is also important to understand how an organization and organizational communication can be viewed as a system.

A system is a network of elements (e.g., people, machines, materials, ideas) that are interdependent in nature and have an effect, *usually intentional,* on one another. The basic systems model utilizes five elements: **inputs, transformation processes, outputs, feedback,** and **boundaries.** These are shown in Figure 8–1.

Inputs are the resources (people, machines, materials, and information) the organization requires in order to conduct its affairs and achieve its objectives.

Transformation processes include basic and support activities that "use up" the inputs to generate outputs. Examples include production, purchasing, maintenance, advertising, and sales.

Outputs are the final products and services that result from the treatment or processing of inputs.

Feedback consists of impulses or units of information that allow the system to control itself through modification or corrective action and move toward goal accomplishment. Feedback may be positive or negative and informs the system whether its output is consistent with plans and if it should maintain the current input mix and transformation activities.

For example, bank managers learned that one way to improve banking operations is to have friendly tellers. If an unfriendly teller is hired, output is diminished because customers take their business to another bank. The decrease in customers and deposits is a form of feedback that tells the manager to hire a new input (i.e., a more friendly teller).

A fifth element shown in Figure 8–1 is the system's **boundaries.** While not specifically a part of the system, boundaries are the physical, psychological, and social characteristics that distinguish the system from its environment. Boundaries are discontinuities between the organization and the environment that define and differentiate it from other parts of the environment.

Boundaries include buildings, products or services, public image of the organization, reputation of the organization's employees, and community participation. A socially responsible image can help to create a

FIGURE 8–1   The Basic Systems Model

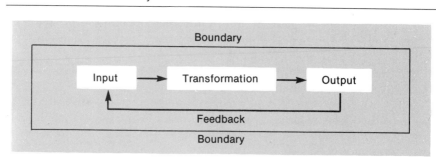

positive distinction between the firm and its competitors. The reputation of a firm's employees in the community can also add to the distinctiveness of the firm.

Systems theory helps to weld the diverse parts of an organization into a coherent whole so that we can see how these parts fit together. A resulting benefit is increased awareness of the interdependence between organizational components. The systems approach also makes it clear that an organization does not operate in a vacuum. While an organization is made up of numerous subsystems, it is also part of a larger suprasystem (see Figure 8–2). Viewing an organization in this fashion increases the manager's awareness of the interdependence between the organization and its environment.

INTERDEPENDENCE

When the work of departments or organizations contributes to the welfare and productivity of each other, a state of interdependence exists. The ability to understand and take advantage of interdependence is important to the coordination and success of an organization. In *The Art of Japanese Management* Pascale and Athos noted that organizational relationships are based on interdependence. In comparing American and Japanese management, the authors observed that Americans are culturally underequipped to grasp the nature and importance of these relationships.[1] It is essential that we understand the impact of interdependence on the coordination and communication patterns within and between organizations.

Highly interdependent organizations are referred to as **open systems,** while those with little or no interdependence are referred to as **closed systems.** According to Baker, "An ideal closed system would be one which receives no energy from an outside source and from which no energy is released to its surroundings."[2]

Examples of closed systems, especially social systems, are difficult to find because, by definition, there is no interaction with the environment. Relatively closed systems might include monasteries, organized crime syndicates, the Ku Klux Klan, and the Veterans of Foreign Wars. Because these organizations are not totally open to information exchange and environmental influence, they typically find themselves in an increasingly hostile environment.

An important consequence of a lack of interdependence in closed systems is **entropy.** Entropy is the degradation of energy in a system that leads to a state of inertia and maximum disorder. If a system is truly closed and accepts no inputs from the environment, its energy will eventually dissipate, and the elements will become randomly arranged. An or-

FIGURE 8–2   Systems, Subsystems, and Suprasystems

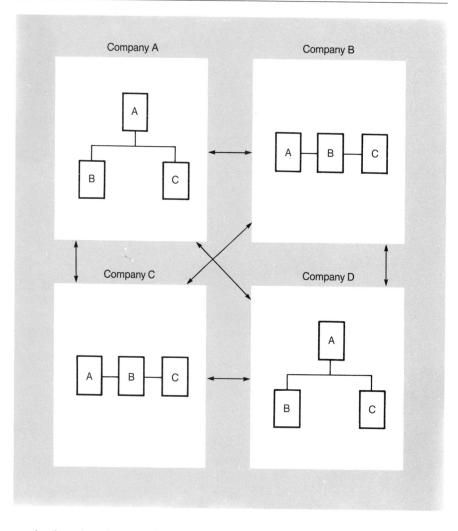

ganization that does not bring in outside energy or information ultimately runs down and dies. Robbins makes this point clearly:

> Survival requires a steady replenishment of those resources consumed. Raw materials must be secured, vacancies . . . must be filled, declining product lines must be replaced, changes in . . . tastes of customers or clients need to be anticipated and reacted to. . . . Failure to replenish will result in the organization's decline and, possibly, death.[3]

To avoid such disaster an organization should be maintained as an open system. An open system is one "in which a continuing flow of com-

ponent materials from the environment and a continuous output of products of the system's action back to the environment occurs."[4] Openness also refers to the quantity and quality of interaction and information flows between and within organizations.

Numerous factors determine the degree of interdependence and, therefore, the need for openness. The manager who is aware of these factors can do a better job of controlling the functional and dysfunctional effects. Identification of some of the primary factors and their impact on communication follows.

Structural Stability

Structural stability refers to the intensity and frequency of change in the relationships between elements within an organization. The more things remain unchanged, the less need there is for interaction. However, as instability increases, so does the need for information exchange.

Stability is characterized as either rigid or flexible. Most bureaucracies are considered to be rigid in structure because change occurs within them at an extremely slow rate. At the other extreme, adhocracies (in which structure is only temporary) are subject to immediate and drastic change.

Summarizing the work of several organizational theorists, Hage, Aiken, and Marrett stated that organizations can coordinate their efforts through either *planning* or *mutual adjustment*. Organizational linkages can be in the form of blueprints: rules, policies, and procedures. Alternatively, they can be based on the flexibility of feedback, intensive interaction, and continuous mutual adjustment.[5] A typical bureaucracy relies heavily on blueprints, and information and decision making move slowly, while in a typical adhocracy mutual adjustment is relied on, information sharing is more intense, and decision making is quicker.

In a classic study, Burns and Stalker examined the impact of changing environmental conditions and technology on organizational structure and management processes. They were able to identify two basically opposing structures which they labeled organic and mechanistic.[6]

Organic structures are open, flexible, and adaptive. Coordination occurs through a free flow of mutual influence and feedback, especially in a horizontal direction. Influence is based on personal competence rather than position power. Organic organizations are, as the name implies, alive and dynamic, constantly changing to meet environmental demands. For example, a custom print shop, a consulting firm, and the emergency room of a hospital would exhibit organic characteristics because they have to respond to whatever is generated by their environment. Communication would be frequent, and behavior would be adjusted based on the sharing of information.

Mechanistic structures are much the opposite. They tend to be rigid, inflexible, and very slow to change, if at all. Coordination is based on

programmed behavior and sanctions to ensure that organizational members conform to behavioral blueprints. While such organizations are high in formality and complexity, tasks are simple and routine. Characteristics of a mechanistic structure might be exhibited by a U.S. military training camp, a religious order, or the manufacturer of a relatively unchanging product (e.g., cardboard boxes, ball bearings).

Burns and Stalker did not label either type of structure as good or bad. Their position was that the best type of structure was the one that would best fit the organization's environment. In an environment that is highly stable where coordination can be achieved with behavioral blueprints, a mechanistic structure may be most appropriate. A high level of volatility and constantly changing information requirements indicate that the organic structure may be most appropriate.

Technology

Another area of study that provides some insight into the nature of interdependence and the variability of coordination and communication requirements concerns the impact of technology on organizational structure. An important contribution was made with the work of J. D. Thompson.[7]

Thompson developed a connection between various types of technology and the requirements for effective organizational structure. Of particular interest are the requirements for coordination and communication. For each of his three major technology types, Thompson identified a different kind of interdependence between organizational units and a different set of communication and coordination requirements (see Figure 8–3).

Because it links independent clients or customers, *mediating technology* allows for a pooling of resources into separated functions or departments. The departments experience minimal interdependence and can rely heavily on standard operating procedures and other formalizing mechanisms for coordination and communication.

Examples of such organizations include banks, insurance companies,

---

FIGURE 8–3 Thompson's Classification of Technology and Interdependence

Technology Type	Interdependence Type	Need for Communication	Type of Coordination
Mediating	Pooled	Low	Standardization
Long-linked	Sequential	Medium	Planning
Intensive	Reciprocal	High	Mutual adjustment

SOURCE: J. D. Thompson, *Organizations in Action* (New York: McGraw-Hill, 1967).

and utilities. Each department provides a specific and limited function that requires little interaction with other departments. For example, the loan officer in a bank does not have to consult with the employees responsible for attracting and managing deposits. The functioning of the loan department is guided by a complex set of standard procedures and regulating statements.

Departments in an organization which utilize *long-linked technology* are sequentially interdependent. Function C cannot be performed until function B is performed, and function B cannot be performed until function A is performed. Sequential interdependence increases the requirements for coordination, and that increases the requirement for interaction. Employees responsible for functions A, B, and C must be in communication with one another.

The employees in the press room of a newspaper cannot do their work without a finished layout. Layout specialists need the advertising and news stories from the appropriate departments. The need for communication is greater in sequential interdependence than in pooled interdependence. It can be accomplished through routine planning, although a certain amount of unscheduled coordinating and synchronizing is characteristic of sequential interdependence. The most sophisticated applications of long-linked technology require the least amount of coordination. Computer-assisted assembly lines (e.g., auto assembly) require relatively little unscheduled interaction.

Organizations that utilize *intensive technology* experience a high level of interdependence which requires constant interaction and updating. It is frequently impossible for individuals in such an organization to do their jobs without being in constant contact with others. Consider the performance of workers in the emergency or operating rooms of a hospital. Construction contractors are sensitive to the need to have various individuals or functional managers interacting with one another, especially if they are working on an unusual or complicated job. Communication is frequently on the spot, with continuous feedback and mutual adjustment.

Task Variability

Task variability and the organization's ability to respond to that variability have an impact on the firm's information collecting and processing needs. Perrow offered some insight into this problem as he distinguished between routine and nonroutine tasks.[8]

> *Routine tasks* are well established tasks for which there is little or no change in method or materials.
>
> *Nonroutine tasks* are tasks about which little is known and for which no established techniques and methods have been developed. There may also be a variety of tasks to be performed.

Perrow identified two dimensions for classifying and treating tasks: the number of exceptions encountered by a firm as it produces a product or service and the degree to which problems (and solutions) are analyzable. The first refers to the variability of the demands and problems presented to the organization in terms of their exceptional nature. The second dimension refers to the ability of the firm to respond to demands placed on it. Depending on the unusualness and difficulty of the task a firm is asked to perform, the firm may or may not be able to come up with an appropriate solution. These two dimensions produce a matrix with four distinct task types (see Figure 8–4).

The information needs for these four different classes of tasks will vary in terms of quality and quantity. The ways information is shared will also vary.[9] In the case of Craftsmanship (Quadrant 1), the firm is dealing with limited exceptions but generally unique, precision tasks (e.g., custom work). The quantity of required information may not be extensive, but the quality or accuracy must be quite high. This calls for intense interaction between the firm or department and its client.

The information needs of firms engaged in routine manufacturing (Quadrant 3) require steady flows of standardized (usually quantitative) information which could be generated by routine scheduled meetings or a sophisticated information system. Unscheduled interactions are minimal in such organizations.

Firms engaged in nonroutine manufacturing (Quadrant 2) would be faced with frequent challenges in the form of unique and complex tasks and would need large amounts of information on a frequent basis. Interaction is intense throughout performance of the task, and would in-

FIGURE 8–4   Perrow's Classification of Task Types

	Few exceptions	Many exceptions
Unanalyzable search	Craftsmanship 1	Nonroutine manufacturing 2
Analyzable search	Routine manufacturing 3	Engineering (heavy equipment) 4

SOURCE: Adapted from C. Perrow, *Organizational Analysis* (Monterey, Calif.: Brooks/Cole Publishing, 1970), p. 83. Used with permission.

clude one-on-one encounters, and group meetings. Unscheduled interaction would be high depending on the uniqueness and difficulty of the task.

Organizations involved in Perrow's engineering type tasks (Quadrant 4) also face a high level of uniqueness, however, they would have the capacity to respond. To do so they would need large, steady amounts of highly accurate, mostly quantitative information. Unscheduled interaction would be frequent in this quadrant also.

The Organization's Environment

It has been well established that the effective business firm operates as an open system, adapting its outputs to the tastes and preferences of its various constituencies *(Megatrends, In Search of Excellence, The Change Masters)*. In a discussion on organizational change, Katz and Georgopoulos offered this observation:

> For organizations to survive . . . in the future, some sizable portion of their resources will have to be committed to enlarging their adaptive subsystems to deal more adequately with external relations and new social inputs. Social effectiveness will have to be added to productive efficiency as an important objective.[10]

This observation focuses on an important change in contemporary managerial philosophy and strategy. Since the beginning of the 20th century and the widespread growth of mass production and distribution, organizations have been traditionally efficiency-oriented, trying to maximize the output-to-input ratio. Toffler aptly observes:

> . . . the new profusion of life-styles, subcultures, ethnic groupings, regional specialties, recreational "affinity groups" all generate demand for a proliferation of varied goods and services.[11]

As consumers and other organizational constituents have become more sophisticated and more demanding, it has become increasingly necessary for management to develop a sensitivity to the changes in constituent's values, tastes, and preferences. Management must continuously address the question: How well is the system's output allowing the firm to meet its objectives? Thus, more emphasis must be placed on the objectives-to-output ratio. This forces management into the difficult task of balancing the goals of maintenance and efficiency (output/input) against those of growth and effectiveness (objective/output).

Efficiency is best achieved in a stable, undisturbed (closed) environment where the system can develop its competencies and refine its processes. The pursuit of effectiveness requires a relatively high level of information sharing between an organization and its environmental

constituents. Regarding the consequences of such interaction Toffler reminds us that:

> the demand for varied new products and services brings with it a proliferation of varied new work processes, alternative work routines . . . so that we wind up with more differentiated individualized people doing more diverse tasks. And this vastly escalates, once more, the costs of coordination. . . . .[12]

The amount and nature of that coordination is, to some extent, a function of the changing nature of the environment. Environmental variability and complexity are vividly depicted in a four-environment model developed by Emery and Trist.[13] The different environments in the model reflect two important dimensions: internal organizational change and interdependence between environmental members. Both dimensions have a direct impact on the complexity and intensity of communication.

The first environment they describe is the **placid-random** environment with little or no dynamic activity within organizations and virtually no interdependence. Placid means undisturbed, and this is how the organizations in such an environment operate. There is little growth-related activity or change within organizations that requires interaction with, or threatens others; therefore, the level of interdependence is extremely low or nonexistent.

In direct contrast to our contemporary environment, self-sufficiency is commonplace in this environment. Communication requirements are low and information needs are easily met by the organization through experience and routine planning.

The placid-random environment might best characterize the early settlement of the United States, especially during the westward migration and settlement. Organizations were established in an almost random fashion and experienced little or no growth or change that affected others in the environment.

The second environment developed by Emery and Trist, the **placid-clustered** environment experiences very little growth by environmental members. However, for a variety of reasons there is a clustering of organizations that increases the level of interdependence. This is exactly what happened during the westward migration and settlement as firms clustered around major transportation routes, resources, and markets. Clustering gradually brings environmental members closer together and leads to increased interaction.

The impact of clustering, of course, is that it makes each organization dependent on the others, creating decision-making uncertainty. Self-sufficiency is less likely in such an environment because needed information is held by others and may not be shared. Consequently, there is the need for some modest level of information collection and analysis.

The third type of environment is the **disturbed-reactive** environment.

In this environment growth and interdependence (internal and external) are at a fairly high level. Organizations are actively involved in research and development; growth is a major objective. This growth and development impacts on the markets and resources of others, and therefore on their activities and objectives.

The impact serves to disturb an organization, and the organization must react to the disturbance. Since information is essential to the decision to react, quick and accurate collection of information is required. The quality and quantity of information gathering and processing will allow the firm to take actions most likely to move it back to a steady state.

This strategy has been employed by many organizations when they move to duplicate the actions of competitors. When Ford introduced the Mustang and Chrysler introduced the minivan, others in the industry moved to offer their versions of these products. As long as disturbances are not too great or too numerous, the firm can eventually collect the necessary information with which to make decisions and respond. When the disturbances become too great or too numerous, the firm finds itself in the final environment described by Emery and Trist.

In the **turbulent** environment the level of change and interdependence is so great that an organization has difficulty staying informed and operates in a chronic state of high uncertainty. The organization's inability to collect and process information immobilizes its decision-making capabilities. The result is that it cannot respond to the collective impact of activities initiated by all other firms in the environment.

Many business failures are a direct result of the severe impact of the actions of other organizations in the contemporary environment. Consider, for example, the computer industry. Competition through product research, development, and marketing has been so intense that many firms have been unable to keep up and have been forced out of the market.

Emery and Trist's environments demonstrate that as the level of activity and change in the environment increases, so does interdependence and uncertainty. In a turbulent environment organizations are unable to predict what others, on whom they are dependent, will do. Decision making and coordination are difficult because conventional planning approaches no longer succeed.

Differentiation and Integration

During the mid-60's, Lawrence and Lorsch reported on the effects of the environment on management practices and organizational structure.[14] Their research focused on two diverse, but related, contemporary organizational phenomena—differentiation and integration. **Differentiation** refers to the distinguishable characteristics that separate various units, oc-

cupational groups, or operational functions within an organization. **Integration,** on the other hand, refers to the connectedness and coordination of those distinct parts of the organization.

The basic hypothesis of this landmark research was that differentiation would increase and the means of integration would change as the environment became more complex, turbulent, and uncertain. Lawrence and Lorsch examined three industries—containers, food, and plastics—and discovered distinctly different environmental and technological characteristics that resulted in major differences in decision making and coordination (see Figure 8–5).

Container firms represented what Burns and Stalker would characterize as a mechanistic structure, while plastics firms resembled more of an organic structure. Container firms were relatively low in environment-generated uncertainty. They relied on routine tasks, coordinated by conventional methods such as standard operating procedures and regulations. Planning and problem solving were accomplished by a traditional management hierarchy.

Plastics firms, on the other hand, were very high in uncertainty created by the environment and relied much more on unconventional coordinating devices such as cross-functional teams and integrative departments and individuals. Food firms placed between plastics and containers, showing moderate uncertainty, and using a combination of decision-making and coordination techniques. Thus, a very clear connection was drawn between environmental complexity, differentiation, uncertainty, and integration.

Complexity

Complexity refers to the extent of differentiation within an organization. Vertical differentiation refers to "tallness" of the hierarchy or the number of levels within an organization. Horizontal differentiation refers to the

---

FIGURE 8–5 Differentiation/Integration across Three Industries

	Plastics	Foods	Containers
Environmental uncertainty	High	Moderate	Low
Differentiation	High	Medium	Low
Using conventional integrative devices	Yes	Yes	Yes
Using nonconventional integrative devices	Yes	Some	None

SOURCE: Paul Lawrence and Jay W. Lorsch, *Organization and Environment: Managing Differentiation and Integration* (Boston: Harvard Business School, 1967).

extent of horizontal separation or departmentation within an organization.

High levels of complexity result in tighter supervision and control, and consequently greater coordination and communication problems because information must move through many levels of management. The opposite is true of flat structures.

The higher the degree of complexity, the larger the number of elements in the system. This suggests the necessity for a greater level of information exchange. It also suggests greater difficulty with coordination and communication on a scheduled basis. For example, Hage et al. found that as the occupational diversity of organizations increased, the frequency of unscheduled interactions and attendance at organization-wide meetings increased.[15]

Formalization

Formalization refers to the degree of standardization within an organization. As formalization increases, there is more reliance on written rules, policies, and standard operating procedures as a means of coordinating the affairs of the organization. Standardization facilitates coordination and decreases variability of action. Formalized organizations may find it useful to direct and coordinate member activities through standardized language. For example, police officers can communicate to their colleagues using such language (e.g., code 3, 10–4) and get highly consistent responses. Football teams use complex signals (e.g., blue, left 64 on 2) to coordinate player actions.

The degree of formalization influences the amount and type of interaction within an organization. Using "completeness of job descriptions" and "job specificity" as measures of formalization, Hage et al. found that job specificity was negatively correlated with the number of meetings and the frequency of attendance at meetings. They also found a strong negative correlation between the existence of job descriptions and the frequency of unscheduled interactions.[16]

INTERORGANIZATIONAL COMMUNICATION STRATEGIES

When complexity and uncertainty are high, more information collecting and sharing is necessary. This means more meetings, more memos, and so forth. As most data is collected and shared in an attempt to deal with uncertainty, the quality or *richness* of information—the information carrying capacity of data—becomes increasingly important.[17] Managers must use a variety of means to get not only quantity of data but quality as well.

To survive and flourish in a turbulent environment, an organization must also be aware of its interdependencies and develop an "environmen-

tal fit"—a state of compatability between the system and its environmental partners. To develop this fit, an organization must adapt to changing economic conditions, altered tastes and preferences, and evolving social and cultural values.

Improving information quality and adapting are dependent on effective information exchange. Alvin Toffler, who has treated these issues extensively, summarized the value of information exchange this way:

> In even the simplest division of labor, workers must expend energy on two different functions: one is actually doing the job; the other is maintaining liaison with others who participate in the process. As the society grows more differentiated the balance between these two components of work—production and liaison—shifts, and more energy must go to the liaison component.[18]

Traditional planning and coordination techniques are appropriate in a stable, formalized environment where plans can be executed and resources coordinated in an unambiguous and timely fashion. When liaison is necessary, adequate information exists and there is ample time to work it through the organization before any harmful effects occur.

In a turbulent environment, however, liaison becomes increasingly necessary, and productivity is diminished. Information is always incomplete, and there is not enough time to move it upward through a cumbersome hierarchy. By the time decisions are made and changes are effected through the traditional hierarchy, it may be too late.

The high level of change and interdependence in a turbulent environment requires a unique set of strategies for coping with the effects of uncertainty on decision making and coordination. As the liaison component becomes more important, organizations must become more proficient at the liaison function. There are several basic strategies available to an organization.

Boundary Spanning

A concept that has developed rapidly into an organizational role is **boundary spanning**—the practice of crossing system boundaries to obtain or give information and to influence the activities of other systems. The boundary spanner is an individual who can move quickly and easily across the boundaries of various organizations within the firm's environment. Boundary spanners operate out of various outreach departments within an organization (e.g., marketing, legal, personnel). Because of the intensity and competitiveness of the environment, boundary spanners have assumed increasing importance. Simon has pointed out that:

> the organization must have an "interface" for ingesting such information selectively and for translating it into formats that are compatible with its internal information flows and systems.[19]

This is the function of the boundary spanner; he or she interfaces and gathers information that originates outside the organization. The boundary spanner can also carry information outside the organization to wherever it is needed.

Controlling the Environment

Controlling the environment to make it more stable and less uncertain is another option. **Merging** organizations is one way of reducing interdependence and uncertainty. If firm A cannot plan because of the unpredictability of firm B's actions, a merger of A and B would remove that unpredictability.

Contracting is another method of controlling interdependence and reducing unpredictability. To ensure the flow of resources or the acceptance of outputs, long-term contracts are quite effective. **Co-opting** (or outright purchase) is another method for controlling the environment. Taking control of competitors or suppliers is an effective way of reducing the effects of interdependence and unpredictability. All these methods reduce incompatibility and increase stability which, in turn, reduce uncertainty, and the need for interaction and information sharing.

INTRAORGANIZATIONAL COMMUNICATION STRATEGIES

The first set of strategies focused on relationships between the organization and its environment. A more important set of strategies are those directly under the control of management.

Reducing the Need for Information Sharing

The objective of the **buffering** strategy is to alter organizational structure or management practices to reduce the need for decision making and information sharing. If an organization can afford to stockpile resources, it doesn't need to make frequent decisions about when to order, how much to order, and so forth. There are fewer occasions to say, "We're out of materials," and therefore fewer orders need to be processed. The obvious and most serious drawback to buffering is the immense cost required to stockpile resources.

One of the advantages of the Japanese system of lifetime employment is less turnover, which has a dual effect. Employees that stay with a firm become more familiar with their co-workers and the firm's operations. Because of the intimacy and sharing of perceptions that develops, less coordination and communication are required.[20] There is also less need to interact with other environmental members (e.g., employment agencies) and less need to depend on them.

Another method to reduce the need for information processing is alteration of the structure of an organization to create smaller independent subsystems. These subsystems can operate on a semiautonomous basis, which reduces their need to interact with other parts of the system. They can make direct contact with resource and output markets in the environment. Additionally, there is likely to be less specialization of inputs, which means less of the liaison component. If, for example, an individual worker is totally responsible for assembling a product, as opposed to working with several others in an assembly group, that worker has no need to coordinate or communicate with others. Information sharing is simplified, uncertainty is reduced, and decision making is easier.

In recent years the Theory Z organization has been popularized as the prototype Japanese operation.[21] A common characteristic of these organizations is environmental stability and the tendency to subcontract volatile tasks. In his discussion of the major implications of information technology, Wilsteed observes the inability of large firms to adapt quickly to change and declares:

> There should thus be a steady move by astute large organizations towards employing smaller organizations on professional contracts, for example, for market research, legal and accounting services, computer systems supply . . . .[22]

There are, of course, certain costs inherent in this strategy. The versatility of outputs of self-contained groups is drastically reduced, as is the quantity because many of the desired effects of division of labor and specialization are lost.

Improving Information Sharing Capabilities

The final strategy for dealing with uncertainty and interdependence is to increase the organization's ability to share information. One very popular method is to create or enhance the organization's information processing system. With the advent of microchips and large scale integration, information technology (IT) has evolved in extraordinarily rapid fashion. It is likely that with very large-scale integration this phenomenal growth will continue throughout the rest of the century. Some experts feel that effective application of IT will be crucial to the survival and profitability of organizations in the future.

Wilsteed has identified some of the major implications of IT on the survival of organizations. The first, he states, is that

> senior managers must create an organization structure and style that is suited to absorbing ideas and changes, as otherwise the enterprise will . . .expire.[23]

Another of his implications relates to decreasing response time for many processes.

> The introduction of IT into manufacturing industries will change many operations radically. Robots enable much shorter production runs, since the setup time in changing to a different product is negligible.[24]

Thus an organization can move to expand its information processing capabilities, taking advantage of highly sophisticated technology. Such technology will allow the firm the opportunity to collect, store, and process more information more quickly. Decision making can occur more rapidly, but more importantly, it can occur more frequently. With the capability of updating information instantaneously and easily, the firm can establish decision rules to be executed by the information system. The major cost considerations stemming from this option are the initial cost of the system, the establishment of decision rules applicable throughout the organization, and the collection of information to be processed by the system.

Organizations must have individuals who are capable of properly using information technology. Simon pointed out some time ago that:

> The information-processing systems of our contemporary world swim in an exceedingly rich soup of information, of symbols. In a world of this kind, the scarce resource is not information; it is processing capacity to attend to information.[25]

There is ample evidence of the impact of computers in the area of decision making and communication.[26] Daft has distilled from the literature a number of effects:

1. Reduction in clerical personnel.
2. Increased power to computer specialists.
3. Greater organizational complexity.
4. Greater decision-making collaboration.
5. Increase in the proportion of professional staff.[27]

A final method for improving an organization's information processing capabilities is to enhance individual and intergroup cooperation. There are several ways to achieve this.

The first and best opportunity for coordination is the line manager who acts as a connecting point, holding diverse individuals together to accomplish the unit's objectives. Likert conceptualized the organization as a series of interrelated groups with the manager acting as a "linking pin."[28] The manager's main task is to coordinate the efforts of his subordinates, bringing them together for purposes of information sharing and decision making.

In a complex and turbulent environment, the accomplishment of objectives may involve several units or groups simultaneously. In such cases it may be fruitful to employ **multiple group memberships.** It might be very informative and productive to have the lead engineer in a product development group serve on other groups in the areas of policy, plan-

ning, or budgeting. The individual could easily share information in both directions because of his joint membership.

A more sophisticated version of group membership is a formalized **integrator**—a liaison person charged with the effective sharing of information between two or more groups or departments. Because of the uncertainties of the turbulent environment, integrator positions have emerged as a formalized method of short-circuiting the chain of command. Integrators can share information more quickly and accurately than those in the chain of command and thus allow the firm to adapt to its environment more effectively. While integrators have position power to accomplish their work, it has been found that they typically are more effective using personal competence and persuasiveness.[29]

Another productive method for information sharing and decision making is the **task force.** Frequently a project will require the expertise of several professional or functional groups. The traditional management hierarchy is simply too cumbersome for the intense interaction involved, and cannot move the necessary amount and type of information in the allotted time. It is better to bring together one or more members from the various groups and let them accomplish the task. Information sharing is improved, and the perspectives of the various members of the group enhance the productivity of the group.

A major drawback is the possibility of perceptual conflict, and consequently, very limited information sharing. Another potential problem is demotivation of members when they are sent back to their home departments, where the routine may seem less exciting and unattractive. Choosing the individuals carefully is a key step in the use of the task force.

A final method of sharing information more quickly and accurately than the conventional hierarchy is **joint group meetings.** While the task force is usually the better method for combining the resources of different groups, joint group meetings are occasionally an effective means of sharing and processing information. If there is no one individual in a particular unit who can effectively represent the unit, or if the nature of the task is such that it requires the expertise of several or most of the individuals involved, then a joint group meeting is an appropriate way of sharing and processing information. The most obvious constraint here is the effort and expense involved in bringing a large group together.

It is necessary for organizations to find more effective ways of interacting with an increasingly complex environment and sophisticated technology. Information from the environment must be quickly and accurately collected and processed so that more appropriate responses can be made. We have suggested strategies to help an organization fit into its current environment. If the organization does not have the ability to adapt to its environment, its performance will suffer and it may not survive.

INFORMATION–SHARING TENDENCIES

We have identified some of the major communication variables and strategies of an organization as a whole. Most of today's organizations attempt to accomplish their objectives in a turbulent environment. The high level of change and interdependence in such an environment creates much uncertainty for management in its attempts to make decisions, both long-run and short-run.

We have suggested some of the more enlightened strategies for dealing with that uncertainty. Regardless of the strategy chosen, the effectiveness of that strategy ultimately depends on the information-sharing tendencies generated and reinforced within a given organization.

Over time, organizations develop characteristic ways of sharing—or not sharing—information. If the tendencies are positive, strong, and adequately reinforced, the organization will enjoy a high level of sharing and productivity. If the tendencies are negative or weak, the firm's productivity will suffer and it will most likely go the way of the dinosaur and the buggy whip factory. To keep this from happening, we offer in this final section a review of some of the barriers to successful information sharing tendencies.

Perception and Language

We already have addressed the information-sharing problems created by inadequate interpersonal perception. If individuals see things differently, it is very difficult for them to share and communicate. Sharing can occur only if individuals possess the willingness and ability to do so, and then only in the proper climate.

If two or more individuals are not familiar with the elements and structure of a given language, it is difficult for them to state and share information in a mutually appropriate fashion.

Power and Status

Information is power. It is also a resource, just like materials, machines, and labor. Those who possess it frequently wield great power and status. Some organizational members may spend much of their time positioning themselves to control the informational resources of an organization to gain power and status. In an effort to retain this power, they refuse to share the information that gives them their power. This can incapacitate the organization.

Information is highly perishable, and will lose its value if it is not shared. If the organization is unable to use information to improve its position, it may miss opportunities and experience a variety of crises.

Power and status incongruencies generate social distance between organizational members and this acts as a barrier to interaction and information sharing. In the case of superior-subordinate relationships, the ability of the superior to reward and punish can extend that distance.

Coalitions and the Emergent Structure

An additional effect of power and status concerns the actual operating structure of an organization. As we have pointed out, organizations are coalitions of various interest groups. The individuals who represent these different interests will do all in their power to protect their interests by pooling, withholding, and distorting information.

In most organizations, no one individual or group holds sufficient power and status to completely control the organization. Thus various coalitions will be formed to control the activities of the organization. The more power and status a coalition can mobilize, the more it can control the variables we have discussed and, consequently, the sharing of information.

Interestingly, Jeffrey Pfeffer states that organizations are not structured for effectiveness, but to protect the interests of the power coalition. The result of various groups attempting to influence the structure of an organization is the emergent structure.[30] A manager who is interested in controlling the flow of information should understand the interplay between individuals and groups as they struggle to forge the emergent structure. The dominant coalition can have an effect on the information-sharing tendencies of an organization.

Distrust

We have addressed the issue of creating the proper climate for optimum information sharing. If management creates a positive climate and rewards those who sustain it, the organization should enjoy the fruits of a high level of information sharing. The organization that maintains a defensive climate will experience a great deal of distrust. Regardless of the strategy employed to deal with the environment, information processing will be ineffectual and haphazard.

Channel Overload

The proper structure of an organization allows for the free flow of information. In a very real sense, the information-processing capacity of an organization will dictate its information needs. Organizations frequently attempt to collect and process more information than they can handle. This leads to overload, and forces the organization to cut back on its ac-

tivities because it cannot process the needed information to do more. It will have to adjust its ability to collect and process information to match what it is capable of doing.

Geographic Dispersion

Space is a frequent barrier to communication. A geographically spread out organization may have difficulty establishing, enforcing, and rewarding proper information-sharing tendencies. Information technology has helped somewhat in overcoming this particular barrier, but not to the extent that it could or should.

If an organization is geographically dispersed, management should be sensitive to that condition and attempt to identify and initiate the best possible information-sharing conditions. Ensuring proper training and providing adequate technology are necessary, but setting the proper example should be at the top of management's list.

Psychological Cost of Information

Whenever an individual defers to another in search of information, there is an implicit understanding that the individual seeking the information is less informed than the individual providing the information. This can be a psychologically and socially humbling experience, depending on the behavior of the information provider. Too often individuals who possess information will make information seeking and sharing a painful experience. They remind the information seeker of his ignorance; perhaps even extort various favors for the information. If the cost of seeking information is felt to be too great, the seeker may refuse to play the game, opting instead to operate in ignorance. Consequently, the choices and actions of the seeker may be to his detriment and that of the organization. It behooves management to create a climate of open, cost-free seeking and sharing of information.

Informal Groups

A properly developed and updated organization chart demonstrates to employees where their positions are and how they fit into the organization. The lines connecting the various positions and departments are intended to represent the lines of coordination, communication, and control. Positions or groups traditionally are departmentalized on one of four bases:

Function—The nature of the work done by the unit (e.g., production, sales).

Product—The different types of products or services provided by a firm (e.g., GM's motor divisions).

Customer—Firms cater to different consumer groups (e.g., households, industry, government).

Geography—Physical regions (e.g., southeast, northeast).

Despite an organization's attempts to develop and maintain a rational structure, individuals will "restructure" the organization to suit their personalities, needs, and so forth. Figure 8–6 shows the formal-rational struc-

FIGURE 8–6 Formal Organization Chart

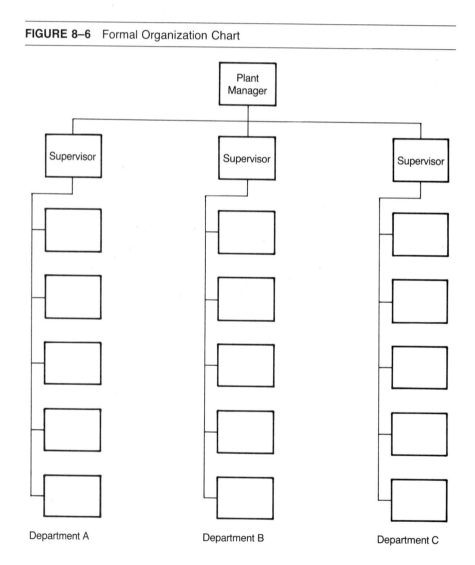

Department A   Department B   Department C

ture of an organization. Figure 8–7 shows the actual information-sharing patterns of the employees. Such groupings will have a direct impact on the firm's productive ability because they influence the sharing of information.

SUMMARY

It is frequently necessary and helpful to view an organization as a system to see all the parts of the organization *and* how they fit together. Systems have basically four components: inputs, outputs, transformation processes, and feedback mechanisms. A fifth aspect of a system, although not a part of it, is the system's boundaries, which separate the system from its environment.

Organizations as systems can be characterized in terms of their interdependence and structural stability. Interdependence refers to the level of interaction and influence between two systems or subsystems. Systems that are subject to a high level of influence by others are referred to as open systems. Systems that do not depend on others and are infrequently influenced by others are referred to as closed systems.

Structural stability refers to the amount of movement and change in relationships within a system. Those organizations that experience long-term stability with little change in inter-unit relationships are referred to as mechanistic. Those that experience a high level of change are referred to as organic.

The environment in which an organization operates varies from random-placid (simple) to turbulent (complex). As the environment evolves from simple to complex, the amount of change, interdependence, and uncertainty increases. Consequently, it becomes more difficult for an organization to respond using traditional planning and coordination methods.

Successful business firms must operate as open, somewhat organic systems in order to respond appropriately to the environment. To reduce uncertainty and make effective decisions, firms must improve their ability to collect and process information from the environment. Three broad strategies exist for doing so. The first is to control the environment. To the extent that a firm can control the environment, it can make the future predictable. Such predictability removes uncertainty and makes decision making easy. A second strategy is to reduce the need for processing information. Organizational processes and structures can be changed so that the requirements for information sharing are no longer necessary. The third strategy is to improve the information-sharing capabilities of the organization and its members. This can be achieved through improved technology, improved communication skills, or by changed structural relationships.

FIGURE 8–7 Informal Groupings

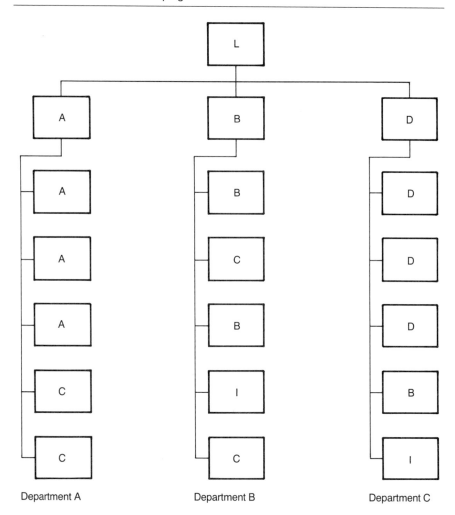

Department A   Department B   Department C

A = Group A.
B = Group B.
C = Group C.
D = Group D.
I = Isolate.
L = Liaison.

Finally, if an organization is to become effective at information sharing it must understand and improve on the information-sharing tendencies of its members. Improper perception, power and status imbalances, distrust, channel overload, and geographic dispersion will influence the information-sharing tendencies of employees. The impact of these factors on information sharing must be clearly understood so that any negative effects can be eliminated.

DISCUSSION QUESTIONS

1. What is a system? Define the basic components of a system and show how they are related.

2. Discuss how and why systems theory is important to the contemporary manager.

3. Explain specifically why systems differ from one another. Discuss systems characteristics in your answer.

4. What does entropy mean? Explain its importance in systems theory.

5. Systems can be open or closed. What are the basic differences between open and closed systems? Why is it important for an organization to recognize whether it tends toward an open or closed system?

6. Burns and Stalker identified two basically opposing organizational structures. Compare and contrast these two structures. Which type is most suited to adaptation to a rapidly changing environment?

7. Discuss efficiency and effectiveness as they relate to systems theory. Indicate whether an open or closed system is more conducive to achieving organizational effectiveness.

8. Emery and Trist have developed a four-environment model to depict levels of environmental variability and complexity. Review the four environment model. Use an example to illustrate each of the four environments.

9. List three different ways to characterize organizations as systems. Describe the bipolar values possible for each characteristic and discuss whether or not organizations tend to exist at the extremes of the bipolar scales.

10. Describe the problem that an organization faces when it must deal with a rapidly changing environment. How does Alvin Toffler describe the problems that arise, given this type of environment?

11. What does liaison mean in the context of organization theory? Why is the liaison component important to an organization in a turbulent environment?

12. In general, there are three basic strategies available to an organization for processing information in a turbulent environment. Describe each of the strategies and indicate how management might employ them.

13. Discuss three strategies to improve an organization's information-processing capabilities.

14. List three barriers to successful communication and information sharing. How can they be overcome?

NOTES

[1] R. T. Pascale and A. Athos, *The Art of Japanese Management* (New York: Warner Books, 1981), Chapter 5.

[2] Frank Baker, *Organizational Systems* (Homewood, Ill.: Richard D. Irwin, 1973), p. 5.

[3] Stephen P. Robbins, *Organizational Theory* (Englewood Cliffs, N.J.: Prentice-Hall, 1983), p. 28.

[4] Baker, *Organizational Systems*.

[5] J. Hage, M. Aiken, and C. Marrett, "Organization Structure and Communications," *American Sociological Review* 36 (October 1971), pp. 860–71.

[6] Tom Burns and G. Stalker, *The Management of Innovation* (London: Tavistock, 1961).

[7] J. D. Thompson *Organizations in Action* (New York: McGraw-Hill, 1967).

[8] C. Perrow, *Organizational Analysis* (Monterey, Calif.: Brooks/Cole Publishing, 1970), pp. 75–85.

[9] R. Daft and N. Macintosh, "A New Approach to Design and Use of Management Information," *California Management Review* 21 (1978), pp. 82–92.

[10] Daniel Katz and B. Georgopoulos, "Organizations in a Changing World," *The Journal of Applied Behavioral Sciences* 7 (1971), pp. 342–70.

[11] Alvin Toffler, *The Eco-spasm Report* (New York: Bantam Books, 1975), p. 30.

[12] Ibid.

[13] Fred Emery and E. Trist, "The Causal Texture of Organizational Environments," *Human Relations* (February 1965), pp. 21–32.

[14] Paul Lawrence and J. Lorsch, *Organization and Environment: Managing Differentiation and Integration* (Boston: Harvard Business School, 1967).

[15] Hage, et al., "Organization Structure and Communication."

[16] Ibid.

[17] H. Simon, *Administrative Behavior* (New York: Free Press, 1976), chap. 14; R. Daft, *Organizational Theory and Design* (St. Paul: West Publishing, 1986), chap. 8.

[18] Toffler, *The Eco-spasm Report*, p. 31.

[19] Simon, *Administrative Behavior*, p. 294.

[20] W. G. Ouchi, *Theory Z* (New York: Avon Books, 1981).

[21] Ibid.

[22] Richard Wilsteed, "Organization Implications of Information Technology," *The Hong Kong Manager* (February 1984), p. 13.

[23] Ibid.

[24] Ibid.

[25] Simon, *Administrative Behavior*.

[26] N. Carter, "Computerization as a Predominate Technology: Its Influence on the Structure of Newspaper Organizations," *Academy of Management Journal* 27, no. 2 (June 1984), pp. 247–70.

[27] Daft, *Organizational Theory*, pp. 328–30.

[28] R. Likert, *New Patterns of Management* (New York: McGraw-Hill, 1961).

[29] P. Lawrence and J. Lorsch, "New Management Job: The Integrator," *Harvard Business Review* (November–December 1967), pp. 142–51.

[30] Jeffrey Pfeffer, *Organizational Design* (Arlington Heights, Ill.: AHM Publishing Co., 1978).

SUGGESTED READINGS

CORBETT, WILLIAM J. "The Communications Tools Inherent in Corporate Culture." *Personnel Journal* (April 1986), pp. 71–74.

GREENBAUM, HOWARD H.; ELLSWORTH J. HOLDEN, Jr.; and LUCIAN SPATARO. "Organizational Structure and Communication Processes: A Study of Change." *Group and Organization Studies* 8 (March 1983), pp. 61–82.

LEIPZIG, JOHN S., and ELIZABETH MORE. "Organizational Communication: A Review and Analysis of Three Current Approaches to the Field." *Journal of Business Communications* 19 (Fall 1982), pp. 77–92.

PODSAKOFF, PHILIP M., and CHESTER A. SCHRIESCHIEM. "Field Studies of French and Raven's Bases of Power: Critique, Reanalysis, and Suggestions for Future Research." *Psychological Bulletin* 97, pp. 387–411.

TELEM, MOSHE. "The Process Organizational Structure." *Journal of Management Studies* 22, no. 1 (January 1985), pp. 38–52.

WALTMAN, JOHN L. "Entropy and Business Communication." *Journal of Business Communication* 21 (Winter 1984), pp. 63–80.

Part Three

Communication

Activities:

Sending and Receiving

Chapter 9

Problem Solving and Reporting

Chapter 9 Case

You are the manager of a plant manufacturing metal containers. You have been on the job three months, having been promoted and transferred in from a similar plant in another city. You've just begun to feel that you know your staff and things have been going well. For the past few days, though, one of the production lines has experienced a dramatic drop in quality. By the time it was brought to your attention last Friday afternoon, the problem was severe. If it continues to worsen, the line may have to be shut down, and you may not be able to fill a special order that has had all the lines working overtime. The line foreman, a longtime employee who came up through the ranks, believes the problem is caused by aging machinery that is about to give out. The maintenance supervisor has checked the machinery and informed you that there's nothing wrong with it, but suggests sabotage. A couple of the line employees confide that purchasing has been known to release inferior materials more than once in the past. You know that the employees have been under a lot of pressure lately to get this order out, and rumblings of discontent have reached all the way to your office. You've learned the hard way what can happen when employees start thinking rebellion and are ready to start making accusations, but something is holding you back. What should you do?

INTRODUCTION

Contemporary management textbooks agree on what constitutes the manager's job. Managerial functions include planning, organizing, directing, and controlling. A fifth function is decision making; we feel that decision making is such an integral part of managing that it cannot be separated. The authors of one management text make this point clearly.

> Decision making is so basic that no management function can be performed without it. For management purposes, decisions are required in planning, organizing, actuating, and controlling. Due to its vital role, the question may be asked, "Should decision making not be considered one of the essential

functions of management?" Some authorities do treat it as a separate function. But, for our purposes, the decision-making process is considered to be an activity inherent in all management functions and not a function by itself.[1]

A further complication arises from studies of actual management behavior that indicate that the functional description of the manager's job is something of an oversimplification.[2] According to these studies the manager does not spend long periods of time engaged in reflective thinking in a relaxed, quiet environment. Instead, managers spend most of their time in brief encounters with others, reinforcing relationships, collecting, processing, and transmitting information about current activities.

Thus the manager is an information processor, and the importance of that role is clearly described by Drucker:

> The manager has a specific tool: information. A manager does not "handle" people; but instead motivates, guides, organizes people to do their own work. The tool—the only tool—to do all this is the spoken and written word or the language of numbers.[3]

In any occupation, the jobholder must know how to use the tools of the trade and the professional manager is no different. To survive, she must be skilled at using information. She must understand the decision-making process and the procedures inherent in it.

In their decision-making roles managers are frequently referred to as "trouble shooters," "disturbance handlers," and "problem solvers." Because the environment of most firms is volatile, routine planning is of limited value and disturbance handling and problem solving tend to occupy a significant part of the manager's time.

Whether the issue is an interpersonal conflict between two employees or the need for a more effective means of advertising, managers are constantly confronted with problems to be solved. Consequently, understanding the problem-solving process is important to the manager's success. In this chapter we will outline a basic approach to problem solving and examine some of the behavioral and procedural issues involved in the process.

RATIONAL EMPIRICISM

Most authorities on problem solving suggest a scientific approach referred to as **rational empiricism.** This is a systematic rationalizing process that involves three basic steps:

1. Careful problem identification through analysis of relevant available information.
2. Identification of alternative solutions.

FIGURE 9–1   The Rational Decision-Making Process

---

1. Define the problem
   a. Collect available information as needed
   b. Organize information
   c. Identify symptoms, their relationships, and causes
   d. Define the problem
2. Develop alternatives
   a. Identify decision objectives
   b. Specify decision criteria
   c. Collect additional information as needed
   d. Organize information
   e. Develop a list of alternatives
3. Select and implement the solution
   a. Evaluate alternatives based on decision criteria
   b. Select solution based on decision criteria
   c. Consider the impact of the solution
   d. Choose the time and method of implementation
   e. Discuss the implementation plan with relevant others
   f. Implement the solution
   g. Monitor the implementation and make adjustments

---

   3. Selection and implementation of a solution that comes closest to maximizing the problem solver's objectives.

This process consists of a logical sequence such as that in Figure 9–1.

Acceptability of Rational Empiricism

While such an approach is widely suggested, there is some question regarding its acceptance and use in organizations. Experts point to the many "seat-of-the-pants" decisions that are made in business firms each day. Even after intensive education in rational empiricism, business students may not automatically favor such an approach. In their study of problem-solving styles, F. Hoy and W. Boulton found that business students overwhelmingly favored an intuitive approach over a rational one.[4] Part of the difficulty with accepting and practicing rational empiricism stems from its inherent assumptions and limitations.

Assumptions and Limitations of Rational Empiricism

The ability to employ a rational-economic approach for successful problem solving requires certain assumptions that limit its effectiveness:

   1. We are capable of identifying all alternatives.
   2. We are capable of realizing all of the consequences of each alternative.

3. We are capable of complete personal detachment.
4. We have perfect information.
5. We are capable of choosing a maximizing solution.

Bounded Rationality. The most obvious shortcoming of these assumptions is that they call for ideal conditions which exist neither in the environment nor within the individual. Herbert Simon recognized this limitation with his concept of **bounded rationality:**

> This then, is the general picture of the human organism that we will use to analyze organization behavior. It is a picture of a choosing, decision-making, problem-solving organism that can do only one or a few things at a time, and that can attend to only a small part of the information recorded in its memory and presented by the environment.[5]

According to this concept the problem solver cannot arrive at a perfect decision because he is confined by internal psychological constraints as well as external environmental constraints. As a result the problem solver:

1. Has access to only limited information regarding the problem situation.
2. Can deal with only a limited number of alternatives.
3. Tends to suboptimize, applying something less than maximizing criteria.
4. Is aware of only some of the consequences of a decision.
5. Employs his own personal values and perceptions.

It is unlikely that a problem solver could be aware of all possible solutions to a given problem. Such omniscience would require perfect information which, of course, no problem solver ever enjoys. Even if such information were available in the environment, it is unlikely that a problem solver would make the effort to gather it. Instead, problem solvers will frequently *satisfice*, which is the practice of seeking a solution that will meet certain *minimal* criteria rather than optimal criteria. Satisficing is an effective way for a problem solver to "make everyone happy" and avoid unnecessary personal risk.

Consider, for example, a manager who is screening applicants for a professional position in his department. He interviews two applicants who have outstanding technical qualifications and experience, but whose personalities are not "compatible" with the personality of the department. A third applicant minimally meets the technical requirements and has a rather innocuous personality. The manager stops his search and selects the third applicant on the assumption that this individual will do the job and not "rock the boat."

The employee probably will get the job done without creating any

interpersonal conflict. There is little risk in this option for the manager. The "less desirable" candidates that were passed over may have been outstanding performers for the organization. Other possible outstanding performers were also excluded because of the manager's satisficing behavior when the search stopped after finding an "acceptable" candidate.

Decision-Making Styles. The greatest limitations of rational empiricism stem from our information-processing propensities, which are heavily influenced by our perceptual sets (See Chapter 5). Those factors that constitute the perceptual set are influential in the development of an individual's characteristic approach to problem solving. Psychologist Carl Jung developed a theory of personality that contains two major dimensions useful for categorizing problem-solving behavior: **perception** and **judgment.**[6]

Perception influences our information *gathering* tendencies which, at the extreme, can be accomplished either by sensation (S) or intuition (N). Judgment influences our information *processing* tendencies which, at the extreme, can be accomplished either by thinking (T) or feeling (F). These dimensions are illustrated in Figure 9–2.

Sensation-oriented individuals are fact oriented; they analyze the facts they gather in a highly impersonal manner. These problem solvers are practical, experience-based, and achievement oriented. Their time frame is short, dealing in the present rather than the future. They prefer problem situations high in structure and low in ambiguity. The sensation-oriented problem solver is more comfortable with problems that can be solved quickly and straightforwardly, and dislikes a lot of detail.

Such problem solvers rely on facts, but will not spend a great deal of time sifting for details. Typical occupations for sensation-oriented types include physician, pilot, athlete, and salesperson.

Intuition-oriented problem solvers enjoy novelty; they dislike routine problem solving. They are quick to become impatient, dislike gathering facts, and would rather rely on feelings and intuition. They are imaginative, open to all sorts of possibilities, and somewhat impractical. Their

FIGURE 9–2 Behavioral Dimensions of Problem Solving

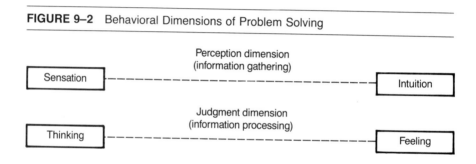

time frame is future oriented, and their outlook is global. Occupations of intuition types include writer, professor, researcher, and entrepreneur.

Thinking-oriented individuals are logical and impersonal in their analysis of a situation. They are unemotional and disinterested in personal feelings. They are methodical, fact-oriented problem solvers, who prefer order and structure. These problem solvers are likely to be efficient and deliberate in the collection and analysis of information.

Because of their methodological nature they will likely go through several repetitions of information collection and analysis before arriving at a solution. Occupations shared by thinking types include lawyer, accountant, engineer, and statistician.

Feeling-oriented individuals are emotional types that make decisions based on human interaction. They are impulsive, spontaneous problem solvers who prefer subjectivity to cold logic. Their problem-solving behavior is tied closely to their human responsiveness.

Such problem solvers are likely to emphasize the people in a situation and base their decisions on personal factors. Occupations of feeling types would include salespersons, social worker, psychologist, and entertainer.

Combining the extreme positions of the two dimensions yields four discrete possible decision styles as shown in Figure 9–3.

Classifying decision styles in this fashion has enabled researchers to identify and study various characteristics of the individuals who subscribe to each style. Figure 9–4 contains one such attempt at categorizing characteristics of each style.

The style an individual subscribes to will make a significant difference in what information is perceived and collected, and subsequently, how that information will be analyzed and interpreted.

What Jung and others have demonstrated with their work on decision styles is that rational empiricism does not always lend itself to human problem solving. Those factors that contribute to our individuality frequently preclude us from rationally collecting and analyzing information

FIGURE 9–3 Decision Styles

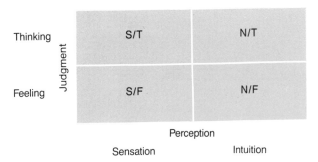

FIGURE 9–4 Characteristics of Decision Styles

	Left Hemisphere			Right Hemisphere
	←———————— DECISION STYLE ————————→			
	ST Sensation/Thinking	NT Intuition/Thinking	SF Sensation/Feeling	NF Intuition/Feeling
Focus of attention	Facts	Possibilities	Facts	Possibilities
Method of handling things	Impersonal analysis	Impersonal analysis	Personal warmth	Personal warmth
Tendency to become	Practical and matter of fact	Logical and ingenious	Sympathetic and friendly	Enthusiastic and insightful
Expression of abilities	Technical skills with facts and objects	Theoretical and technical developments	Practical help and services for people	Understanding and communicating with people
Representative occupation	Technician	Planner	Teacher	Artist
	←———————————— MANAGER ————————————→			

SOURCE: "Minds and Managers: On the Dual Nature of Human Information Processing," *Academy of Management Review* 6, no. 2 (1981), p. 190. Adapted with permission.

and arriving at optimal solutions to our problems. Having stated these shortcomings of the scientific approach, let us now take a rather detailed look at it and become sensitive to its weaknesses and its strengths.

DEFINING THE PROBLEM

Recognition of a problem results from communication with one's self or with others. A problem typically manifests itself as a set of symptoms. The keys to defining a problem are the knowledge and ability to clearly:

1. Recognize and measure symptoms.
2. See possible relationships between symptoms.
3. Pinpoint and evaluate likely causes of those symptoms.

For example, if you were simultaneously experiencing fever, nausea, and loss of appetite, you might initially attempt to treat each symptom separately. If the symptoms persisted you would eventually consult a physician. The physician would have the knowledge to verify your symptoms, see a connection between them, and diagnose their cause (e.g., virus, chicken pox, nephritis, appendicitis). Once the most likely cause was established the physician could prescribe treatment. In some cases, before a problem can be diagnosed and treated, the problem solver will find it necessary or desirable to gather pertinent information.

Collecting Information

In many instances the individual who first identifies a "problem" or brings it to your attention (e.g., boss, subordinates, customers) is actually presenting a set of symptoms. That individual may be close to the problem and have a vague sense of what the problem is or how various symptoms fit together and what is creating them. It is still necessary to collect additional information and organize it into a comprehensible pattern. After moving through several iterations of collecting, organizing, and analyzing information, you should be able to identify the problem and generate an optimal solution.

In the previous example, the physician would rely heavily on your description of what you are experiencing because you are closest to the symptoms. If not satisfied with the information you provided, she would conduct her own investigation, including examination and tests. As a result, she might detect other symptoms (e.g., sensitivity to touch on your right side). This additional information would aid her in ruling out several possible relationships and causes, and pinpointing the exact cause of the symptoms (e.g., appendicitis).

Determining what information you need is a basic step in the problem-solving process because the ultimate quality of a solution depends almost entirely on the quality of information. We have included a brief discussion of the types and sources of information available to problem solvers to assist you in collecting information.

Internal Information. In most decision-making situations the problem will concern some aspect of an organization's operations. The information needed to make a decision is usually stored within the firm in some form. Consequently, information collection requires a familiarity with the company's information recording and retrieval system. Knowledge of the types of information generated by the firm should be accompanied by knowledge regarding how, where, when, and by whom it is recorded.

There is great diversity in the level of sophistication and effectiveness of information systems. They range from an old shoe box full of sales receipts in a storeroom to a highly developed, fully computerized system.

In the latter case, the problem solver can have the appropriate information accessed by the firm's information specialists. In the former case, a great deal of questioning, searching, sifting, and patience may be necessary for the problem solver to get what is needed.

The development of the microprocessor has made the personal computer a reasonable answer to many internal information-management problems. The availability of "user-friendly" software packages (e.g., dBase III, 1-2-3 from Lotus) has dramatically enhanced the ability of many small and medium-size firms to maintain relatively sophisticated information storage and analysis systems. Such systems have applications in traditional areas such as accounting and production, as well as in marketing and personnel. Being computer literate will be immensely helpful to problem solvers as information technology continues to advance.

External Information.   A second major classification is external information. This refers to information generated and held by outside individuals and organizations. Sources in this category consist mainly of public and private information agencies.

Public organizations are dominated by the federal government and much information is available from the various federal agencies and bureaus. The majority of information pertaining to business is maintained by the Departments of Commerce, Labor, and Agriculture—although there are many others that have business-related information. Other public sources include state and local governments, public institutes, and university research bureaus.

Private sources consist mainly of professional-technical organizations that collect and maintain information pertinent to their specialized interests. Examples of such organizations are Moody's Investor Service, Standard & Poor's, American Management Associations, chambers of commerce, The Conference Board, and the American Institute of Certified Public Accountants. Additionally, there are countless private consulting and research firms that will provide information on a proprietary basis.

Collecting external information requires a thorough knowledge of the various source organizations and the types of information collected by each. Information provided by these external sources is often available on request, especially in the case of the federal government. Private organizations may require membership or a subscription fee. Because of the costs and time required to obtain information from many external sources, the best approach is often a library. The library is the main storehouse of secondary information.

Secondary Information.   Information can also be classified as primary or secondary. Secondary information has already been compiled and is available in published (print and nonprint) form. A firm's information

system, books, periodicals, newspapers, videotapes, microfilm, and microfiche are sources of such information.

Locating and accessing *internal* secondary information depends on the features of the organization's information system. The effective problem solver, therefore, learns to interact with, and utilize the services of the organization's information system.

Because of its importance as a collection point for *external* secondary information, you should have a working knowledge of a library and its contents. Three external secondary sources that you will find most helpful are *books, periodicals,* and *newspapers.* Each source varies in terms of its scope of coverage and currentness. Books (e.g., textbooks, directories, encyclopedias) are useful if you are looking for broad treatment of a given subject. If, for example, you were looking for information on the economy of a given state or country you could consult an encyclopedia or an economic atlas. If you were seeking a description of the field of personnel management, a textbook on personnel management might be most informative. Because of the time required for writing, reviewing, and printing, however, books may not contain the most current information available.

If you wanted up-to-date information on a specialized aspect of personnel, articles appearing in recent issues of personnel periodicals would be a good source. These articles would contain the most recent information collected by researchers and/or research organizations.

Daily newspapers provide very current and specific coverage. Newspapers can provide up-to-date information (e.g., stock market transactions, police arrests, births, and deaths) on a variety of topics, and they are easily accessible. Most libraries subscribe to the newspapers of the nation's largest cities.

Become familiar with the use of indexes, which are available in most libraries. Indexes contain an alphabetical listing of article titles on a variety of topics. An index may carry titles from only one publication (such as *The New York Times Index*) or may list articles from a variety of publications (the *Readers' Guide).* Articles are usually listed by topic, author, and title.

An index saves enormous amounts of time and effort by giving you a comprehensive list of articles on a topic, all in the space of perhaps a few pages. Most indexes are compiled and published quarterly or annually so you can identify the most recent information by beginning with the most recent edition of the index.

The most useful bibliographic index for business-related topics is the *Business Periodicals Index* (BPI). The BPI catalogs articles carried in well-known journals such as the *Harvard Business Review* and the *Academy of Management Journal.* Other valuable indexes are the *Readers' Guide to Periodical Literature, The Wall Street Journal Index, The New York Times Index, Social Sciences and Humanities Index, The Accountants' Index, Funk and Scott Index of Corporations and Industries, Psychological Abstracts,* and *Sociological Abstracts.*

There are many multiple-issue numeric publications prepared by the federal government. *The Statistical Abstract of the United States* presents an annual summary of statistics in such areas as population, education, employment, income, prices, transportation, and manufacturing. *Survey of Current Business,* published monthly by the Department of Commerce, presents detailed information on just about all phases of industrial activity. There are a variety of other weekly, monthly, and annual publications available. While the sources cited here are not exhaustive, they do represent the most often used ones for business-related problem solving.

With the rapid development of electronic and photographic technology a wealth of information is now available in nonprint form (e.g., film, videotape, microfiche). Most major libraries now have a separate nonprint section for information available in nonprint media. For example, many university catalogs and business directories that were available only in print are now available only on microfiche. Films and videotapes are available for those interested in a variety of topics from aerobics to economic development.

Computers have become capable of storing increasing amounts of information. And even though we are in the age of the super computer, it is neither possible nor desirable to store all information everywhere. As a result, an exciting, highly effective method called **networking** has developed for accessing remote information. A network is a computer system involving remote terminals (or other input/output devices) and data communication lines linking the terminals through a central processing unit. Data, facsimile reproduction, and video transmission are possible through such networks.

There are numerous applications of networks available. For example, an individual can shop by computer by subscribing to a private network that "publishes" a catalog of goods and services available around the nation. Members of the network can use electronic funds transfer systems (EFTS) to transact business.

For problem solvers there are a variety of research networks available for gathering data. Critical information in business, medicine, law, economics, and other areas can be assessed worldwide by subscribing to a network service.

For example, networks have aided researchers and problem solvers immensely with a variety of on-line computer search services available in most libraries. These services (e.g., Bibliographic Retrieval Services, Dialog Information Services) provide instant access to hundreds of different databases (e.g., NNI, ERIC, PSYCINFO) which provide an up-to-date, cumulative listing of articles or other publications on a given topic. Figure 9–5 illustrates how these services are structured.

The service technician is provided with a number of key words called **descriptors**. These descriptors are entered into the computer which will then search whatever databases the library subscribes to. If there are any

FIGURE 9–5 On-Line Computer Search Service

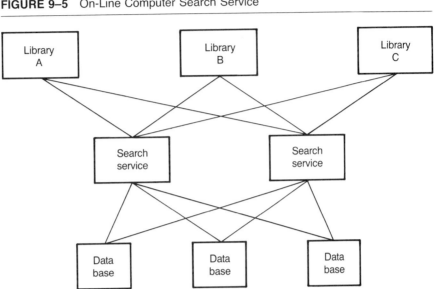

publications containing these descriptors, you are provided a bibliographic reference and, depending on the database service, an annotation.

Generally, three kinds of databases can be searched on-line. *Bibliographic* databases contain references to information in journals, books, reports, patents, and other sources. Abstracts or summaries are often included. *Factual* databases contain organization names, addresses, technologies available for licensing, and so forth. *Numeric* databases contain economic statistics, market data, and other manipulable information.

Primary Information.   In most problem-solving situations you will need current information and occasionally your information needs may be so current and/or unique that there is no secondary information available internally or externally. In these instances you will have to collect *primary information.*

Primary information is collected first-hand from original sources. Suppose a university administrator was interested in providing a new commuter service for students. If the service was new and unique, there probably would be no definitive information available from secondary sources to serve as the basis for deciding whether or not to provide the service. Consequently, the administrator would have to find out directly from the students how receptive they would be to such a service. There are several methods the administrator could use to gather primary information: *questionnaire, interview, observation,* and *experimentation.*

Questionnaire. Questionnaires are most useful when you have to contact a large number of individuals or organizations and need only a limited amount of information from each. If a situation seems appropriate for the use of the questionnaire, there are several features to consider—*design, response rate, response time, type of information,* and *cost.*

Design is the most troublesome issue for a number of reasons. The questions used on the questionnaire must be carefully designed to elicit the precise information desired. Once the questionnaire is prepared and distributed, there is no opportunity to observe respondent reactions and personally answer their questions. If not carefully designed, the questionnaire could be worthless. An extremely beneficial procedure is to pretest the questionnaire on a small sample of respondents. This "debugging" could prevent unnecessary grief and expense.

Interview. The interview can be used to overcome two of the major weaknesses of the questionnaire—lack of immediate feedback and low response rate. It can also add objectivity and accuracy to the information collected.

The interview affords immediate feedback and clarification of questions. This cannot be done with the questionnaire. The information collected via the interview is more complete and useful. This assumes, however, that the interviewer is a trained specialist who can restate and clarify an item and still elicit natural responses.

The use of interviewers introduces a potential weakness—the possibility of human error or bias due to interaction with the interviewee. Even well-trained persons may allow some bias to enter their efforts, but the information gained from immediate feedback usually offsets the human error potential.

One of the most recent innovations in the use of technology is something called electronic interviewing. Computers using interactive programs ask respondents a series of questions regarding a particular service or product. The machines can be placed at the site where the product or service is consumed or delivered (e.g., hotel or restaurant lobby, shopping mall).

Electronic interviewing is essentially a cross between the interview and questionnaire, and consequently has a mixture of advantages and disadvantages. Electronic interviews can overcome some of the human bias problems because there is no human interaction with the respondent. Also, there is no need for trained interviewers. While specific feedback cannot be provided, a well-written program can anticipate many respondent reactions or problems and provide detailed clarification. Disadvantages include initial machine and program cost, the acquisition of well-written programs, and the typical human resistance to high technology.

Observation.   A third survey method is observation. Rather than asking how often an individual does something, you simply watch and count. This method permits increased objectivity because usually there is no direct interaction required between the observer and the observed; therefore, no respondent bias or contamination exists. This is the major strength of observation as a means of gathering information.

The major limitation of observation is that it is restricted to observable phenomena and can be used to collect only descriptive information (e.g., how many consumers purchased Brand X). Because of the absence of interaction and feedback, it does not offer any explanation as to why the observed activity occurred (e.g., why consumers purchased Brand X). The benefits of observation must be carefully considered and weighed against the costs. Time requirements and the need for trained observers make observation very slow and expensive and it suffers the same drawbacks as the interview. However, given the level of objectivity necessary and the type of information required in some situations, the cost may be justified.

Experimentation.   Some problems require that you determine the value of certain variables; others that you determine the unknown nature of interaction between variables. In order to examine such interaction, experimentation may be necessary. Experimentation is investigation under controlled conditions. Control is the quality that enables you to direct the elements of the experimental situation in whatever fashion you desire in order to meet your objectives (e.g., identify relationships, solve problems). Because of their importance to experimentation we need to identify a subtle difference between manipulation and control.

Experimentation may take place in the natural setting where a phenomenon or relationship exists (field experimentation) or in a contrived or artificial environment under simulated conditions (laboratory experimentation). Control is a major consideration in deciding between laboratory and field experimentation. In order to investigate a relationship between two or more variables, it is often necessary to neutralize or screen out other "interfering variables." One alternative is to move to the laboratory where a simplified version of the natural setting is created thus introducing only those variables essential for investigation. One danger of laboratory experimentation is that when you move back to the natural setting to apply your findings they may be worthless because of interaction between the many uncontrolled variables in the natural setting. Consequently, it may be better to use the second alternative, field experimentation.

When investigating problems in the field, control is seldom absolute and complete; therefore, it may not be possible to manipulate variables as you would in the laboratory. But while total manipulation is not possible, control is. R. L. Ackoff stated it in this manner:

The astronomer cannot manipulate the stars and planets, but he can conduct controlled inquiries. . . . Similarly, the social scientist may not be able to manipulate the group of people he studies, but if he can determine what the important properties of the group are, he can investigate . . . in a controlled manner.[7]

Once you identify relevant and controllable variables and determine their values, you can "manipulate" them by controlling or allowing for their effects. Such manipulation or control has been greatly enhanced by modern statistical methods (e.g., multivariate analysis, factor analysis).

Experimentation frequently may not appear to be a very useful or acceptable means of collecting information in an organizational setting because of the effort and control required. It is most appropriate in situations where change is to be introduced. If a firm is preparing to respond to changes in its environment and there are multiple options available to the firm, experimentation may be the best way to "field test" the options and select the most attractive choice. Many marketing decisions are made on the basis of field research which involves some form of field experimentation. The Coca Cola Company would have done well to conduct more extensive field experimentation before introducing "New Coke" and entering into the embarrassing situation they created.

Once the problem solver determines his particular information needs, chooses the method of collection, and collects the information, the next task is to organize that information.

Organizing Information

To organize information effectively, it may be necessary or convenient to dissect the problem by sorting the information regarding symptoms or characteristics into different groupings. Such division is a simplifying device for analyzing information and piecing it together, and for generating solution alternatives. The particular nature of the problem and the objectives of the decision will usually suggest a basis for a divisional network. (Refer to the discussion on idea arrangement in Chapter 2 and the section on organization for oral reporting in Chapter 11.) Some examples of organizing bases are:

Chronology (time sequence).
Geography (spatial relationships).
Cost versus benefits.
Qualitative versus quantitative factors.
Operational functions (production, marketing).
Managerial functions (planning, organizing).
Social groupings (employees, consumers).
Behavior patterns (high performers, low performers).

Consider the personnel director who is experiencing a high turnover rate and is asked to come up with recommendations for reducing it by some specified amount within a specified time period. The director will want to determine the different reasons for the turnover. How much is voluntary? How much is involuntary? Where is the turnover occurring? Is it prevalent throughout the organization? Or localized in one or two departments? The director might find it beneficial to collect and organize information on a departmental basis. Then, within each department, turnover information could be categorized on the basis of type of separation.

The most effective way to develop a breakdown is to raise specific questions about the various aspects of a problem. This will help to generate working hypotheses and additional questions that will prove helpful in the next step of the scientific process: *identifying symptoms, relationships, and causes.*

Identifying Symptoms, Relationships, and Causes

It is important to realize that analysis permeates the entire problem-solving process. Some analysis is required when you first determine that there is a problem, when you decide what your informational needs are, when you decide where and how to collect that information, and when you organize the information into a meaningful pattern. Analysis is the ongoing task of deciding on the importance of information, what the information tells you, and how it all fits together.

Analysis is essentially the act of trying to put together the pieces of a puzzle. If you have ever put together a commercial jigsaw puzzle, you at least had a picture of the finished product and knew something of the overall pattern and relationship between the pieces. The shapes and colors of the pieces suggested how they fit together. In most real-world problem-solving situations, however, you do not have that advantage and to be effective, a systematic approach for testing and fitting pieces of information together is required.

As you identify symptoms and attempt to develop relationships between them, it may be useful to reflect on similar past problems. While past problems may be suggestive, remember that each problem is somewhat different, with its unique cause-effect pattern and, ultimately, its own solution. As you make your way systematically through the analysis stage, you should be especially sensitive to three key issues: *the role of assumptions, comparability of information,* and *types of relationships.*

The Role of Assumptions.   An important aspect of analysis is the identification of assumptions made during analysis because these assumptions may impact on the validity and applicability of solutions. Consider, for example, the personnel director who is trying to develop a solution to his

firm's turnover problem. Because of low inflation in recent years, the director assumes that there will be no significant upward pressure on wages, and therefore, no wage competition. The assumption of relatively steady wage rates allows the director to develop his solution to the turnover problem. However, due to volatile economic conditions things do not remain unaltered, and wage pressures build quickly. The assumption of no change in wage rates results in inadequate recruiting and hiring.

Decision makers often make assumptions subconsciously and do not realize the impact of those assumptions on their analysis and development of alternatives. Therefore, it is important to note explicitly and recall any assumptions that are made to keep the analysis and problem solution consistent with reality.

For example, if the personnel director focused his turnover investigation on one department, he might find it necessary or convenient to isolate the department *for information collection purposes*. This isolation might cause him to assume *subconsciously* that activities in other departments have no effect on turnover in the department under investigation. Such an assumption would probably be inappropriate; but if it is made, it should be explicit so that conclusions and recommended actions can be tempered by that assumption.

Comparability of Information.   You cannot add apples and oranges, nor can you compare and analyze them. As you analyze pieces or sets of information, therefore, their comparability should be determined first. To illustrate this point consider the following profit figures for a firm:

1980	$500,000
1985	$600,000

An immediate conclusion might be that the firm's profitability has improved considerably. But what if inflation increased the general price level over the five-year period by 20 percent? Given only the dollar amount, such a conclusion could be quite misleading. Only when we compare the price-level change with the profit figures does the full impact become clear. In effect, these two sets of figures—dollars from different years—may be useless for purposes of comparison.

To compare pieces of information that differ in nature, it is helpful to develop some type of transformation function. This is a measure or statement that transforms one item into terms of another, thus making them comparable. A common transformation scale for most of us is the Consumer Price Index, which can be used to evaluate purchasing power in light of inflation. Using the figures above as an example, the firm's profitability would be as follows:

1980	$500,000
1985	$500,000

There are an extraordinary number of instances where transformation and comparability are difficult to achieve. Consider, for example, the lack of comparability in many employee-related decisions that are made by a manager. Job applicants do not all have exactly the same types of qualifications and experiences. Employees do not all meet promotion criteria in the same way. The lack of comparability in such areas should not be ignored. Instead, we should accept the challenge of making information usable in the problem-solving process by designing more sophisticated and valid transformation techniques.[8]

Types of Relationships.   A significant part of decision making is understanding the relationships between the different pieces of information that you have collected. There are two basic kinds of relationships that may be detected: **correlation** and **cause-effect**. The differences between them are important.

Two variables may be related but not causally connected. The values of the two variables may change together either directly or inversely, yet neither may be necessary for the occurrence of the other. Consider, for example, something as simple as taking a shower and going out on the town. Many individuals shower before going out for the evening. If we were to tabulate the instances of showering and going out, we would find a positive relationship between these two activities; however, neither is necessary for the occurrence of the other. They can and frequently do occur independently. People may shower before going to work or to bed; others may go out on the town without taking a shower.

Observing and measuring relationships between activities in this fashion does not tell us why they occur, only that they do. Even so, such information can be quite valuable for prediction. If we observed that Joe Smith regularly takes a shower before going out on the town, we could predict when he will go out by observing when he takes a shower. Of course, if he also takes a shower before going to bed or to work our predictive ability is somewhat diminished.

Consider an example closer to the business environment: the relationship between job qualifications and success on the job. Employers would like to be able to predict which job applicants will be successful employees *before* hiring them. In an attempt to increase their accuracy of prediction, many employers attempt to identify correlates of job success such as education level, past experience, and personality type.

If these characteristics show a statistically significant relationship with job success, employers can measure them prior to hiring, thus ensuring more accurate selection and a lower turnover rate. Note carefully that the basis of the relationship is not known. The cost of finding out the exact nature of the relationship, when compared with its usefulness, may not be justified.

Cause-effect relationships are different from correlation in that they describe a relationship and also explain it. In a cause-effect relationship one variable is said to be the cause of another if the occurrence of one is both sufficient and necessary for the subsequent occurrence of the other. Hence, when X, then Y. Cause-effect is a deterministic relationship, since the occurrence of X will always determine the occurrence of Y. Our "natural laws" are all deterministic. When you heat water to 212 degrees, it begins to boil. This result will be the same every time.

Quite often the relationship between two variables is probabalistic rather than deterministic in that the effect that one variable has on the other depends on the given environment. (This obviously could be said of all relationships, even those in the physical sciences, but environmental conditions are much more stable in the physical than in the social sciences.) Consequently an established relationship may be nullified if the proper environmental conditions do not exist. For example, the environment in outer space nullifies certain relationships that exist here on earth. This fact has created problems for NASA in the exploration of space.

Identification of cause-effect relationships is quite difficult and frequently controversial. For example, there is a great deal of controversy concerning the health effects of smoking. Opponents of smoking contend that there is a cause-effect relationship between smoking and various diseases. Proponents of smoking claim that there is no evidence to support that claim. The research findings, they say, are only correlational. Apparently, only certain people are affected by smoking because they have a certain predisposition that makes them susceptible to harmful effects. Like many other aspects of the environment, the smoking-disease relationship may be probabilistic.

Environmental volatility is much more prevalent in social organizations than in the physical environment. The volatile and complex nature of the environment in most business firms often leads to erroneous notions of causation. Often this leads to a common weakness in problem solving—confusing symptoms and problems. All situations are not the same, and problems are not always as simple and obvious as they appear. This is the reason management educators and practitioners now embrace various contingency theories.

A problem is defined when you feel confident that you have:

1. Studied and understood the available information
2. Clearly identified the symptoms (e.g., lower sales, decreased consumer loyalty, increased employee turnover, increased employee complaints)
3. Reasonably related the symptoms to one another and to a common explanation with no unexplained or "leftover" facts or questions.

The explanation referred to in item 3 is the basis for stating the problem. With a clear statement of the problem, the problem solver can then move to developing alternative solutions.

DEVELOPING ALTERNATIVES

Before actually setting forth a number of alternative solutions, there are two issues that must be addressed: **identifying decision objectives** and **specifying decision criteria**.

Identifying Decision Objectives

In all problem-solving situations the overriding objective is, of course, to solve the problem. But beyond that, the problem solver and other individuals may have more personal or ulterior objectives in mind. Consequently, it is a good practice to have a clear statement of what the outcome of the solution should be.

In some situations the problem solver may be satisfied with a minimally acceptable solution; in others the problem solver may be striving for an optimal outcome. For example, if a tax accountant resigned from a firm at the start of the tax season, the manager would immediately have to find a replacement to avoid turning away clients. Should the replacement be a marginally competent temporary employee or a highly qualified tax specialist who, in all probability, would be impossible to find at that time of year?

When a problem is being examined, various individuals will have an interest in the solution, and each may desire a slightly different outcome, based on his or her interests. Too many conflicting objectives may preclude the identification of a satisfactory solution, and the objectives of each individual must be clearly recognized and either eliminated or incorporated into the final objective.[9] Otherwise, a totally inappropriate solution may be chosen.

For example, in an organization facing declining sales, decreasing consumer loyalty, and a shrinking market share, representatives from various departments may be asked to help identify and solve the problem(s) responsible for these symptoms. Members of the production department may see this as an opportunity to update and expand the production facilities while the personnel director may want to upgrade the firm's personnel. Each member, in turn, may have a different, perhaps private, objective. If each member of the problem-solving group attempts to serve his or her interests, the welfare of the organization as a whole may not be served. To avoid this the problem solver should clearly state and reinforce the objective of a decision—a well-stated objective helps in the identification of criteria.

Specifying Decision Criteria

The choice of an alternative is based on that alternative's ability to fulfill the decision objective better than any others. This ability is typically measured in terms of some set of standards or criteria.

In a business setting, the decision criteria usually come from one of two sources—the organization or the individual problem solver. Organizations have many quantitative standards that are used in problem solving (e.g., ROI, market share, sales, personnel turnover rates, standard costs, reject rates, scrap rates). For the vast majority of problems, identifying alternatives and choosing a solution will be tied to such criteria.

Sometimes a problem is so unique that there are no criteria specified by the firm's system of objectives and policies to guide the problem solver in choosing a solution. The individual is faced with the choice of applying personal values or taking the time and effort to establish a new set of organizational criteria.

Of course, problem solvers always invoke their personal value systems to some extent, but only as a guide for applying criteria set forth by the organization. In the absence of prescribed criteria, the individual must decide whether those values are appropriate for choosing an alternative. If not, group problem-solving approach may afford a better synthesis of values.

Regardless of the source of the criteria, it is essential to establish a set of standards against which various alternatives can be evaluated. The use of criteria will simplify the choice process and provide for a clearer, more accurate decision. Criteria must be consistent with, and representative of, the objectives of the organization or the problem solver. With such assurances, the problem solver can then proceed to develop a list of alternatives.

Developing Alternatives

Many problem situations are repetitive, and searching past experiences for alternatives can be an excellent source of guidance for future actions. Your own experiences, and the experiences of other members of your organization who have handled a similar problem, can be tapped for advice and guidance.

If no individual within the organization can offer any advice, the problem solver can resort to his informal network of professional contacts in other organizations. Such individuals are frequently willing to share their expertise and experience to help solve a particular problem. There is just one caveat to keep in mind: environments are never exactly the same. The past and future may be two entirely different environments and conditions within your organization and other organizations are different. Therefore, do not *habitually* rely on old solutions or those from

your network of contacts without ascertaining that the previously used solution is appropriate.

There are basically two schools of thought regarding the development and evaluation of alternatives. The first states that the problem solver should identify as many alternatives as possible, employing as many sources as possible. Only after all sources have been exhausted and all alternatives have been listed should the evaluation process begin. This approach is favored because it precludes suboptimization based on premature selection of an alternative. However, it does require more time and expense to develop an exhaustive list of alternatives, many of which may be useless.

The second approach to developing and evaluating alternatives is to search for solutions and evaluate them as they are listed. The problem solver usually goes to the most lucrative sources for the best alternatives early in the search. Therefore, the later alternatives are less attractive and the marginally most expensive ones on the list.

Thus, the problem solver searches for alternatives up to the point where the cost of obtaining additional ones is greater than their potential advantage. The major disadvantage of this approach is that the individual may never be exposed to the best possible situation. The advantage is the lower cost and time required to identify a solution.

A number of interesting techniques have been developed to assist the problem solver who uses either approach. For the individual who chooses to search out as many alternatives as possible from as many sources as possible techniques such as nominal grouping, brainstorming, and Delphi are available (see Chapter 7). For the individual who chooses to pursue alternatives on a cost-benefit basis there are quantitative techniques that can assess the expected value of additional information.

Because environmental volatility has made problem solving such an important part of the manager's job, it has become increasingly important to understand and foster creativity. Creativity can be invaluable in the generation of alternatives, especially for nonroutine problems.

Creativity is the generation of new ideas. These ideas should be of value to the problem solver or their "newness" may be totally worthless and not considered creative at all. The creative process appears to require several steps.[10]

1. Problem identification: the individual focuses on a particular problem to work on.
2. Preparation: the problem solver gathers information about the problem and potential areas of solution and immerses herself in that information.
3. Incubation: the problem solver organizes and re-organizes the information trying out many different combinations and patterns. Such simulation may go through numerous iterations.

4. Insight: as a result of step three the individual will eventually discover a combination that appears to achieve the desired effect or meet the necessary test. Such results often come in "aha!" fashion when least expected.

5. Verification: the individual establishes that the solution does indeed meet the necessary requirements to be considered the solution. Essentially, the solution is tested, refined, and applied.

In Chapters 6 and 8, we examined the need for, and benefits of an open organization. We illustrated how open information sharing would improve the effectiveness of individuals and the organization as a whole. This openness is the proper environment for heightened creativity.

Barriers to creativity include fear, anxiety, and defensive behavior. For example, White has shown that anxiety is inversely related to creativity.[11] Bowers demonstrated an inverse relationship between defensiveness and creativity.[12] Thus, the maintenance of Gibb's supportive climate (see Chapter 6) could be crucial to developing quality alternatives and solving problems effectively.

Too much rigidity in organizational structure is another barrier to creativity. Inflexible relationships and policies that induce too much conformity also inhibit the creative process. To foster a creative environment and improve the quality of problem solving, it is beneficial to maintain an open, organic type of organization.

SELECTING AND IMPLEMENTING THE SOLUTION

Once the alternatives have been generated, the problem solver can invoke the decision criteria that have been established. Because a decision rule has already been prescribed, the actual choice among alternatives is straightforward. The alternative that most favorably meets the criteria and the decision objective can be selected for implementation.

The problem solver should carefully think through the effects of the solution that has been chosen. The individuals and systems that will be affected by the solution should be identified. New pressures created by the solution on employees, policies, and procedures should be recognized and compensated for. The probable responses of affected individuals should be anticipated so that adjustment can be made where necessary.

Depending on the nature of a problem and its solution, there may be a good time and a bad time for implementation. Individuals often perceive things to be sequentially related. Consider the implementation of a solution in terms of present and future events. Just as there may be good and bad times, there may be good and bad methods of implementation.

For example, assume that a firm is faced with declining productivity and a reduction in forces is necessary. What would be the best time to

announce the layoff? What would be the best method for announcing the layoff? Would it be appropriate to place a layoff notice in the employees' last pay envelopes? Or, should management call an employee meeting weeks in advance and review the decision with employees? Could the employees' immediate supervisors be instructed to make the announcement? Obviously, in this case there is no good time or method; the only thing to do is determine the least harmful time and method and make the best of a bad situation.

Once the time and method have been chosen, discuss it with others who have some familiarity with the situation. This requires more time and effort, but others may see things that you do not and may be able to improve on your implementation plan. When you have time to utilize the experiences and perceptions of others, it is usually a good idea to do so.

You must carefully monitor the outcome of your solution. It is better to be aware of its shortcomings so that you can chart course corrections. This is why, for example, a physician prescribes treatment and instructs the patient to return if the treatment does not work. The physician is not absolutely certain the treatment will work and wants to be able to make any necessary changes in his solution. If the patient cooperates with the physician, both individuals will eventually benefit.

REPORTING

To fulfill the role of problem solver the manager must often share the results of a problem-solving effort with others inside and outside the firm. A conventional and convenient form of sharing information is the report.

A report can be many things, serve many purposes, and take on numerous forms.[13] It can be long or short, formal or informal, simple or complex, personal or impersonal, written or oral. As a working definition, a report is a detailed presentation, account, or statement concerning some issue, problem, or phenomenon under consideration, possibly containing conclusions and recommendations. The exact nature of any given report is dependent on a number of factors.

Purpose

Recognizing the purpose of a message is a fundamental aspect of effective communication. Clarity is as much a state of mind in report preparation as in any other form of communication. If the purpose of the report is clear in the mind of the sender, the report will be accurate and effective. It is important to identify the purpose of a report. Reports may serve any or all of three general purposes: *describing*, *explaining*, and *prescribing*.

Descriptive Reports. Frequently the purpose of a report is to describe some aspect of organizational operations or external conditions. Descrip-

tive reports contain nothing more than a figure, picture, statement, or model expressing a condition or state of existence. Examples of this type of report are a periodic progress report, a trip report, an income statement, and a state of the union report.

Explanatory Reports.   Many reports not only describe an organizational activity, but also explain the activity. They enumerate facts and relate those facts. Consider, for example, a report prepared by a personnel director concerning the problem of personnel turnover. A descriptive report is limited to describing the extent and nature of turnover. The explanatory report explains the reasons for the turnover, perhaps showing a cause-effect relationship between turnover and other variables (e.g., working conditions, compensation).

Prescriptive Reports.   Descriptive and explanatory reports convey information that is used to *arrive* at a decision. The prescriptive report is used to *convey* a suggested decision or decision alternatives. It is the most complex type of report and encompasses aspects of the other types in that it contains description and explanation, but it goes a step further by proposing a decision for the receiver.

The prescriptive report is labeled "analytical" by many authorities, but this is something of a misnomer because most reports require some degree of analysis. For example, analysis is required to determine the purpose of a report or the nature of a problem. Analysis is required to determine information needed as well as the sources of that information. And information, once collected, must be analyzed to provide explanations, draw conclusions, and provide recommendations. Consequently, the term *analysis* characterizes all reports.

Using the example of personnel turnover, the complexity of the prescriptive report can be illustrated. After providing an appropriately detailed description of the turnover, the reporter then provides an explanation of why the turnover is occurring. The last phase of the report is to present one or more solutions for reducing turnover.

The three functional types, in the order introduced, involve successively higher levels of complexity in that each requires a more sophisticated level of investigation and analysis. Thus it is important to recognize the purpose for which a report is prepared.

Subject

Before preparing a report you should give serious thought to the nature of the subject. The quantity and quality of information that is available and accessible about a particular subject may dictate the length and/or quality of a report. If you were attempting to prepare a report on the effects and advisability of using Nutrasweet, your ability to provide expla-

nations, reach conclusions, or develop recommended actions may be severely limited because there is not much conclusive information available on the subject.

The nature of a subject may also limit the analytical treatment of information. For example, financial information can be subjected to rigorous quantitative treatment, whereas information concerning behavioral phenomena may not lend itself to such treatment.

Some subjects are quite sensitive and controversial and must be treated with great caution, tact, and formality. Contrast, for example, a report about the impact of a new production technology on personnel with a report on the installation of a new cooling and heating system. Assuming that both reports would be shared with the firm's personnel, the former would require greater care and skill because of its impact.

Use

The use that will be made of the report may dictate how detailed the report can be and the specific content to be included. It may also influence which aspects of the subject are the most important and therefore should receive the greatest emphasis. A report used for internal purposes only can be prepared informally. If the report is to be used to effect changes in external relationships, it may be necessary to prepare a highly impersonal and formal report.

A good report is objective. Occasionally, a subjective report (referred to as a *persuasive* report) is necessary to sell a prescribed outcome. The most common reports of this type are proposals. Specific examples are a report by a personnel director attempting to persuade top management to approve a new compensation program or a report by top management to persuade stockholders to adopt a new management control system. A careful distinction is noteworthy regarding persuasive reports—only the presentation should be subjective, not the information presented.

Receiver

The preparation of a report, whether written or oral, requires careful consideration of the person who will receive and use the information contained in the report. Consideration of this individual may dictate a great deal about how a report is prepared and what goes into it. Review the material presented in Chapter 2 regarding selection of information—it will assist you in pinpointing report content for a given audience.

SUMMARY

In this chapter we have taken a rather detailed look at the scientific approach to problem solving referred to as rational empiricism. This

approach suggests certain specific steps in which a problem solver must engage. Specifically, he or she must gather and analyze necessary information, clearly define the problem, develop alternative solutions, and select and implement the most effective of those solutions.

Information used in the process can be primary or secondary, internal or external. Methods of collecting information include questionnaires, interviews, observations, and experimentation. Information, once collected, must be organized and analyzed to identify symptoms, relationships between the symptoms, and possible causes of the symptoms. Using such information, the problem solver can pinpoint the problem and develop a list of alternative solutions.

Once a solution has been identified, the problem solver must methodically implement it. Implementation requires attention to timing and method. There is usually a proper time and a proper method for most effective implementation. Only by monitoring implementation of the solution can the problem solver become aware of any weaknesses and make corrections.

Frequently problem solvers are required to report their actions. A report, whether written or oral, will be one of three basic types: descriptive, explanatory, or prescriptive. Each type is progressively more complex. The type of report a problem solver uses depends on the purpose of the report, the nature of the subject, and the audience. When these are determined, the problem solver can choose the most appropriate form and content for the report.

DISCUSSION QUESTIONS

1. Should decision making and problem solving be considered as a separate management function? Defend your answer.

2. Review the assumptions of rational empiricism. What weaknesses do you see in each assumption? How do those weaknesses affect the usefulness of the scientific process?

3. List four types of information sources. Briefly explain each source and the type of information found in each source. Give an example of each source.

4. Describe in detail three secondary sources available for researching a business problem.

5. Discuss the pros and cons of using the various methods of primary information collection.

6. What factors must be considered when a questionnaire is chosen as the means to gather primary information?

7. How is experimentation used to gather primary information? Would it be suitable to use experimentation to solve a business organization problem?

8. Use of assumptions, comparison of information, and determination of rela-

tionships are important aspects of the systematic analysis of information. Discuss the importance of these to problem analysis.

9. Describe the range of decision objectives. Why should the type of decision objective be made explicit?

10. What kinds of decision criteria are common in the business setting?

11. Describe the two approaches to developing and evaluating solution alternatives.

12. Define a report and list various types of reports. Discuss three factors that are important in determining the type of report that is suitable for a particular situation.

13. What consideration should the report preparer give to the user-receiver of the report? Describe how user-receiver characteristics influence the report.

14. How do you view yourself in terms of Jung's decision-making dimensions? Do you feel that you have developed a style?

15. Depending on your answer to question 14, how has it affected your choice of academic major and career goals? Do you think there is a particular style for people in your chosen career? What is it?

16. Study the classification system used in the classified advertising section of a local newspaper. Is the system complete? Are there any gaps? Overlaps? Can you identify any weaknesses in the system? Can you suggest any improvements?

EXERCISES

1. Identify a problem or issue that you would like to see solved. This could be a problem at your workplace, at home, at school, or in your community. Dissect the problem and develop a thorough divisional breakdown that would suggest the types of information you would need and would allow you to organize information for analysis and solution.

2. Choose a topic in which you have an interest. You could use the problem from Exercise 1. Go to your school or public library and develop a list of sources containing information on the topic.

3. Review the guidelines for improved language usage in Chapter 2. Choose one of those guidelines and develop a detailed research design to test its validity.

4. Write a proposal for a research project that would determine the best method of student evaluation of teachers. Keep in mind that this method will eventually be used nationally.

5. Select a controversial issue or service at your college or university. Carefully pinpoint the nature of the controversy. Then design a questionnaire to measure the nature and strength of student attitudes toward the issue.

6. Determine your communication style by filling out the following questionnaire.

What Is Your Style?

Before communicating effectively with others, you must first identify the communications mode that fits you best.

For more than 30 years, psychologists have known that each of us has a recognized habitual communication style. The famous Swiss psychologist, Dr. Carl Jung, divided these styles into the four classic types shown below. And this test—a very condensed and simplified version of the I-Speak survey—can help you identify the communications mode you presently use!

Instructions. For each self-descriptive statement below there are four different endings. Rank order **each** ending using 4 for the ending most like you; 3 next most like you; 2 next most; and number 1 least like you.

---

1. I am likely to impress others as
   a. practical and to the point   a. ____
   b. emotional and somewhat stimulating.   b. ____
   c. astute and logical.   c. ____
   d. intellectually oriented and somewhat complex.   d. ____

2. When I work on a project, I
   a. want it to be stimulating and involve lively interaction with others   a. ____
   b. concentrate to make sure it is systematically or logically developed.   b. ____
   c. want to be sure it has a tangible "pay-out" that will justify my spending time and energy on it.   c. ____
   d. am most concerned about whether it "breaks ground" or advances knowledge.   d. ____

3. When I think about a job problem I usually
   a. think about concepts and relationships between events.   a. ____
   b. analyze what preceded it and what I plan next.   b. ____
   c. remain open and responsive to my feelings about the matter.   c. ____
   d. concentrate on reality, on things as they are right now.   d. ____

4. When confronted by others with a different point of view, I can usually make progress by
   a. getting at least one or two specific commitments on which we can build later.   a. ____
   b. trying to place myself in the "others' shoes."   b. ____
   c. keeping my composure and helping others to see things simply and logically.   c. ____
   d. relying on my basic ability to conceptualize and pull ideas together.   d. ____

5. In communicating with others, I may
   a. express unintended boredom with talk that is too impersonal.   a. ____
   b. convey impatience with those who express ideas that they have obviously not thought through carefully.   b. ____
   c. show little interest in thoughts and ideas that exhibit little or no originality.   c. ____
   d. tend to ignore those who talk about long-range implications and direct my attention to what needs to be done right now.   d. ____

Analysis of Answers

To obtain an approximate indication of your primary communication style, enter below the number (1, 2, 3, or 4) you wrote next to each ending:

	Intuitor	Thinker	Feeler	Senser
Question 1	d.____	c.____	b.____	a.____
Question 2	d.____	b.____	a.____	c.____
Question 3	a.____	b.____	c.____	d.____
Question 4	d.____	c.____	b.____	a.____
Question 5	c.____	b.____	a.____	d.____
Totals	____	____	____	____

Now total each column. The column that has the highest sum indicates your favored communication style; the column with the smallest total is your least-used style.

The Intuitor

Intuitors are individuals who look forward to the future with a global perspective. They are good with concepts and often are able to relate diverse thoughts and ideas into meaningful wholes. Most Intuitors display good innovative ability and skill in looking at "the big picture." Most planners are Intuitors.

The Thinker

Most Thinkers focus on being precise and systematic in their approach to problems. Since facts and data are the tools with which one thinks, Thinkers usually develop good analytical skills in dealing with these facts. Thinkers also want to know about a broad spectrum of information related to a decision: the factors that have led up to it (historical background), what is

(continued)

(concluded)

happening now, and what the outcome will be.

The Feeler

Feelers usually prefer to deal with situations according to "gut reactions." Feelers are highly sociable and use empathy and understanding in their solutions to problems. Most of them are perceptive of others' needs and are able to discern what lies beneath the surface. Their time orientation is essentially toward the past. Many sales persons are Feelers.

The Senser

The Senser's time orientation is immediate: the here and now. As a result, most Sensers respond to things they can touch, see, and feel—things of an immediate nature. They tend to be action oriented and are often valued for their ability to get things done. Sensers are often found in production and high-pressure job situations.

NOTES

[1]Robert Trewatha and M. Gene Newport, *Management: Functions and Behavior,* rev. ed. (Plano, Tex.: Business Publications, 1979), p. 72.

[2]Henry Mintzberg, *The Nature of Managerial Work* (New York: Harper & Row, 1973); Henry Mintzberg, "The Manager's Job: Folklore and Fact," *Harvard Business Review* (July–August 1975).

[3]Peter Drucker, *People and Performance* (New York: Harper's College Press, 1977), p. 56.

[4]F. Hoy and W. Boulton, "Problem-Solving Styles of Students," *Collegiate News and Views* (Spring 1983), pp. 15 ff.

[5]James G. March and Herbert A. Simon, *Organizations* (New York: John Wiley & Sons, 1958), p. 11.

[6]C. Jung, *Psychological Types* (London: Routledge and Kegan Paul, 1923; Princeton, N.J.: Princeton University Press, 1971). Also see W. Taggart and D. Robey, "Minds and Managers: On the Dual Nature of Human Information Processing and Management," *Academy of Management Review* 6, no. 2, pp. 187–95; I. Myers, *The Myers-Briggs Type Indicator* (Palo Alto, Calif.: Consulting Psychologists Press, 1962).

[7]R. L. Ackoff, *The Design of Social Research* (Chicago: University of Chicago Press, 1965), p. 4.

[8]For a discussion of decision theory and models of utility transformation see E. F. Harrison, *The Managerial Decision-Making Process* (Boston: Houghton Mifflin, 1981), especially chap. 9.

[9]For a detailed discussion of dealing with conflicting objectives see D. E. Bell, R. L. Keeney, and H. Raiffa, *Conflicting Objectives in Decisions* (New York: John Wiley & Sons, 1977).

[10]J. F. Mee, "The Creative Thinking Process," *Indiana Business Review* 31, no. 2, pp. 4–9.

[11]K. White, "Anxiety, Extraversion-Introversion, and Divergent Thinking Ability," *Journal of Creative Behavior* 2, no. 2, pp. 119–27.

[12]P. G. Bowers, "Effect of Hypnosis and Suggestions of Reduced Defensiveness on Creativity Test Performance," *Journal of Personality* 35 (June 1967), pp. 311–22.

[13]For a more exhaustive discussion of classification schemes and report types, see: J. Menning, C. Wilkinson, and P. Clarke, *Communicating through Letters and Reports* (Homewood, Ill.: Richard D. Irwin, 1976), chap. 13.

SUGGESTED READINGS

BARABBA, VINCENT P. "How Kodak's Market Intelligence System Cuts Risk, Speeds Decisions." *Management Review* 73, no. 8 (August 1984), p. 813.

MILLER, MARC. "Putting More Power into Managerial Decisions." *Management Review* 73, no. 9 (September 1984), pp. 12–16.

NUTT, PAUL C. "Types of Organizational Decision Processes." *Administrative Science Quarterly* 29, no. 3 (September 1984), p. 414ff.

SUMMERS, IRVIN, and DAVID E. WHITE. "Creativity Techniques: Toward Improvement of the Decision Process." *Academy of Management Review* (April 1976), pp. 99–107.

Chapter 10

Policies, Procedures,

Handbooks, and

Training Manuals

Chapter 10 Case

You are the assistant manager of a firm that manufactures children's clothing. Your duty has been to welcome new junior executives and see to their orientation into the company. You have your welcoming speech down pat, but have always turned the new employees over to your secretary for information on rules, regulations, insurance, pay, vacation, and so on. Unfortunately, with three newly hired account representatives fidgeting in your office, you have just learned that your trusted secretary has called in sick. You believe you know enough about employee rights and benefits to wing it, but you also know that getting all the right forms signed is important. You've found what appears to be a policy and procedures manual, but from the looks of it, the last update took place in 1980. What steps should you take this morning? For the future?

INTRODUCTION

Business and industry understand the value of good communications, an effective communication program, and a climate of mutual trust. It has even been stated that without communication there is no organization! Unfortunately, some business communicators realize the value of good communications only after a crisis has arisen and the trial-and-error method has been used to solve the crisis. Once solved, the situation that precipitated the crisis may slip into the background and business continues as usual. *Real* understanding of the value of good communications is more than how good or effective it is in a single crisis situation. Effective communication is a cumulative process and has a cumulative effect with the final result successful in direct proportion to *all* that has gone into it. The same is true of policies and procedures: a sound policy and effective

procedures are a cumulative process and have a cumulative effect. Once this philosophy—or *raison d'etre* is understood and accepted, policies and procedures take on new meaning for an organization.

An organization faced with a sudden internal crisis (such as a high number of resignations or imminent unionization activity) would find little comfort in initiating and developing a complete communications program. However, the cumulative effect of already having and maintaining a sound communications program—on wages and salaries, company philosophy, policies and procedures, conferences, and interpersonal relations—could do much more than crisis communication at this stage.

What is the total, long-range effect of a policy or procedure? What is the company philosophy behind the policy? Why should it be stated? Whom does it affect? How does it affect other people or departments? How does it affect *other* company or department policies? How should it be communicated? These are all important questions that must be considered before the cumulative effect can be assessed.

DIFFERENTIATING OBJECTIVES, POLICY, AND PROCEDURE

A well-planned and executed policy and procedure manual is one of the most useful management tools. However, an organization's use of policy and procedure statements as an effective communications tool is directly related to the quality of those statements. Bloom comments, "Many managers believe that their manuals reflect and communicate current policy and procedure completely, clearly, and concisely."[1] In most cases, nothing could be further from the truth. Many managers do not distinguish between objectives, policy, or procedure. And even if they conceptualize those differences, they have great difficulty expressing them completely, clearly, and concisely.

Objectives differ from policy in that objectives are *goals* or ends, whereas a policy, while it may contain a brief statement referring to a desirable goal, is a statement of a *means* to attain a goal. A procedure serves to *implement* a policy by outlining *who* does *what, when*.

POLICY

Definition and Characteristics

Policy is defined in various ways. "Broad interest," "direction or philosophy," "statement of corporate principles," "guides to action," "principles and objectives," "consistency for recurring situations," and "standard practice" are a few examples. Policies may be concrete or abstract, formal or informal, short range or long range, and require complete rigidity or allow absolute flexibility.

Four elements are stated or implied in most definitions of policy:

1. Reference to the achievement of an objective.
2. An organizational principle or belief.
3. A recurring situation.
4. A guide to action.

A synthesis of these four elements provides a good definition of a business policy: *A policy is a general statement of a group of related principles (company philosophy) that serves as a guide to action for a recurring situation that facilitates the achievement of a goal.*

In addition to the four basic elements mentioned above, Dauton lists the following distinguishing characteristics of policy:

1. Policies are action-oriented.
2. Policies are standards for solving problems.
3. Policies energize, direct, focus, channel, restrict, regenerate, and modify.
4. Policies include objectives and values as master policies.
5. Policies have as their most conspicuous characteristic the idea of "relatedness."
6. Policies exist in a hierarchy.
7. Policies are both formal and informal.
8. Policies relate to the present and to the future and are *flexible* blueprints for action.
9. Policies relate to every aspect of the organizational hierarchy.
10. The motivational or energizing forces of policies are people's needs, wants, goals, and desires.
11. Policies must be flexible, so that the firm will be in a position to cope with the many uncertainties that cannot be accurately predicted.[2]

A policy statement is composed of two parts: the preamble and the actual policy or guide to action. The preamble consists of two parts: a statement of the objective, which reflects the philosophy of management, and a statement of the principle or principles involved in the situation for which the policy is written. In essence, the preamble tells the "why" for the policy, and the policy statement tells what guidelines are to be followed. A complete policy, including preamble, policy statement (guide to action), and format will be illustrated in a later section.

Policy Determinants

Two major determinants that affect all policies are: (1) those imposed from outside sources are external, and (2) those generated from within the organization are internal. The internal factors are more easily recognizable since they tend to be more predictable. These include the value system of top management, the history of the company, the company's

leadership style, past experience with policies, and management's perception (realistic or not) of the present condition of the company.

The external factors are more complex due to the many unknowns and the constantly changing environment. Most important are the general economic conditions of the country, the industry, and the company. Others include shifting social values, government constraints, and pressures from groups with some vested interest in the industry or company.

Policy Administration

One person should be in charge of guiding the policy from its inception to implementation. Frequently, this person is the board or company secretary, the assistant to the president, or the personnel director.

If the company is technical or manufacturing, the administrator may be an operations executive. A typical line-staff company generally has a staff policy administrator. A retail or service organization may rely more on the personnel director as the administrator of its policies.

The size of an organization also affects the quantity and style of policies. A small company has fewer and more informal policies than a larger firm. A parent or holding company has few specific policies. The more decentralized the company, the greater the possibility that the administrator is at the local level; a centralized organization tends to have all policies generated by top management, but implemented by the local administration. Also, the more group-management oriented the company, the greater the likelihood that there is a policy administrator.

In those companies with a full-time policy administrator, that person drafts policies and also supervises their coordination and review. She has responsibility for preserving consistency between new and existing policies and maintaining complete, accurate, and updated policy manuals. According to Bloom, "Policy (and procedures) must be known, understood, and used. To be known, statements must be properly disseminated. To be understood, statements must be clearly and concisely written. To be used, statements must be up-to-date."[3]

FORMULATION, IMPLEMENTATION, AND EVALUATION

Formulation

What prompts management to review its policy statements or develop new ones? Bloom says that typically, one or more of the following problems may exist:

1. Too many manuals are in use.
2. An excessive number of middle and upper managers are involved in the production and distribution of statements.

3. Inconsistencies of content, style, and format exist among statements.

4. Different in-house publications contain duplicate policy and procedure statements.

5. There is no authoritative single-source answer to questions.

6. Violations of policy and procedure exist, with resultant increases in costs, loss of revenues, and exposure of the company to increased business risks.

7. Top management is spending increasing amounts of nonproductive time writing memoranda reemphasizing or explaining policy and procedure.

8. The cost of maintaining policy and procedure materials is increasing at an unacceptable rate.

9. Changes in the organization—reorganizations, acquisitions, divestitures, company culture, management style, etc.—have invalidated many policy and procedure statements.

10. There is an immediate need to address a specific problem.[4]

The first step in policy development is recognition of the need for the policy. This may come from management, or it may arise from an upward communication flow. Once the need is recognized, the policy is developed. The actual writing of a policy was once considered the prerogative of top management; however, that function is frequently delegated to others, either individuals or a committee.

Once written, the policy should be reviewed and coordinated with all officials, departments, individuals, and groups affected by it. Final approval is given by the top executive prior to implementation.

Employees at all levels should be thinking about and participating in the development of company policies and procedures. Many companies believe that employee involvement creates a better alliance between the company and employees. If employees help create policies and procedures, isn't it logical that they will be more likely to implement and adhere to them?[5]

Implementation

Announcement. Verbal and/or written announcement of new policies or changes in existing policies should be made prior to the effective date. Copies may be posted on bulletin boards or distributed for inclusion in company manuals. Any outdated policy should be removed from the manual. Because many employees may not read notices on bulletin boards and look hurriedly, if at all, at intra-organizational mail, this form of notification may go unnoticed. The most effective announcement is usually through department meetings, and it can lead to the next step, indoctrination.

Indoctrination.   This is perhaps the most crucial step in implementing policy. The purpose is to educate, inform, and overcome any resistance to change. An established or routine training program or department meeting can serve as the vehicle for indoctrination. Actual or hypothetical examples of how the policy is to be implemented should be discussed in detail until all concerned see the value and the benefits of the policy's implementation.

Evaluation

All policies should be reviewed regularly to ensure that they are providing and allowing for (1) consistency of action, and (2) specificity. A policy should be consistent, yet flexible enough to adapt to changing conditions. It must also be specific, but broad enough to allow individual creativity. Other questions that can aid in evaluating a policy are: Is the policy clearly and concisely stated? Has it been communicated to all those affected by it? What are the ramifications of the policy? How effective is the implementation of the policy? At what future date should the policy be reviewed?

A Case in Point.   Now that we have considered some of the factors when developing or implementing a policy, consider the following case.

ROOM 406

It was 4:56 P.M. on Tuesday, on the surgical floor of John Randolph Memorial Hospital. Nurse Rhonda Flint, an efficient woman with 15 years of service in the hospital, was in charge of the floor that afternoon. She was making her final check of the rooms prior to the arrival of her relief, who came on at 5:00 P.M. In room 406 she found that Mr. Henry Youstra, who had undergone surgery the week before, and who had not responded after surgery, had finally died. Mentally, she began to notify various administrative departments including admissions and reception, wrap [the] body, and so forth. Suddenly recalling that she had a dental appointment at 5:15 P.M., she decided to ask her relief, who generally arrived early, to handle the procedure.

While depressed with the death, Flint couldn't suppress a feeling of relief, for bed space was a critical problem at the hospital. She would tell her relief to prepare the room immediately for a new patient. She returned to the floor desk which was located near the elevators. The night nurse, Ann Simmons, had already arrived and was waiting at the desk.

"Anything new, Rho?" Ann asked.

"406 just died, so that room's all set to go again. I hate to see them go that way, but we can certainly use the space. I'm pressed, will you take over?" Rhonda replied.

"Sure. Does the office know that 406 is ready?" Simmons asked.

"No, you can call them after you get things cleaned up."

Nurse Flint then left, and Nurse Simmons went about her routine duties.

At about 6:30 P.M. Nurse Simmons called the office and told them that room 406 was ready for occupancy, though she had not checked the room herself. She was told that a Mr. Leopold would be down from emergency surgery later on and would be given that bed.

Visitor's hours began at 7:00 P.M. and Mrs. Henry Youstra left home at 6:00 P.M. to arrive just at 7:00 P.M. Over the weeks of visiting her husband, she had acquired the habit of asking for her visitor's card by the room number. The girl at the front desk gave her the card prepared for visitors of Mr. Leopold, and she took the elevator to the fourth floor. Nurse Simmons recognized Mrs. Youstra as a nightly visitor and smiled professionally at her, not recalling which patient she visited, nor looking at the name on the card. Nurse Simmons placed the card in the desk file and Mrs. Youstra went down the hall.

At 8:00 P.M., the end of visiting hours, Nurse Simmons checked each room to see that all visitors had left. In room 406, she found Mrs. Youstra dead on the floor beside the bed containing her husband's body.[6]

The ramifications of this case are many and complex, but a number of things are apparent: (1) the case identifies a recurring situation faced by hospitals every day, (2) the situation is one on which hospital boards and administrators should reflect and express their philosophy, (3) a desirable goal can be stated, and (4) general guidelines to action can and should be enumerated. The policy in Figure 10–1 might be appropriate for this case. Note that the content includes references to the organization's beliefs, a philosophy, a recurring situation, and general guides to action. Also note that the physical format includes: the name of the organization and location, a policy number, a subject line, and a signature and title of the person responsible for issuing the policy.

A Case in Point.   All organizations are faced with employee absences. This is a recurring situation, which, without company philosophy and guidelines, could easily get out of hand. Uncontrolled absences could result in lowered employee morale, inefficient company operations, and reduced profits. Taken to the extreme, it could mean individual employee terminations, or a general layoff.

Let's assume that a company has been faced with just such a problem. Top management has sent the word down to the supervisors that overtime costs are out of line—a result of too much unexcused absenteeism. One supervisor interprets this to the department staff by saying, "This business has got to stop! You've been getting away with highway robbery, two or three days off a month with no reason. From now on, everybody has to convince me he's on his deathbed before I OK a day off with pay." Another supervisor may see the situation quite differently and report to the employees: "Well, the folks in the front office are a little huffy today. We're going to have to watch the time off with pay for a while. Give them a couple weeks and a few good orders and they won't notice the overtime."

FIGURE 10–1 Hospital Policy for Patient Expiration

J. R. M. Hospital
Bay City, Minnesota
April 10, 19—

Policy #1112   Subject: Patient Expiration

We believe that it is the responsibility of the hospital personnel to attend to the details arising from the death of a patient, promptly and with genuine respect for the feelings and wishes of the family of the deceased, and to insure that no undue hardship will be suffered by members of the immediate family or other patients.

Therefore, it is our policy that (certain) measures be followed at the time of the patient's expiration. Hospital personnel shall perform with minimal confusion the tasks of:

1. Proper notification of family.
2. Verification of death (by family or hospital physician).
3. Immediate notification to all hospital units affected.
4. Efficient follow-up.

/s/ _____
Hospital Administrator

Again, this is a recurring situation, and one on which companies should express their philosophy and goals and suggest guidelines for action. An appropriate policy statement for this case is shown in Figure 10–2.

The policies suggested for the two cases do not, by themselves, solve any problems. The policies—and any accompanying procedures—must be carried out to avoid any future problems. Therein lies some of the "cumulative effect" of policies and procedures mentioned earlier in the chapter. Someone must check to see whether they are being carried out and must constantly update them to reflect the company philosophy and method(s) of operation.

Advantages of a Policy Manual

If policies are communicated, accepted, and carried out, many advantages will accrue including: greater consistency in evaluation, discipline, and operating routine; less confusion by all employees in carrying out their duties and responsibilities; and, if communicated properly by management, greater knowledge and acceptance by employees of company philosophy.

FIGURE 10–2 Company Policy on Absenteeism

XYZ Manufacturing Company
Springdale, Arkansas
April 5, 19___

Policy #112   Subject: Absences

We believe that excessive absenteeism is a detriment to the national economy and puts an unfair burden on the great majority of our employees who demonstrate their responsibility by maintaining their regular work loads. This burden is further detrimental to our company's goals of maximum production efficiency and minimum overtime costs.

Therefore, in order to treat all employees fairly, the following guidelines will be followed (specific procedures are outlined in Procedure #P-112):

1. First unexcused absence—the employee will receive a written reprimand, a copy of which will be placed in the employee's personnel record.
2. Second unexcused absence—suspension without pay for two days.
3. Third unexcused absence—dismissal.

(Note: Appeal procedure is covered in Procedure #P-112.)

/s/ _____
Vice President

A policy specialist for an international company says,

The company benefits from continuity of management if and when one manager is replaced by another. The policy manual serves to orient and guide the new employee, who will have to administer it in roughly the same way. Another advantage is reassurance to outsiders. Potential investors, clients, stockholders all tend to breathe easier when they see that instructions on how to operate the company are available on nearly every desk.[7]

PROCEDURES

Policies offer the "why" of a company decision, and procedures illustrate the "how." Theoretically, every policy should have an accompanying procedure, and vice versa.

Definition

Procedures are the step-by-step means by which all repetitive business functions are coordinated and carried out. They tell *who* does *what* and in what *sequence*.

In preparing a procedure, the writer must understand and analyze the people affected by and carrying out the procedure. The language, the illustrations, and the directions must be stated to aid complete understanding. A procedure that is not understood is as ineffective as one that is not carried out!

A procedure may be presented in essay or narrative form, or in visual or flowchart form. Both ways identify who does what in what sequence, but the flowchart offers the advantage of presenting the entire sequence at a glance.

A procedure in essay form for the hospital case is illustrated in Figure 10–3. Figure 10–4 illustrates the flowchart format for the same case.

COMPANY HANDBOOKS

Glancing through company handbooks, one finds many differences. One handbook might be an orientation booklet citing company history, philosophy, various rules and regulations, and providing information on such things as parking locations, lunch and coffee breaks, and employee discounts. Another handbook might be a collection of company policies and procedures covering absenteeism, promotion and transfer, equal opportunity, purchasing and procurement, and safety.

One writer who specializes in the development of employee written communications suggests that employee handbooks should achieve the following purposes:

1. Provide potential and new employees with a favorable first impression of the organization.
2. Serve as a complement to the new employee orientation program, providing reinforcement and expansion of the topics covered in the orientation.
3. Provide employees with information concerning the fundamental policies and procedures of the organization.
4. Provide the employee with an overview of what he can expect from the organization and what the organization will expect from him.[8]

Purpose and Determinants

The size of the organization, the number of employees, the volume of business, the number of plants, locations, the product or service, and the number of suppliers all may contribute to the rationale behind a company handbook. In one case, the company may be a small local department store concerned with customer service and employee welfare. The need for formalized policies and procedures may not be warranted, and the philosophy behind a company handbook is one of presenting general in-

FIGURE 10–3 Narrative Procedure

J. R. M. Hospital
Bay City, Minnesota

Procedure # 1112-A

Subject: Patient Expiration

1. Person finding body.
   a. Notify the nurse in charge of the floor that the deceased is on.
   b. Lock room if it is a private room.
   c. If not a private room, use the curtain dividers.
2. Nurse in charge.
   a. Notify attending doctor.
   b. If the attending doctor is not available, notify any doctor on duty.
   c. Notify Supervisor of Nurses.
   d. Call an undertaker at the earliest opportunity.
   e. Notify the following:
      (1) Supervisor of Nurses.
      (2) Admissions.
      (3) Administrator.
      (4) Reception.
      (5) Social Services.
   f. Notify cleaning crew.
3. Attending doctor.
   a. Examine the body and pronounce death.
   b. After the family has arrived at the hospital, the attending doctor should advise them that the patient has expired.
4. Supervisor of Nurses.
   a. Call the family to come to the hospital.
   b. Do not say that the patient has expired, simply state that there has been a serious change in his/her condition.
   c. Appoint two employees to inventory deceased belongings.
5. Employees taking inventory.
   a. Make an inventory report.
   b. Make said report in the presence of next of kin.
   c. Have a member of the family sign the report.
   d. Both employees sign and date said report.
6. Reception.
   a. Pull card from in-patient swing file.
   b. Enter notice-of-death on the roster so that no visitors will be allowed.
7. Social Services office.
   a. Calculate any benefits that the patient may have coming from Medicare, Medicaid, Medi-Pac, etc.
   b. Forward to the Admissions office.
8. Admissions.
   a. Pull the deceased patient records and tabulate bill.
   b. Send copy of closing to administrator.
   c. Do not open room for new patients until verification has been received from the nurse in charge that the room has been cleared and cleaned.

FIGURE 10–4 Flowchart Procedure

Procedure # 1112-A   J. R. M. Hospital Bay City, Minnesota   Subject: Patient Expiration

Nurse	Physician	Family	Orderly or aide	Admissions	Director of Nursing	Medical Records	Morgue	Housekeeping
1. Notify physician.	2. Examine to legitimize death and sign death certificate.		7. Tag body for identification.	9. Notify morgue of patient death.			11. Refrigerate the body until autopsy is performed or body is claimed.	
4. Notify Admissions of patient expiration.	3. Notify the patient's family.		8. Tie and wrap body and place on a stretcher.	13. Take responsibility for belongings of patient and notify family of their availability.				16. Prepare room for occupancy.
5. Notify Director of Nursing of expiration and send patient's records to her/him.		14. Family picks up belongings.	10. Transport body to the morgue.	15. Notify Housekeeping of death.	19. Authorize receipt of records and send them to Medical Records.	20. Prepare and close the patient's record.		17. Notify Admissions when room is available for occupancy.
6. Instruct orderly or aide to tag the body.				18. Schedule room for occupancy.				
12. Package personal belongings of the deceased and send to Admissions.								

formation in easy-to-read narrative form. In another case, the organization may be a large manufacturing company that has several plant locations, thousands of employees, is unionized, deals with a variety of suppliers, and employs several manufacturing representatives. Just the physical separation of the plants, the salespersons, and the suppliers may call for greater coordination and control than would be necessary in the first case. Coordination and control may be achieved by having a policy manual or company handbook. A company handbook should be tailored to the situation, the company, and those who will need and use it.

An example of a table of contents for a company handbook designed primarily to orient new employees to the organization is given in Figure 10–5. This type of handbook probably could be written in a very informal, natural, and easy-to-read style. It might even contain cartoons to illustrate some points. By glancing at the table of contents, you can tell that it probably contains all the information that an employee might need to know. An example of a more detailed collection of organizational policies, procedures, and orientation materials is illustrated in Figure 10–6.

Once the need for a company handbook has been determined, the style of writing can reflect a great deal about the company. Most management texts reflect the trend to implement Theory Y in the management process.[9] Briefly stated, McGregor suggests that behind every managerial action are assumptions about human behavior. Theory X suggests:

1. Most persons have a dislike of work and will avoid it.
2. Most persons must be controlled, directed, or threatened with punishment.
3. Most persons avoid responsibility and lack ambition.

In contrast to these assumptions, Theory Y suggests:

1. Most persons do not inherently dislike work.
2. Most persons can and will exercise self-direction in achieving objectives.
3. Most persons accept and even seek responsibility.

Theory X leads to authoritarian management, while Theory Y takes advantage of the natural desire to work. Challenging objectives are set and people are held accountable for the results. Unfortunately, many company handbooks do not reflect this trend.

Style

To be successful, a handbook must be written in a manner that can be easily read and understood by the majority of employees. However, in one survey of 50 handbooks, the researcher found "on the average, the reading level of most [handbooks] was at the third year of college,"[10] but

FIGURE 10–5 Company Handbook

TABLE OF CONTENTS

a majority of the employees who were asked to read the handbooks had a high school education or less!

In many situations, employees cannot or do not communicate upward. Instead, they turn to their employee handbooks for guidance. While the information presented may be clear, concise, and complete—all

FIGURE 10–6 Policy and Procedure Manual

J. R. M. Hospital
Bay City, Minnesota

Section	Topic	Page
Organization	Introduction	1
	Board of Directors	1
	Organization Chart	2
	History	3
Policies	Job Security	4
	Equal Opportunity	4
	Employment of Relatives	5
	Recruitment	6
	Promotions/Transfers/	
	Demotions	7
	Dismissals	8
Orientation	Orientation/Processing	9
	Training/Evaluations	10
	Job Assignments	11
	Termination	11
	Records	12
Benefits	Wage and Salary	13
	Sick Leave	14
	Holidays	14
	Insurance	15
	Food Service	15
Administration	Attendance	16
	Cleanliness	16
	Communications	16
	Discipline	17
	Safety	17
Departmental		
Responsibilities	Accounting	18
	Business	19
	Dietary	20
	Housekeeping	21
	Laboratory	22
	Medical Records	23
	Nursing Service	24
	Personnel Department	25
	Pharmacy	26
	Purchasing	27
	Surgical	28
	X-Ray Department	29

desirable characteristics—the *style* or tone of the writing may reflect a lack of trust in the employee. In turn, this may bring about lowered morale and distrust, and may propagate a philosophy of Theory X.

Note the examples in Figure 10–7 and ask yourself which company you would rather work for.

SUMMARY

Perhaps the greatest danger in the administration of policy, the implementation of procedures, and the development and adherence to company handbooks, training, and office manuals is a "hardening of the arteries." This lack of flexibility or inability to change may be because management does not recognize current trends. Policies and procedures can become sacred ground on which no person should tread, and policies, procedures, or office handbooks become static rather than ongoing dynamic tools. Consequently, their usefulness is severely limited.

Another key concept that causes problems is the absence of consistency among the policies, procedures, and company handbooks. One policy should be consistent with another, with the procedures developed to implement a policy, and with the company handbook, which explains and interprets the policies and procedures. Many times these are written by different persons, and the inconsistency that may exist among them compounds administrative difficulties.

Lack of understanding of a policy or procedure can be corrected if it is recognized early, and feedback is important to this. All these tools should be viewed as communication interchanges between the organization and any of its publics—within or outside the organization. It is important for the organization's top management to know how these tools interact with others.

Motivation is a crucial factor in policy administration and procedure implementation. Lack of motivation on the part of those expected to carry out policy can do nothing but ensure its ineffectiveness. A close identification between the goals of the company and the needs of the individuals concerned must be made at an early stage. Close personal supervision during the initiation of any new (or change in) policy or procedure plays a major role in its success.

A final comment concerns the motivation and behavior of top management who represent the organization and have ultimate responsibility and authority for the tools described here. One writer notes: "The gap that often exists between what executives say and how they behave helps to create barriers to openness and trust, to the effective search for alternatives, to innovation, and to the flexibility in the organization."[11]

Thus, an administrative system that encompasses policies, procedures,

FIGURE 10-7   Theory X and Theory Y Handbooks

Company X   *Company Y*

Introduction

I extend to you a welcome to the Springs Plant of Pixie Manufacturing Company. The company was founded in 1912 and is the second largest producer of corset snaps in the world. The Springs Plant started in 1958.

The firm takes pride in producing quality products and hopes we can take pride in you as a productive worker.

As an employee of our company you will be expected to uphold the standards and promote business of Pixie Manufacturing Company.

Please read this handbook and be familiar with its contents.

/s/ _____
President

We extend to you a most sincere and cordial welcome to the Springs Plant of Pixie Manufacturing Company. Our company was founded in 1912 and is the second largest producer of corset snaps in the world. This plant began operation in 1958 and has been judged the "Outstanding Plant" of Pixie for the last three years!

We take pride in producing quality products and providing our customers with the best possible service. We take pride, too, in our employees and realize that the success of any endeavor depends on the people involved.

We think you will find our company a good place to work, and hope you will enjoy your job. We are pleased you have joined us, and I am looking forward to meeting you personally.

/s/ _____
President

Responsibilities

Hours

The work day will be divided into three eight-hour shifts. You will work the shift assigned to you by your foreman. There will be a one-hour lunch break approximately in the middle of each shift. There will be two ten-minute breaks, one before and one after the lunch break, for each shift. The specific time for each break will be posted by each shift's foreman. Overtime work will be assigned by the foreman.

Hours

The work day will be divided into three eight-hour shifts. Preferential assignment to certain shifts will be given on a seniority basis. However, if you have a valid reason for needing to work on a certain shift, this can be worked out through the Personnel Department. Contact the personnel manager in regard to this. There will be a one-hour lunch break approximately in the middle of each shift. There will be two ten-minute breaks, one before and one after the lunch break for each shift. The specific time for each break will be posted by your foreman. Overtime work will be assigned on a voluntary basis with seniority rank taking precedence.

Procedures

Entrance and exits

Enter the building only at the employee parking lot door. Exit by the same door. In the event of fire, employees will exit through the nearest fire escape.

Entrance and exits

For your convenience and safety, employees are encouraged to enter and exit from the door located at the south side of the employee parking lot. Fire exits are located for your safety in all work areas.

Parking

Park only in those areas that are designated for employees.

Parking

Parking is provided for your convenience on the north side of the plant.

FIGURE 10-7 *(concluded)*

Company X

Company Y

Lost and found
Take all found items to the lost and found box in the main office immediately.

Transfers
If it be in the best interest, transfers from one department to another can be arranged when there are openings available. Such transfers must be approved by the foreman.

Promotions
Promotion recommendations will be handled by the supervisor of your department.

Holidays
There are seven paid holidays. Your foreman can give you information about arrangements for any particular holiday.

Community service
Once a year solicitations are made for contributions to the United Fund campaign. To make it easier for our employees to contribute, a payroll deduction system has been worked out through which employees can fulfill their pledges. Dixie Manufacturing strongly encourages support of this program.

Smoking
There will be absolutely no smoking in areas of the plant designated as "No Smoking" areas.

Lost and found
Please turn over found items to your foreman.

Transfers
If it seems to be in the best interest of both the employee and the company, transfers from one department to another can be arranged when there are openings available.

Promotions
Promotions will be granted according to years of service, skills, and work habits. Your supervisor usually makes the initial recommendations. Lack of skill can be more than compensated for by hard work.

Holidays
Paid holidays include New Year's Day, Memorial Day, July Fourth, Labor Day, Thanksgiving, and two days at Christmas. Your foreman can provide you with additional information.

Community service
At various times of the year, charities solicit contributions. If you want to contribute, a payroll deduction plan can be arranged.

Smoking
For your safety and well-being, "No Smoking" areas of the plant must be observed.

Employee benefits

Life insurance
Every full-time employee of Dixie Manufacturing Company receives a life insurance policy, including accidental death and dismemberment coverage, the premium on which is paid entirely by the company. The amount of this policy is based on your earnings, which are reviewed annually. This coverage becomes effective after you have been employed for two months.

Life insurance
As an added convenience, Dixie Manufacturing gives a life insurance policy to all its employees. The premiums are paid by the company. The amount of the policy is determined by seniority. If you wish to increase the amount of the policy, you can contribute through payroll deductions. Personnel in the Employee Relations department will be happy to answer your questions and provide claim forms and assistance with matters pertaining to your insurance benefits.

company handbooks, and training manuals is only as successful as the time, effort, enthusiasm, commitment, and motivation that top management and the writers put into it.

DISCUSSION QUESTIONS

1. Define organizational objective, organizational policy, and organizational procedure. Why is it important to distinguish between these three concepts? How are the three related?

2. What is meant by saying that effective communication is a cumulative process and has a cumulative effect?

3. Define business policy and discuss the various elements of policy.

4. Discuss four conditions that give rise to review of current policy or development of new policy.

5. How can new policy be effectively introduced?

6. Discuss three advantages of a policy manual.

7. Discuss three advantages of developing a company handbook.

8. Contrast Theory X and Theory Y management styles. Give some examples of how one could determine a company's management style by analyzing company manuals and handbooks.

9. What is the most significant barrier to effective business policy administration and implementation? How can it be overcome?

EXERCISES

1. Write a policy and procedure for Valley National Bank on coffeebreaks. It will be issued by Sam Brown, Vice-President for Personnel.

2. Write a policy and procedure for any organization you are familiar with on a subject of your choice.

3. Develop an appropriate Table of Contents for an employee handbook for an organization you have worked for part-time or summers. (What would you have liked to know?)

4. Write several passages for items from Exercise 3, above. How might they be written by a company officer—based on your knowledge of company philosophy/leadership style? How would you write/rewrite the same items?

NOTES

[1]Stuart P. Bloom, "Policy and Procedure Statements that Communicate," *Personnel Journal* 62, no. 9 (September 1983), p. 711.

[2]Paul M. Dauton, Jr., "The Policy Formation Process," in *Business Policy Cases, Incidents and Readings*, ed. F. J. Bridges and K. W. Olm (Boston: Allyn & Bacon, 1966), p. 398.

[3]Bloom, "Policy and Procedure Statements," p. 714.

[4]Bloom, "Policy and Procedure Statements," p. 711.

[5]For a discussion of the advantages and disadvantages of employee participation in the formulation of policies and procedures, see C. Roland Christensen, Norman A. Berg, Malcolm S. Salter, *Policy Formulation and Administration* (Homewood, Ill.: Richard D. Irwin, 1980), p. 9, and Lloyd L. Byers, *Strategic Management: Planning and Implementation* (New York: Harper & Row, 1984), p. 10.

[6]William V. Haney, *Communication and Organizational Behavior*, 4th ed. (Homewood, Ill.: Richard D. Irwin, 1979), pp. 326–27.

[7]Terry W. Smith, "Developing a Policy Manual," *Personnel Journal* 61, no. 6 (June 1982), p. 446.

[8]Debra L. Heflich, "Developing a Readable Employee Handbook," *Personnel Administrator* 28, no. 3 (March 1983), p. 80.

[9]For a discussion of Theory X and Theory Y, see Douglas McGregor, *The Human Side of Enterprise* (New York: McGraw-Hill, 1960).

[10]Heflich, "Developing a Handbook," p. 81.

[11]H. N. Broom, *Business Policy and Strategic Action* (Englewood Cliffs, N.J.: Prentice-Hall, 1969), p. 62.

SUGGESTED READINGS

AMERICAN MANAGEMENT ASSOCIATION. *How to Prepare and Write Your Employee Handbook.* New York: AMA Publications Group, 1984.

TRAVIS, A B. *The Handbook Handbook: The Complete How-to-Guide to Publishing Policies and Procedures.* New York: R. R. Bowker, 1984.

Chapter 11

Oral Reports

Chapter 11 Case

You are justifiably proud of the project you've just finished. After all, you put nearly six months of your heart and soul into it, not to mention countless hours of your own time. You and the company president have discussed it informally all the way through, so you know she's on board. She's told you, however, that she needs the approval of the board of directors before launching a project of this size, and she's asked you to give a formal report at the next board meeting, just eight days away. You need to condense the information into a 15-minute presentation, and you need to be persuasive. How will you prepare? How much technical information will you include? What kind of visual aids, if any, will you need?

INTRODUCTION

This chapter will review some principles of oral communication and focus on the oral report. It cannot replace a formal class in speech communication or substitute for valuable, actual experience before a group.

The oral report is one of the most widely used forms of communication in business today. Oral communication is used during 70 to 90 percent of the day by managers and a large part of that percentage includes oral reporting. Success in business, as elsewhere, depends on presenting ideas in an orderly, persuasive, and compelling way. Business needs effective leadership, and leadership depends on the ability to communicate to others so they will react as one wishes. In a sense, business managers make speeches every time they speak.

Peter Drucker summarizes the need for communication skills: "No matter whether the manager's job is engineering, accounting, or selling, his effectiveness depends on his ability to listen, to read, to write, and to speak."[1] Managers use many forms of oral communication during their daily activities to perform their responsibilities efficiently and effectively.

A manager or supervisor may have to report to superiors about the production schedule; a personnel specialist may report to a group of department heads on tardiness or absenteeism; a manager might present information about safety standards to a group of employees or indoctrinate new employees into the company. A business manager could present information on the economic outlook to a number of company officials. A vice president may need to review the advantages and disadvantages of the economic and environmental conditions relating to a new plant location. The president of a company may have to present an annual progress report to the board of directors. A businessperson might be asked to lend his or her experience to a local civic group. All of these are forms of oral reports—some short, some long, some with detailed information, some with only minimal documentary evidence. The content in each of the above situations would depend on the particular situation and audience. They do have one thing in common: they give information to someone or to a group. The planning, preparation, organization, and presentation will vary depending on the number of receivers, their knowledge of the subject, the topic being presented, and the environmental factors.

PLANNING

Before you can begin collecting information, preparing for specific audience adaptation, or practicing, a number of questions need to be asked:

What is the purpose of this presentation? To inform? To convince? To entertain? To get some action? A combination? Are you just informing a group about a new form to be used in the company, or are you also expecting them to know how to complete it? Are you giving a group of company executives information about profits or are you also attempting to get a vote on building a new plant?

Who is the audience? Number? Age? Sex? Interests? Level of knowledge about the subject? Attitudes and values? Some or all of these audience demographics should affect the preparation of your presentation. Is your preparation the same for 10 people in a conference room as it is for 300 in an auditorium? Do you prepare in the same way for those who have the same level of knowledge as you? Finally, what is the audience *expectation* of you and your presentation?

What is the occasion, time, place, event? Your presentation does not occur in a vacuum; others may come before or after you on the program. What will be the topics of their presentations? How much time will you have? Can you adapt to either expanding or cutting your presentation? Should you refer to the occasion, place, or event? Should you refer to a person or group for special recognition?

You must determine the purpose and know a number of things about the audience and occasion before any specific preparation and organization can take place. One useful plan that identifies many of the factors for audience/event analysis is given below.

Speech Preparation Plan[2]

The Particular Circumstances

1. When will the speech be given?
2. Where will the speech be given?
3. What will be the medium of presentation, and who is the actual audience?
4. What kind of atmosphere have recent speeches created?
5. What recent events are fresh in the minds of listeners?
6. What are the demographic and group personality features of the audience: age, politics, religious profile, level of education, likes and dislikes, heroes and villains, issues on which individuals disagree?
7. Who are the leaders and who are the followers?

Psychological Dynamics

1. How can I give my subject priority in the minds of listeners?
   a. What universal human motives might it involve?
   b. How might I make use of my hearers' sensitivity to proximity, continuity, magnitude, contrast, and conflict?
2. How can I bring my subject most clearly into focus?
3. Can I develop my subject in a form that satisfies my listeners' need for coherence, causal relationships, symmetry, and the sense of cumulation?
4. Can I meet the tests of comprehensiveness, reliability, and authenticity of communication?
5. Can I create and stimulate an urge to power among my listeners? Can I excite them and involve them in a group ready for action?

PREPARING

For the novice, the amount of work involved in the planning, organization, and presentation of any type of speech or report may seem almost insurmountable. The oral report offers the novice the opportunity to develop skill and self-confidence before a group because it is not as complex as other forms of reports.

There must be preparation before the presentation, organization during the presentation, and follow-up concluding the presentation. Under all circumstances, the speaker must be knowledgeable about the subject! How do you choose the information to be included in an oral report? The material in Chapter 9 suggests some sources for this information, and we will set out a few sources here.

Personal Experience.   This is the best place to start searching for information when preparing for any written or oral report. What has been your experience or observation? The information you may have gained while visiting in a foreign country a month, a week, or even a couple of days can add more valuable information than reading about that country. You may be the only person in a group with experience working on an assembly line. Be careful when using personal experience or observation—it was *your* experience or observation based on *your* frame of reference, attitudes, likes, dislikes, beliefs, values, and moods. Your experiences should not be generalized to others.

Company Documents.   These are valuable sources of information, especially if the report needs to include material on inventory, production figures, sales, or personnel data. It should be a fairly simple task, with today's electronic retrieval systems, to compile information based on company documents.

Library Materials.   You have literally millions of books available to you in your public, university, or company library. However, don't overlook the periodicals—magazines, journals, and newspapers, or the nonprint materials—films, records, tapes, and videotapes. The nonprint materials may be useful for research as well as aids for your presentation. A number of libraries, especially university and metropolitian ones, have access to a growing number of on-line databases. These collections can be accessed by computer terminal and searched via telephone. There may be a nominal charge for this service, but it may be well worth it if it means the difference between getting the "right" information and not getting it at all.

Interviews.   Personal interviews with experts on a subject can lend credibility to your own or others' experiences or observations. The information you gain from this source may not be available elsewhere and should be looked on as adding a unique insight to the subject of the report.

Questionnaires.   Survey research, including questionnaires, can offer the most compelling evidence and documentation of any sources of information for an oral report. However, it must be emphasized that for the conclusions drawn from survey data to be considered valid and reliable a number of factors need to be considered. At the very least, the research hypothesis needs to be stated accurately, the research instrument (questionnaire) needs to be validated, the sample must be representative of the total population, and the statistical tests used must be appropriate for the data. Any survey research that does not meet these minimum standards (and many classroom project surveys do not) should carefully identify all

qualifications, restrictions, or limitations. In meeting these minimum standards, a student can make good use of information and skills from courses such as sampling, questionnaire construction, statistics and programming, especially SAS or SPSS.

ORGANIZING

Organization is the key to effective speaking. A report must be logical, clear, easily understood, and concise. The oral report may be divided into three parts: gaining attention, adapting to the audience, and presenting the information. The length and content development involved in gaining attention and adapting to the audience vary depending on some of the circumstances mentioned in the planning stage. If the listeners are familiar with the subject, their attention has already been drawn to the issue, and they are fully aware of the need to hear the material to be presented. These two parts of the report may be quite short or even eliminated. The speaker determines the listener level of interest and familiarity with the subject, and then develops the entire presentation.

Gaining Attention

Gaining and holding attention can be accomplished in a variety of ways. The right opening depends on the purpose of the report and on the audience. Usually, one or two of the following are sufficient: personal greeting, reference to the subject or occasion, a statement of fact or opinion, humor, a quotation or testimony, a question, or an illustration.

Personal greeting and reference to the subject or occasion are more appropriate for the formal presentation as they provide an easy introduction to the subject and help establish rapport with the audience and direct their attention. For example, "Good morning, members of the ABC sales team! It is a pleasure to have this opportunity to speak to you on the 25th anniversary of the company and to tell you of our progress and pride during those 25 years." In just two sentences the speaker has greeted the audience, made mention of the occasion, and identified the topic of the speech or report.

A statement of fact or opinion documents the importance or seriousness of the problem or topic and serves to get the speaker's point of view into the open. If a subject is controversial, however, the speaker might do well to hold his or her opinion in reserve until such time as that position has been established with other evidence. Otherwise, the audience might hear only the opinion and mentally start to debate the issue. However, if the speaker has analyzed the audience properly and feels they are in agreement, a statement of opinion or personal observation might help to establish a common frame of reference and rapport.

The use of humor, if *relevant* and *appropriate*, is always welcomed by a group. Audiences warm up quickly to good storytellers. Keep in mind, though, the overall purpose of the presentation. If a person can amuse as well as inform, humor is an excellent technique for holding the attention and interest of the audience. Telling a joke or humorous anecdote just for the sake of humor may be speaker suicide. A joke with no particular relevancy to the remainder of the presentation may lose the attention of the audience. Since the audience is made up of individuals, each person may have a different concept of humor than the speaker.

A quotation or testimony can direct audience attention and document the subject from an outside source. This device is beneficial in focusing the attention on a specific issue. Keep in mind that an opening quotation should not overshadow the presentation and should not be just a task of reading; it should enhance the meaning of the presentation.

A question can be used to create a sense of suspense and promote audience attention throughout the presentation. If the question is not answered immediately, the speaker should be sure the material presented in a later part of the report does provide the answer. If it does not, the audience may assume the speaker did not follow through with the original plan and is disorganized. A rhetorical question, however, is one designed not to be answered, but to make the audience THINK.

Illustrations and specific instances can be used at any point in a presentation: gaining attention, relating the subject to the audience, or presenting the major part of the report. Illustrations are *detailed* examples and include who, what, when, and where. If appropriate, the why may also be added. Some form of imagery can be used to give added detail to these basic facts. "Imagery" is an extension of "image" or "imagine," and that should give you a clue to its meaning.

If someone asked you what you did yesterday morning you might reply, "Oh, I got up about seven o'clock and went to a friend's house for breakfast." That identifies who, what, when, and where, but it does not contain any imagery. You might have said, "I got up about seven o'clock because a friend had invited me to breakfast and to study for an exam. But, when I went outside, I was surprised to find 10 inches of snow on the ground and wind blowing about 30 miles an hour. Although it was only a few blocks, the snow was blowing in my eyes and the wind almost gave me frostbite on my ears. When I finally arrived, the aroma of freshly brewed coffee and that delightful scent of bacon and eggs greeted me. My tastebuds started working overtime just by smelling the bacon and eggs and the coffee." Well, do you smell the coffee? If so, that's imagery: a sense of smell, touch, taste, hearing, seeing, physical exertion, or internal sensation produced by words alone.

Finally, an illustration may be either hypothetical or factual. A specific instance, however, is usually thought of as factual and it contains only the four w's. Did you ever see that famous TV show or the movie "Dragnet"

and hear that classic line, "All we want are the facts"? The "facts" included only the four w's and no imagery. Those were specific instances in their finest form.

Adapting to Your Audience

Adapting to the audience is not a separate part of any presentation, but should pervade the entire presentation. Audiences are people, and people are individuals with different sets of interests, knowledge, and purposes for being present. The report must relate to specific material; it must be important to and somehow affect the audience.

The speaker should ask himself the questions: Why should this group want or need to know this information? Will it have some bearing on their health, wealth, knowledge, or other interests? Will it affect their relationship with others in the organization? Will it prepare them to carry out some task or project? How will this group benefit by listening to this information? The answers to these questions, in the form of some hypothetical or factual illustrations, will continue to hold the group's attention while moving into the real content of the topic.

If, for example, you are giving a class report on the principles of effective interviewing techniques, you might include one of your classmates in a hypothetical illustration: "Chris, let's suppose you are interviewing with a company that really interests you. Do you know what will happen during that interview? Do you know the questions the interviewer may ask? Do you have questions prepared that you want to ask? No? Well, relax! In this report, I'm going to tell you everything you ever wanted or needed to know about interviewing techniques."

Or, consider yourself a training supervisor conducting a session for employees on new company safety measures: "Tom, faced with a situation in which one of your employees was handling materials improperly, would you know how to show and tell that employee about our safety program? By the time I have finished this report—about 20 minutes— you should have all the information you need to promote our 'Safety First' program in your department."

Both situations place persons in the audience in a hypothetical—but potentially realistic—situation in which they might want or need to know the information about to be presented. Once you have the audience hungry for more information you can proceed to the most important and detailed part of the report.

Presenting the Information

The heart of the oral report is the presentation of the content material. The organization for this information can be accomplished best and most

easily by adhering to the old saying, "Tell 'em what you're going to tell, tell 'em, and tell 'em what you've told them." A more formal way of saying this is to include (1) an initial preview, (2) some detailed information (including illustrations, statistics, testimonies, and other forms of evidence to support your main points), and finally, (3) a summary. This method of organization helps focus the audience's attention, direct their thoughts to the issues, categorize and classify information, and summarize.

The initial preview of the report should include the purpose, how the audience will benefit (if you haven't included that in the previous step), and an outline of the points that will be covered during the report. Audiences appreciate organization in order to develop mental comprehension.

After the preview, detailed information is given in the body of the report, beginning with the central purpose and following through with two to five main points. Each point should be supported with some forms of illustration or evidence.

The sequence of your main points depends on the nature of the material being presented. Some traditional and logical methods of ordering the main points of a report include: (1) time, (2) space or geographical relationship, (3) cause-effect, (4) deductive, (5) inductive, and (6) special topical.

The time sequence is used to emphasize that the first point must be accomplished first, before items two, three, and so on. How would you instruct someone to change a flat tire? You *must* start by getting the lug wrench and jack out of the trunk. You don't do that in the third or fifth sequence, but the first.

Space or geographical relationships are used frequently to describe a production sequence—how raw materials move from the loading dock, through various processes, to the final product. Sales reports can be organized easily and logically depending on regional or district offices or divisions.

If you are presenting information on a subject such as absenteeism or tardiness, then the cause-effect, effect-cause, or effect-effect methods may be useful. The specific method can identify where you wish to place the emphasis in your report. For example:

- Poor supervision (cause) leads to absenteeism (effect).
- Absenteeism (effect) is a result of poor supervision (cause).
- Absenteeism (effect) results in lower production (effect).

In the last situation, the cause has not been identified—it may be unknown or it may be implied. Depending on the chosen method, the emphasis can be placed on poor supervision, or absenteeism, or lower production.

Deductive and inductive methods of sequencing information are the

most classical. In deductive reasoning, an accepted general statement is applied to an individual case (e.g., all cats are animals; this is a cat; therefore this is an animal). In inductive reasoning, several cases are studied, and, from the observations made, a general principle is formed. When the general premise for deductive reasoning is true, the deduction from it would be certain for all individual instances. However, the principle formed in inductive reasoning would be certain only when all possible instances had been examined. Thus, in giving a presentation, you could cite your evidence first and draw a conclusion last; or, you could begin with the generalization and support it with specific pieces of data. The choice depends on where you want to place the emphasis.

Some topics do not lend themselves to any of the methods mentioned above. If there is no logical sequence to the points in your report (i.e., it doesn't matter which point comes first or last) then you can place them in any order. This is a special topical sequence. If you are discussing the special properties and handling techniques of several chemicals a plant produces, the order in which these are discussed may not matter. However, even here you have a choice of sequencing depending on what you want to emphasize: (see Figure 11–1).

Thus, while sequencing information may vary from general to specific, or specific to general, or may emphasize time or space, the method of organizing that information depends on the purpose of the report and what is most effective for that purpose.

Finally, a summary of the main points with appropriate conclusions and recommendations may be added. This section provides a review and reinforcement of important points. A speaker could actually remind the audience that he or she is about to conclude and their attention again is focused on the main points of the presentation. Again, the purpose of the presentation determines the method chosen for the summary. If you are

FIGURE 11–1   Examples of Sequencing

Plan A	*Plan B*
Chemical X	Special properties
Properties	Chemical X
Handling techniques	Chemical Y
Chemical Y	Chemical Z
Properties	Handling techniques
Handling techniques	Chemical X
Chemical Z	Chemical Y
Properties	Chemical Z
Handling techniques	

persuading a group to buy a product, change a policy, or *do* something, the summary tends to be persuasive; if giving information, you simply repeat the main points.

Outlining the Presentation

Outlining the presentation helps the speaker by providing some tangible evidence that the material is clear, concise, well organized, and that all relevant material has been included. An abbreviated outline is shown in Figure 11–2.

THE TRANSACTIVE NATURE OF COMMUNICATION

Most of the material in this chapter deals with speaking in public. This form of speech interaction is not like the old bow and arrow or ping-pong theories of communication. The bow and arrow theory suggests that the speaker is the arrow and the audience is the target. Either you hit it or you don't. The ping-pong theory suggests that the ball is in your court or

FIGURE 11–2 Sample Outline

TOPIC:

PURPOSE:

AUDIENCE DEMOGRAPHICS:

I **Introduction**
  A. One to three attention getting methods
  B.
II **Audience adaptation**
  Ask, then answer—using illustrations—why does this group need or want to know this information.
III **Body**
  A. Preview
    1. Briefly preview the main points to be covered
    2.
    3.
  B. Detailed information
    1. Discuss in detail two to five main points supported by illustration and other forms of evidence, and sequenced by time, space, etc.
    2.
    3.
  C. Final summary
    1. Briefly review the main points
    2.
    3.

mine. We view *all* speech interaction as transactive in nature and, as such, it is reciprocal. The interplay between the participants is crucial to the ultimate success of the interaction. Gail Myers and Michele Myers comment:

> This transactional process is like a spiraling process and makes the analysis of communication difficult since every facet of the process is likely to be both cause *and* effect, stimulus *and* response, source *and* receiver, message *and* medium.[3]

At this point you may want to review Transactional Analysis in Chapter 6 and the nature of small group communication in Chapter 7.

USING VISUAL AND AUDIO AIDS

Main points, statistics, floor plans, and other parts of a report can be emphasized and made more understandable by the use of an appropriate visual aid. If a report is somewhat complex, there is a potential for confusion. Visual aids can be used to emphasize and clarify points or relate other information. The chalkboard, a chart easel, a prepared chart, mimeographed material, photos, tape recordings, models, or the actual object of discussion are examples of these aids. Visual aids should extend and enhance, not overshadow or take the place of an effective presentation. Some guidelines to follow are:

1. Use only relevant and appropriate material.
2. Prepare the material in advance of giving the report.
3. Keep it simple.
4. Make it big enough to be seen.
5. Place it where everyone can see it.
6. Address the audience, not the visual aid.
7. When not in use, put the visual aid out of sight.

People enjoy watching something other than the speaker if it is appropriate and can illustrate a point. This should be determined during the preparation step, and the visual aid should be included in the natural sequence of the total process. Points that are condensed and shown on a visual aid are likely to be remembered longer.

THE QUESTION AND ANSWER PERIOD

Most presentations should allow for an audience question and answer period. Assuming the audience is "friendly" and the questions are not asked to embarrass the speaker, he or she should show sincere interest in attempting to satisfy the questioner. The most direct method is to give ad-

ditional information and it is probably what the questioner wanted. Another method is to compare the effects or results of a proposed solution with the results of one suggested by a listener. The use of the speaker's prestige, personal experience, or knowledge may be used where credibility needs to be established or emphasized. Be honest with your audience; if you do not know the answer, suggest sources the person may consult or offer to find the answer and report back to the person. End this segment of the presentation in as friendly and courteous a manner as possible.

PHYSICAL AND VOCAL PRESENTATION

While content and organization are generally considered the most important aspects of an oral report you need to give some attention to the physical and vocal aspects. "Stage fright" is a normal reaction for anyone presenting information before a group and actually can be healthy. If a person is concerned enough about the presentation to become nervous about it, he or she often gives an effective presentation. The speaker who has thoroughly prepared for the report is in command of the situation and any early nervousness usually subsides quickly.

Before starting a presentation, pause and take a normal and relaxed breath. Be thoroughly familiar with the introduction, the personal greeting, humorous anecdote, reference to the occasion or whatever method you have chosen. This will help give you the start that you may need.

Gestures can be used effectively to enhance points of the presentation. However, being natural in movement and speech is essential in order to enhance and not distract. Gestures should be well timed and vigorous, but relaxed. Posture should be relaxed; eye contact should be definite and directed to all parties in the group (this assumes the audience is not larger than 20 or 25 persons), and facial expressions should supplement the idea and intent of the speaker.

The vocal qualities of the speaker should be pleasing to the audience. Some variety in pitch, force, and rate of speech gives added clarity and emphasis to the content of the report and helps hold the attention of the audience. An enthusiastic speaker conveys meaning and keeps the audience listening.

If either the physical or vocal presentation is distracting to the listeners, they may well miss the content. On the other hand, physical movement, gestures, rate, and force of the presentation that are natural, relaxed, and enthusiastic, can add to the effectiveness of the total presentation. Practice the presentation—the more familiar you are with the material, the more relaxed you will be as a speaker.

The extemporaneous presentation has all the advantages and few, if any, of the disadvantages of the impromptu, manuscript, or memorized

presentations. It can be embarrassing to a speaker to lose her place in a manuscript or have a memory lapse. By definition, the extemporaneous presentation calls for planning, preparing, and practicing and is therefore far superior to an impromptu presentation.

SUMMARY

A prerequisite to effective oral communication (just as with written communication) is sensitivity to the receiver. This sensitivity helps you adapt your writing as well as your verbal messages to the specific audience. The receivers' frame of reference, (general background, education, likes, dislikes, attitudes, values, and moods) should be taken into account when preparing for an oral report. While it may be impossible for a speaker to adapt to every individual in an audience, he should make every attempt to adapt to group characteristics. This is why an early determination of audience demographics is important. Once the demographics and needs of the audience have been evaluated, the speaker can organize and develop the content of the report to better adapt to those characteristics.

Gaining and holding attention, pointing out the need for the audience to know or be convinced of the ideas presented, and finally, giving the desired information are parts of a simplistic but effective method of organization.

The content and organization of a presentation can be enhanced by other factors: effective vocal and physical delivery, attractive and well-timed use of audio-visual aids, and a confident but sincere approach during a question and answer period.

Public speaking, whether in the classroom or the board room, is both an art and a skill. Effective communication *can* be learned, but it must be approached with sincerity, discipline, and practice!

DISCUSSION QUESTIONS

1. Discuss sources of information that might be explored when preparing an oral report.

2. An oral report can be divided into three main parts. The first part is gaining attention. Discuss the first part and the two remaining parts of an oral report.

3. Presentation of the content of a report should have a threefold organization. Describe this organizational procedure.

4. Describe three of the six traditional methods for sequencing the main points in a report.

5. What are visual and audio aids? Discuss some guidelines for their usage in oral reporting.

6. What are some pointers that a speaker can use to improve the physical or vocal presentation of a report?

7. Why is the extemporaneous presentation method considered superior to the memorized or impromptu methods?

EXERCISES

1. Choose an article from a recent issue of a professional journal. Outline the content to illustrate (a) attention devices, (b) audience (reader) adaptations, and (c) initial preview, development, and summary of the major issues.

2. What changes would you make if presenting the same basic information to members of your class? To a group of business people? To newspaper/television interviewers?

3. Make the presentation to your communication class members. Develop appropriate audio-visual aids and plan to have a question-answer period after the presentation.

NOTES

[1]Peter Drucker, *The Practice of Management* (New York: Harper & Row, 1954), p. 346.
[2]Michael Osborn, *Speaking in Public* (Boston: Houghton Mifflin, 1982), p. 158.
[3]Gail E. Myers and Michele Tolela Myers, *Communicating When We Speak* (New York: McGraw-Hill, 1978), p. 26.

SUGGESTED READINGS

GROGG, PATRICIA MARCUM. "You Can Be a Better Speaker." *Supervisory Management* 29, no. 9 (September 1984), pp. 15–17.

KELLY, CHARLES M. "Effective Communications: Beyond the Glitter and Flash." *Sloan Management Review* 26, no. 3 (Spring 1985), pp. 69–74.

KIRKPATRICK, DONALD L. *How to Plan and Conduct Productive Business Meetings.* Chicago: Dartnell Corp., 1976.

KLUMPH, NED. "Effective Meetings: A Management Must." *Supervisory Management* 29, no. 12 (December 1984), pp. 28–32.

LALIBERTE, ROBERT E. "Management and the Action Presentation: A Process Model." *Optimum* 15, no. 3 (1984), pp. 68–84.

PAGE, WILLIAM T. "Helping the Nervous Presenter: Research and Prescriptions." *The Journal of Business Communication* 22, no. 2 (Spring 1985), pp. 9–19.

VARDAMAN, GEORGE T. *Effective Communication of Ideas.* New York: Van Nostrand Reinhold, 1970.

ZELKO, HAROLD P. "Better Seminars and Workshops for Both Sponsors and Participants." *Personnel Journal* (February 1986), pp. 32–34.

Chapter 12

Listening

Chapter 12 Case

"Ladies and gentlemen, our speaker for today's session, Dr. Mary Steele, labor relations expert and Professor of Management at the University of . . ." *Ah, yes, that last labor relations seminar was great. San Francisco . . . great food . . . great company . . . those redwoods were really something . . .*

". . . and then the president signed executive order number 11491 . . ." *This stuff is all too technical for me, anyway. After all, I've got Sally to take care of the union for me. Yes, indeed, that San Francisco trip was one of the very best. I wouldn't mind living on one of those houseboats someday.*

". . . negotiators are growing more and more professional, and therefore more dangerous . . ." *What's that? Sirens? Did I unplug the coffeepot this morning? I always do—automatic response, but this morning?*

". . . the cost of a lengthy strike can be averted . . ." *This woman is good, but I wish I'd had something besides that coffee for breakfast. I wonder if this guy next to me can hear my stomach growl? Applause? Great. I'm starved. There's the boss: she's always up for a good lunch.*

"Mike, glad I caught you. This was a great presentation. Let's discuss those ideas about interim negotiations over lunch." *Oh, no.*

What went wrong?

INTRODUCTION

In most books and articles oriented toward business and industry, you will observe such words as *rumor, communication, grapevine, speech, telephone,* and *interview. The words* **listen** or **listening** are seldom mentioned but are implied directly or indirectly. This chapter focuses on the importance, types, and problems of listening. If you develop an understanding of these factors, you are well on the way to becoming a better listener.

DEFINITION

In one of the classic articles on listening, Ralph G. Nichols states:

> Obviously, hearing and listening are not identical. Rather, they seem to be two distinguishable phases of a total process which we might call aural assimilation. Hearing is the perception of sound; listening is the attachment of meaning to aural symbols.[1]

What Nichols is suggesting is that listening goes beyond the mere perception of sounds and involves the ability to discriminate sounds and ideas, to comprehend, and to attach some meaning to the messages that are selected. Ronald B. Adler and George Rodman differentiate between hearing and listening when they point out that hearing is the process wherein sound waves strike the eardrum and cause vibrations that are transmitted to the brain. Listening occurs when the brain reconstructs these electrochemical impulses into a representation of the original sound and then gives them meaning.[2] A broader definition of listening may also include silence. "Silence is golden," but in this case, it is the *interpretation* of silence that may have meaning.

IMPORTANCE OF LISTENING

Perhaps it is begging the question to say that listening is important! Nevertheless, some people do not seem to understand just how important it is. In one of the first studies in this area, Paul T. Rankin discovered that 70 percent of an average adult's waking time is spent in some form of communication. It breaks down to 9 percent in writing activities, 16 percent in reading, 30 percent in speaking, and 45 percent in listening activities. Rankin also reported that reading (the second least-used communication skill) received 52 percent of the emphasis in classroom instruction, and listening (the most-used communication skill) received only 8 percent of the emphasis.[3] Because of this lack of emphasis in teaching listening skills, some educators have dubbed listening "the orphan of education."

During the 1940s, two studies reported the following major conclusions regarding listening activities: we can listen and comprehend at a rate three times faster than most people speak and 98 percent of all that we learn in our lifetimes we learn through our eyes or through our ears.[4] In spite of these and Rankin's statistics, our educational institutions have been sorely remiss in developing and implementing any systematic and orderly programs of instruction in listening. A notable exception has been at the University of Minnesota under the direction of Professor Ralph Nichols.

The importance of listening can be seen in our everyday work life. A

common question included in many employee surveys is, "What is the single, most important attribute of an effective manager?" The results frequently indicate that listening to individual employees is the most important single factor!

Researchers suggest that from 50 to 90 percent of a person's working time is spent in some form of communication and that half of that is spent listening. Using an annual salary of $30,000 and Rankin's percentages, the importance of communication activities is $21,000 per year, while listening activities account for more than $10,000. In today's communication-oriented business world, these figures may be even greater.

The ability to take instructions in a classroom, on the job, or in everyday life, is vital to achieving success in any task. In order to carry out these instructions, one must listen effectively. One of the leading causes for failure in business is that people tend to hear, but not listen. Think of all the telephone conversations, interviews, conferences, and training sessions that go on in organizations around the world and the amount of listening activities that occur. No matter how qualified a person may be for a job, that person's ultimate success may well depend on his or her communication abilities—especially listening.

TYPES OF LISTENING

Listening intensity varies with the situation, the topic of conversation, the immediacy or relevance of the subject to our needs, and the persons involved. Three general types of listening are classified here.

Casual or Marginal Listening

A student listening to the radio while studying for an exam, a homemaker listening to a television soap opera while doing chores, and a businessperson engaging in light conversation in the hallway are examples of the casual or marginal listener. The person may be thinking of other things, and listening in the immediate situation is secondary in importance. This particular type of listening could be considered a reprieve to our minds. It can be used as an exercise for our mental processes even though the person is under no pressure to learn or comprehend.

Attentive Listening

If the radio announcer suddenly breaks into the middle of a record to announce a tornado watch, the student studying for the exam may suddenly listen more attentively. The immediacy of the situation has created in the listener a need for more attention to the weather conditions. An

employee who hears his or her supervisor say, "Your next progress review and merit raise may depend on how well you carry out these instructions" will probably listen very carefully. In both of these cases, the person has some motivation to hear, understand, and remember. That person has determined that there is a need to obtain some information for immediate or future use. If, in the process of gathering that information, the individuals have given meaning to that information, then they have been productive, attentive listeners. Attentive listening should be one of the characteristics of an effective communicator.

Projective or Empathic Listening

Counseling and conflict situations call for projective or empathic listening. To understand what a speaker has experienced, one must imagine himself or herself in the other person's position. This type of listening is often difficult since barriers such as disliking the person, disagreeing, passing judgment, and giving advice could hinder the process of communication. The ability to put ourselves in another person's place with no preconceived ideas is an asset, but it is difficult to do. How many times have you heard a person say, "This is the way *I* did it," instead of listening to *your* situation and analyzing it from *your* point of view.

To become an effective, empathic listener, it is necessary to subordinate your own emotions and opinions. That is not an easy task; it requires fine tuning to another's experience and feeling. But, that is exactly what Carl Rogers, the noted psychotherapist, suggests. To overcome our natural tendency to judge and evaluate another person we must learn to "listen with understanding."[5]

FACTORS INFLUENCING LISTENING

There are many factors that can and do affect listening. First, there should be an organically and biologically sound and complete hearing system. A person must be aware of any deficiencies that might be present and be able to deal with the defect effectively.

The physical environment of the area of interchange must be as conducive as possible. Noise and other distractions, an uncomfortable temperature in the room, and improper lighting all inhibit proper communication between the speaker and listener. It becomes the listener's responsibility to overcome these inefficiencies.

As an attentive listener, place yourself in the best environment for listening—do not sit near doorways or under air-conditioning vents. Have the necessary supplies and be organized. If necessary, take notes; however, do not let notetaking distract from your listening ability.

The listener must have a common frame of reference with the speaker to understand the speaker's vocabulary, organization, inferences, and conclusions. If there is not enough overlap in the frame of reference, there is little chance that communication will be effective. The receiver may be hearing, but not listening or attaching meaning to what he or she is hearing.

It is difficult to put priorities on these factors, but a proper attitude on the part of the listener is the most important. Boredom, narrow-mindedness, egocentricity, prejudice, and impatience can all contribute to an "improper" attitude. In other words, a listener must *want* to listen effectively if he or she expects to gain knowledge and understanding of what another person is saying. To do that, one must *consciously* rule out those attitudinal factors that may contribute to the ineffectiveness of the interchange.

One study identifies some important factors in poor listening as disinterest, overt criticism of the speaker, an argumentative attitude, an interest only in facts, voluminous notetaking, half listening, and a lack of effort on the part of the listener.[6] All of these can be eliminated or changed to pave the way toward becoming a more effective listener.

Listening is more than an absence of speaking. It assumes a certain level of hearing acuity, an adequate physical environment, a common frame of reference between the parties, and, perhaps most importantly, an "accepting" attitude that is supportive and not defensive or judgmental.

BARRIERS TO EFFECTIVE LISTENING

Listening is not a separate communication entity, but involves two complementary skills—the skill of the sender and the skill of the receiver. The sender can control much of the communication interaction by gaining attention, showing relevancy of the topic to the receiver, choosing appropriate and interesting examples, and using vocabulary that is within the common frame of reference. The receiver can, in a sense, control the communication interaction almost completely—simply by not listening.

We can listen and comprehend three times faster than the 100–200 word per minute rate that most people attain in speech. However, we can read, think, and yes, listen approximately three or four times as fast as we speak—or as fast as someone speaks to us. This leaves us with 350 words per minute "vacant" in our thoughts during the listening process. How we use this spare time is vital to becoming a good listener. Many listeners react to distractions or find other ways to waste that spare time. The following are some of the most common distractions and barriers to effective listening.

Physical Distractions

Much of our behavior is automatic and involuntary, and sometimes it is difficult *to not* attend to some distractions (e.g., a loud noise, a growling stomach). It is usually not difficult to return to a conversation or listening to a speech or report after one of these temporary distractions. However, we should make a conscious effort to return to the communication inter-action as quickly as possible. The longer we keep our attention on the distraction, the more difficult it is to get back into the conversation or speech.

Mental and Emotional Distractions

Fake attention occurs when a mental or emotional distraction occurs. This could happen while we daydream or make private plans. Perhaps an emotional problem has our undivided attention. The conversation may not hold our interest and we think of other things—an exam in a class next period, a production problem that has to be solved, a human relations problem, or the route of a vacation.

To overcome this problem, you must be aware of what is happening and give conscious attention to the communication interaction. Be aware of such problems and overcome each individually as quickly as possible to gain full comprehension of the communication interchange.

Detouring

Detouring is like distractions except the detouring usually concerns the mental process involved in the interchange itself rather than a physical or audible noise. We are detouring when we allow ourselves to become distracted by words, phrases, or concepts during a conversation. Perhaps we do not understand a particular term, or certain terms bring out emotions that distract our minds for a short period of time. We may "fade-out" for a while, then suddenly get back into the interaction.

If, for example, a speaker mentions Mexico in a conversation, what is likely to happen (especially if you were there on a recent vacation)? Your thoughts probably turn to pleasant—or unpleasant—experiences: the weather, an interesting event, or an expensive souvenir. If so, you were detouring, and during that "fade-out" you may have missed some very important points of the speaker.

Debating

Although most of us "fade-out" and come back into an interaction rather quickly with distraction, daydreaming, and detouring, the problem of de-

bating is created when the listener mentally stops listening. As a listener, if you suddenly find yourself disagreeing and planning your response, you may miss the speaker's point.

People have an inherent tendency to evaluate others, whether or not there is a basis for such a reaction. You may begin to evaluate a presentation, the person's appearance, opinions, research, knowledge, or sincerity. As a supervisor listening to complaints from the line, you may be preparing your rebuttal as the person is trying to explain an incident; therefore, you can miss the most important information by mentally pronouncing judgment before the evidence is in. To overcome this problem, learn to listen completely first, then ask questions or raise issues.

The barriers to effective listening mentioned above are illustrated in Figure 12–1. Think of the straight line as the conversation line and follow

FIGURE 12–1 Barriers to Effective Listening

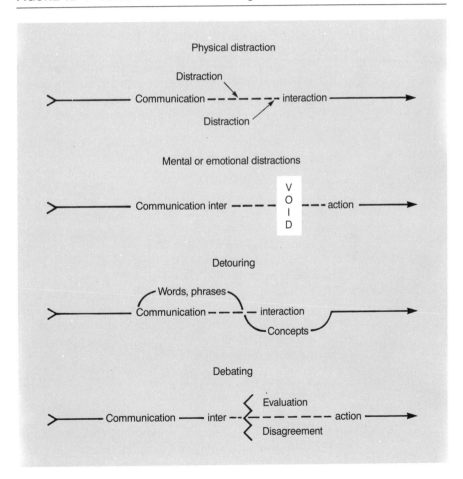

how distractions, daydreaming, detouring, and debating interfere with the free flow of that conversation. In some cases, it may be impossible for us to *not* give our attention to some of these distractions, but it is imperative to reduce the amount of time we give to them to get the full impact of the speaker's message.

FEEDBACK

Feedback determines whether a speaker's message has been received as a reasonable facsimile of what was sent and intended. Feedback can be verbal, nonverbal, or a combination of the two. A nod of the head may suggest that the listener has heard and understood the message. A question implies that the message has been heard and understood, at least in part. The technique of paraphrasing the speaker's message is an excellent form of feedback because it allows the speaker to check it for accuracy and completeness. Once this has been done the conversation can proceed. To do this with *all* communications would be silly and redundant. However, paraphrasing can be very beneficial when giving and receiving instructions, responding to the expression of a strong opinion, or when the nonverbal aspects of the communication seem to contradict the verbal message.

Robert Rasberry and Laura Lemoine point out the importance of feedback when they say:

> In interpersonal communication the knowledge gained by feedback is essential: Feedback tells us when our instructions are misunderstood, how our comments lack necessary relevancy, and how our nonverbal behavior contradicts what we say verbally. For feedback to be helpful to the person receiving it, information must be given clearly, be understood, be accepted, and be usable in making changes to both verbal and nonverbal messages.[7]

SUGGESTIONS FOR IMPROVEMENT

In order to become an effective listener, the following suggestions are given.

Take time to listen. Listen for information, suggestions, complaints, and feelings. Since you may not comprehend and store every word in your memory, you can obtain main ideas, pros and cons, key words, facts, and opinions. Be able to distinguish opinions from facts.

Control the physical environment as much as possible. If conditions are uncontrollable, place yourself in a strategic point with as few distractions as possible.

Be prepared physically and mentally for the appropriate situation. If you are

in an organizational meeting, staff meeting, one-to-one interchange, or group discussion, do your homework before the interchange. Survey the particular encounter and prepare for any new terminology and background information about the persons, company, organization, or issues. Have an open mind—listen to a person completely before passing judgment or preparing your rebuttal. The ability to learn from others is a continuous process.

Be organized. Take notes if it is necessary. However, take only main points, and you will remember the secondary ones if you have listened effectively. Use the "spare" time effectively by organizing your own thoughts on the particular topic as you listen.

Notice the nonverbal communications of the speaker. Expressions, gestures, and voice inflections are ways of ascertaining implied meanings. (Nonverbal communication is covered in more detail in Chapter 3.)

Finally, *be alert and give your full attention* to the speaker. It takes two to engage in a communication interaction—a speaker and a listener. The moment a listener assumes the role of a sender, the listening process has ended for that person and the two of you have exchanged roles. Both must assume responsibility for the success of that interaction.

The Starns' Wines, Inc. Case[8]

The Starns' Wines, Inc. Case illustrates many poor listening habits by all of the participants. As you read through it, jot down as many of the poor listening habits as you can. Also take note of the different forms of feedback and how (or if) they were interpreted correctly (or at all).

Background

Established in 1965, the Starns' Winery overlooks the beautiful Alexander Valley in northern Sonoma County, California. Using money he had saved and dreams he couldn't put aside, Jason Starns, then 39, broke ground for the winery he hoped would produce some of the finest wines ever made.

In 1965 and 1966, Starns and his assistant, Robert Swinzel, worked vigorously selecting the proper grape varieties, testing the soil, and measuring rainfall and temperature variances in an effort to determine the best possible location for the Starns' vineyards. Endless months preparing and planting the vineyards followed.

Since it would take two or three years of nurturing the vineyards before the grapes would be mature enough to make wine, Starns and Swinzel carefully selected grapes from other vineyards in the area to produce wine.

In the fall of 1967, the first Cabernet Sauvignon and Chardonnay wines were produced by the Starns' Winery and placed in small French oak barrels for the long fermentation process necessary for truly great wines.

When the vineyards planted by Starns were mature enough to be harvested, grapes from these vineyards were used to produce the two great wines which Starns specialized in. This guaranteed the Starns family the year-to-year consistency they wished to maintain in their wines.

Other family members became involved in Starns' Wines, Inc., as it was eventually named, as the years passed. William Starns, Jason's oldest son, currently runs the marketing department at the winery, while Shannon Starns assists the chief winemaker, Swinzel.

With the help of Swinzel and his family, Jason Starns' Premium Cabernet Sauvignons and Chardonnays have become known worldwide as two truly great wines. The 1970, '72 and '75 Cabernets all have won numerous gold medals in major wine competitions both in the United States and abroad.

Although Starns' Winery produces only about 40,000 cases of its two wines, the company has seen fantastic success and growth in its 20-year history (see Figures 12–2 and 12–3). The winery's main concern has always been to maintain "quality in the bottle" and let the price fall where it may. Starns' wines retail in the $14–20 range, while most California varieties sell in the $5–10 price range.

Currently, the company produces only the two wines spoken of earlier, Cabernet and Chardonnay. These two grape varieties are known and

---

FIGURE 12–2   Cases of Wine Sold, 1967–1985

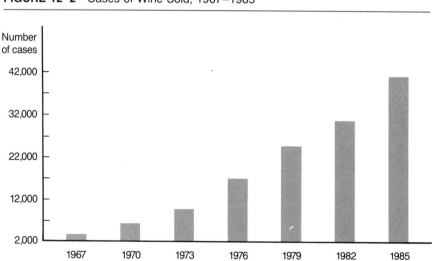

FIGURE 12–3   Wine Sales, 1967–1985

respected worldwide as two of the highest quality, which is why Starns has chosen to produce only these two. Current production mix of the two wines is shown in Figure 12–4.

Company Organization

Today, the CEO and President of Starns' Wines, Inc. is still Jason Starns. The vice president is Frank Jones, 45, a financial wizard who joined Starns over seven years ago. William Starns, 28, is vice president of mar-

---

FIGURE 12–4   Sales Mix

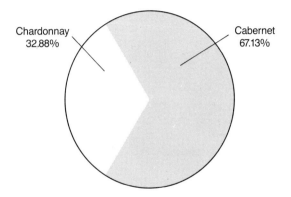

keting, while Shannon Starns assists Robert Swinzel, 58, in the winemaking department. There are also departments at Starns' for distribution, finance, and research and development. See Figure 12–5 for an organizational chart.

New Wine at Starns'?

In 1986, William Starns noticed that a new category of wines was catching the interest of the American public. "Blush" wines, as the category is labeled, are technically white wines made from red grapes. The process involves removal of the grape skins early in the fermentation process allowing limited skin contact and a lighter tasting wine.

William called a meeting of the top executives to introduce an idea he had formulated. Present at the meeting were his father Jason, Swinzel, Shannon Starns, Frank Jones, and two local vineyard owners who had expressed an interest in the project.

"We have an idea that may revolutionize our company," William Starns said as he opened the meeting. "In the coming 12 months we could sell two to three times as much wine as we've ever sold before."

As he spoke, William noticed Swinzel whispering to Shannon Starns. This continued throughout William's presentation.

FIGURE 12–5   Organizational Chart

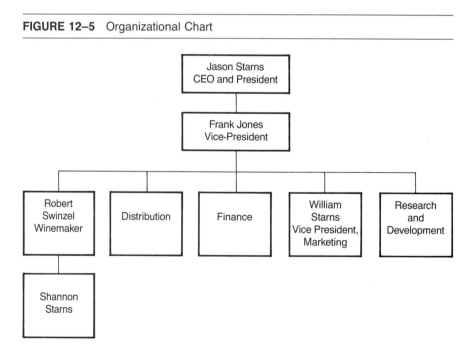

"With the help of these two gentlemen I've asked to join us today, I have discovered an area of the wine industry that we can't afford to over-look," continued the younger Starns. "Last year, over 100,000 cases of blush wines were produced in Sonoma County alone. We could reap a bonanza from this category by producing our own blush wine."

As William finished his statement, Jones looked up from his notetak-ing and inquired, "Is this blush wine profitable based on your research?"

As the financial discussion continued, Shannon's attention focused on the noisy truck hauling grapes past the boardroom window. The sight of the grapes reminded her of the weekly status reports she must have ready by Friday.

Discussions between the vineyard owners and the executives of Starns' continued for over an hour. One of the vineyard owners began to explain the enormous quantity of grapes available to the prospective winemakers, but Swinzel spoke out: "You don't know the first thing about making wine! Owning a vineyard full of zinfandel grapes doesn't make you the world's foremost authority."

At this point, Jason Starns, CEO, felt that the discussion had become too heated to accomplish anything, and he asked for adjournment for the day.

That evening, Frank Jones and some friends met for dinner. While looking at the restaurant's wine list, Frank noticed a blush wine by Ster-ling vineyards. He mentioned to one of his companions that Starns' was investigating the possibility of producing a similar wine. "These wines seem to have a broad appeal," Jones said. "They are light in taste and semisweet in nature. Most of the ones on the market are priced under $6."

While Jones was speaking, his friend fidgeted with his napkin and wondered where the waitress was with his drink.

The following morning, Swinzel arrived at the winery early and ran into William Starns in the hall. "I thought your comments yesterday were unnecessarily harsh. . . " William began. Swinzel turned and walked away.

The prospect of producing a new wine continued to be discussed among the executives of the company in the weeks that followed. William, frustrated with the long wait, burst into his father's office and said, "I think we've put this decision off long enough. I think we should begin production right away."

"I don't care what you think," Jason replied firmly. "Neither a quality wine nor a quality business decision should be made quickly."

Objective

The case illustrates some of the most frequent communication problems associated with listening behavior. Throughout the case, examples of poor

listening behavior crop up. Making an early evaluation of what's being said, physical distractions, lack of interest in the subject matter, and feeling that the speaker lacks credibility on the topic being discussed are all common listening problems.

Since executives spend at least 90 percent of their time communicating with people, and approximately 63 percent of that time listening this is an important area in the field of communication.[9]

CASE QUESTIONS

1. What are your overall impressions of the way the various members of Starns' Winery handled their listening responsibilities?

2. How could the listening behaviors exhibited in this case be improved?

3. How did each person's preconceived ideas about those they were listening to affect their listening behavior?

CASE DISCUSSION

Stop Talking   As William Starns opened the board meeting, he noticed Robert Swinzel whispering to Shannon Starns, apparently in response to what was being said by William. Consider the following admonitions: "There is no way in the world you can be an effective listener if you're talking,"[10] and "Many times there is much more to be gained by listening than by talking."[11]

Ask Questions   As William Starns completed his introduction concerning the new wine, Frank Jones was already preparing a question to ask Starns. This is one of the best ways to show the speaker that you are listening. Ask questions.

Distractions   Noisy trucks passing the window of the boardroom captured Shannon's attention while the financial side of the wine question was being discussed. "Good listeners tend to adjust quickly to any kind of abnormal situation; poor listeners tend to tolerate bad conditions."[12] Block out any and all distractions if you are to become an effective listener.

Debating   "You don't know the first thing about making wine!" Robert Swinzel yelled. What Swinzel's problem appears to be is that he simply doesn't think that a vineyard owner (i.e., farmer in his mind) is credible enough to be explaining the benefits of producing a new wine. Something the vineyard owner has said has set Swinzel off and he's apparently closed his mind off from what's being said.

"Effective listeners keep an open mind to what is being said."[13] Effective listeners try to identify and to rationalize the words or phrases that

are most upsetting emotionally. Swinzel has put a fence around his mind because he feels that "I know the wine business and you don't."

Disinterest While at dinner with his friends it is obvious that Jones has lost the attention of at least one companion. This is more of a general lack of interest in the subject matter than anything else. "Bad listeners usually judge the subject dry after the first few sentences. Once this decision is made, it serves to rationalize any and all inattention."[14]

Evaluation–Judgment Swinzel had no desire to listen to William in the winery's hallway. He had committed yet another common listening fault known as evaluation-judgment. "It is a well-known fact that a speaker can gain or lose his audience in the first 30 seconds of his presentation," writes Jud Morris in *The Art of Listening*. "Human beings have an irresistible tendency to judge before they really understand."[15]

Swinzel evaluated what William was saying and judged it to be something he was not interested in hearing. The next few sentences spoken by William might have been of some interest to Swinzel, but he walked away after judging the early content of Starns' message.

Private Planning In addition to the noisy trucks distracting Shannon, the sight of the grapes also reminded her of the weekly reports she needed to prepare—when she would be able to complete them, whether they would be late, and what the consequences might be. She may have missed many valuable points in William's presentation and the discussion.

IDCWYT "*I don't care what you think*," Jason replied firmly to his son. Even though his son, William, might have researched the question of producing a new wine, and may have numerous points that backed up his statement, his attitude and tone of voice led him into trouble.

The IDCWYT syndrome (using acronyms developed by Eric Berne in his book, *Games People Play*) occurs when the listener has made up his mind about what it is you are saying. There is probably nothing to say that will overcome this "I don't care what you think" attitude.

SUMMARY

Listening is more than just hearing; it is the attachment of meaning to symbols. It should include a responsiveness to the sender and it implies a closure—a complete loop in the communication cycle. The necessity for effective listening is well documented in research studies and is seen and experienced in our everyday lives. Many studies show that poor listening is the single most important cause of problems in organizations; and, our own experiences in everyday life support the importance of good listening in our interpersonal relationships.

Casual or marginal listening, when listening is secondary to other activities, occurs most frequently during our daily activities. Projective or empathic listening (the ability to put ourselves in another's position) is

often difficult because of our lack of genuine sensitivity to others. Attentive listening is when we process the message, give it meaning, and attach a "need to know" to the message.

Listening is affected by our biological mechanism, the physical environment, our frame of reference to the other person, attitude, and our perception of "the need to know." These factors may lead to a variety of barriers to effective listening: physical distractions, mental or emotional distractions, detouring, and debating.

As a sender, one method to evaluate the listening of others is the feedback we get. As a receiver, one method to show that we are listening is the feedback that we give. Feedback provides closure and completes the cycle in the communication process.

We can improve our listening by taking time to listen, controlling the physical environment, preparing ourselves physically and mentally for the situation, using our "spare" time effectively, being responsive to nonverbal cues of the sender, and by being alert and giving our full attention to the sender and the situation. A mental response to this question can focus our attention and give added meaning to the message coming our way: *Why is this person saying this, to me, at this time?* The answer should provide the reason why we should be an attentive listener.

DISCUSSION QUESTIONS

1. Differentiate clearly between hearing and listening. Why is it important for communicators to be aware of these differences?

2. Describe in detail the three general types of listening. Which type of listening should be a characteristic of an effective business communicator?

3. Describe four factors that influence listening ability.

4. List the various categories of barriers to effective listening. Explain two of the categories in detail.

5. How do both the sender and the receiver of a message control and affect listening?

6. Define detouring and debating as barriers to listening. What should a listener watch for in order to avoid these barriers?

7. What specific guidelines should a manager use to become an effective listener?

EXERCISES

1. As a third party to a conversation of your choice, observe the listening habits of the two participants. Did they interrupt? Debate (too soon)? What were their nonverbal behaviors?

2. Your instructor will read a short passage and then ask questions. What will be/ was your listening behavior in this instance (knowing in advance you would be questioned) *versus* a class lecture? Is there, or should there be, any difference?

NOTES

[1]Ralph G. Nichols, "Listening: Questions and Problems," *Quarterly Journal of Speech* 33 (February 1947), p. 83.

[2]Ronald B. Adler and George Rodman, *Understanding Human Communication* (New York: Holt, Rinehart & Winston, 1985), p. 74.

[3]Paul T. Rankin, "Listening Ability," *Proceedings of the Ohio State Educational Conference* 9th Annual Session, Columbus, Ohio (1929), pp. 172–83.

[4]Ralph G. Nichols and Thomas R. Lewis, *Listening and Speaking: A Guide to Effective Oral Communication* (Dubuque, Iowa: Wm. C. Brown, 1954), p. 2, and Richard Hubbell, *Television Programming and Production* (New York: Murray Hill Books, 1945), p. 12.

[5]Carl R. Rogers, *On Becoming a Person* (Boston: Houghton Mifflin, 1961), pp. 330–31.

[6]Ernest G. Bormann, William S. Howell, Ralph G. Nichols, and George L. Shapiro, *Interpersonal Communication in the Modern Organization* (Englewood Cliffs, N.J.: Prentice-Hall, 1982), pp. 123–27.

[7]Robert W. Rasberry and Laura Fletcher Lemoine, *Effective Managerial Communication* (Boston: Kent Publishing, 1986), p. 168.

[8]The Starns' Wines, Inc. Case was prepared by Kent Starr, M.B.A. candidate, University of Arkansas, April 1986.

[9]William F. Keefe, *Listen Management* (New York: McGraw-Hill, 1971), pp. 9–10.

[10]Keith Davis, *The Dynamics of Organizational Behavior*, 3rd ed. (New York: McGraw-Hill, 1967), p. 334.

[11]Jud Morris, *The Art of Listening* (Boston: Cahners Books, 1967), pp. 141–42.

[12]Davis, *Dynamics of Behavior*, p. 334.

[13]Ralph G. Nichols, "Listening Is a Part Skill," *Nation's Business* (July 1957), pp. 56–60.

[14]Ibid.

[15]Morris, *Art of Listening*, pp. 39–60.

[16]Ibid., pp. 101–6.

SUGGESTED READINGS

BROWNELL, JUDI. "Listening: A Powerful Management Tool." *Supervisory Management* 29, no. 10 (October 1984), pp 35–39.

CALLARMAN, WILLIAM G., and WILLIAM W. McCARTNEY. "Identifying and Overcoming Listening Problems." *Supervisory Management* 30, no. 3 (March 1985), pp. 38–42.

CRAIG, MARY BETH VASILE. "Listen, Really Listen to Your Members." *Association Management* 34 (September 1982), pp. 79–80.

POWELL, JON T. "Stress Listening: Coping with Angry Confrontations." *Personnel Journal* (May 1986), pp. 27–30.

SHIELDS, DOYLE E. "Listening: A Small Investment, A Big Payoff." *Supervisory Management* 29, no. 7 (July 1984), pp. 18–22.

STREET, RICHARD I., JR.; ROBERT M. BRADY; and RAYMOND LEE. "Evaluative Response to Communicators: The Effects of Speech Rate, Sex, and Interaction Context." *Western Journal of Speech Communications* 48, no. 1 (Winter 1984), pp. 14–27.

Chapter 13

Principles and Types

of Interviewing

Chapter 13 Case

You are the district manager for a major national electronics firm. Part of your job is to recruit three new sales reps from the state university. Your company requires engineers for these positions and prefers some business background as well. It is important to do a good job in selecting the new employees, both for the company and for your own career. How would you go about it? What arrangements would you make with the school? What kind of questions would you ask the students you'll be interviewing? Since the interviewees are going to tell you what they think you want to hear, how can you discover their talents, their ambitions, and whether they would really fit in with your firm?

INTRODUCTION

The interview, often defined as a conversation with a purpose, is one of the most important interpersonal communication techniques available to the business communicator. Pearson defines the interview as a "formal and preplanned form of interpersonal communication which has a specific purpose, is well organized, and involves two parties who ask and answer questions."[1]

As with any communication interaction, no two interviews are ever alike. Each is carried through to success or failure by the unique contribution of the participants. Consider a personnel manager conducting screening interviews for new employees. The interviewer is faced with certain constraints, such as the criteria that any prospective employee must meet, time limitations for the interview, and physical surroundings. Also, the interviewee brings to the interview situation his or her own attitudes and feelings about many things (the company, the job, even the economic situation of the country). The interviewee also has certain

knowledge of the company and job, attitudes toward certain subjects, feelings, and even biases. Thus, the parties create an interaction or relationship that is different in every interview situation.

To better understand how this relationship develops, we turn our attention to more specific purposes of interviews, the different types of interviews, some of the basic principles for effective interviewing, the planning that must take place before an interview, and some of the potential problems that may arise during the interview.

PURPOSES

The *purpose* of an interview contributes to the development of the relationship between the parties. Three basic purposes, or some combination, for most interviews are: (1) to secure information, (2) to give information, and (3) to influence behavior.

Securing Information

Securing information is the primary purpose of job analysis, polling (attitude and opinion seeking), and separation and post-exit interviews. In each of these cases, the interviewer is seeking information about the interviewee's level of knowledge, skills, attitudes, and feelings. The end result of these interviews is to summarize and categorize the data necessary to develop standards, determine trends, identify problem areas, or propose changes.

Giving Information

Giving information is the main purpose for induction, progress and appraisal, training, and retirement interviews. Here, the interviewer attempts to give information about company policies and procedures, gives explanations for certain evaluations, explains procedures and methods, or identifies information that will affect the interviewee and his or her relationship with the organization.

Giving and Securing Information

To give and to secure information are equally important purposes in employment, transfer and promotion, and complaint or grievance interviews. The amount of time spent in these interviews may be equally divided between the interviewer, who explains hiring procedures, company philosophy, differences in job categories, salaries, and so forth, and the interviewee, who discusses goals, strengths, or dissatisfaction with a product or company procedure.

Influencing Behavior

Influencing behavior, while a separate and very important purpose, should be an avowed goal only after securing and giving complete and accurate information. This is a crucial purpose of disciplinary or reprimand and counseling interviews. It is also the purpose of sales interviews (in the sense of influencing the behavior of an individual or group to purchase a product or service).

Although each of these may be a primary purpose for an interview, many situations call for two or all three to be met. An interview contributes to an organization as a vehicle to gain information, to help understand attitudes and relationships, and to suggest changes or modify behavior. Properly conducted, the interview may be a powerful technique capable of detecting incomplete or inaccurate information, developing an accurate information base, and getting access to material that is not otherwise available. Improperly handled, the interview may become a source of inaccuracies and distortions that seriously impede the flow of communication and, ultimately, achievement of the purpose.

PRINCIPLES FOR EFFECTIVE INTERVIEWING

Attitude

The emphasis given to the words **interaction** and **relationship** is quite intentional. The dynamic interaction that takes place between the parties of the interview and the resulting relationship are the keys to an effective interview. The attitude of the interviewer is one of the most important factors in this relationship. If the interviewer views each interview as a different situation and each interviewee as an individual, the interview will take place in a positive and constructive atmosphere. But if the interviewer has become callous to the job and views the interviewee as "just another 30 minutes" before quitting time, the interview is doomed to failure regardless of the interviewee's level of knowledge, skills, or personality characteristics.

The interviewee's attitude may be equally important in many interview situations. In the employment interview, it can be assumed that the interviewee has voluntarily chosen to be interviewed and consequently will arrive wanting to put his or her best foot forward. In a disciplinary interview, the situation may be quite different. The employee-interviewee may be very defensive or even hostile during the interview, and attitude becomes an additional burden for the interviewer to overcome.

Climate

A second principle for effective interviewing is the creation of a positive, constructive climate in which the interaction can develop. This atmo-

sphere may be physical in nature (a pleasant room, comfortable sitting and writing arrangements, attractive surroundings, lack of interference), or it may be a "mental set" or an extension of one or both parties' attitudes. If each party not only hears what the other says, but listens and responds, an atmosphere is created for an interaction to become a basis of mutual confidence.

Orientation

It is important that the interviewer orients the interviewee. What is the purpose of the interview? How is it to proceed? Will the interviewer give information first? What is expected of the interviewee? Knowing these things at the start of an interview organizes the limited time that may be available and gives both parties some guidelines of what to expect and how to proceed.

Frame of Reference

A fourth factor that contributes to the effectiveness of the interview is the system of symbols used by both parties. Certainly a common language is essential, and the more common the frame of reference between the interviewer and the interviewee, the greater is the likelihood that effective communication will take place. Words, symbols, job functions, and technologies that are commonplace in a company, but may not be known to the interviewee, should be fully defined and explained by the interviewer. (You may want to review "frame of reference" in Chapter 4.)

Objectivity

Objectivity is essential to an effective interview. The interviewer must strive to be just and fair in the evaluations of the interviewee, and train to be a good listener and to be open-minded and objective. Objectivity will be discussed in more detail as one of the more serious potential problems of interviewing.

TYPES OF INTERVIEWS: AN OVERVIEW

Personnel interviews probably account for the greatest number of interviews in business today. There are other types—problem-solving, decision-making, sales, public relations, labor relations, psychiatric, and legal, but our main interest is personnel interviews, with special attention given to employment, appraisal, complaint, and reprimand interviews. The following is intended to help you "walk through" a series of interviews.

You are about to graduate from college and you would like a job in which you use your education, training, and experiences. You want a

company in which you can take pride, one concerned with the welfare of its employees, and that offers opportunity for advancement. These may be very general goals and ideas for most graduating students. You may also have some very specific criteria for making a final decision (salary requirements, geographic location, etc.). How do you go about finding a company, a job, a location?

The **employment** or **hiring interview** is one of the most widely used forms of oral communication. This type of interview is used to gain information that cannot be obtained by other means. Initially, you participate in a preliminary interview (usually 20 or 30 minutes long) that may be conducted on campus at the university placement service or at the location of the company. If you pass the initial screening in the preliminary interview, you may be invited to one of the regional or district offices of the organization to participate in a second or even a series of interviews.

If you decide to join an organization and report to work, you will probably go through an orientation session. Quite often, this takes the form of an **induction** interview to orient the new employee to the company, its policies, procedures, techniques, standards, history, products, sales, and services. Anything that you should want or need to know to make you a well-informed employee should be included in the induction interview.

After 30, 60, or 90 days, an **appraisal** or **progress review interview** may be scheduled. This may be conducted by your immediate supervisor or a representative of the personnel department. The purpose of this interview is to offer feedback to you, to offer suggestions for improvement, and to get an evaluation from you regarding your adjustment to the company and job.

At some point during your tenure with the organization, the company may decide to poll all the employees or some group of them about some subject. This can take the form of a questionnaire or a **polling interview.** The questionnaire is used if the questions asked are clearly stated, short, and if the responses can be conveniently categorized. The interview is preferred if the questions are open-ended (not easily categorized, and more detail is wanted). The purpose of this interview is to gain information, attitudes, ideas, and feelings from many people on specific topics.

The **job analysis interview** may be scheduled routinely or only on occasion. Its purpose is to gain information about the nature of a job, what is being done, what should be done, what changes could be suggested, what relationships need to be reevaluated, and what the standards are and whether they need to be altered.

If you have made adequate progress in your position, you have a **promotion** or **transfer interview** to secure information from you and give you information about the new position, the nature of the job, the level of responsibility, and the location. It is at this time in your career that you

are faced with many evaluations and decisions, especially if the promotion means a new location. Where am I going? Where do I want to be in five years? How will the new position affect my future, my family, and my relationship with the organization? These are difficult questions to answer and should not be approached on a crisis basis, but instead faced early in your planning so it will be easier for you to evaluate the total consequences when this interview situation arises.

After accepting a promotion and/or transfer, a **training interview** may be in order. This interview is similar to the induction interview, but usually does not include the basic information about the company. The training interview instructs a new employee (or even a senior employee) about a new job. This type of interview is also very common when instructing employees (individually or collectively) about new or different safety standards or equipment or policies.

On occasion, you may find yourself in conflict with the company rules, regulations, or standards. A **reprimand** or **disciplinary interview,** combined with a **counseling interview,** may be appropriate. This interview is to allow the interviewer to secure complete and accurate information. In addition, the interviewer should attempt to influence your behavior in such a way that the conflict is reduced or eliminated.

The **complaint** or **grievance interview** combines gaining information, giving information, and perhaps even influencing behavior. The person who is complaining wants to give information—what is wrong with a product, a service, a fellow employee, a company standard. The interviewer also may give information—an explanation of why, what, or where something was done. Either party may ultimately seek to influence the behavior of the other or to cause some action to be taken.

A **separation** or **post-exit interview** may be requested by the company when you leave the organization. This interview may take place before you actually terminate employment (separation) or after you terminate employment (post-exit). The purpose is basically the same: to gain information about why you are leaving and to get suggestions about improvements that could be made. Occasionally, employees are not entirely honest in their responses in these interviews for fear of reprisals. Extreme care must be taken by the interviewer so that the interviewee feels free from fears.

The **retirement interview,** a final personnel function, is designed to acquaint the new or potential retiree with benefits and services that may be offered or given by the company. Retirement benefits in the form of annuities, life insurance, hospitalization, office space, or reduced prices for company products become of primary concern to the new retiree. It is simple courtesy on the part of an organization to make sure that each former employee is fully aware of these benefits.

Figure 13–1 identifies the different types of personnel interviews and their primary purpose.

FIGURE 13–1 Personnel Interviews

Type of Interview	*Primary Purpose*
Employment/hiring	Secure/give information
Induction/orientation	Give information
Progress/appraisal	Give information
Polling	Secure information
Job analysis	Secure information
Transfer/promotion	Secure/give information
Training	Give information
Disciplinary/reprimand	Secure/give/influence
Counseling	Influence behavior
Complaint/grievance	Secure/give/influence
Separation/post-exit	Secure information
Retirement	Give information

STRUCTURE OF THE INTERVIEW

The interview can be casual, structured, or focused.

The Casual Interview

The completely casual interview is most common in psychiatric interviews where the interviewer is attempting to draw out the interviewee. The end result of the interview is usually unknown at the start, and the content that emerges during the interview determines the time and the direction of the interview. Time is not a constraining factor during the casual interview—this type of interview may take hours to complete. (In fact, it may never be complete but merely extend into another interview.)

The Structured Interview

At the other extreme, in the patterned or structured interview the questions are carefully worded and ordered. Two factors suggest or demand the use of the structured interview: (1) time is a crucial factor for the interviewer, and (2) large numbers of people are to be interviewed and those in charge of the interviews want to reduce the interviewer variability in asking questions. Hence, in a structured interview the sequence of questions and the questions themselves will be the same. This may be especially important when there are two or more interviewers conducting many interviews during a short time.

The Focused Interview

The focused or planned interview allows for both casual *and* structured approaches. During the employment interview, for example, the inter-

viewer may want or need to ask some standard questions while allowing for free interaction with the interviewee. Thus, certain general areas of interest are covered, but not necessarily with the same wording or sequence as a previous or following interview. This is also true of most induction, progress and appraisal, transfer and promotion, training, and complaint or grievance interviews.

DOMINANCE OF THE INTERVIEW

Directive

The amount of dominance exerted by either party during the interview can greatly affect the relationship between them. If an interviewee leaves an employment interview feeling that he has not had the opportunity to ask any questions, he may develop a different feeling about the company, the job, and certainly the interviewer than if he had been allowed to raise some issues that were not covered by the interviewer. This dominance by one party is a directive interview and is most common in polling interviews. It is used in highly patterned or structured interviews.

Nondirective

The nondirective interview, in which neither party dominates, is more characteristic of the casual interview. During this interchange, there is complete give-and-take and freedom of exchange of information, ideas, and feelings. The problem with a nondirective interview is that neither party may feel that very much was accomplished.

Combination

The combination approach usually is used in conjunction with the planned or focused interview. One party may dominate for a short time, asking very specific questions. Once a series of items has been sufficiently covered, the other party may assume the leadership and move into other areas of concern.

Figure 13–2 identifies the types of interviews and the most common structure and form of dominance associated with each.

GENERAL PROBLEMS OF INTERVIEWING

There are many variables that can affect the interview. An interview is an interaction between people and, as such, is subject to many errors. Some errors are random and vary from one interview to another; others consis-

FIGURE 13–2 Types, Structure, and Dominance during the Interview

Types	Structure	Dominance
Employment/hiring	Focused	Combination
Induction/orientation	Focused	Combination
Progress/appraisals	Focused/ structured	Combination/directive
Polling	Structured	Directive
Job analysis	Focused/ structured	Combination/directive
Transfer/promotion	Focused/casual	Combination
Training	Focused/ structured	Combination/directive
Disciplinary/reprimand/ counseling	Focused	Combination
Complaint/grievance	Focused	Combination
Separation/post-exit	Focused/casual	Combination
Retirement	Focused/ structured	Combination/directive

tently affect the interview results. Gottlieb draws the analogy between the interview and a chess game when he says:

> During the opening game of a chess match, the players focus their attention on the control of the center of the board. Each player attempts to discover the other's strategy and to place pieces in effective locations for future development. . . . The opening-game phase of the interview has many of the same characteristics. As in chess, this is an extremely important part of the interview because the format for the entire encounter will be established here.[2]

This section will identify some of the most frequent and serious problems common to interviews. Other more specific pitfalls will be enumerated in Chapter 14.

Interviewer Bias

Interviewer bias is one of the most troublesome problems affecting an interview. Each individual comes to the interview with certain knowledge, education, attitudes, goals, objectives, likes, and dislikes. In addition, there are certain factual states associated with each of the parties to the interview: age, sex, and ethnic background. These states cannot be debated; however, they can be a source of bias. The fact that an interviewee has a Spanish surname or is Catholic has little to do with whether the person should be hired or disciplined, or whether a complaint is justified. These factual states, where known or observed, must be dealt with simply as demographic data, and the interviewer must constantly be on guard to avoid using this information in the decision-making process.

A person's goals or objectives can also present a serious source of bias

based on the perception or interpretation of the interviewer. If an interviewer asks the rather common question, "Where do you want to be in five years?" and the interviewee responds, "I would like to be vice-president of the company," the interviewer may interpret this statement as characteristic of a very confident, well-trained, enthusiastic, hard-working individual and mentally or verbally praise this determination. On the other hand, the interviewer may see this comment as reflective of an insolent, unknowing, discourteous young buck. Before either interpretation is made, further probing of the interviewee's goals, objectives, and motivations are needed.

Stereotyping

A special form of interviewer bias is stereotyping and the interviewer who gives in to first impressions is usually guilty of this fault. If a supervisor does not like long hair on men, she may tend to rate a man with long hair lower than men who have short hair, regardless of how the individual actually performs his work. Although an interviewer's experience may suggest that there is a close association between some physical trait and a personality "type," the interviewer must constantly keep in mind that each interview is different and each interviewee is different. Several common misassumptions include: red hair means a fiery temper, nervous behavior indicates emotional maladjustment, or neatness in dress and appearance suggest neatness in work habits.

Halo Effect

The "halo effect" is closely associated with stereotyping. This is the tendency to rate a person either high or low on *all* points of his or her performance because the rater likes or dislikes *one* aspect of the interviewee's responses or performance. The interviewee who is neat in dress and appearance *may* have neat work habits, but to rate that person high on dependability and cooperation without supporting evidence is an example of the halo effect.

Probing

The inability to probe is a problem of the novice interviewer. The untrained or novice interviewer may be overly concerned with the amount of time available for an interview or with being sure all questions are covered. The lack of appropriate probing usually can be traced to an interviewer who is more concerned with the interview mechanics than with the interaction that should take place between the parties. The trained interviewer will probe and pry (in a friendly and professional manner). He will find out not only *what* the interviewee did on the previous job but

also *how, why,* and *how well* he or she did it. Probing requires listening with sincere interest and responding with relevant follow-up questions or answers.

Record Keeping

Errors in record keeping can create serious problems for both parties. Many interviewers use an interview guide to jot down notes, ideas, and evaluations during the interview as a record of what took place. Many interviewers prefer to record their observations and evaluations after the interview. The interviewer should never rely on memory, especially after conducting several interviews. It is too easy to confuse evaluations with different persons and the consequence of this action could be disastrous.

Questioning

The nature of the communications between the interviewer and interviewee can result in obtaining inaccurate or unreliable information. For example, the form of a question can have a significant effect on the answer obtained. The change of an article in a question such as "Did you see *the* umbrella?" instead of "Did you see *an* umbrella?" can affect the reliability of an answer.

THE GROUP INTERVIEW

Most interviews are conducted as a one-on-one situation; there is one interviewer and one interviewee. Occasionally, and usually for specific reasons, an organization may conduct group interviews. These interviews are also used to accomplish one or more of the purposes already discussed, *and* to create a stressful situation.

Instead of separate interviews, two or three new college graduates are gathered around a table, given a discussion topic, and told to "have a go" at it. Company executives sit on the sidelines and watch how well the candidates use words, think, persuade, and win respect from the others around the table. The executives grade the candidates independently, then later compare notes and decide whom to hire.

In another form of a group or stress interview, a group interviews a single person, asking questions so rapidly that the person does not have time to think or express opinions. This interaction is designed to create conflict and raise anxieties in the person being interviewed. Because it injects a new element of human interaction into the interviewing process, the group or stress interview stands apart from other types of interviews.

Objectives

The objectives of the group interview are to observe how the interviewee functions, mentally and physically, under situations of stress. The immediate purpose may be simply to test the stability of the interviewee, or it may be to simulate future stressful situations that the interviewee may encounter. In some cases, it may be used to verify information when the truthfulness of the interviewee is in doubt. The use of stress interviews can be observed in the widely divergent areas of the military, education, and business.

During World War II, stress interviews were used by both sides in the selection of strategic military personnel. The German military command selected officers on the basis of an evaluation by a board of psychological examiners. Such interviews usually lasted up to two days under varying conditions of stress. The objective was to obtain an evaluation of intelligence, the use of planning and clear thinking, energy, expressive movements, and the limits of capacity.

Stress interviews were also used by the U.S. Office of Strategic Services during World War II to discover how people would behave under conditions of extreme stress. Interviews were conducted under conditions of intimidation, embarrassment, emotional stress, and physical exhaustion.[3] Following the subjection of American prisoners of war to brainwashing during the Korean War, stress interviewing has been included as a training device to prepare American military personnel to withstand comparable conditions.

The stress or board interview is also used in the academic world. Usually a committee conducts this type of interview, called an oral comprehensive examination, before granting an advanced degree. Also, some organizations use this method to screen candidates. One nonprofit foundation relies heavily on the board or group approach, while another uses a single interviewer who bombards the interviewee with questions.

A third area, and the one that is most important here, is the use of the group or stress interview in business—particularly in the hiring interview.

The primary goal of the stress interview is to evaluate attitudes and personality; to break through any pretenses an interviewee may have established. The premise that this interview can be evaluated—tested and measured—rests on the assumption that the interviewer is trained to identify these things and to relate them to the needs of the organization.

Types of Questions

During the stress interview many irrelevant questions may be asked. In fact, 50 to 90 percent of the questions may have nothing to do with the position or job for which the person is being interviewed. The open-

closed series of questions is used most commonly. The open question gives the interviewee an opportunity to explain thoughts and feelings: "How do you feel about your choice of major in school?" "What are your views on the U.S. foreign aid policy?" During the time the interviewee is responding, he or she is asked a closed question. This question, related to the open question, requires a specific response: "Do you like your choice of major?" "Do you agree with the U.S. foreign aid policy?" This type of questioning throws the interviewee off guard and shows how well the person adapts to the change in the situation.

Closely related to the open-closed questions is a series of direct-indirect questions: "Tell me about your university." "Tell me about this state's social welfare program." These questions, quite indirect, can be followed or interrupted by the direct ones: "Tell me about your courses or instructors or advising and registration practices in the college."

The either-or-question, also known as the double question, forces the interviewee to choose from a limited number of responses, usually two. "Do you prefer to paint or read?" "Would you rather be paid by salary or receive tips?" "Do you like to get up early in the morning or stay up late at night?" If the interviewee refuses to be trapped by the either-or question, it tends to show individuality. After all, there may be several shades of gray between the choices given.

Other Factors

In addition to the variety of questions that may be asked of the interviewee, the manner in which they are asked can provoke frustration. One common method is to bombard the applicant with questions. A series of four or five questions may be asked at once. Because the interviewee is unable to remember or have time to answer all of them, the one or two responded to identify the interviewee's main thoughts and give an indication of the person's interests. Physical disturbances are frequently used as additional nuisances during the group interview. The interviewer may walk around the room, and other people may appear and disappear in the room or make telephone calls. All of these may be distracting and frustrating to the interviewee, but are planned to help evaluate how well he or she maintains composure. Other items that may be used to determine stability, resourcefulness, and composure are: motor skill tests, brain puzzlers (with several solutions or with one solution), different geometric forms that must be put together in a single predetermined design, cryptograms, and mazes.

Evaluation

The philosophy behind the use of the group or stress interview by an organization must be carefully scrutinized. It should be based on defined

principles and goals. The success in achieving these goals is closely related to the competence of the interviewers, and to this end, the interviewers must be well trained. A significant reservation is raised because many interviewers do not possess the necessary experience. A further reservation is the difficulty of restoring mutual respect and rapport between the interviewer and interviewee after a group or stressful situation. It is important to end every interview on a positive note, and the possibility of doing this in group interviews seems in doubt. The interviewee may never feel quite the same and the injection of stress may extend beyond the immediate interview situation to affect future relationships among the people involved. Before an organization decides to use this form of interview, the advantages must clearly outweigh the disadvantages!

SUMMARY

The spectrum of personnel interviews ranges from the employment to the retirement interview. Between those two, one may find a variety of other interview situations: induction, appraisal, polling, job analysis, promotion, training, disciplinary and reprimand, and complaint or grievance. Special attention will be given in the next chapter to the most common interviews: employment, appraisal and progress review, complaint, and reprimand and counseling.

This chapter has identified some of the basic principles and problems of interviewing for both one-on-one and group settings. The purpose of the interview must be clear in the interviewer's mind. Is it to secure information, give information, influence behavior, or some combination? Once the purpose is determined, attention can be focused on developing a positive attitude, a supportive climate, an appropriate orientation, and objectivity. The interview is not complete, however, until the interviewer has converted all the raw information collected in the interview into some appropriate evaluation, plan, or decision.

DISCUSSION QUESTIONS

1. Compare the three basic purposes of interviews. Discuss the benefits of properly conducted interviews and the hazards of improperly conducted interviews.

2. Describe four factors that influence effective interviewing. Give an example of an interview situation that illustrates how each factor or principle affects the success of the interview.

3. What is meant by the "system of symbols" used by the interviewer and interviewee? How does this factor affect interview effectiveness?

4. From hiring interview to retirement interview, the typical employee encounters many different interview situations in a business firm. Briefly describe the progression of interviews from hiring to retirement that most employees encounter.

5. Interviews are generally structured in one of three ways. Compare and contrast each interview mode.

6. What does dominance in an interview mean? Discuss the differences between directive and nondirective interviews, and indicate interview situations in which each is appropriate.

7. List and define four of the most frequent and serious interview problems. Give an example to illustrate each problem type.

8. Describe three common but serious interview problems. What can be done to remedy the problems?

9. What are the characteristics of a stress interview? When and why are stress interviews employed? What safeguards might be used to ensure that this type of interview generates positive outcomes for both the company and the interviewee?

EXERCISES

1. Identify an organization of your choice (national, regional, local) for a possible employment interview. Develop a plan to research the company, product, services, location, and so forth. Carry out the plan and do the research.

2. Develop your own personal resume and cover letter. Vary both depending on making application to at least three organizations specializing in different products, services, and in different locations.

3. Assume you are recruiting/interviewing for a company of your choice. Develop a one- or two-page information brochure for the company, its products, and locations. Research the duties and responsibilities for two or three positions in the company. Plan a focused interview guide for each possible interview.

NOTES

[1]Judy C. Pearson, *Interpersonal Communication* (Glenview, Ill.: Scott, Foresman, 1983), p. 260.

[2]Marvin Gottlieb, *Interview* (New York: Longman, 1986), p. 17.

[3]Robert L. Kahn and Charles F. Cannell, *The Dynamics of Interviewing* (New York: John Wiley & Sons, 1957), pp. 175–76.

SUGGESTED READINGS

BAYNE, ROWAN. "Selecting the Selectors." *Personnel Management* 15 (June 1983), pp. 42–44.

DIPBOYE, ROBERT L. "Self-Fulfilling Prophecies of the Selection-Recruitment Interview." *Academy of Management Review* 7 (October 1982), pp. 579–86.

EDWARDS, MARK R. "OJQ Offers Alternative to Assessment Centers." *Public Personnel Management* 12 (Summer 1983), pp.146–55.

KIKOSKI, JOHN F., and JOSEPH A. LITTERER. "Effective Communication in the Performance Appraisal Interview." *Public Personnel Management* 12 (Spring 1983), pp. 33–42.

LITECKY, CHARLES R. "Better Interviewing Skills." *Journal of Systems Management* 36 (June 1985), p. 36.

MATHENY, PHILLIP R. "How to Hire a Winner." *Supervisory Management* 29 (May 1984), pp. 12–15.

PALMER, ROBIN. "A Sharper Focus for the Panel Interview." *Personnel Management* 15 (May 1983), pp. 34–37.

"Performance Appraisals." *Personnel Administrator* (March 1984), entire issue.

Chapter 14

Applications of Interviews

Chapter 14 Case

You are a new supervisor for a large government agency, and it's time for your first round of annual performance appraisals. You are apprehensive about it, but you've been to school to learn the nuts and bolts of the process. You know what forms to use and how to advise employees of their grievance rights, if that becomes necessary. All things considered, you're pretty lucky. You have a great unit—all hard-working, enthusiastic people who do good work—all except Joe. Joe's work has been below standard during the entire time you've supervised him. To top that off, he's belligerent and hard to deal with. It's going to be a difficult interview, but it's got to be done. What type of preparations should you make? What kind of documentation should you have available?

INTRODUCTION

Most of the principles of interviewing that were discussed in Chapter 13 are applicable to any of the interview situations enumerated. Here we will focus on four of the most common and frequent types of interviews: employment and hiring, appraisal and progress review, complaint, and reprimand.

It is critical that the interviewer form objective judgments and evaluations in each of these situations. The interviewer—with her knowledge, experience, interviewing technique, and ability to analyze and evaluate—is the major determinant in accepting or rejecting a candidate for employment, in evaluating an employee for receiving a merit raise, in evaluating and responding to a complaint, and in initiating some change in the behavior of an employee. With better and more effective interview procedures, the skilled interviewer can reduce the number of pitfalls.

THE EMPLOYMENT AND HIRING INTERVIEW

Organizations are faced constantly with employees who voluntarily quit, employees who are discharged, deaths, and transfers. Consequently, the organization must continually replenish itself with new employees. A wrong hiring decision can be one of the most frustrating experiences to confront a personnel administrator and can cause problems for many years. The majority of poor hiring decisions can be eliminated by having an orderly and predetermined procedure established by the personnel department. The steps in the procedure generally include recruiting, screening, investigation, and the interview.

Recruiting

A single interview that takes place on a college campus or in the office of a personnel director does not take place within a vacuum. The organization is always on the lookout for a good employee and its search may encompass many avenues and several weeks or months. Employment agencies can serve as a convenient source for new employees. Agencies serve as brokers, receiving notice of vacancies from organizations and maintaining information on many applicants, to provide a service of matching applicants and jobs. They may include testing and evaluation as part of their service—an invaluable aid to a company with a small personnel department (or none at all) that cannot afford to set up and carry out volumes of interviews and tests. The fee, usually paid by the company, may be considered a wise investment, especially if the company finds qualified applicants through this source.

Advertising at the local, state, regional, or even national level may be an important and necessary step in recruiting. An organization seeking to fill a single, high-level position may find the best applicants through newspaper or trade journal advertisements. Because of the expense and the opportunities to locate applicants through other sources, this is not true if the company is looking for several middle management or operative employees. The biggest single advantage to widespread advertising is the number of persons who potentially become aware of the vacancy.

Most colleges and universities operate a placement service that assists students and alumni in the investigation of career opportunities, maintains liaison between registrants and employers, and provides research information related to placement activity. Interviews with companies and government agencies are scheduled throughout the year. Companies may send one or more interviewers to a college campus once or twice a year to interview graduating seniors for full-time employment or any student for part-time or summer work. The interviewers are normally highly trained personnel familiar with all aspects of the company and responsi-

ble for making decisions about the candidates regarding future interviews and/or employment. The interviewers are usually representatives of the personnel department (seeking sales trainees or general management trainees) or department heads (e.g., engineering, industrial management, accounting) who are concerned with evaluating the applicants' in-depth knowledge of a specific area. Thus, the college placement service is a convenient source of many applicants and allows maximum concentration of time and effort to both the interviewer and the applicants.

Leads from current employees are a frequent source of new workers. Employees usually have direct contact with others of similar social, educational, or professional background who may be dissatisfied with their existing employment and informally or discreetly looking around for a change of job. This can serve as a supplementary source of job applicants. Caution must be taken, however; a company must be careful to comply with the equal employment laws to ensure that this method does not become a "closed system" of recruitment.

Screening

Once the criteria for a job have been established and the method of recruitment determined, the rest of the hiring procedure can proceed. An applicant may have a short preliminary interview when initially inquiring about a particular job. The personnel specialist can very quickly determine whether the applicant meets the minimum standards. Prior to or immediately following the preliminary interview, the applicant completes an application form. At middle or high management levels, a personal data sheet or resumé serves this purpose.

The application requests name, address, education, previous employment experience, military record, memberships in professional associations, and skills.[1] Requests for age, race, religious preference, or marital status should not be included on an application form. One recent study conducted in Ohio and Kansas found 73 percent of all application forms surveyed contained one or more illegal preemployment inquiries. The most frequent illegal categories were gender, race, physical characteristics, marital status, personal history, and inquiries about dependents.[2] Once an applicant has passed these initial steps successfully, some tests may be required. An organization must be able to show the need and relationship between any given test and the specific job; tests cannot be discriminatory except for the purpose of determining specific qualifications for a given position. Any test or other pre-employment requirement must be a *bona fide occupational qualification* (usually shortened to BFOQ). The most common types of tests used today are designed to determine aptitude and skills. Intelligence, interest, and emotional stability tests are not commonly used.

Investigation

At some point in the screening process, each applicant may be investigated to ascertain information not available through other means or to check the accuracy of information supplied by the applicant. This may be by letter or telephone call to the applicant's previous employers or others who are familiar with the person's employment record. Before employers limit or eliminate reference checking, they should consult the recent U.S. Department of Commerce statistics. One report stated that 30 percent of all business failures result from employees' dishonesty; internal theft occurs at a rate 15 times higher than external theft; embezzlement causes an annual loss of over $4 billion; and employee pilfering costs business $5–$10 billion annually.[3]

The Interview

The interview is usually the next step in the hiring process and is probably the most widely used tool of selection.[4] The results should provide information about the applicant's attitudes, character, expressive ability, and capacity for growth and advancement. Interviewers may include some or all of the following types of questions:

1. What knowledge, skills, abilities, and other worker characteristics (commonly referred to as KSAOs) does the applicant possess? A high school or college transcript or an application form may show that the interviewee has had a course in accounting, but the interviewer may probe deeper to ascertain just how knowledgeable the applicant is in the area of cost accounting methods.

2. Questions on motivational and emotional areas of concern, such as the needs for security, ethics, maturity, and independence, provide information of vital concern to the interviewer.

3. Questions dealing with the attitudinal and behavioral facets of an individual provide insight into the applicant that can be quite revealing to the trained interviewer. Some common questions here center around attitudes associated with life, previous jobs and companies, and other people. These questions most frequently take the form of a hypothetical case posed by the interviewer. The critical incident technique lends itself to the development of this type of question.

Frank S. Endicott, placement director at Northwestern University, has listed the 50 most frequently asked questions by employers during an interview with college seniors:

1. What are your long- and short-range goals and objectives, when and why did you establish these goals, and how are you preparing yourself to achieve them?

2. What specific goals, other than those related to your occupation, have you established for yourself?
3. What do you see yourself doing five years from now?
4. What do you *really* want to do in life?
5. What are your long-range career objectives?
6. How do you plan to achieve your career goals?
7. What are the most important rewards you expect in your business career?
8. What do you expect to be earning five years from now?
9. Why did you choose the career for which you are preparing?
10. Which is more important to you, money or type of job?
11. What do you consider to be your greatest strengths and weaknesses?
12. How would you describe yourself?
13. How do you think a friend or professor who knows you well would describe you?
14. What motivates you to put forth your greatest effort?
15. How has college prepared you for a business career?
16. Why should I hire you?
17. How do you determine or evaluate success?
18. What qualifications do you have that make you think that you will be successful in business?
19. What do you think it takes to be successful in a company like ours?
20. In what ways do you think you can make a contribution to our company?
21. What qualities should a successful manager possess?
22. Describe the relationship that should exist between a supervisor and those reporting to him or her.
23. What two or three accomplishments have given you the most satisfaction? Why?
24. Describe your most rewarding college experience.
25. If you were hiring a graduate for this position, what qualities would you look for?
26. Why did you select your college or university?
27. What led you to choose your field of major study?
28. What college subjects did you like best? Why?
29. What college subjects did you like least? Why?
30. If you could do so, how would you plan your academic study differently? Why?
31. What changes would you make in your college or university? Why?
32. Do you have plans for continued study?
33. Do you think that your grades are a good indication of your academic achievement?

34. What have you learned from participation in extra-curricular activities?
35. In what kind of work environment are you most comfortable?
36. How do you work under pressure?
37. In what part-time or summer jobs have you been most interested? Why?
38. How would you describe the ideal job for you following graduation?
39. Why did you decide to seek a position with this company?
40. What do you know about our company?
41. What two or three things are most important to you in your job?
42. Are you seeking employment in a company of a certain size? Why?
43. What criteria are you using to evaluate the company for which you hope to work?
44. Do you have a geographical preference? Why?
45. Will you relocate? Does relocation bother you?
46. Are you willing to travel?
47. Are you willing to spend at least six months as a trainee?
48. Why do you think you might like to live in the community in which our company is located?
49. What major problem have you encountered and how did you deal with it?
50. What have you learned from your mistakes?[5]

As mentioned earlier, one form of interviewer bias is the manner in which a question is asked. This can lead an applicant to answer differently under differing circumstances. Current equal employment laws affect whether an organization includes certain questions on an application form or whether an interviewer asks certain questions. Lipman G. Feld, in his article, "Fifteen Questions You Dare Not Ask Job Applicants,"[6] states that simple courtesy is no longer enough; the interviewer must avoid areas and questions that could seem to be discriminatory, even if not meant to be. In general, a question is improper if it seeks to elicit information about race, religion, age, sex, or ancestry. Feld suggests that questions in the following areas may be questionable, if not illegal:

1. **Address.** Specific inquiries into foreign addresses that would reveal national origin are illegal.
2. **Organizations.** Questioning applicants about membership in professional groups is permissible as long as inquiries are not phrased in such a way as to elicit information on race, religion, or national origin.
3. **Photo request.** An organization cannot require a photo before or with an application. Requiring a photo after the interview, but before hiring, is also illegal. However, it is acceptable to require

a photograph after hiring for identification purposes and it is legal for an applicant to submit a photo at his or her option.

4. **Relatives.** The name and address of a *person* to be notified in case of accident should be requested instead of the name and address of the nearest relative.

5. **Recommendations.** Instead of asking for recommendations from one's present employer, only the names and addresses of several people who can give references should be requested.

6. **Military experience.** The interviewer may only ask about military experience or training and not about the applicant's general military service.

7. **Academic background.** Whether a school is private or its curriculum includes religious instruction are topics to avoid. Questions about what degrees the applicant holds are permissible.

8. **Educational level.** A company may legally require specific educational levels only when they are directly related to job performance.

9. **Arrests and convictions.** An arrest is merely an accusation. It is legal to ask if an applicant has ever been convicted of a crime.

10. **Social security status.** It is illegal for an employer to specify that he will hire only persons receiving social security benefits. However, it is within the rights of the employer to ask a social security recipient how many hours he or she can work due to restrictions on income.

11. **Employment tests.** Validated tests are permissible; however, they must be specifically related to the requirements of the job. They must be fair, reasonable, administered in good faith and, of course, be impartially evaluated.

12. **Height requirements.** An EEOC decision states that such questions as "how tall are you" have a "chilling effect" on potential workers.

13. **Weight.** Weight should have no bearing on an applicant's suitability unless it is distinctly job-related. Even then, standards must be applied on a uniform basis.

14. **Marital status.** It is illegal to refuse to hire an engaged or married woman on the assumption that the turnover rate is high; this would be based on a stereotyped sex characterization and is discriminatory.

15. **Car or home ownership.** Requesting information about the ownership of a car or home discriminates against certain minority groups who must be given a fair chance for employment. Car information is permissible if a car is specifically needed in the work execution.

Planning for the Interview.

From the interviewer's perspective.   The trained interviewer, with adequate experience, knows that the planning that occurs before an interview is certainly the "ounce of prevention." One of the first things an interviewer must do is plan (or at least be aware of) and adjust to the physical setting. From the time the applicant walks through the door, opinions are being formed. A cramped, dirty, uncomfortable room or lobby may provide the initial basis for a decision by the applicant. The size of a waiting room or interview room may be beyond the control of the interviewer, but the room should be clean, orderly, and aired. Telephone calls or other interruptions are a frequent source of irritation to the interview situation and are within the interviewer's control. Explicit instructions should be given about conditions that warrant an interruption.

The interviewer should be familiar with all aspects of the company, its locations, products or services, and job requirements. Since the interviewee may have searched out information about the company prior to the interview, the interviewer's knowledge about the specific position and the job requirements are the primary focus of interest to the interviewee. A well-informed interviewer can attract a highly qualified applicant based not only on information about the company but also on knowledge about the position.

The interviewer should be aware of and study the applicant's record if advance information is known (e.g., an application form). This can shorten the time of the interview or give added minutes to a discussion of points not otherwise covered by this record.

From the interviewee's perspective.   The interviewee should arrive for the interview at the scheduled time and avoid breaking an appointment without notifying the company or the interviewer. Not to do so could be interpreted by the interviewer as undependable and irresponsible.

The interviewee who knows something about the company, locations, products, and service prior to the interview may have a definite advantage over other applicants. This information can be obtained easily from a college placement service, a local library, or directly from the company. Consider the ramifications of this actual case: a student who planned to interview with the XYZ Company and thought it was a pharmaceutical firm. When he arrived, the XYZ Company turned out to be a paper box company! The amount of time, effort, money, and embarrassment proved to be quite sizable in this instance.

Appropriate and neat attire, letters of reference, and application forms completed prior to the interview are essential. Anything that the interviewee can plan and prepare for—including sample questions—enhances the reception and relationship with the interviewer.

Conducting the Interview.

From the interviewer's perspective. Many factors affect the outcome of an interview, and it should not come as a surprise that the opening minutes play a big role in that outcome. Calling the interviewee by name, giving a firm handshake, and making a few remarks designed to establish some common ground all contribute to the informal atmosphere necessary to put the interviewee at ease. Although an informal, permissive climate is a desirable goal, the interviewer should avoid too much familiarity. The climate that is established is to a large extent the result of the interviewer's attitude and interviewing skills, being frank, friendly, honest, self-confident, and even aggressive at times—but with a sense of humor. Above all, the interviewer must be a good listener and eliminate all objectionable traits, habits, or mannerisms.

Operationally, the interviewer must maintain control of the situation and keep the interview moving along. At the same time, the interviewee's appearance, attitude, abilities, knowledge, mannerisms, physical abilities, mental alertness, and emotional stability, as well as the facility with which she responds, should be noted. The best method of accomplishing this is to keep notes and record the important points and high spots of every interview. An evaluation form is shown in Figure 14–1.

In gaining information, one of the stated objectives of this interview, the interviewer must plan the time needed for the interview and gauge the time in accordance with the immediate situation. Questions should be formulated in advance to bring out attitudes, experiences, capacities, and personal facts but should avoid prying beyond necessity or seeking information that may already be available.

The traditional, informal, or casual interview has several potential disadvantages: it is susceptible to bias, distortion, and legal attack; it is rarely totally objective since the interviewer may look for qualities that she prefers; and, it is highly inconsistent. For these reasons, many writers and practitioners vigorously defend and use the structured interview method. One group states there are seven essential criteria for the development and evaluation of interview questions. They should:

1. Be accurate, complete and unambiguous.
2. Be strictly and clearly job-related.
3. Assess only knowledge, skills, abilities, and other worker characteristics (KSAOs).
4. Assess only job requirements.
5. Reflect as nearly as possible the content of the job.
6. Be geared to the appropriate complexity level of the job.
7. Be reviewed carefully to eliminate any bias.[8]

Finally, one of the most important characteristics of the successful interviewer is the ability to follow through, to guide "leads" in the conver-

FIGURE 14–1

EMPLOYMENT INTERVIEW PERFORMANCE FORM

_____ _____ _____

Date   Div.   Applicant

Applicant criteria   *Comments*

Personal conduct
Physical appearance _____
Mental alertness _____
Language usage _____
Courtesy and tact _____
Cooperative attitude _____
Voice and articulation _____
Enthusiasm _____

Job characteristics
Meets job requirements _____
Able to work with co-workers _____
Accepts working conditions _____
Future prospects for advancement _____

Presentation of goals
Knowledge of prospective
    employer _____
Knowledge of prospective
    company organization _____
Reasons for wanting this job _____

Qualifications
Academic training _____
Professional experience _____
Handling of potential weaknesses _____
Focus on favorable points _____

Interview procedure
Anticipate questions _____
Thorough answers _____
Effective transitions _____
Close _____
Apparent purpose, direction _____

sation to logical conclusions, and to thoroughly check the applicant for omissions and obvious disqualifications.

The employment and hiring interview is a two-way street; the interviewer must also give information. To do this, the interviewer must anticipate and answer all the applicant's questions about company policies, various programs such as insurance, suggestion systems, safety, products, rates of pay, shifts, and opportunities for advancement. When the interview is conducted at a company location, the interviewer may conduct a tour of the plant. If the interviewee is being considered for a specific position, the duties—both undesirable and desirable—should be discussed. The applicant should be shown the work and be given sufficient information in order to make an intelligent decision about the position.

From the interviewee's perspective.   The primary goal of the interviewee should be to offer sufficient information to the interviewer to make possible a fair judgment. In so doing, the interviewee's own thoughts may be so clarified that a better decision concerning the desirability of the job can be made. The interviewee should be willing and eager to talk about former jobs, employment, and professional experiences. Statements should be clarified and explained, avoiding a simple yes-no answer to most questions. There should be no attempt to carry the conversation into areas where little pertinent information will be obtained or given.

The most successful interviewee behavior includes: following the pattern the interviewer sets, maintaining good eye contact, and being alert but as relaxed as possible. Speak in a normal tone. Get your strong points across without being boastful. Be interested. The preparations that you have made help to reflect this interest.

Some of the positive factors you should emphasize are: interview preparation, career planning (including ambitions and goals), your willingness to work, scholastic effort, previous work experience, and attitude. One writer suggests that interviewers want to know the answers to only three questions:

1.   Will you do the job competently if hired?
2.   Will you get along well with other members of the staff?
3.   Do you have the temperament, stability, flexibility, and dependability required for the job?

If you can convince the interviewer that the answer to each of these questions is "yes," then you may be on the way to a job.[9]

Regardless of how many questions you may be asked during an interview, "all talk and no show" is just that. Be prepared to document your accomplishments. If you have initiated some new project in an organiza-

tion, show a news release or a picture, or a commendation from an officer of the group attesting to your **initiative.** An "A" term paper with the professor's comments may illustrate good **research** ability. Without being boastful, you can quote others who have commented on your positive characteristics by saying, "My residence hall supervisor recommended that I apply for the counselor position this year" **(confidence, trust),** or "My boss was especially pleased with the way I handled a particular work problem while he was gone" **(resourcefulness).**

The interviewee should avoid: lying, being rude, showing a lack of interest in the interview, exhibiting a belligerent or overly aggressive attitude, giving incomplete or inaccurate information, being concerned only about salary, displaying a lack of initiative, and being indecisive.

Closing the Interview.

From the interviewer's perspective. The interview closes when the interviewer decides that all the information needed to make a fair and sound decision has been obtained. The termination should be handled to give the interviewee the impression that a sincere interest is shown by the interviewer and the organization—whatever the outcome. This does not include giving encouragement to the applicant who is obviously not qualified; nor should the interviewer make promises or commitments that cannot be honored. If a decision is made to reject the applicant, the interviewer should carefully explain the reasons for this decision. If the interviewer needs more time to evaluate the candidate or wants another interview, the interviewer should be as specific as possible regarding future arrangements.

From the interviewee's perspective. During the entire employment interview process, the goal is to "sell yourself," and that must remain foremost in your mind. If you are told that you do not meet the qualifications, it does little good to criticize the interviewer, the company, or its hiring practices. Just as the interviewer wants you to leave the interview with a good feeling about him or her and the company, so too should you want the interviewer to have a positive feeling about you.

Carlson summarizes the employment interview process by commenting:

> The selection interview should be made an integral part of an overall selection procedure, and to accomplish this, new and additional materials are needed. The new materials should include a broad-gauge, comprehensive, structured interview guide; standardized evaluation and prediction forms that aid the interviewer in summarizing information from all steps in the selection process . . . .[10]

The complete selection process is illustrated in Figure 14–2.

FIGURE 14–2 Selection Process and Reasons for Rejection

Items	Possible rejection
Stage I (screen) Initial interview ———————→	Does not meet *minimum* qualifications (education, experience, etc.)

Stage II (develop detailed
  information)
  Application form ⎫
           ⎬ ————→
  Second interview ⎭
	More detailed information available (not determined in screening interview) and cause for rejection

Stage III (verification)
  Education/experience ⎫
            ⎬ ————→
  References ⎭
	Inappropriate, inaccurate information supplied by applicant
	Weak/negative references—especially regarding work history

Stage IV (specific
  qualifications)
  Tests (if appropriate) ⎫
            ⎬ ————→
  Physical exam
    (if appropriate) ⎭
	Does not pass tests or physical examination

Stage V (recommendation) Final interview ———————→	Rejection only for very specific cause
Hire	

THE APPRAISAL AND PROGRESS REVIEW INTERVIEW

The appraisal interview is also known as a progress review, merit-rating, or performance review. Regardless of what it is called—and there may be some technical differences—the purposes are basically the same: to determine how well the employee has adjusted to a position, to find out whether the person is meeting company goals, and, where necessary, to offer constructive suggestions for improvement. This interview may evaluate an employee for future training and development, promotion, or compensation. Benefits from this form of interaction should accrue to both the employee and the organization.

This interview should never take the place of daily contact between an employee and the supervisor. On-the-job training, immediate correction of an employee for improper work methods or activities, and occasional surveys of employee attitudes are in a different category. The employee should always know exactly where he or she stands with the supervisor. A good supervisor constantly keeps the employees informed of job performance and under this theory, an appraisal interview may be

entirely unnecessary. The view taken here is that after employment a follow-up interview is necessary.

The schedule for these interviews is, of course, up to the company. An initial progress review may occur within the first week or month of employment. Another may occur after 60 or 90 days. Thereafter, this formal evaluation may occur only once a year. A sample 30-day review form is shown in Figure 14-3.

The appraisal should never become a ritual that loses its meaning to one or both parties. To avoid this, the interviewer—a supervisor or a representative of the personnel department, singly or together—must constantly focus on the relevant factors. A manufacturing plant may consider quantity of production a relevant factor; a bank may consider "human relations" or lack of customer complaints the most important. The focus of this interview should be on employee **performance.** Some writers claim that traditional approaches evaluate employees on the basis of personality traits: attitudes, judgment, honesty, emotional maturity—all the wrong things. "Experience has shown, however, that by focusing on personality traits, appraisals overlook the most relevant factor—performance. The link between possession of specific traits and performance is tenuous at best and more importantly lacks practical validity."[11]

Performance-based appraisals determine which objectives were accomplished, how well they were accomplished, or what corrective measures need to be implemented in order that the objectives can be achieved. Consider the following statement: "In order to get ahead around here you'll have to shape up." That kind of comment tells an employee absolutely nothing. The manager could have said, "Your product output is below the established standard. How can your supervisor help you to achieve this standard?" Although these two sentences are but an abbreviated version of what a complete appraisal would include they do accomplish a number of things: first, the appraisal identifies the minimum standard; second, it evaluates the employee in relation to that standard; and, third, it offers the employee an opportunity to get some help in correcting the situation. In addition, the tone is such that it does not damage the ego of the interviewee.

The steps in developing a performance-based appraisal system are:

1. Identify the major duties and responsibilities of a job.
2. Select the key areas (two to five) that correspond to and could have the greatest impact on the organizational goals.
3. Rank, weight, or assign percentages in order of priority.
4. Develop performance standards. A performance standard is a quantitative baseline against which an employee's performance can be measured and evaluated.
5. Finally, set performance objectives. These are statements that are

FIGURE 14–3

EMPLOYEE 30-DAY FOLLOW-UP INTERVIEW

Name _____ Date of interview _____

Date employed _____   Present
                                position _____

Are you happy in and satisfied with your present job assignment? _____

_____

Do you feel that your present job assignment is "in line" with your qualifi-

cations and interests? _____

_____

Have you been apprised of and instructed in the details of your present

assignment by your department manager? _____ By

your associates? _____ Who was your sponsor?

_____ Was your sponsor helpful to you? _____

_____

Have your associates been congenial, cooperative, and willing to help

you? _____

What suggestions do you have? _____

_____

_____

Do you have any questions regarding your work? _____

_____ Company policies? _____

_____

What other type of employment in the company appeals to you? _____

_____

                                         _____
                                               Personnel Director

expected to be achieved. These objectives should be consistent with the organizational goals, feasible, tied to some time frame, and most important, capable of being measured and evaluated.

Dr. Thomas Gordon suggests that supervisors *and* the employees should co-develop **quantitative measures** whenever possible. However, he cautions that for certain functions, precise quantitative measures may not be available.[12] The following represent some of the quantitative and subjective performance measures that can be used in the appraisal interview. These are the items that should be the focal point during the interview.

Performance Standards for Appraisal Interviews

Quantitative Measures	*Subjective Measures*
Number of errors	Appearance
Number of complaints	Telephone courtesy
Dollar sales volume	Customer satisfaction
Dollar cost reduction	Pleasantness
Number of deadlines met	Creativity
Number of new customers	Innovativeness
Number of items produced	Cooperation

A sample worksheet used during this interview is given in Figure 14–4. Any of the performance items mentioned above would need to be included as a part of the worksheet.

A staff appraisal worksheet is illustrated in Figure 14–5. Although this example includes some personality traits to be evaluated, the focus is still on **performance**.

The Significance of Communication

Setting performance standards and developing a worksheet are the vehicles to the evaluation process. It is the *communication* that takes place between the supervisor and employee that is the key to the success of the appraisal interview. Regardless of the final evaluation, that communication must be open, honest, sincere, and well intentioned if the employee is to benefit. Active listening is crucial to the entire process. Gordon offers one final piece of advice: "Remember to keep the discussion forward looking—the past is gone."[13]

THE COMPLAINT INTERVIEW

If every action in an organization is guided by the principle of doing "what is best for the organization as a whole," it may be necessary to have

FIGURE 14–4 Performance Review Worksheet

Employee _____

Department manager _____

Check opposite of this employee:

	Performance Requirement		
	Minimum	*Average*	*Maximum*
Progress in learning job	☐	☐	☐
Quality of work	☐	☐	☐
Quantity of work	☐	☐	☐
Cost overruns	☐	☐	☐
Time	☐	☐	☐

What is employee's strong point? _____

_____

What is employee's weakness? _____

_____

How can this weakness be corrected? _____

_____

Performance objective: _____

_____

_____

_____   _____
     Employee's signature   Manager's signature

a reconciliation of differing personal perceptions and directions to achieve this goal. However, before such reconciliation can take place, the differing personal perceptions and directions need to be made known to the concerned parties.

Accepting another person's point of view is not simple and few people can listen to and gather information from another person without reacting along the lines of their *own* problems or experiences.

Complaints, reprimands, and counseling interviews provide the organizational communicator with a great challenge and opportunity to use his interpersonal skills.

Everyone has complaints at some time—a student in the residence halls doesn't like broccoli, a customer decides she doesn't like the shade of green in her purchase, an employee prefers to be on the day shift—each *thinks* he or she has a justifiable complaint. These "complaints" may be grouches and grumbles—a way to express a general unhappy feeling. In some cases the complaints may be the result of poor planning, and no one else is really to blame. Some complaints are honest dissatisfactions with something or someone. Possibly a third party can bring about some improvement in the situation.

FIGURE 14–5 Staff Appraisal

Name_____
Position_____

| Date employed _____ | Salary range _____ | Date last increase _____ | Present salary _____ |

Training courses completed:

1. _____ 3. _____
2. _____ 4. _____

Describe in detail any job complexities that make your work assignment different or more difficult than others in the same classification.

	Performance Requirement		
	Minimum	*Average*	*Maximum*
Job knowledge, familiarity with all phases of regular duties	☐	☐	☐
Quality of work, degree of excellence of work completed	☐	☐	☐
Quantity of work, amount of work completed daily for any given period	☐	☐	☐
Judgment, degree of efficiency in matters affecting action, good sense, and discretion	☐	☐	☐

Public contact
  In person
  By telephone
  By mail
	☐	☐	☐

Personal factors
  Appearance
  Attitude and co-operation
  Punctuality
  Attendance
	☐	☐	☐

How has your work performance improved and your value to the company increased since your last apprasail?_____
_____

How can you be helped or what additional assignments can be given you for you to better understand your job?_____
_____

Performance Objective:_____
_____
_____

_____   _____
Signature of staff member   Signature of supervisor

Factors Precipitating Complaints

Frequently, an employee will rush into a supervisor's office, ranting and raving about something that has just happened. In reality, the employee may be just "blowing off steam"; even the employee may not know what can or should be done about the situation. Another employee, after tolerating a situation for weeks or months and giving it careful consideration, may approach the supervisor with a complaint *and* an economical and efficient solution to the problem. These cases have different problems and people involved and yet there are some similarities. The supervisor or the personnel specialist must be able to sort out the really significant differences and know when and how something can be done about them.

In the two cases cited, both employees may have legitimate complaints; the difference in the presentation can give one an added advantage in getting the problem solved. The discerning supervisor or interviewer must not let personalities determine whether a person has a complaint; the investigation must go beyond that. Certainly the "chronic complainer" can be identified very quickly and must be dealt with in an appropriate way. That person must be educated to the difference between an irritation and a complaint.

When a student says, "This is only March . . . another two months of school," or an employee comments, "This is only Wednesday . . . two more days of work," these expressions may be simple observations of fact. They are recognizing the inevitable. On the other hand, they could be expressions of dissatisfaction and symptoms of some real problems.

What Is a Complaint?

A complaint may be any one of the following:

1. A simple difference of preference may become the source of a complaint and manifest itself in the infringement of one person's rights by another. If, for example, management allows employees to bring radios to their work stations, who determines which station to listen to and the volume? One employee may like soft music; another may prefer loud rock and roll music. One employee may prefer a window open; another may prefer it closed. Ultimately, these cases may result in complaints.

2. Unfairness or perceived injustice is a second source of complaints. The supervisor who gives "all the easy jobs" to one employee or who rates an employee below average when that person feels he or she has been doing as well as anyone else usually generates a number of complaints. In the academic world, grades (and how the professor arrived at them) become the source of many student complaints.

In these cases, the complaints stem from perceptions—an employee who thinks or feels some jobs are easier than others, or a difference in

perception between what the supervisor and the employee call average and below average, or the student who thinks she has done just as much work as another student.

3. While the first two types of complaints involve two or more people and their differences in preferences or perceptions, the third type centers around one individual. Questions like "How was my pay calculated?" or "Why am I scheduled to work late?" can be headed off as potential complaints with complete and accurate information. When this information is not forthcoming, the questions and lack of information balloon into a full-fledged complaint that may have major significance to the individual.

4. A fourth source of complaints may stem from technological or organizational factors. "This machine has never worked right." "The materials are not on time or are defective and keep me from doing my job." "If only someone could tell me where to go to get something done around here." These complaints may appear to be "external" to the situation, but many times the problems are subject to correction.

Suggestions for Handling Complaints

Although each situation is different, some suggested approaches include the following:

1. Whether listening to the employee who is "blowing off steam" or to the one who approaches the supervisor with the well-thought-out problem and solution, the interviewer must remain calm and uncommitted until the employee has presented the entire story. The main job of the interviewer in this first step is to listen intelligently, understandingly, and skillfully to the other person. The interviewer should ask questions in an effort to get all the important details: Who? What? When? Where? At this stage, the interviewer should be as objective as possible and avoid agreeing or disagreeing with the interviewee. Repeating the complaint may add discrepancies or errors as a result of the emotion of the immediate situation.

2. Once the complaint has been verbalized and all the facts are disclosed, try to agree on what the complaint is about. Is it a difference in preferences or perception? Is it an organizational problem or one involving machines or materials? Is it a basic human right that has been violated?

3. After the complaint has been received and the basic issue agreed on, the next step is to consider possible solutions. The complainant should be allowed, and in fact invited, to participate in this step. However, keep in mind any laws or company rules that must be observed no matter what solution is proposed. If it is a matter of a delayed shipment of materials or defective equipment that had to be returned, the complaint may be justified but the situation cannot be corrected. If it is a matter of interpre-

tation of company rules or perceptions of evaluations, the basis for the interpretation should be given. Attacking other people or companies, questioning the sincerity or intelligence of the complainant, or passing the buck does not eliminate the complaint or soothe the person who feels an injustice has been done.

4. Based on the possible solutions that are discussed and reached in the previous step, the interviewer can identify what actions will be taken. If further checking is necessary, the interviewer should avoid a definite commitment to any specific action and promise to do the further checking. Since timing is often a crucial factor in many complaints, the interviewer should advise the complainant when to expect an answer.

5. The interview should be terminated in a manner that is satisfactory to both parties. No one should take unfair advantage of the other party.

6. The interviewer must follow up by checking the facts, checking company rules, examining records, and taking action. If necessary, the interviewer should inform others of the action and of possible consequences (changes in work procedures, relationships with other people, and the like).

THE REPRIMAND AND COUNSELING INTERVIEW

The most obvious difference between a complaint and the reprimand and counseling interview is the origin of the situation. The complaint interview stems from a customer or employee who is dissatisfied. The person receiving the complaint may have little time to prepare for the confrontation. The reprimand and counseling interview stems from the organization—a supervisor or personnel representative who is dissatisfied with the performance or behavior of an employee—and the interviewer must be fortified with all the relevant information in advance to be effective.

For our purposes here, the reprimand and counseling interview will be presented as a combination interview. The reprimand may be appropriate when an employee (1) has violated some company policy, procedure, rule, or regulation; (2) does not meet standards of performance due to a cause that can be shown to be within the control of the employee; or (3) engages in some personal activity that is disrupting to the company or the morale of other employees (e.g., sleeping on the job, fighting, etc.). In each of these cases, there is some specific principle that has been neglected or violated. Assuming the employee has primary or complete control over the causes, the employee can be instructed or required to take some action to correct the situation. The primary focus is on the employee and his ability to adjust to the policy, procedure, production standard, and needs of the company or peers. It is hoped that the solutions to the problems brought out in a reprimand interview can be initiated

immediately; and, once "solved," the problems may never recur. Essentially, the reprimand is an attempt to **change behavior.**

The counseling interview is an attempt (1) to change **attitudes and behavior**, or (2) to identify and correct some (long range) problem—usually attitudinal or physical. Thus, the counseling process may take weeks or months of gathering facts, unfreezing existing attitudes, identifying physical or emotional problems, or training and retraining an employee.

Let's consider an employee caught sleeping on the job. After being discovered once or twice, the employee would probably receive a reprimand. The employee might offer some reasons for the behavior such as "I was out too late last night and was tired." The interviewer might dismiss the situation if it was the first time and if the employee's action created no damage or threat to the company. If the employee was a night guard for a chemical company and this action might have resulted in disaster to the company or even to the entire community, the employee would probably receive a severe reprimand and some form of discipline. After four or five such instances, it might be determined that the employee suffered from narcolepsy (tendency to sleep or doze). To identify the real problem and take some corrective action might involve a physician, a psychologist, a training specialist, or several supervisors (to train or retrain the employee for a new job)—even might involve union officials (to get exception to seniority rules within the plant). This could take three to six months. In most business and industrial situations, every reprimand should include identification of any attitudinal, emotional, or physical problems or limitations as well as some agreed-on action to correct the problem situation. Therefore, the reprimand and the counseling interviews are presented as a combination interview.

Suggestions for Handling Reprimands

Basic Prerequisites.   The first thing the interviewer must do before issuing a reprimand is to collect all the facts! Are they complete? Are they accurate? If gathered from a third party, is that person a reliable source? If they involve company records (production, inventory, etc.) are they documented? Remember, opinions are not facts; hearsay evidence is no good. There should be witnesses who saw the action or violation. Are the facts relevant? What has been violated? A company rule? An accepted principle? Common courtesy?

After gathering all the facts, the interviewer must plan for the interview. The interviewer's attitude must be one of fairness, and the location must allow for strict privacy. Feeling confident that one knows the facts, picking a time and place conducive to the situation, and having a positive attitude all aid the interviewer in achieving the purpose of this interview.

That purpose is to identify and get agreement on the problem and the proposed solutions (corrective action), and to get the employee to accept responsibility for improvement.

Identifying the Problem.   Most dissatisfactions fall into one of three categories: knowledge, skill, or attitude. The interviewer must deal with the problems and not with personalities. If it is a company rule, policy, procedure, or custom that has been violated, the interviewer must cite when, where, and how the violation occurred and what the result was. It is crucial to communicate the consequence of the action to the employee, to the company, and to other employees. Although the interviewer may have all the facts, the employee's side of the story should be heard. The interviewer should repeat the story objectively to make sure it is understood accurately. Any differences in the two versions should be discussed and reconciled. The interviewer should ask more questions, if necessary, to get any details.

If the problem stems from a dissatisfaction with the employee's skill (which may result in low output or unacceptable quality), the source of the problem must still be identified. Is the employee aware of the company standards? Has there been adequate training? Is the supervisor at fault? Correcting skill problems involves criticism, which attacks a worker's security and the need for approval—two things an employee wants. The object of the correction or reprimand should be improvement, not punishment. Thus, proper identification of the problem and correction head off the need for further discipline.

Problems caused by "unacceptable" attitudes are more difficult to discuss with an employee. The best short-range approach is to show how the attitude affects the employee, the relationship with the supervisor or other employees, and the company. The process of changing the attitude and consequent behavior may take several sessions between the employee and the supervisor or personnel specialist.

Identifying Corrective Action.   Once the problem has been identified correctly, it should not be too difficult to identify what action is necessary to improve the situation. If the problem is a lack of knowledge or improper use of materials, more training may be prescribed. Regardless of what corrective action is recommended, the employee must understand and accept the idea that she will benefit—in greater productivity, more praise, increased earnings, and other advantages.

Getting the Employee to Assume Responsibility.   The employee should be encouraged to help identify the problem and the necessary corrective action because involvement enhances the possibility of success. The employee also must understand what responsibility he has in the overall plan. If additional training has been prescribed, when and where

will it take place? What materials will be needed? What follow-up procedures will be executed? Once the employee knows what is expected (when, where, how, and what benefits will accrue) the responsibility for corrective action can be placed with the employee.

Terminating the Interview.   When the employee agrees to whatever corrective action is necessary, both parties to the interview should think in terms of the future and the positive benefits that will accrue. The interview should close on as friendly a note as possible.

Following Up.   The personnel specialist or supervisor will evaluate both the progress and performance of the employee and should get the employee involved in this activity.

SUMMARY

The relationship that develops between an interviewer and interviewee is crucial to the success of any interview. This is especially true in the four types of interviews discussed in this chapter: employment and hiring, appraisal and progress review, complaint, and reprimand. Each of these calls for the interviewer to show objectivity, a supportive attitude, and a sincere interest in the interviewee. If the interviewer can provide these three inputs to the interview, the potential candidate for a position or the employee being appraised should feel that he or she is being evaluated fairly. The customer or employee with a complaint or the employee being reprimanded should feel that he or she is being heard and that some action will be taken or there will be positive suggestions for improvement. By creating this positive climate, the interviewer can increase the likelihood of success of any of these interview situations.

DISCUSSION QUESTIONS

1. Discuss the steps in the employment/hiring process.
2. Discuss the kinds of questions that are illegal in an interview. Indicate the basic requirements that must be met in designing and administering tests to prospective employees.
3. What three kinds of questions are generally asked in the hiring interview?
4. What specifically should the interviewer and interviewee each do to prepare for the job interview?
5. Discuss the advantages and disadvantages of the informal or casual interview.
6. Some practitioners hold that there are seven essential criteria for the development and evaluation of interview questions. List five of these seven criteria.

7. Describe the behavior of a successful interviewee during the interview. What factors should the interviewee tend to stress or emphasize?

8. What should be the focus of the appraisal/progress review interview? Discuss why the traditional appraisal interview has come under criticism.

9. List and then explain the basic steps in developing a performance-based appraisal system.

10. Give three suggestions that should help an interviewer to handle a complaint interview.

11. Give three suggestions that should help an interviewer to handle a reprimand interview.

12. What specifically should an interviewer do to ensure that the object of a reprimand is to encourage improvement rather than to punish?

EXERCISES

1. Based on your preparation from Chapter 13 exercises, carry out the appropriate interviews as *(a)* applicant, and/or *(b)* interviewer.

2. Participate in the following interviews as either (as assigned) interviewer or interviewee:
   (a) merit rating
   (b) complaint
   (c) reprimand
   (d) stress/group

NOTES

[1] Title VII of the Civil Rights Act of 1964 and the Equal Employment Opportunity Act (EEOA) of 1972 deal with a number of these issues. The Age Discrimination Act of 1967 and the Rehabilitation Act of 1973 preclude discrimination based on age and disability, respectively.

[2] Carl Camden and Bill Wallace, "Job Application Forms," *Personnel Administrator* (March 1983), p. 31.

[3] Carole Sewell, "Pre-Employment Investigations," *Personnel Journal* 60, no. 5 (1981), p. 376.

[4] Elliott D. Purcell, Michael A. Campion, and Sarah R. Gaylord, "Structured Interviewing: Avoiding Selection Problems," *Personnel Journal* 59, no. 11 (1980), p. 909.

[5] Frank S. Endicott, *Trends in Employment of College and University Graduates in Business and Industry* (Evanston, Ill: Northwestern University, 1974), pp. 9–10.

[6] Lipman G. Feld, "Fifteen Questions You Dare Not Ask Job Applicants," Excerpted from *Administrative Management*, © 1974 by Geyer-McAllister Publications, Inc., New York.

[7] See Appendix A for a transcript of a sample employment interview.

[8] Purcell et al., "Structured Interviewing," p. 910.

[9] Shirley Sloan Fader, "Those Intimidating Interview Questions," *Business Week's Guide to Careers* 2, no. 3 (1984), p. 26.

[10] Robert Carlson et al., "Improvements in the Selection Interview," *Personnel Journal* 50, no. 4 (1971), p. 273.

[11]Kent Baker and Stevan R. Holmberg, "Stepping up to Supervision: Conducting Performance Reviews," *Supervisory Management* 27, no. 4 (1982), p. 22.

[12]Thomas Gordon, *Leader Effectiveness Training* (New York: Bantam Books, 1977), p. 250.

[13]Ibid., p. 252.

SUGGESTED READINGS

CONNELLY, WILLIAM J. "How to Navigate the River of Legal Liability When Hiring." *Personnel Journal,* May 1986, pp. 32–46.

DEETS, NORMAN R., and D. TIMOTHY TYLER. "How Xerox Improved Its Performance Appraisals." *Personnel Journal,* April 1986, pp. 50–52.

EDWARDS, CATHY. "Aggressive Recruitment: The Lessons of High-Tech Hiring." *Personnel Journal,* January 1986, p. 40ff.

JACOBS, RICK, and STEVE W. KOZLOWSKI. "A Closer Look at Halo Error in Performance Ratings." *Academy of Management Journal* 28, no. 1, pp. 201–12.

LOWE, TERRY. "Eight Ways to Ruin a Performance Review." *Personnel Journal,* January 1986, pp. 60–62.

MAIER, NORMAN R. F. *The Appraisal Interview: Three Basic Approaches.* LaJolla, Calif.: University Associates, 1976.

MORGAN, PHILIP I., and H. KENT BAKER. "The Complaint Interview: Two Approaches to a Productive Meeting of the Minds." *Supervisory Management* 29, no. 7 (July 1984), pp. 34–39.

WEBSTER, EDWARD C. *The Employment Interview: A Social Judgment Process.* Schomberg, Ont., Canada: S.I.P. Publications, 1982.

Chapter 15

Conflict Management

Chapter 15 Case

You are the president of a medium-sized publishing company; your firm has grown under your leadership from a small local printer of ladies' club cookbooks and regional poetry to a force in the national market for hardback specialty books (photography collections, how-to books, and nonfiction). You have just come from a meeting of your executive staff in which you presented what you consider to be a major opportunity—a chance to expand into the rapidly growing paperback market for genre books (westerns, science fiction, and romances). It's a highly competitive market and will require expansion, but you can swing it. The only problem is Frank and Wayne. Those two guys have been at each other's throats for months, and today their animosity and bickering got so bad that you had to terminate the meeting. They just don't like each other—no one seems to know why. This expansion, if you decide to do it, is going to require everyone working at 100 percent; you can't afford that kind of hostility. What can you do?

INTRODUCTION

The organization should be a place where highly motivated people come together to achieve predetermined objectives. Unfortunately, this is not always the case. Ineffective leadership styles, organizational change, and interpersonal conflict are a few factors that frequently prevent or inhibit the attainment of those objectives. Conflict is one of the most pervasive factors that must be handled. The type, degree, or intensity may vary, but conflict is very much a part of our organizational lives. Himes sums it up when he states that "people are aggressive, conflicting creatures."[1]

The potential for conflict exists whenever people are required to interact with one another. Until recently, managers were negative toward conflict, but currently there is agreement that conflicts within organizations can have a positive value. In an article titled "Three Cheers for Con-

flict,"[2] author King cites 15 reasons or propositions that make conflict an asset to an organization. We will discuss these positive aspects and some of the dysfunctional factors surrounding conflict in this chapter.

DEFINITION

Lee Thayer states, "the way we describe and define things places limits on our ability to think about those things."[3] Perhaps the traditional negative view of conflict is because many definitions and examples of conflict describe it as a negative process.

One classic definition of conflict is offered by Morton Deutsch. He defines a conflict as "a situation in which incompatible activities occur. An action which is incompatible with another action prevents, obstructs, interferes with, injures, or in some way makes it less likely or less effective."[4] Thus, when the interests of two parties are mutually exclusive, the resulting interaction will result in some form of conflict. Dictionary definitions include "competitive or opposing action," "an antagonistic state," or "divergent ideas, interests, or persons." These emphasize the negative, or incompatible, aspects of conflict.

Pfeffer describes conflict as "a desire on the part of both contestants to obtain what is available only to one, or only in part."[5] Katz and Kahn treat conflict as a collision of actions: "two systems (persons, groups, organizations, nations) are in conflict when they interact directly in such a way that the actions of one tend to prevent or compel some outcome against the resistance of the other."[6] Conflict can include differences in desires, wants, outcomes, or objectives, and those differences can occur anywhere on a continuum from simple mental disagreement to actual physical violence.[7]

One of the few definitions that focuses on the possible balance between positive and negative functions of conflict is that of MacCrimmon and Taylor. They deal with conflict as existing in situations where multiple participants have different outcome preferences, and act in such a way as to affect the outcomes of others.[8] Note that the word *affect* does not suggest either a strictly negative or a strictly positive focus. Instead, the connotation can be one of both competition *and* cooperation.

TYPES AND SOURCES OF CONFLICT

Different explanations for the existence of conflict can be found. In a very generic sense, conflict exists (1) between different organizations, (2) between an organization and individuals, and (3) between different individuals. In each of the types of conflict mentioned, people are involved in

some respect. We will concentrate on the interpersonal conflicts that occur between people within organizations and between individuals and the organization.

Conflicts that occur between people within organizations where one person or group competes with others are common in many work situations. These rivalries may originate from a number of sources—such as differences in information, beliefs, values, interests, and desires—or from a scarcity of some resource such as money, power, time, space, or position. Conflicts that occur between individuals and the organization can stem from the difficulty of the task, differences in skill levels, the pressure to conform or to avoid failure, and the relative importance of an individual's decision.[9]

Other writers[10] list the following as types of conflict:

1. Goal conflict occurs when a desired goal has both positive and negative aspects, or when there are two or more competing goals and the person must choose between them.
2. Role conflict occurs when we face a situation where we have to choose a particular role or act out an expected behavior pattern and we do not wish to do so.
3. Institutionalized conflict results from organizational attempts to structure work assignments. This is most evident when a group of persons in related fields or departments becomes concerned with their own needs at the expense of other departments or the organization.

Jeffery Gandz identifies three distinct types of conflict in human and industrial relations management:

1. Pseudoconflict: when one party misunderstands the motives or actions of the other. For example, the transfer of an employee from one machine to another may be viewed by the employee as a demotion.
2. Common-problem conflict: when two parties are trying to achieve objectives that are not opposed; for example: a formerly stable employee who develops a drinking problem and who is subjected to disciplinary action.
3. Conflicts of interest: when the parties involved have diametrically opposed objectives. Conflicts such as this may be negotiated, or arbitrated, but are seldom settled to the satisfaction of both parties.[11]

Although not all inclusive, D. J. Harris's classification scheme probably identifies the most frequently encountered types and sources of conflict. He groups conflict problems into three general categories:

1. Problems based on individual differences.
2. Problems resulting from perceptual differences.
3. Problems deriving out of differences with and within the organization.[12]

These three problem areas will now be discussed in some detail.

Individual Differences

No two people are alike; some are aggressive, others are passive. One individual may prefer to make decisions alone; another may seek out the opinions of others. One employee may withstand criticism with a high degree of tolerance; another may react emotionally. Any one of these traits may in and of itself create a conflict situation. Such a situation is commonly referred to as a personality clash or conflict, and is one of the most difficult situations to resolve.

Perceptual Differences

Most people view their work environment as either supportive or threatening and respond accordingly. Our perceptions of activities, events, and our co-workers have a direct impact on the development of conflict. When an employee perceives something in the environment that appears to be supportive or favorable, his perception will be more accepting. However, when an event or another person appears to be destructive or threatening, the employee will usually resist and fight back. In both these cases, the behavior of the employee is a direct result of his or her **perception.** The value and importance of perception has been established in Chapters 1, 2, and 5. What we experience through our senses is what we ultimately respond to, act on, and communicate to others. Unfortunately, our perception is frequently inaccurate and leads us into a conflict situation.

Organizational Differences

Conflict is frequently encouraged by constraints and demands of the organization or the responsibilities to be performed by an employee. Scarce resources may generate competition between employees. When individuals are placed in a win-lose situation, competition (conflict) for rewards becomes fierce. If employees perceive that their success can only be obtained at the expense of another, there is potential for conflict. This often results in an individual asserting her rights while denying others' rights. These and other effects of conflict will be the focus of attention in the next section.

EFFECTS OF CONFLICT

Although conflict clearly plays a positive role in individual and group interactions it is a double-edged sword. Traditionally, conflict is viewed as negative.

Destructive Effects of Conflict

Visualize a recent encounter with a parent, spouse, teacher, or supervisor. Did the situation cause some inappropriate reaction or behavior on your part or the part of the other person? Did it result in a polarization of perception or sentiment? Did you withold information in order to gain some type of advantage? Were you tempted to deceive the other by saying things in a manner that would cause the other to come to an erroneous conclusion? Were you unwilling to share your ideas, and even if these ideas were expressed, were they seriously considered by the other party? Did the conflict lead to rivalry and hostility? Did it delay or make a decision more difficult? Were your emotions "out of control?" Did you show signs of ineptitude, or lack of ingenuity or creativity? Did you have the feeling, "I want to win this one" even at the expense of the other person? These are just a few negative aspects of conflict. Most of these questions—and their responses—stem from a verbal communication or a nonverbal communication behavior. It is easy to see the relationship between communication and conflict.

It is difficult to control conflict once it has begun. Destructive conflicts tend to expand and escalate, and rely on strategies of power and tactics of threats, coercion, and deception. Communication between the parties becomes unreliable and impoverished, and leads to suspicious and hostile attitudes. According to Morton Deutsch, "Along with impairing the perceptual and cognitive processes, intensification of conflict polarizes thought, causes stereotyped responses, and produces defensiveness."[13]

These negative effects are summed up in the results of a study by Warren Schmidt and Kenneth Thomas. Various groups of executives were asked to think about the results of recent conflicts in their companies. According to these executives, as a result of conflict:

1. People felt defeated and demeaned.
2. Distance between people was increased.
3. A climate of distrust and suspicion developed.
4. People and departments that needed to cooperate did not.
5. Resistance developed where teamwork was needed.
6. Turnover increased.[14]

Most of these negative outcomes resulted from the personality differences and the ensuing emotional tensions generated by the communication (or lack of it) between the participants.

The negative aspects of conflict are summed up by psychoanalyst Karen Horney when she states: "Living with unresolved (or negative) conflicts involves a devasting waste of human energies, occasioned not only by the conflicts themselves but by all the devious attempts to remove them."[15]

Constructive Effects of Conflict

Many writers, researchers, and businesspeople contend that conflicts can be productive in some cases. The positive outcomes can be traced to an interaction of ideas and viewpoints among individuals with a diversity of personalities, educational backgrounds, experiences, and abilities—all of which can produce the most effective solutions to individual and organizational problems. Thus, unless a supervisor wants to keep everyone functioning at a low level, conflict is probably inevitable and may be a positive force to be encouraged. It can lead to innovation and change; it can energize people and can be a source of increased organizational effectiveness. Functional or issue-oriented conflict may force communication where there was none. In this sense, conflict is an essential element to effective problem solving, especially in those situations leading to and needing consensus. Conflict can lead to innovation, creativity, prevent stagnation, and lead to the challenging of existing norms and practices.[16]

Businesspeople uphold the notion that conflict can be productive and that conflict management is a necessary skill. In a study by the American Management Association, 293 of the managers surveyed perceived conflict as an important part of their organizational life. Some of the findings of the study included:

1. Managers spend about 20 percent of their time dealing with conflict situations.
2. The ability or skill to manage conflict has become more important over the past 10 years.
3. The managers rated conflict management as equal to or higher in importance than topics presently taught in the AMA programs. This includes topics such as planning, leadership, motivation, and decision making.[17]

If conflict is neither inherently good nor bad, what is the crucial difference in whether a conflict situation results in something constructive or something destructive or dysfunctional? To answer that, you must determine whether the conflict is **functional** or **issue oriented,** or whether it is **emotional** or **personality oriented.** How is the conflict "managed" or resolved? When the manager can channel the energy generated by a conflict into a productive direction, he will have learned to develop a healthy approach to a potentially explosive situation. The recognition of conflict as an important human process is basic to conflict resolution. This means

an open encouragement of constructive conflict is necessary, perhaps even supported by rewards to employees who are effective in this effort.

CONFLICT SCENARIO

Conflict does not occur in a vacuum—it is a dynamic, ongoing process involving a relationship between two or more individuals, organizations, or nations. The conflict itself has a "life." Certain conditions precipitate the conflict, these conditions must be perceived, the impact of the conditions must be evaluated and felt, the conflict becomes visible and open, and finally, there is an aftermath. Louis R. Pondy analyzes the characteristics of conflict in a sequence of five stages.

1. Latent conflict: This stage represents the basic cause or issue over which the conflict arises. The antecedent conditions may be incompatible goals, scarcity of resources, or a desire for autonomy. Usually at this stage, it can be determined whether the conflict is functional, issue oriented, or personality oriented. If it is perception oriented, it may or may not be determined whether the perception is accurate. Unfortunately, that determination is usually not made until much later during the conflict situation, if at all.

2. Perceived conflict: In this stage, the individuals involved in a situation become aware of the incompatibility of their relationship with each other. What was latent as an antecedent condition now becomes exposed. Or, this conflict may be perceived when no conditions of latent conflict exist. If this is the case, then it is a problem of perceptual inaccuracy. It may be that conflict conditions are present but are not perceived—this is also a problem of inaccurate perception.

3. Felt conflict: This stage recognizes the emotional consequences resulting from the perceived conflict. For example, tensions, stress, anxiety, hostility begin to be felt by one or both parties.

4. Manifest conflict: The anxieties felt within the individual in the previous stage are vented. The conflict now becomes visible in various expressive behaviors ranging from mild disagreement to open warfare. Aggression, including physical violence and verbal abuse, are the extremes.

5. Conflict aftermath: If the conflict episode is actually resolved to the satisfaction of all the participants, then a foundation is laid for productive cooperation. On the other hand, if the incompatibility and antagonism are not resolved, but only suppressed, then the original conditions will be present in the relationship, and there may be new eruptions of conflict.

Therefore, conflict within an organization can be understood best as a dynamic process underlying a wide variety of behaviors. The term *con-*

flict refers to its antecedent conditions, a perception of those conditions, overt manifestations, and residues of feeling. This structure, taken together as a history, forms a conflict episode.[18]

When analyzing Pondy's sequencing, one thing becomes apparent. At some point in the sequence (usually stage 1 or 2) the conflict or potential conflict becomes "good" or "bad." This value judgment is directly related to the perceived outcomes of the conflict. We identify those conflicts with perceived positive outcomes as functional, issue, or perception oriented. The destructive or dysfunctional outcome usually stems from an emotional or personality-oriented conflict. Other destructive outcomes may result from functional or issue-oriented conflicts which degenerate into emotional or personality conflicts. Thus, the nature of the conflict and the way it is managed—rather than suppressed, ignored, or avoided—will determine whether the conflict outcomes will be constructive or dysfunctional. Several strategies to reduce or optimize conflict are discussed in the next section.

Conflict is contextual; there are no absolute right or wrong ways to deal with it. The difference between conflict that results in positive growth and conflict that causes disruption depends on personalities, relationships, issues, and environments. Possible outcomes must be considered before final decisions about strategies are made. However, recent research indicates a trend toward a more integrative approach to the handling of conflict. The following section will consider some of the traditional approaches to conflict as well as some of the more recent integrative approaches.

CONFLICT MANAGEMENT

A new term, *conflict management* is emerging in business circles today. What is it and how does it work? It is more than just reducing or ignoring conflict; it is the planning and control of conflict through stimulation, encouragement, and resolution. This philosophy recognizes and encourages conflict so that the manager has a better chance to control it. Conflict management only works when top management makes it known that they believe functional or issue-oriented conflict is desirable.

Historical Approaches to Conflict

Traditionally, managers have not been very good at conflict management. The historic approaches to conflict resolution have included withdrawal, suppression, smoothing, forcing, and perhaps at best, compromise. None of these gets at the root problem.

Withdrawal simply bypasses those in conflict, while suppression requires witholding information. Both utilize the communication process in

its most negative sense: filtering, distortion, and even the lack of communication. Stimac comments that these methods may not always be bad: "If a person who has thought through when, where, and how to confront an individual concludes that confrontation will be disastrous, then it is more functional to avoid it."[19] However, he emphasizes that in this instance the person has at least thought through the situation. If the party has not analyzed the situation or considered confrontation as an alternative, perhaps the person is taking the path of least resistance.

Smoothing is playing down the differences between individuals and groups while emphasizing common interests. It is only a superficial resolution, and is used mainly when a temporary solution is needed. The communication activity used with smoothing is deceptive, misleading, and ultimately will not avoid a recurrence of the conflict situation.

Forcing, which results in a win-lose situation, is another approach to conflict management. Here the gain by one of the participants necessitates the other's loss. This method imposes the goals, methods, or values of one participant to the other. Strategies are aimed at defeating the opponent. Communications are judgmental and accusatory and feedback is not encouraged or allowed.

Compromise is the most frequently used technique to resolve conflicts, and is the most socially acceptable or democratic. There are no winners or losers since each party is required to sacrifice something. The most traditional example of compromise is union-management negotiations. During bargaining, each side will agree to give up a demand if the other side will do the same. Although some satisfactory solutions can be reached, the long-run effects are that each side feels they have surrendered something of value.

Integrative Conflict Management

Confrontation, third-party interventions, and **creative problem solving** are often described as separate techniques in the handling of conflict. We present all three as a unit since each can be used to supplement the others, and the use of all three may be the best approach. The word or name used in each of these techniques should give you a clue as to its definition, characteristics, and process.

A confrontation occurs when involved parties directly engage each other and focus on the conflict between them. The purposes of such a meeting may include: diagnosing the conflict to get at its root problem, improving the relationship between the parties, acknowledging a commitment to a common goal, or identifying ways to de-escalate the conflict.

A neutral setting and sufficient time are necessary to facilitate a productive confrontation. The parties must have open minds and a sincere desire to resolve the conflict. Repeating and summarizing the other person's comments, clarifying your own messages, and diagnosing and ana-

lyzing difficulties are useful steps toward resolution.

Schmidt and Tannenbaum contend that third party interventions and creative problem solving can produce the most effective conflict resolution. They feel that a third party is invaluable in suggesting a greater variety of possible solutions. Also, a third party can listen with understanding (rather than evaluation) to clarify the issues and determine whether they are based on different perceptions. Finally, a third party can recognize and accept such feelings as fear, jealousy, anger, or anxiety without making a judgment.[20] All of these stand as definite advantages to the use of third parties, but must be weighed against the time, cost, and convenience involved.

Creative problem solving is an attempt to arrive at a conflict solution that is of high quality *and* acceptable to the parties involved. The content of the discussion or confrontation should be free from accusations and value judgments. The parties should direct their energies toward defining and defeating the problem, not each other. This requires a commitment to a common goal, frequently referred to as a **superordinate goal,** that supersedes all of the individual goals sought by either participant.

Finally, confrontation and creative problem solving, with or without a third party, demand an exhaustive and nonjudgmental search for alternative solutions and a decision-making process that is based on critical evaluation and agreement.

Sensitivity Training

A final approach to conflict resolution that has been used with some moderate success is sensitivity training. Laboratory education, more commonly known as sensitivity training, was popular in the 1960–75 period. Although this experience received severe criticism from many and gradually waned in its popularity, it is now being revived as a strategy to deal with conflict. It is perhaps most useful if viewed as an on-going process in an attempt to develop awareness rather than as a technique for confronting specific conflict situations.

This group experience attempts to provide opportunities for individuals to expose their behavior, give and receive feedback, experiment with new behavior, and develop awareness and acceptance of self and others. There are no set agendas, standards, or group norms except those set by the participants. If negative feelings develop, irritations are expressed openly and without malice. This promotes an understanding of the conditions that facilitate group processes. Other advantages are increased self-insight and knowledge, and the development of skills for diagnosing and analyzing individual, group, and organizational behavior. Some individuals may learn a great deal in this experience; others reject the process. Consequently, this technique must be approached with caution and with a good facilitator.

Approaches to conflict resolution are tools—not ends in themselves. There are no magic cures to conflict; each approach may be appropriate in different circumstances. A manager needs to have the awareness, capacity, and flexibility to select the most effective method depending on the situation.

RESEARCH RESULTS

Eleanor Phillips and Ric Cheston reported the results of their research in an article titled, "Conflict Resolutions: What Works?" This study investigated two contradictory strategies for conflict resolution: the tough guy approach and the problem-solver approach. Some 25 mid-level managers, with at least 10 years of experience, who were attending the Sloan School of Management were asked to describe two conflicts from their own experience—a "good" conflict and a "bad" conflict. Incidents were analyzed and classified by the study team. Some of the conclusions were: "Structural conflict caused by struggles between departments or groups was the most common type described by study participants; next was conflict due to personal value or personality. Communication conflict was least common."[21]

The authors say that forcing was the method most commonly used to resolve the conflicts and that compromise was the least used. In a number of instances, the manager first attempted to use one method and when it failed, would fall back on another. Forcing was also the most commonly used "fallback" method. Figure 15–1 identifies the conflict resolution methods used by type of conflict, and Figure 15–2 identifies the fallback methods of conflict resolution.

The authors point out that positive outcomes from the use of problem-solving are most likely to occur if

1. There is goal agreement and good communication between the participants.

FIGURE 15–1 Conflict Resolution Methods Used, by Type of Conflict

Conflict Resolution Method Used	Types of Conflict			Totals: Methods
	Communication	Structure	Personal	
Forcing	2	10	11	23
Problem solving	5	7	0	12
Compromise	0	5	0	5
Avoidance	2	6	4	12
Totals:Types	9	28	15	52

SOURCE: Eleanor Phillips and Ric Cheston. "Conflict Resolution: What Works?" *California Management Review* 21 (Summer 1979), p. 78

FIGURE 15–2 Fallback Methods of Conflict Resolution

First Method Attempted		Fallback Resolution Method		
	Forcing	Problem Solving	Compromise	Avoidance
Forcing	5	1	3	1
Problem solving	10	10		
Avoidance	2	2		

SOURCE: Eleanor Phillips and Ric Cheston. "Conflict Resolution: What Works?" *California Management Review* 21 (Summer 1979) p. 78

2. There is equal power between the parties, or if power is not an issue.

3. There is equal representation of the involved parties.

4. There is trust and a sincere regard for others, open-mindedness, and no previous history of conflict.

5. The conflict is inherent in the structure of the situation.[22]

In a study titled, "Communication, Conflict, and the Corporate Connection," Dale Level and Shelby Morton identified types of conflict and their resolution. They asked 124 business managers, enrolled in an evening MBA program, to describe a conflict situation in which they had been involved at work within the last six months. They were asked to classify the conflict situation as: (1) issue-oriented, (2) personality- or emotion-oriented, or (3) an issue-oriented conflict that degenerated into a personality clash. The managers were then asked to indicate if the conflict had been resolved and to briefly describe the method of conflict resolution. Figure 15–3 summarizes the results.

The results indicated that the business managers who participated experienced approximately the same number of issue, personality, and issue-to-personality-oriented conflicts. However, there was a 62 percent greater chance of having that conflict resolved if it was issue-oriented. The researchers did not specify methods of resolution, but the open-ended responses by the managers indicated that problem-solving and

---

FIGURE 15–3 Types of Conflict and Number of Resolutions

	Number	Resolved	
		Yes	No
Issue-oriented	44 (35%)	36 (82%)	8 (18%)
Personality-oriented	40 (32%)	9 (23%)	31 (78%)
Issue-to-personality	40 (32%)	7 (18%)	32 (80%)
Total nonissue	80 (65%)	16 (20%)	63 (79%)
	N = 124		

---

forcing were the two primary methods used.[23] These results are in general agreement with those reported by Phillips and Cheston. The data reported by Level and Morton were gathered during a modified sensitivity training session. In this session, the types and characteristics of conflict were defined and illustrated. Mock conflict situations were developed, discussed, and an opportunity for role playing was given. Most participants felt this type of session helped increase their awareness of conflicts and the various processes that can be used to resolve these conflicts.[24]

Earlier in this chapter reference was made to three types of conflict identified by Gandz: pseudoconflict, common-problem conflict, and conflicts of interest. Although not a research-based study, Gandz states that each type of conflict requires a different method of resolution behavior by those involved. For example: pseudoconflict requires **information exchange;** common-problem conflicts necessitate a range of **problem-solving behaviors** that include the exchange of information, searching for, and evaluating alternative solutions; and conflicts of interest may be resolved, or at least regulated, either by **bargaining** or by **adjudication.**

The final points to be made here, substantiated by the research results of Phillips and Cheston, and Level and Morton, and by the statements of Gandz are: (1) each technique may be appropriate in different circumstances, and (2) communication is vital to the conflict resolution process.

POWER AND CONFLICT

A discussion of conflict without a discussion of power would be incomplete. Just as conflict exists, so does power. Perhaps it would be equally correct to say, just as power exists, so does conflict. Either can come first and lead to the other.

Power and the related concepts of control and influence frequently create conflict. Person A has power over person B to the extent that A can get B to do something that B would not otherwise do. That one person has the power to coerce another suggests that one exerts a force in total opposition to some or all of the previously existing forces. This is potential conflict!

Let's look at two competing concepts to control the behavior of an employee: a supervisor urges the employee to speed-up production while group norms demand the opposite. There is external conflict between the supervisor and the peer group. In their attempt to exercise power over the employee they cause an internal conflict for the employee.

Conflict could also be present without the group pressure. The employee cannot escape some sense of conflict when urged to speed-up. The employee's production level is a combination of his need for money, aspirations for promotion, physical condition, skill, personal drive, values, attitudes toward the supervisor, and many other things. To produce a

change, a new frame of reference must be established, and the forces that contributed to the older production level must be changed.

If the employee has no power over the supervisor, the internal or perceived conflict of the employee may not be expressed. He may try to comply, and no overt conflict results between the two. If the employee has and exercises some reciprocal power, it may be used to resist attempts at influence.

The more frequently conflict occurs in an organization, the greater the need for power. Power is the ability to induce change in the behavior of others. Out of the desire to induce such changes, each member of the organization becomes a seeker of power and, if the search is successful, a wielder of power.

Power is a function of what each person values and the nature of the relationship between the participants. Five types of power are referred to by various authors.

1. Reward power occurs when person A is in a position to control the rewards that B will attain. Supervisors frequently make recommendations for employees regarding salary increases and promotions. Although these decisions should be based on merit, the supervisor is still in a position to recommend or control these benefits.

2. Coercive power is the reverse of reward power. A has some form of punishment to level against B if B does not do what A wants. Being assigned all the dirty jobs and told to work overtime may be expressions of coercive power.

3. Legitimate power stems from A's position in the organizational system. A supervisor has legitimate power over an employee while at work; a teacher has legitimate power over a student while in the classroom; and a parent has legitimate power over a child while that child remains at home. Frequently, all three of these power bases are used together; usually they create resentment in the employee, student, or child toward the supervisor, teacher, or parent.

4. Referent power occurs when person B identifies strongly with person A. The relationship may be personal or work related, but there is a strong agreement in attitudes, opinions, values, and feelings. Person A becomes something of a role model for B.

5. Expert power occurs because person A has some special knowledge or expertise that is useful to B. If student B is studying with student A (who has special expertise in the subject) and A suggests that they go for a beer, B will probably comply with the hopes that he or she will be able to gain some of A's insight into the subject.

Currency is another term used in conjunction with power. Currencies are sources of power used in conflict situations. When others value the currencies of person A (and see A as the only way to attain them) then A can exercise some degree of power. The major currencies that people call

on are: (1) economic (reward or coercive power), (2) position or status (legitimate power), (3) interpersonal linkages (referent power), and (4) knowledge (expert power).

Another relationship between power and conflict is the distinction between absolute and relative power. When a person's goals are specific and limited, the person will seek relative power. Absolute power, which maximizes conflict potential, is a power that is greater than the power possessed by others.

Conflict and power are related at the interpersonal level, the organizational level, and at the national level. If you doubt this relationship, consider the American hostages in Iran, the Russian invasion of Afghanistan, the American and Russian withdrawals from the 1980 and 1984 Olympics, Cuba's determination of who would be sent to this country, or any conflict at home or work. Possibly, conflict is another word for power, and power is another word for ego.

SUMMARY

Most conflicts arise when people are compelled to live and work together. No one is certain whether a conflict-free organization has ever existed or if it would be a desirable goal to attain. Antagonisms, tensions, aggressions, negative attitudes and the frustration of perceived conflict will always be present whenever we live and work with others.

In addition to identifying various types, sources, effects, and assumptions about conflict, several measures to combat the problems of conflict have been proposed in this chapter. Typical measures include avoidance, forcing, compromise, confrontation, third-party intervention, problem solving, and sensitivity training. Most encourage dissemination of correct information to break down false prejudices and unfavorable stereotypes. Others appeal to ideals of fair play and openmindedness. Whatever technique is employed, managers should place emphasis on improving communication.

A conflict-free organization is not necessarily a desired goal. Conflict can reflect a healthy atmosphere in which all parties are actively pursuing the attainment of organizational goals.

Communication behaviors and activities can play an important role in establishing an organizational environment that encourages constructive conflicts. Through open communication, many worthwhile exchanges can occur that may prove beneficial to organizational goal accomplishment. This will occur, however, only if the groundwork for establishing trust and openness has been established. The manner and content of communications can go a long way in establishing the framework for the constructive use of conflict situations.

DISCUSSION QUESTIONS

1. How does the definition of conflict affect the way we think about conflict? Define conflict without using negative terms. Indicate positive and negative outcomes of an organizational conflict situation.

2. What are the sources of conflict between people within an organization? What are the sources of conflict between individuals and the organization?

3. Harris' classification scheme identifies the three most frequently encountered types and sources of conflict. Explain the Harris classification system.

4. Enumerate five negative consequences of conflict in an organization.

5. List four potential positive consequences of conflict in a business organization. What implications should management draw from the positive aspects of conflict?

6. Discuss the five stages that characterize conflict according to Louis R. Pondy. What general conclusions regarding conflict can be drawn from the Pondy sequencing scheme?

7. What is conflict management and what are the new assumptions regarding conflict management?

8. How can tension be healthy for an organization?

9. Contrast traditional and modern conflict management techniques and orientations.

10. Define and compare these conflict management techniques:
    a. Confrontation.
    b. Third-party intervention.
    c. Creative problem solving.

11. Discuss the benefits of third-party intervention.

12. What is creative problem solving and how is it used to reduce conflict?

13. According to the Phillip and Cheston research study, what conditions are most conducive to ensuring positive outcomes from using problem solving in resolving conflict?

14. Compare the results of the Phillips and Cheston research study on conflict and that of Level and Morton.

15. Define the five types of power. How are power and conflict related?

NOTES

[1]Joseph S. Himes, *Conflict and Conflict Management* (Atlanta: University of Georgia Press, 1980), p. 2.

[2]Dennis King, "Three Cheers for Conflict," *Personnel* 58, no. 1 (January–February 1981, pp. 13–22.

[3]Lee Thayer, *Communication and Communication Systems in Organization, Management and Interpersonal Relations* (Homewood, Ill.: Richard D. Irwin, 1968), p. 13.

[4]Morton Deutsch, "Conflicts: Productive and Destructive," *Journal of Social Issues* 25 (1969), p. 7.

[5]Jeffrey Pfeffer, *Power in Organizations* (Marshfield, Mass: Ballinger Publishing Co., 1981), p. 74.

[6]Daniel Katz and Robert L Kahn, *The Social Psychology of Organizations,* 2nd ed. (New York: John Wiley & Sons, 1978), p. 613.

[7]For more detailed definitions, see for example, Jaynette Hineline and Dale Level, "Strategic IntraOrganizational Conflict" (Fayetteville: University of Arkansas, 1986), working paper in progress.

[8]Kenneth R. MacCrimmon and Ronald N. Taylor, "Decision Making and Problem Solving," *Handbook of Industrial and Organizational Psychology*, ed. Marvin D. Dunnette (Chicago: 1976), p. 1424.

[9]Steward L. Tubbs, *A Systems Approach to Small Group Interaction* (Reading, Mass.: Addison-Wesley Publishing, 1978), p. 244.

[10]Brian L. Hawkins and Paul Preston, *Managerial Communication* (Santa Monica, Calif.: Goodyear Publishing, 1981), chap. 10; Andrew Szilegyi and Marc J. Wallace, Jr., *Organizational Behavior and Performance* (Glenview, Ill.: Scott, Foresman, 1983), chap. 8; and James H. Donnelly, James L. Gibson, and John M. Ivancevich, *Fundamentals of Management,* 5th ed. (Plano, Tex.: Business Publications, 1984), chap. 13.

[11]Jeffery Gandz, "Resolving Conflicts: A Guide for the Industrial Relations Manager," *Personnel* 56; no. 6 (November-December 1979), p. 25.

[12]O. J. Harris, *Managing People at Work* (New York: John Wiley & Sons, 1976), p. 361.

[13]Morton Deutsch, "Conflict: Productive and Destructive," *Journal of Social Issues* 25 (1969), pp. 7–41.

[14]Warren H. Schmidt and Kenneth W. Thomas, "Conflict: A Powerful Process for (Good or Bad) Changes," *Management Review* 63 (1974), p. 4.

[15]Karen Horney, *Our Inner Conflicts* (New York: Charles Scribner's Sons, 1945), p. 27.

[16]Bobby R. Patton and Kim Giffin, *Problem Solving Group Interaction* (New York: Harper & Row, 1973), p. 90.

[17]Alan Weiss, "Conflict: It's What You Make It," *Supervisory Management* 19 (1974), p. 30.

[18]Louis R. Pondy, "Organizational Conflict: Concepts and Models," *Administrative Science Quarterly* 12 (1967), p. 306.

[19]Michele Stimac, "Strategies for Resolving Conflict: Their Functional and Dysfunctional Sides," *Personnel* 59, no. 6 (November-December 1982), pp. 54–64.

[20]W. Schmidt and R. Tannenbaum, "The Management of Differences," *Harvard Business Review* 38 (1960), pp. 107–15.

[21]Eleanor Phillips and Ric Cheston, "Conflict Resolution: What Works?" *California Management Review* 21 (Summer 1979), pp. 76–83.

[22]Ibid.

[23]Dale Level and Shelby Morton, "Communication, Conflict, and the Corporate Connection," Paper presented to the International Business Communication Association convention, New York City, November 1983.

[24]Ibid.

SUGGESTED READINGS

BLAKE, ROBERT, and JANE S. MOUTON. *Solving Costly Organizational Conflicts.* San Francisco: Jossey-Bass, 1984.

BROWN, DAVID. *Managing Conflict at Organizational Interfaces.* Reading, Mass. Addison-Wesley, 1983.

FERRARO, VINCENT L., and SHEILA A. ADAMS. "Interdepartmental Conflict: Practical Ways to Prevent and Reduce It." *Personnel* 61, no. 4 (July-August 1984), pp. 12–23.

FOGG, RICHARD W. "Dealing with Conflict: A Repertoire of Creative Peaceful Approaches." *Journal of Conflict Resolution* 29 (June 1985), pp. 330–58.

FRASER, NIALL M., and KEITH W. HIPEL. *Conflict Analysis: Models and Resolutions.* New York: North-Holland, 1984.

JONES, ROBERT E., and CHARLES S. WHITE, "Relationships among Personality, Conflict, Resolution Styles, and Task Effectiveness." *Group and Organization Studies* 10 (June 1985), pp. 152–67.

POWELL, JON T. "Stress Listening: Coping with Angry Confrontations. *Personnel Journal* (May 1986), pp. 27–30.

ROWEN, MARY P., and MICHAEL BAKER. "Are You Hearing Enough Employee Concerns?". *Harvard Business Review* 84 (May-June 1984), p. 127ff.

TURNER, STEVE, and FRANK WEED. *Conflict in Organizations.* Englewood Cliffs, N.J.: Prentice-Hall, 1983.

VAN DE VLIERT, EVERT. "Escalative Intervention in Small Group Conflicts." *The Journal of Applied Behavioral Science* 21, no. 1 (1985), pp. 19–36.

Part Four

Communication

Enhancement

Chapter 16

Organizational Change

and Development

Chapter 16 Case

How did this staff meeting get out of hand so quickly? Only a few minutes ago, you made the announcement that workmen would arrive this morning to begin installing the new computer system. With a terminal on every desk and direct access to the home office computer, this system will revolutionize the way your service organization does business. You are excited about the opportunities that will come with the new efficiency and speed of operations and know everyone will like the system once they get used to it. You have a small staff that has worked well together over the years. You genuinely like them and wanted to surprise them with your "new toy." But two of the women have left the room literally in tears, Jim is red-faced with anger because he says he can't type so he can't possibly use the "new-fangled thing," and it looks like open revolt is about to break out. What did you do wrong?

INTRODUCTION

Our perceptions, attitudes, and motives are constantly growing and changing. We learn more each day about ourselves and our environment, experiencing an ever-expanding reality. The learning experiences we encounter influence how we respond to and accept change as well as how we respond to one another. If we are to maintain effective interpersonal relationships, we must understand the change process and how it affects our relationships. The contemporary environment is turbulent, uncertain, and changing; consequently, an organization cannot operate as a closed system. Instead it must be in touch with and sensitive to the environment if the organization is to survive. And to survive, it must change.

Here we will enumerate the more important pressures for change and development. After identifying the operational steps that constitute the

change process, we will introduce a model outlining the organizational development process. Simultaneously, we will consider the role of communication in change and development, and demonstrate how effective communication can improve the ability of an organization to manage change and development.

PRESSURES FOR CHANGE

Change is ubiquitous. It has been said that the only true constant in our lives is change. In the introduction of his widely acclaimed book about the connection between the past, present, and future, John Naisbitt said:

> That is the intention of *Megatrends*—to discover the many ways in which America is restructuring, to understand how the pieces fit together, and to try to see what the new society looks like.[1]

In the conclusion of his book Naisbitt tells us that we are living in a "time of parenthesis" which lies between two eras. About this time and its people he said:

> Those who are willing to handle the ambiguity of this in-between period and to anticipate the new era will be a quantum leap ahead of those who hold on to the past. The time of the parenthesis is a time of change and questioning.[2]

It is a time of change because there are so many continuous pressures that make change inevitable. Let us consider the most prevalent of those forces.

Technological Development

Technological development is perhaps the primary source of pressure for change, and the greatest vehicle for ushering change into our lives. The development of the plow allowed farmers to drastically increase food production to the point that they created surpluses. This created a need for, and development of, markets, transportation, warehousing, bookkeeping and so forth in order to dispose of the surpluses.

As one piece of technology is devised, it seems to induce the creation and development of another almost in chain reaction fashion. This was certainly so during the 19th century when so many agricultural breakthroughs occurred. One piece of machinery after another was invented, and the agricultural world was carried along by the unebbing flow of technological discovery.

This has also been true in the high-tech area of the late 20th century. Computer technology has gone rapidly through transistors, microchips, large-scale integration and very large-scale integration. With quantum physics we moved quickly into microwave and laser technology. Thus, technology serves as a vehicle carrying change constantly along and into

our lives. These changes intensify the need for interaction and communication and force people to initiate information-sharing encounters.

Advancing Communication

Technology has had an effect on communications: the printing press, telegraph, telephone, television, and the computer. Modern information technology has improved communication to the point where we really do have what Marshall McLuhan called a "global village."[3] The peoples of the world now live in what is essentially an ultra-large village where the sharing of relevant information is instantaneous. When a plane crashes in a remote part of the world, or terrorists strike in one of the world's major cities, we are informed within minutes. We know about significant breakthroughs in medicine or the pursuit of peace almost immediately. News of such occurrences, whether in politics, art, or finance, has profound effects on us. We must understand these effects and be prepared to cope with them.

Increasing Interdependence

Because we now live in McLuhan's global village, we not only know more about one another, but have to come to depend more on one another. The level of economic, social, and political interdependence has increased dramatically, and organizations have developed various methods to minimize the unmanageable level of uncertainty stemming from such interdependence. In the United States a new merger movement began in the 1980s. Takeovers have included many popular names: GE purchased RCA, GM bought out Hughes Aircraft, Phillip Morris now owns General Foods. Internationally, we have become mutually dependent through military pacts, trade agreements, and exchange programs in the arts and education.

This interdependence means that we are greatly affected by what others do. Remember the energy crisis of the 70s? The frequent acts of terrorism throughout the world? The continuing search for peace and human rights? More and more, the have-nots have the opportunity to see what the haves have—and that brings about greater pressure for social, political, and economic change. Part of that change must be a new set of responses to cope with the new reality. Once again, the need for increased communication is evident.

Changing Value Systems

Accompanying, and sometimes resulting from these pressures, are drastic, traumatic changes in values. In South Africa, for example, the people, black and white, exist in a state of shock, frustration, and confusion trying to assess what has happened to their lifestyle and where they are headed.

Those who interact with South Africa are equally concerned. They must assess the change taking place there and be prepared to respond properly.

In the United States major upheavals have occurred in our value system as a result of the Vietnam War, severe economic problems, and changing roles for men and women. We have househusbands and female astronauts, role reversals that would have been totally incongruous just 20 years ago. Such shifts create new relationships and the need for new patterns of behavior and communication.

The Legal System

The legal systems of most industrialized societies are a major vehicle for delivering change into our presence. The U.S. Constitution, numerous federal statutes, and case law provide the foundation of our business law. Examination of the impact these canons on business policies and practices clearly illustrates the role of law as a powerful change vehicle.

For example, changes in employer-employee relations are far-reaching because of the National Labor Relations Act. The 1964 Civil Rights Act drastically altered the treatment and political role of minorities and females—on and off the job. The growing body of case law concerning issues such as performance evaluation and employment-at-will is precipitating further changes in the relationship between employer and employee. Court proceedings and legislative actions are changing the relationship between business firms and their consumers, creditors and their clients, and doctors and their patients. As the legal environment is reshaped, so are behavioral expectations, and interaction and information-sharing are necessary to learn what those expectations are.

Education

Education is another powerful force driving the machinery of change. In a sense, education *is* change since the purpose of education is to provide a learning experience, and by definition, learning is a long-term change in behavior. Public school systems and institutions of higher learning have as one of their goals the development of students into something more than or different from what they were before they entered the educational process. Thus, education brings into the lives of its recipients a greater understanding of their environment and a greater range of responses for coping with life.

Reference Individuals and Groups

We have identified major institutions—technology, law, and education—as vehicles for change. People can also be vehicles for change. Powerful

reference individuals can provide leadership or inspiration that will elicit change—Lincoln, King, Kennedy, Ghandi, and Hitler serve as powerful examples and incite large segments of society to new ways of thinking, feeling, and acting. They may provide a sense of self worth, pride, or courage that allows the affected individuals to transcend their previous level of expectations and behavior.

Occasionally a reference group will have the same effect. The members of such a group can develop an identity or a cause with which large numbers of individuals can identify. Through persuasive action, such groups can usher in major changes in the behavior and lifetime outcomes of affected individuals.

Professional associations (AMA, AICPA), ethnic and religious organizations (NAACP, Catholic Church), and issues groups (MADD, Sierra Club) can all have profound lifetime effects on their members as well as the culture in which they function.

THE CHANGE PROCESS

Some organizations identify the major sources of change, monitor them, and when necessary, react to the pressures they create. However, this response may not be enough to ensure organizational survival. Therefore, a proactive approach to organizational change and development becomes not only attractive, but necessary.

One of the most frequently cited explanations of the change process is the model developed by Kurt Lewin.[4] Lewin's model involves three basic stages: **unfreezing, changing,** and **refreezing.** (See Figure 16–1.)

Drawing an analogy between the behavior of an individual and a frozen liquid helps to illustrate Lewin's approach to change. Once a liquid is frozen into a particular form, it must be unfrozen *before* it can be changed into another form. Once unfrozen, the liquid can be poured into a container of another form (i.e., changed), and then refrozen in the desired shape.

Similarly, before an individual's behavior can be changed, existing undesirable patterns must be thawed and discouraged. Subsequently new response patterns can be formed and solidified through proper reinforce-

---

FIGURE 16–1 Lewin's Process of Change

Stage	Goal	Technique
Unfreezing	Discouraging undesirable behavior	Extinction
Changing	Teaching new behavior	Coaching, demonstration
Refreezing	Solidifying new behavior	Positive and negative reinforcement

ment. Before we examine the Lewin model, there are several concepts from behavioral psychology that will expedite our examination and discussion.

The Law of Effect and Reinforcement

We begin with an understanding of Thorndike's **law of effect.**[5] This principle of learning says that behavior is a function of its consequences: if an individual feels good after doing something, the probability of repeating that behavior increases. If an individual feels bad after doing something, the probability of repeating that behavior decreases. A most important concept for applying the law of effect is **reinforcement.**

To increase the probability of occurrence of a particular behavior pattern, it should be reinforced when it occurs. Behavior is reinforced by introducing rewards or **reinforcers** after the performance of some desirable behavior. Reinforcers can be positive or negative. A positive reinforcer, when introduced, makes the individual feel good (e.g., money, food, a pat on the back, a kind word, an opportunity to learn). Negative reinforcers make the individual feel bad (e.g., pain, offensive statements). Providing these reinforcers is referred to as positive reinforcement and negative reinforcement.

Positive reinforcement makes the individual feel good *after doing something desirable.* It is the most constructive way to alter behavior because it creates a positive outcome and it focuses on a desired response. A simple example would be to say "thank you" to someone immediately after he has done a task you asked him to do.

Negative reinforcement is the act of removing something considered undesirable by the individual (e.g., hard work, pain) *after doing something desirable,* thereby making the individual feel good. It is the next most constructive way to alter behavior because it too focuses on a desired response and creates a positive outcome. An example would be for a teacher to excuse students from homework because they performed well in the classroom.

Punishment is the act of applying painful stimulation or the threat of such stimulation. Contrary to popular tendencies, punishment is the least constructive way to alter behavior because it is the act of providing something undesirable after the individual *does something undesirable.* Punishment is not an effective means of behavior modification because the only message the individual gets is that what he did was wrong without informing the individual as to what is correct.

Because of changing circumstances (e.g., new technology, new relationships due to reorganization), it may become desirable or necessary to eliminate certain behavior patterns that were previously reinforced. A very useful concept at this point is **extinction.** Psychologists refer to extinction as the act of withholding reinforcement following the occurrence

of some behavior which was previously reinforced. The individual would no longer feel good after engaging in the behavior. As a result, according to the law of effect, the probability of occurrence of the behavior would diminish.

Two additional terms that are useful for our discussion are **change agent** and **change target.** A change agent is an individual or group responsible for designing, introducing, and effecting change. A change target is the individual or group that the change agent is trying to influence.

Unfreezing Behavior

To change archaic, irrelevant, or undesirable present behavior patterns, it is first necessary to unfreeze them and bring the change target into a pliable state where behavior can be reshaped. The individual must realize that her current behavior is no longer rewarding.

To convey that message, it is necessary to either discontinue reinforcement or refuse to acknowledge the behavior. Eventually the individual will become aware of the absence of reinforcement, and will gradually experiment with new behaviors or seek clues and direction for appropriate behavior. When the individual begins to exhibit experimenting or searching behavior, the current behavior is considered "unfrozen." The manager should be ready to provide the proper direction and definition of the new behavior.

Changing Behavior

The principal task during this stage of the change process is to specify the appropriate new behavior, and to influence the individual by explanation, demonstration, and coaching to adopt that behavior. There are, according to Kelman, three processes of social influence: **compliance, identification,** and **internalization.**[6] The former requires only superficial obedience while the latter requires intense commitment from the individual.

Compliance. Compliance occurs when an individual is "interested in attaining certain specific rewards or in avoiding certain specific punishments that the influencing agent controls."[7] The individual adopts behavior not because of a belief in the inherent value of it, but rather because it is instrumental in achieving a particular end. For example, it is easy to observe motorists traveling in excess of 55 miles per hour on most interstate highways, *except* when law enforcement agents are present. Likewise, employees who are seeking good performance evaluations will placate and patronize a superior by carefully observing rules and protocol in which they do not believe.

The most significant feature of compliance is that the force which

induces the behavior is outside the individual, as in the case of a police officer or a supervisor. And the instant the police officer or the supervisor leaves the situation, the individual may revert to other less desirable behavior patterns. Consequently, behavior prompted through compliance is temporary at best. At worst the individual may come to despise the forced behavior and the force, and eventually leave the situation.

Because of the requirement for external force, formalized communication and control mechanisms are essential. The required behavior must be constantly "displayed" (e.g., signs, posted rules) and employee behavior must be monitored.

Identification.   Identification occurs when "an individual adopts behavior derived from another person or a group because this behavior is associated with a satisfying self-defining relationship with this person or group."[8] This kind of behavior is highly imitative, and quite common in the presence of strong referent individuals.

Commercial advertisers often employ celebrities (e.g., sports figures, actors and actresses, politicians) to endorse products, issues, and programs. The rationale is that if consumers identify with the celebrities, and the celebrities are seen using a product or supporting an issue, the consumers will be persuaded to buy the product or support the issue. So, for example, when Bill Cosby drinks Coke in front of a national TV audience, those for whom he is a role model will drink Coke. And when Jerry Lewis issues a plea to support muscular dystrophy, those who identify with him and his position will contribute to MD programs.

Here again, the most significant feature is that the force inducing the behavior is outside the individual. As long as the relationship is satisfying, and as long as the referent individual is present, the adopted behavior will persist. But if the relationship should change and become dissatisfying, or if the referent individual should be removed from the situation, the influence may stop and the behavior will cease. Behavior change brought about by identification is likely to be stronger and last longer than that induced by compliance, but because it is outside the individual, and because the individual does not directly subscribe to the behavior, it is subject to change.

Internalization.   Internalization occurs when "an individual accepts influence because the induced behavior is congruent with his value system."[9] In the case of internalization the individual analyzes both the behavior and the reasons for it, and accepts them because they are consonant with his beliefs and feelings. An individual might read a series of articles outlining the merits of driving only 55 miles per hour, such as saving lives and saving energy. If these reasons are consistent with his beliefs and feelings, he internalizes the behavior and drives 55 miles per hour.

The major feature that distinguishes internalization from compliance

and identification is the fact that internalization comes from inside the individual. Consequently there is no need for enforcers (e.g., police officer, supervisors) or referent individuals. The force for change is inside the individual, therefore, the behavior induced by internalization is stronger and longer lasting.

Internalization is the preferred process to effect a change in behavior. Internalization requires careful development and sharing of information so that the individual can reason and subsequently make the decision to adopt the desired behavior. Unfortunately, managers are too frequently reluctant to take the time to develop or present the information that will allow employees to internalize beliefs and behaviors beneficial to the welfare of the organization. They don't want to give employees the time or freedom to reason and make decisions, but prefer to rely on compliance to achieve desired outcomes. The result is indifference, a lack of commitment, and no real change in performance. The benefits of internalization are distinctly superior, and once again underscore the need for effective communication.

Refreezing Behavior

Once an individual has been persuaded, by whatever means, that her current behavior is inadequate (unfreezing), and she has been given direction for new behavior (changing), it is time to solidify the new behavior. The key to refreezing is proper reinforcement of the appropriate behavior and this will occur only if the reinforcers (e.g., social approval and recognition, opportunities for personal development, advancement, monetary compensation) are matched to the change target's values and needs. Managers often project to employees those things that the managers value, and rather than strengthening desired behavior, this provokes employee resentment, frustration, and turnover.

Reinforcement can occur in a variety of patterns called **reinforcement schedules** that can be either continuous or intermittent.

Continuous reinforcement requires that the change agent provide a reward *every time* the individual demonstrates the newly adopted behavior. To encourage a secretary to type errorless letters, it would be necessary to provide reinforcement every time a letter was typed without an error; letters with errors would not be reinforced. Continuous reinforcement will support an individual when he is learning and engaging in a new behavior pattern. Behavior that is reinforced on a continuous basis will also extinguish very quickly.

Instead of using continuous reinforcement, a number of **intermittent** schedules are possible. Intermittent schedules can be structured in two ways: **fixed** and **variable.** Each of these types can be varied on the basis of **response frequency** or **elapsed time.** Combining these features yields four possible schedules.

Fixed interval: Provides a reinforcer after the passage of a specific amount of time (e.g., every five minutes). The most common example of fixed interval reinforcement is the conventional pay period (e.g., every week, every two weeks).

Variable interval: Provides a reinforcer after varying time periods (e.g., after two minutes, then after three hours, then after thirty minutes.) Variable interval schedules are not commonly used in industry. An example might be a fisherman who sits on the lake all day and catches fish in a random pattern during the day.

Fixed ratio: Ratio here refers to the number of reinforced responses to nonreinforced responses. Thus a fixed ratio would involve providing a reinforcer after a given number of responses (e.g., after every fifth response). An example would be to compliment a secretary after every third error-free letter.

Variable ratio: This schedule would require randomly varying the ratio (e.g., after third response, then after fifteenth response, then after eighth response). A common example of this would the pattern of winning from playing the slot machines in Las Vegas.

The application of these different reinforcement schedules will depend on the objectives, individuals, and time frame of a given situation. It is frequently wise to use continuous reinforcement in the initial stage of refreezing, then move to an intermittent schedule when the behavior begins to solidify.

The Role of Communication

As we examine the influence process, especially the long-term benefits of internalization relative to compliance, the role of communication is underscored. In their description of an integrated change program Huse and Bowditch reported:

> One of the first tasks of the change agents was to open up better communication channels so that the organization members could develop mutual trust and understanding before new and more profound changes were made.[10]

Progress toward change is frequently impossible without open communication and a free flow of information. In their discussion of goals for organizational change and development Porter, Lawler, and Hackman's two primary goals were trust and open communication. About trust the authors said:

> Presumably, it means that members of organizations, no matter what their positions, can rely on the integrity of what other members say and do—in short, where there is trust there is the feeling that "others will not take advantage of me."[11]

Porter and his colleagues make it clear that the amount of success in or-

ganizational development efforts is clearly a function of the level of trust management develops. The authors point out that a high level of trust and open communication go hand in hand:

> This goal [open communication] follows naturally the goal of the development of a high level of trust, for without the existence of a general level of trust it is virtually impossible to achieve open communication. Open communication involves, basically, the free provision of accurate information . . . regardless of what the facts are.[12]

Open communication is self-reinforcing, and conducive to internalization because it reduces the negative and threatening consequences of sharing of information. Trust and open communication are not normal responses in organizational life. But the reduction of threat allows change targets to experiment and learn how to respond in a trusting environment.

The success of change depends on the persuasiveness of the change agent. And often, the success of influence efforts by a change agent is a function of her credibility. Change agents can increase their credibility by adapting their messages to their receivers and by conveying those messages in the proper fashion. Perhaps the most successful means of enhancing credibility is through trust and open communication.

ORGANIZATIONAL DEVELOPMENT

Thus far we have addressed change on an individual level; the need for maintaining a proper organization-environment fit requires the management of change on an organization-wide basis. What is needed is a comprehensive approach for bringing about productive change.

Organizational development has evolved as a collection of theories, models, and techniques over the last 30–40 years. One definition, by Warren Bennis, states that organizational development

> is a response to change, a complex educational strategy intended to change the beliefs, attitudes, values, and structure of organizations so that they can better adapt to new technologies, markets, and challenges, and the dizzying rate of change itself.[13]

Bennis' definition amplifies the far-reaching role of OD in organizational life. Achieving the right environmental fit is predicated on the ability to recognize and adapt to changing technology and markets.

French and Bell offer additional insights into OD and communication with their definition of OD as a

> long-range effort to improve an organization's problem-solving and renewal processes, particularly through a more effective and collaborative management . . . with the assistance of a change agent, or catalyst, and the use of . . . action research.[14]

French and Bell specify problem-solving processes as the ways in which an organization diagnoses challenges in the environment and then makes decisions relative to those challenges. Their idea of renewal refers to the prevention of decay and entropy. Most important is their reference to action research that embraces the need for collaboration via "data collection," "data feedback," and "data exploration." These data-related activities emphasize the indispensible role of communication in OD.

A description by Aronson of the initial sensitivity sessions conducted years ago vividly conveys the integral role of information sharing:

> As it happened, one of the educators joined the group just as the observers were discussing her behavior and interpreting an episode that she had participated in the preceding morning. She became very agitated and said that the observer's interpretation was all wrong. She then proceeded to give her version of the episode. The discussion proved very exciting. The next night, all 50 of the participants showed up and gleefully joined the discussion, frequently disagreeing with the observations and interpretations of the trained observers.[15]

One can sense from this account that there was some very real interpersonal sharing going on. The individuals involved were truly trying to share their perceptions of reality. This is the substance of OD. It is an attempt to change our stored beliefs, emotions, and behaviors so that our responses are more appropriate and productive. The information-sharing essence of OD is seen in each step of the OD Process.

THE ORGANIZATIONAL DEVELOPMENT PROCESS

OD theorists and practitioners have identified a series of steps that generally constitute the OD process. These may occur in linear fashion, or more than one may occur simultaneously; They may occur very quickly, or over a long time. Let's consider each step in the process.

Felt Pressure for Change

The OD process begins when top management begins to experience pressure, senses a problem, and is prompted to take some action to solve the problem. These pressures may be manifested internally or externally. Specific sources of external pressure might be a union, domestic and international competitors, suppliers, population dynamics, shifts in consumer values and tastes, or governmental actions. Internal pressure sources could include employees, archaic technology, or outdated policies and procedures.

Perhaps the most specific and dramatic manifestation of a need for change is high employee turnover. If the most competent people are leav-

ing the organization, the need for change is imminent. Other manifestations might include a lack of direction, an inability to identify or serve organizational constituencies, a demotivating climate, and continuous complaints of a lack of effective communication.

Identifying the sources of pressure is essentially an information collecting and sharing activity. If internal conditions are not conducive for information sharing by organizational members, it may be necessary to introduce a change agent.

Introducing the Change Agent

Members of top management often identify an individual or organization to act as the agent of change. Change agents are frequently outsiders such as consultants, or members of corporate management who have an outside perspective. Sometimes the change agent is an enlightened insider who happens to have the proper knowledge and skills to bring about the effort needed.

The change agent must have appropriate credentials. When a CA is hired by management she will, of course, be given legitimate authority with which to function. But most often CAs can work best on the basis of their expertise and interpersonal skills, much like an integrator. The exercise of personal competence is usually more effective than the use of legitimate authority. Organization members must perceive the CA in the proper light if the CA is to be effective.

Change agents are expected to be knowledgeable and creative, with the ability to come into a situation and apply rational empiricism to solve the organization's problems. The background of the CA determines, in part, how the CA functions. Her education, experiences, values, and attitudes will influence how and what she perceives as important and how she interacts with members of the organization.

Perhaps the most indispensable of the CA's credentials are the trust and credibility that allow her to be persuasive. Because trust is so important, outsiders are frequently an obvious choice over insiders who, in the eyes of employees, would not meet Porter's definition of trust. Change agents must guard against becoming overly familiar with the change targets by maintaining a certain amount of social distance. Those CAs who do not maintain some distance run the risk of being identified as part of the organizational culture (i.e., an insider). When this happens the CA's credibility may be severely damaged.

A third factor influencing the CA's impact is the leadership climate in the organization. Members of top management are in the best position to set the tone for organizational change and development. They can influence employees to expect and accept change by clearly communicating their plans and expectations in a timely fashion.

Every aspect of a change program should be communicated and con-

ducted within a climate of complete trust. Management should announce the presence of the change agent to minimize anxiety and consequent resistance. With trust and good communications, the CA's credibility is protected and employee acceptance and participation will be enhanced.

The technology and structure of the organization must also be compatible with the desired efforts of top management. If the CA does not have the appropriate resources with which to work, or if the policies and procedures (e.g., controls, reward system) act as a straightjacket constraining the CA, her efforts will be ineffective.

Diagnosing the Organization's Condition

Once the CA has been chosen and successfully introduced, he can begin to move about the organization, meeting initially with high-level and middle-level management groups to collect needed information for diagnostic purposes. Initial contacts may be in the form of interviews or small group meetings, but may include some attempts at survey utilization.

Communication at these encounters is usually pleasant, but it is also formal and constrained. Managers are not quite sure what to disclose or how to disclose it. The change agent must be especially perceptive to detect resistance on the part of management. Managers frequently need to be encouraged and reassured to get maximum participation.

After the initial series of contacts the CA will meet again with top management to share the collected information and to provide an assessment of the situation. As a result of this high-level examination, the CA and top management will agree on a possible set of objectives and a strategy for reaching those objectives.

Fact-Finding and Collaboration

At this point the CA begins to work with individuals and groups at various levels to collect more extensive information by means of surveys, interviews, and observations. Armed with all the necessary information the CA will begin a collaborative effort with managers and employees to identify specific treatments or interventions. Frequently there will be a sharing of collected information and intense analysis to identify areas that are most deserving of OD efforts.

There are various roles that the CA can play.[16] The **medical model** suggests that the CA act as diagnostician, studying the available information, clarifying options, and recommending solutions to top management. In the **engineering model,** management has diagnosed the problem and engages the CA to implement a solution designated by management. The **process model** is more collaborative. Neither the CA nor management unilaterally dictates the problems and their solutions, but works together to identify problems and solutions.

When specific interventions are chosen, methods are also chosen. They may include courses to impart knowledge, exercises and training sessions for skill building, or group (sensitivity) sessions to enhance teamwork.

As can be seen from Figure 16–2, there are eight modes of OD intervention. The first is **training and education,** which involves direct teaching or experienced-based learning such as classroom lectures, discussions, and simulations. The second mode is **process consultation**—observing, discussing, and directing ongoing operations to improve them. **Confrontation** is the third mode and it involves bringing individuals or groups together in an attempt to improve previously poor communication and relationships. This may be accomplished by sharing previously collected information, or simply sharing perceptions of one another. The fourth mode is **data feedback** or the collection of information by surveys, interviews or observation, and feedback to appropriate individuals for planning or problem solving purposes.

The fifth mode is **problem solving,** which involves meetings essentially for the purpose of identifying, discussing and solving problems. **Planning** is the sixth mode and is essentially the development of organizational objectives and strategies. The seventh mode is **task-force establishment,** an organization-wide response to OD. It encompasses the identification and function of various individuals or groups who will be responsible for an ongoing OD effort in the organization. The final mode is **technostructural activity,** which involves the alteration of the organization's structure and work processes.

Figure 16–2 also indicates that the focus of attention can be at various levels: individual, group, intergroup, and total organization. Figure 16–3 provides a listing of the various techniques by level of focus.

Institutionalizing OD Outcomes

A specific intervention is usually followed by feedback and evaluation. The outcome of one intervention may suggest another. As the results of OD interventions become clear and useful for the organization, management can institutionalize the results. These OD results can be a permanent part of the organization's culture, structure, policies, and procedures. In effect, if the outcome is good for the organization, it should be adopted formally by the organization.

RESISTANCE TO CHANGE

The major problem which change agents and organizations encounter when engaging in OD is resistance to change. Resistance to change is a

FIGURE 16–2 The OD Cube

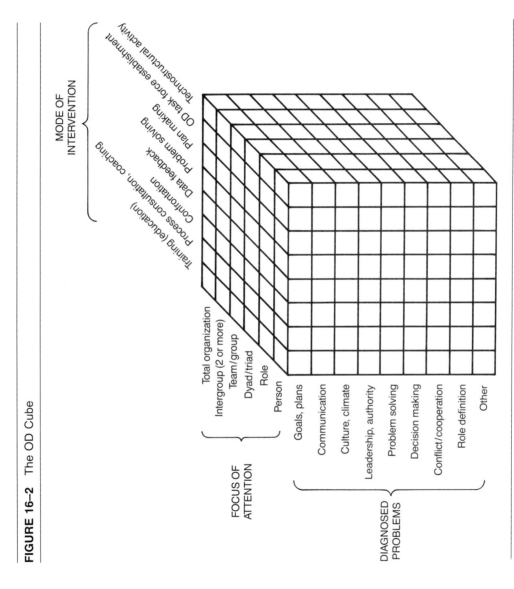

SOURCE: Richard A. Schmuck and Matthew Miles, *Organization Development in Schools* (LaJolla, Calif.: University Associ- ates, 1976).

FIGURE 16–3 OD Modes for Various Levels of Intervention

Level	Intervention Activity
Individual	Classroom training
	Coaching and counseling
	Sensitivity training
	Job design
	Career planning
Group	Training and education
	Team building
	Process consultation
	Sensitivity training
	Survey feedback
	Problem solving
Intergroup	Training and education
	Organizational mirroring
	Process consultation
	Survey feedback
	Problem solving
Organizational	Survey feedback
	Technostructural activity
	Confrontational meetings

---

human characteristic, and following are a number of the more important reasons why people resist change.

Fear of Uncertainty

Various theories of motivation (such as Maslow's Need Hierarchy) have postulated a generalized need for safety and security. Most people like a certain amount of predictability in their lives and will go to great lengths to ensure that predictability. We travel the same route to school or work each day. We use the same types and brands of products consistently. We interact with the same people, shying away from new encounters. Change or even talk of change clearly threatens those habits and relationships.

Fear of Economic Loss

The patterns of behavior we have established were chosen because they are in some way rewarding. We do the work we do, where we do it, the way we do it, because we know there are certain economic incentives—at the end of each week or month there will be a paycheck. We have a home, food, medical and life insurance because we can do the work that earns us those things. Change threatens all those things because we do not know if it will offer us the same rewards.

Fear of Changed Social Relationships

The need for affiliation and belonging is another strong need. We establish close and intense relationships with others on and off the job to satisfy that need. We can count on not being alone because we have established such social ties. But change threatens those ties, and changing work methods or technology may force the dissolution of them. Resistance is a natural form of defense.

Lack of Competence and Esteem

Change programs frequently require skills that are foreign to an individual's repertoire, and totally unattainable. The transition seems monumental, and the individual's knowledge of the new behavior is so limited that he believes that the new behavior is beyond his capabilities. This can generate a level of anxiety that feeds the fear, and makes the individual feel even less able to cope with the new behavioral demands.

STRATEGIES FOR SUCCESSFULLY INTRODUCING CHANGE

Any form of resistance diminishes an individual's ability to function as a productive member of the organization. If resistance is too intense, or spread throughout an organization, it can paralyze and eventually destroy the organization. There are a number of methods for reducing or eliminating resistance. Kotter and Schlesinger have identified the following six approaches to introducing change that minimize resistance.[17]

The first approach is **education and communication.** This approach correctly assumes that resistance to change is rooted in a lack of information and understanding. An information void or unclear communication leaves much room for interpretation of facts and, perhaps more importantly, managerial intentions. Communication and open discussion in an open trusting climate before the change occurs can help employees to understand, accept, and even support needed change. The beauty of this approach is that the change targets essentially become change agents, helping one another to learn the new pattern of responses.

Participation and involvement is the second approach to overcoming resistance. Getting employees ego-involved and actively participating in the change process can be beneficial in a number of ways. Their participation will ensure a greater sharing of information and therefore better understanding of the need for change, as well as the change itself. Additionally, their understanding will increase acceptance. Finally their ego-involvement will help to induce greater commitment. Participation and involvement also converts change targets into agents. The only serious drawback to this approach is the time consumed.

A third approach is **facilitation and support.** This approach requires

the maintenance of a supportive climate such as that discussed in Chapter 6. Employees confronted with the prospect of change experience fear, anxiety, and hostility, and management should provide outlets for these emotions. It may even be advisable to allow time away from the job so that employees can unwind, rebuild, and refresh themselves. This is an expensive approach, but if it allows individuals to recuperate before destroying their involvement and commitment, it may be worthwhile.

The fourth approach listed by Kotter and Schlesinger is **negotiation and agreement.** In some change situations individuals (e.g., informal leaders, scarce talents) or groups (e.g., labor unions) may be resistant, but overwhelmingly important to the change effort. If so, some kind of compromise effort may be in order. It may become necessary to sit down and negotiate certain incentives (pay, privileges, policies) with these individuals so that they will accept and endorse the change program. This may be an expensive tactic, but it may also be indispensable. At all costs, however, management must retain firm leadership and control over the change effort.

The fifth approach is **manipulation and cooptation.** When the previously mentioned approaches have failed or seem inappropriate, management may have to resort to manipulation. We discussed three levels of influence earlier in this chapter, and indicated that internalization is preferred over compliance and identification. There are occasions, however, when management must engage in manipulation of employees, information, and other resources. Tactics such as employee "arm-twisting," withholding information, or making threats become a means of last resort. Coopting or consorting with powerful individuals to get their support or endorsements may also be necessary. The danger with these tactics is that they may backfire as employees attempt to manipulate management, and the entire change effort may be destroyed.

Approach number six is **coercion.** Coercion can be explicit or implicit. It is also highly negative because of the use of threats to do economic, psychological, or physical harm to the change target. Frequently it involves threats of a plant closing, pay reductions, unfavorable working conditions, demotions, and similar other unfavorable consequences. This approach employs compliance as a means of influencing behavior. It requires a change agent with a great deal of power, and it typically means that whenever the employees get the opportunity, they will resist the change by reverting to old behaviors. That, of course, is the greatest drawback of coercion.

SUMMARY

A time-worn but accurate cliché tells us that the only constant in our environment is change. There are pressures for change continuously developing from our dynamic institutions such as law and education. Research

and development deliver technological change in both revolutionary and evolutionary fashion.

The net result of such pressures is an ever-present requirement for individuals and organizations to adapt and to do so there are orderly processes that must be observed. An understanding of these processes and the role of communication in them is essential for effective management. The individual who hopes to succeed as a manager in our contemporary environment must become familiar with each stage in the rational processes of change and organizational development.

Resistance to change is a fact of life. When change is perceived as positive and helpful, people will embrace it. However, when it is perceived as negative and harmful, people will resist it. In an organizational setting management should view resistance as a symptom signaling that something is wrong. Whenever management is contemplating change, a careful program for introducing and implementing it should be developed.

We have offered models and techniques for organizational change in this chapter. One thing that should be clear from those models, and from our discussion of resistance to change: effective communication is essential. If relationships are to be positive, and if the relationship climate is to be supportive, effective communication is an absolute necessity. Managers who direct a strong communication program will find the introduction of change to be much easier and resistance to be minimal.

DISCUSSION QUESTIONS

1. List seven pressures for change. Discuss in detail three of those pressures. Give concrete examples for each of the three.

2. What did Naisbitt mean when he said that we live in a "time of parenthesis"? Identify some of the challenges that face individuals living in this "time of parenthesis."

3. Explain Thorndike's "law of effect." How is it related to reinforcement of behavior?

4. Compare and contrast positive and negative reinforcement. Distinguish between negative reinforcement and punishment.

5. Compare and contrast punishment and extinction as ways of changing behavior.

6. Explain Kurt Lewin's model of the change process. Emphasize how communication plays a central role in the change process.

7. Discuss the three processes of social influence identified by Kelman. Indicate which process would be most helpful in bringing about permanent change.

8. How does refreezing of behavior take place? Indicate some common problems in refreezing behavior.

9. Distinguish between continuous and intermittent reinforcement schedules. Give examples of several types of intermittent schedules.

10. Discuss the role of communication in the organizational change process. Indicate how and why communication is a key factor in organizational change.

11. Define organizational development. What role does communication play in OD?

12. List the steps in the organizational development process. Briefly explain each.

13. Describe characteristics of the change agent and the organization that are crucial to successful organizational development.

14. Contrast the medical model and the process model for a change agent.

15. Discuss four of the eight modes of intervention in the OD process.

16. Explain why individuals commonly resist change. Indicate how the communication process plays a key role in breaking down barriers to change.

17. Kotter and Schlesinger identified six approaches to introducing change which minimize resistance. List the six approaches. Compare and contrast three of them.

18. Look through a recent issue of a general interest periodical such as *Time* or *Business Week*. How many articles deal with change? What were the sources of change? How many articles describe situations dealing with resistance to change? Try to explain why resistance was present in the latter situations.

NOTES

[1]John Naisbitt, *Megatrends* (New York: Warner Books, 1982), p. xxii.

[2]Ibid. p. 279.

[3]Marshal McLuhan and Q. Fiore, *The Medium Is the Message* (New York: Bantam Books, 1967), p. 67.

[4]Kurt Lewin, *Field Theory in Social Science* (New York: Harper & Row, 1951).

[5]James Deese and S. Hulse, *The Psychology of Learning* (New York: McGraw-Hill, 1970), p. 82.

[6]Herbert Kelman, "Three Processes of Social Influence," *Public Opinion Quarterly* 25, (1961), pp. 57–58.

[7]Ibid.

[8]Ibid.

[9]Ibid.

[10]Edgar Huse and J. Bowditch, *Behavior in Organizations* (Reading, Mass.: Addison-Wesley Publishing, 1977), p. 465.

[11]Lyman Porter, E. Lawler, and J. Hackman, *Behavior in Organizations* (New York: McGraw-Hill, 1975), p. 497.

[12]Ibid.

[13]Warren Bennis, *Organizational Development: Its Nature, Origins and Prospects* (Reading, Mass.: Addison-Wesley Publishing, 1969), p. 2.

[14]Wendell French and C. Bell, *Organization Development: Behavioral Science Interventions for Organization Improvement* (Englewood Cliffs, N.J.: Prentice-Hall, 1978), p. 14.

[15]Eliot Aronson, "Communication in Sensitivity-Training Groups." In *Organizational Development* by French, Bell, and Zawacki (Plano, Tex.: Business Publications, 1983), p. 249.

[16]Andrew Szilagyi and M. Wallace, *Organizational Behavior and Performance*, 3rd ed. (Glenview, Ill.: Scott, Foresman, 1983), p. 539.

[17]John Kotter and L. Schlesinger, "Choosing Strategies for Change," *Harvard Business Review*, March-April 1979, pp. 106–14.

SUGGESTED READINGS

GREEN, JAMES H. "Overcoming Terminal Fright." *Supervisory Management* 29, no. 9 (September 1984), pp. 3–10.

GREENBAUM, HOWARD H.; ELLSWORTH J. HOLDEN, JR.; and LUCIAN SPATARO. "Organizational Structure and Communication Processes: A Study of Change." *Group and Organization Studies* 8 (March 1983), pp. 61–82.

HUNT, RICHARD E., and MARILYN K. RIGBY. "Easing the Pain of Change." *Management Review* 73, no. 9 (September 1984), pp. 41–45.

KOTTER JOHN P., and LEONARD A. SCHLESINGER. "Choosing Strategies for Change." *Harvard Business Review*, March-April 1979, pp. 106–14.

NARAYANAN V. K., and RAGHU NATH. "The Influence of Group Cohesiveness on Some Changes Induced by Flextime: A Quasi-Experiment." *The Journal of Applied Behavioral Science* 20, no. 3 (August 1984), pp. 265–76.

PETERS, JOSEPH P., and SIMONE TSENG. "Managing Strategic Change: Moving Others from Awareness to Action." *Hospital and Health Services Administration* 29, no. 4 (July-August 1984), pp. 7–20.

QUINN, JAMES BRIAN. "Managing Strategic Change." *Sloan Management Review*, Summer 1980, pp. 3–20.

SCHUSTER, MICHAEL. "Cooperation and Change in Union Settings: Problems and Opportunities." *Human Resource Management* 23, no. 2 (Summer 1984), pp. 145–60.

Chapter 17

Conducting Communication

Audits

Chapter 17 Case

You are the manager of a district office of a public relations firm. In addition to the 60 employees in your office, you also supervise five branches located in neighboring states. You have just returned from a week-long seminar at headquarters. One of the topics covered was communications audits. On the way home, the idea kept coming to you: maybe some of the problems you've been having are caused by communications problems. How would you begin an audit? What questions would you ask and to whom would you direct them? What kind of analytical tools might you use to diagnose your firm's communications strengths and weaknesses?

INTRODUCTION

We know that an effective organization depends on effective communication, both internally and externally. To deal simultaneously with the needs of the present and the future, the effective organization must have a healthy and resilient communication system. Management must avoid system entropy—the decay or rundown of the system to a state of inertia—by allocating resources for periodic investigation to detect and eliminate weaknesses, and to enhance the system's strengths. A convenient means for such investigation is the **communication audit.** An audit is a methodical review or examination, including identification, measurement, and analysis, of the various system elements to determine how effectively they are functioning.

A communication audit can be compared to a physical examination. The physician-auditor knows from years of study and practical experience what an ideal system (i.e., a normal body) looks like and how it should function.

The physician begins the examination by dividing the body into various "subsystems"—circulatory, skeletal, digestive, and respiratory. The next step is to identify the relevant components of each subsystem. In the case of the circulatory system, for example, components would include the heart muscle, arteries, and veins. The physician then decides what information is needed to determine the current status of each subsystem (e.g., blood pressure, pulse), and the means for getting that information. Information is collected using various techniques (e.g., interview, physical examination), and tools and equipment (e.g., sphygmomanometer, X ray) with which the physician is familiar.

Once needed information is collected, the physician can compare it with the ideal and determine the health of the examinee. If subsystems are functioning normally, the physician need not prescribe any action. If there is a serious discrepancy between normal and actual, which is not self-correcting, the physician will prescribe some action to resolve the discrepancy—exercise, chemical therapy, surgery, or other corrective treatment.

Before giving advice or prescribing treatment the physician must assess the feasibility and potential success of various corrective actions. To be effective, treatment must be based ultimately on this assessment. For example, an individual patient may be chronically overweight despite repeated warnings and exhortations from the physician to lose weight. The reality that the individual will never maintain even an approximately ideal weight must temper the physician's advice and treatment. Similar recognition must be given to a variety of patient circumstances such as religious objection to some forms of treatment, or inability to pay for some forms of treatment. In effect, the treatment must carefully fit the circumstances.

THE COMMUNICATION AUDIT

The medical procedure described is essentially the same as that required for a communication audit. Viewed as a system, the organization can be divided initially into identifiable subsystems. Organizations are social entities whose objectives and inner workings vary a great deal; consequently, the subsystems will vary from organization to organization. Subsystems which could be crucial communication links in an organization include policies and procedures, selection and orientation, employee relations, rewards, and advertising and public relations.

Once the subsystems are identified, the next step is to determine the relevant features and the desired information about each (e.g., its nature, function, current state of operation). After all informational needs are specified, methods must be selected for collecting the information. The collected information, which must accurately reflect the organization's

current status, can then be compared with what is considered to be an ideal or acceptable standard.

Comparison should indicate the weaknesses and strengths of the organization's communication system and suggest the need for corrective action. Before prescribing treatment, however, there is a caveat. Like the physician, the auditor must recognize the differences between the ideal and what the firm can realistically achieve. For example, a solution that calls for additional personnel and other resources that are financially beyond a firm's grasp is not an alternative to be considered. This critical point is frequently overlooked.

When examining a firm's communication system, it is equally important to bear in mind that the environment is frequently an integral part of the investigation. Because of increasing interdependence, a system's environment has great potential for influencing the system. And anything that has the potential for affecting communication within the system's environment must be accounted for. To do otherwise is to ignore a serious dimension of communication and a major factor in the audit.

We can identify six distinct steps to be accomplished in a communication audit. Each step requires careful thought and decision making based on input from all individuals involved in and affected by the audit.

Step One: Identifying the Focal Unit

The discussion so far has been general and has focused on the entire system or organization. In the most comprehensive audits the entire system would be the focus of investigation. It is frequently desirable and financially necessary, however, to choose a particular division, department, or other unit within a larger organization as the focus of study. Such a study is referred to as a **partial audit,** and begins with identification of the unit to be audited. One helpful way of identifying the focal unit is in terms of the various communication strata introduced in Section II of this book. These three levels are defined as follows.

1. *Intrapersonal:* Those matters or problems that are the domain of a single individual and over which complete or primary control is possible by the individual.
2. *Interpersonal:* Those matters or problems that are outside the control of any one person, and are affected by the interaction of two or more persons (e.g., dyad, small group, mass communication).
3. *Organizational:* Those matters or problems that stem from the particular idiosyncrasies, structure, policies, and procedures of a given organization (e.g., department, division, firm).

These are suggested as general levels from which to contemplate the identification of the focal unit. Of course more detailed classification can be developed depending on the objectives and needs of the auditor.

Step Two: Stating the Purpose of the Audit

The first task is to decide what it is that you want to do. Audit objectives may be problem oriented or research oriented. They may take the form of attitude surveys, skill tests, readability tests, or network analyses. Generally speaking there are three broad purposes for an audit.

The first purpose is **prevention.** Preventive audits are conducted to ensure proper operation and maintenance of the system. Such an audit is similar to an annual physical checkup. Health maintenance organizations, an increasingly popular form of medical insurance, provide not only extensive medical treatment, but also emphasize preventive medicine as a means of maintaining a healthy body. HMO managers believe that a healthy body requires less extensive and less costly treatment than an unhealthy body. Likewise, preventive audits are designed to minimize communication problems and, consequently, yield more time and other resources for productive activity.

A second general purpose of communication audits is **problem solving.** A widely accepted principle of management in U.S. business firms is the **exception principle.** The exception principle is basically a control concept concerned with identifying "exceptions" to logically developed organizational rules and procedures. The presence of exceptions usually indicates that something has caused a violation of the rules or procedures (i.e., a problem exists). Resources must then be dedicated to identifying the cause and removing it.

Typically there is an inverse relationship between the frequency of preventive and problem-solving audits. Effective maintenance sustains the system's strengths and reduces the probability of system failure and the need for problem solving. One of the most frustrating aspects of the problem solving audit is that organization members frequently sense that there are problems but cannot identify or verbalize them. Maintenance audits, on the other hand, are typically designed to test the effectiveness of the current system.

The third general purpose for conducting communication audits is **innovation.** There are occasions when a firm wants to improve its "environmental fit," or stay ahead of the competition by introducing some beneficial change into the system. The purpose of the innovation audit is to generate and test the feasibility of new and better ways of communicating. One way that management can avoid system entropy is to dedicate some resources to research in order to find ways to make the organization's communications stronger and more productive.

To add clarity and practicality to our discussion of audit purposes, a representative sample of specific purposes is offered using the classification strata from Step One.

Sample Purposes at the Intrapersonal Level.

1. To ascertain that individuals have the required training and skills.
2. To verify that individuals are making regular and efficient use of communications "technology."
3. To measure the objectivity of individuals in their intake of data.
4. To determine whether individuals are confusing facts, inferences, and value judgments.
5. To determine whether individuals are overstating or overcomplicating messages.
6. To determine if a different technology or training technique would improve individuals' communication skills.

Sample Purposes at the Interpersonal Level.

1. To determine if individuals in leadership positions are using appropriate leadership and communication styles.
2. To ascertain the existence of appropriate mechanisms for providing interpersonal feedback.
3. To find out if interpersonal status and power differences are being nonverbally emphasized or de-emphasized.
4. To confirm individual awareness and sensitivity to differences in perceptual sets and interpersonal perception.
5. To test the effectiveness of new methods for decreasing filtering.
6. To determine if individual offices or work stations can be arranged more effectively for greater harmony and information sharing.

Sample Purposes at the Organizational Level.

1. To determine whether or not individuals are encouraged to "own" or to share information.
2. To ensure that individuals are fully acclimated to the organization on joining. To ensure that they are made aware of policies and procedures.
3. To determine if the organization tends to favor and encourage the use of one type of channel or medium to the exclusion of others.
4. To ensure that channels are properly utilized. To measure channel usage for overload or underload.
5. To test for the presence of employee obsession or goal displacement concerning the use of forms.
6. To ensure that there is an organizational climate of confidence and mutual trust.

7. To discover if there are different policies or rewards that will encourage higher levels of disclosure and feedback.

Step Three: Identifying Subsystems, Activities, and Variables

Once the focal unit and purpose of an audit have been specified, the next
step is to determine the subsystems and the components of those subsystems to be investigated. Typically this is done in terms of specific activities
and variables. There are numerous subsystem activities and variables that
could be the subject of investigation. A representative sample of activities
and variables that have been studied in past audits and research projects
is shown in Figure 17–1.

What is or is not a pertinent variable or activity must be judged within
the audit situation. One preliminary method for identifying relevant activities and variables is to examine the work of past audits. With the results of previous audits in hand, the next step is to generate questions
suggested by the very nature of your purpose and the unit under investigation. Assume, for example, that a firm is interested in conducting an
organization-wide maintenance audit. Some questions regarding communication policy and procedure for the total system might be as follows.

1. Are there clearly written policies that create and support a sound
communication program? Are there appropriate procedures to
implement the policies?
2. Do the policies reflect the firm's philosophy, goals, and objectives?
Do they commit the organization to a sincere, open, two-way communication program?
3. Do the policies and procedures have the commitment of top and
middle management? Does management actively support and encourage open communication?
4. Are the policies and procedures made known to all who have an
interest in, or need to know them? Are responsibilities for implementation and enforcement clearly defined, assigned, and accepted?
5. Are the policies and procedures reviewed, evaluated, and
changed when necessary?
6. Are all communication activities coordinated? Does one person
have responsibility for overall administration and evaluation of
the program?

Recognizing that individuals and individual behavior are what actually
make any system work, the maintenance audit might reasonably focus on
the existence of assumed knowledge and behavioral expectations. Sample
questions that reflect individual activity and control might include the following.

FIGURE 17–1 Audit Activities and Variables

Authority, responsibility	Message flow
Channels, networks	Content
Linkage	Direction
Propinquity	Distortion
Status differences	Distribution
Interpersonal attraction	Speed
Satisfaction	Rate
Sense of achievement	Internal noise
Traffic density	External noise
Load, people	Efficiency
Load, time	Redundancy
Efficiency	Modes
Environmental contact	Verbal, oral
Expectations	Verbal, written
Interaction	Nonverbal
Ability	Motivation
Retention	Objectives
Comprehension	Operational functions
Satisfaction	Organizational structure
Sense of achievement	Skills
Status differences	Interpersonal
Interpersonal attraction	Perceptual

---

1. Do supervisors know what their roles and responsibilities are in the overall program? Do they understand their authority, responsibility, and accountability for keeping employees informed? Are supervisors given information in a timely fashion? Are they familiar with the channels and media of the system?

2. Are employees encouraged to seek information from their immediate supervisors? How are they encouraged? How does the leadership style affect the climate between supervisor and subordinate?

3. Is the role of all departments (especially personnel) in the total communication program clearly stated and communicated? Does each department facilitate better communication in the total organization? Is communication encouraged through formal line relationships and channels, and is short-circuiting kept to a minimum?

4. Are employees' needs for information reflected in the overall system? Are employees given basic information on wages, job security, advancement opportunities? Are they given information about the organization such as philosophy, objectives, plans, profitability, financial integrity, competition, government regulations, and how all this affects them?

Communication media are usually only a means to an end in the com-

munication process. However, because of their design, use, disuse, or misuse, they can take on major significance and must be considered an integral part of the total communication program. Questions addressing media and their significance in the maintenance audit might include the following.

1. Does the organization have a company handbook? Does it include important information about policies, procedures, and organizational relationships?
2. Is there an in-house publication? Does it contain a variety of information from a variety of sources? Or is it used only for "official" information dissemination? Is it appealing?
3. Are bulletin boards accessible, attractive, and regularly monitored? Is there a distorting pattern (e.g., discriminatory, anti-union) to the types of information regularly displayed?
4. Are company letters regularly and frequently sent to the homes of employees? Does top management personnel sign them? What kind of information is contained in the letters?
5. Is there a suggestion system? Are suggestions and submitters acknowledged and given proper recognition and compensation? Who maintains the system? How are suggestions processed?
6. Are meetings and conferences used for two-way communication, or just one-way downward dissemination? Are appropriate attention, time, and training given to conducting conferences and meetings?
7. Are all types of interviews used? Are those who use the interview given adequate training?
8. Are questionnaires, polls, and opinion surveys utilized? For what purposes? How are results utilized? Are results ever publicized? Is action ever taken as a result of information collected?

Asking such questions of individuals involved in the audit unit can assist in pinpointing precisely what needs to be examined and measured. As answers are developed, the precise activities or variables of interest can be stated, and the auditor can move to the information collection stage.

Step Four: Collecting and Treating Information

As activities and variables are identified for measurement, the auditor can decide where the information can best be obtained. Typically the needed measures will suggest obvious sources. Knowing the information requirements and the sources of information, the auditor has yet another decision to address: *how* to collect the information. There are a variety of collection and treatment techniques from which the auditor can choose. Some of the more popular and frequently used ones are described below.

Content Analysis. This technique is self-descriptive in that the content—elements and structure—of a message can be measured and analyzed in a variety of ways. Units of measure for content analysis might include sentence length, productivity, level of abstraction, diversity or monotony of vocabulary, type and consistency of tone, and repetitive use of words or phrases. Assume, for example, that you want to determine a speaker's attitude toward a minority group. The speaker's tone might be evaluated by classifying (e.g., positive-negative) all descriptive words from a number of speeches before minority and nonminority audiences. The ratio of positive/negative descriptives could be computed for the two different audiences and tested for significance.

Another example would involve the detection of unbalanced or biased language usage by labor and management. A stereotypic response might be to expect management to use words like "strike," "seniority," and "grievance" less frequently than labor. A dictionary—a list of words or phrases used as a limited vocabulary for specific purposes of analysis—could be developed and applied to a representative set of labor and management messages to determine the frequency of usage of the dictionary items.

The success of content analysis, like other techniques, depends on how well you define the unit of measure and, of course, how carefully it is applied. To enhance the usefulness of this technique, computer applications have been developed.[1]

Readability Tests. Readability has been defined as the ability to read a message one time and understand it. Over the years various tests or formulas have been developed to measure readability.[2] Most utilize some treatment and/or measure of words and sentences in a message. Some attempt simply to judge the difficulty of word choice while others evaluate the construction of messages. Others attempt to measure the amount of human interest, and therefore, likelihood of attention and stimulation. The Gunning Fog Index, for example, consists of the following steps.[3]

1. Compute average sentence length by dividing the number of words in a passage by the number of sentences.
2. Count the number of difficult words *per 100 words*. Difficult words are three-or-more syllable words, excluding combination words and verbs formed by adding suffixes such as "es."
3. Add the calculations from steps 1 and 2. Then multiply the sum by the constant .4. The "score" indicates the minimum expected education (grade) level for which the message should be readable.

The Gunning Fog Index is used to determine whether messages are written at an appropriate level for a particular audience. Scores that are consistently out of line with the assumed educational level of the intended

audience indicate a need to revise the level of difficulty of the message upward or downward. Often, for example, company publications are not understood by employees because they are written at the writer's level instead of the reader's.

One of the drawbacks of readability analysis is the amount of data that must be generated and treated. Obviously a representative sampling of messages must be analyzed to offset any extreme measures of a given message or time period. When evaluating a lengthy communication (e.g., book, issues of a newspaper) a large amount of data will be accumulated. Another drawback is that when a formula is applied, the result is just a number, and there is no method for validating that number, other than to use more than one formula as a means of cross checking. This means, of course, more data manipulation. To help make this task more manageable, however, microcomputer software is now available.[4]

Semantic Differentiation. A controlled association technique such as semantic differentiation requires individual respondents to differentiate word associations or meanings using sets of bipolar adjective scales.[5] Sets of carefully selected bipolar adjectives are set at opposite ends of a seven-point scale and paired with a particular concept under investigation. Respondents are then asked to indicate their reaction to the concept using the bipolar scales.

A key task involved in semantic differentiation is identifying appropriate adjectives to be utilized. Original work on the semantic differential by Osgood, Tannenbaum, and Suci indicates that different adjective scales relate to or measure three basically different dimensions: evaluation (e.g., good-bad), potency (e.g., strong-weak), and activity (e.g., calm-agitated).[6] Since SD appears to measure these three dimensions in any concept, scores can be generated and comparisons made across concepts and groups of respondents.

In addition to measuring the strength of word associations, SD has been adapted and used for measuring attitudes. For example, assume you are interested in comparing the attitudes of consumers toward a particular firm, its closest competitor, and what might be considered the ideal organization. In this instance the adjective pairs would be selected and combined with the concept of the "focal firm," the "ideal firm," and the "competitor firm." See Figure 17–2. The consumer-respondents are instructed to indicate the direction and strength of their feelings toward the Focal Firm along the bipolar scales.

The same adjective pairs would then be combined with the concepts Ideal Firm and Competitive Firm. The mean ratings for all consumer-respondents would then be calculated for each set of adjective/concept combinations. These measures could then be plotted and examined to see how the Focal Firm compares with the ideal and the competitor. Significant differences could indicate unfavorable consumer perceptions of the

FIGURE 17-2 An Example of Concept-Scale Pairings

	Focal Firm							
	1	2	3	4	5	6	7	
Friendly	—	—	—	—	—	—	—	Unfriendly
Liberal	—	—	—	—	—	—	—	Conservative
Beautiful	—	—	—	—	—	—	—	Ugly
High cost	—	—	—	—	—	—	—	Low cost

organization, and a need to enhance the organization's image through improved communication.

ECCO Analysis. ECCO is an acronym for Episodic Communication Channels in Organizations.[7] This technique traces a message as it moves through a particular channel or channels within the focal unit. It can yield significant information about channel use, filtering effects by various individuals participating in a channel, elapsed time for a message to move through a channel, and channel redundancy.

ECCO analysis is time-consuming and requires careful application so as not to disturb the "normal" movement of messages. If there is a conscious awareness that an investigation is being conducted it could destroy the natural field setting. Additionally, it requires a user who knows what to look for and what kinds of questions to ask during the trace. Questionnaires may be appropriate if used after a message has been passed through a particular channel and their use will not disturb normal behavior.

Interaction Analysis. Interaction analysis is a useful means of analyzing interaction patterns between individuals or groups of individuals. One version of this technique utilizes a sociogram and matrix. The auditor first determines a classification of message types or purposes. Respondents are then asked to indicate the frequency of interaction with other individuals within the focal unit concerning these particular types of messages. Once the frequencies are determined, the level of interaction between various unit members can be indicated using an x by x matrix. This may then be used to show how the actual rate of interaction (i.e., informal structure) compares with that dictated by the formal structure (i.e., chain of command).

Odiorne's Communication Audit. This technique is representative of a series of questionnaires used in communication audits to measure and compare the perceptions of two or more groups.[8] Essentially the responses elicited by the audit questions are tabulated and compared for

different groups (e.g., superior/subordinate). Significant discrepancies between the sets of responses indicate potential barriers between groups as they attempt to communicate with one another.

Communication Log. Individuals are asked to record certain pieces of information regarding their communication encounters in a listing technique called a communication log. What is recorded depends on the object of the audit. Information could include the medium used, elapsed time of encounter, nature of message, purpose of communication, direction of the message, and sender-receiver role. Respondents may be asked to report on all their communications or just a sample (e.g., every other day for three weeks).

It should be noted that the information generated by this technique is descriptive rather than explanatory, and its success depends on the abilities and cooperation of the respondents. The design of the log is critical. If not carefully thought out and designed to elicit the exact information desired, it may generate a great deal of useless garbage.

Shadowing. This is essentially an observation technique used to collect information similar to that generated by the log. Instead of self-reporting, however, it requires a well-trained observer who knows what to observe and how to record it accurately. The general strengths and weaknesses of observation were discussed in an earlier chapter. Those characteristics should be kept in mind when choosing information collection methods.

The ICA Audit. The techniques described thus far represent a rather incoherent set of methods developed by different individuals with different information needs either in practical audit or research settings. As a result they do not constitute a set of standardized audit procedures and methods. Unfortunately, the audit results using these techniques cannot be compared between firms or with any national norms. Fortunately, there have been a few attempts at developing a comprehensive audit instrument. While none of these audit models has been widely subscribed to, perhaps the most popular one is the International Communication Association (ICA) Audit.[9]

The ICA Audit utilizes a series of five complementary instruments that can be used individually or separately: questionnaire, interview, network analysis, critical incidents, and a log. The full audit requires about 25 weeks to implement, and yields an organizational profile, a communication network, and reports on critical communication experiences and behaviors. Perhaps the most attractive feature of the ICA Audit is the ability to compare audit results with a national data bank. Such a data bank could serve as the basis for developing criteria with which to measure communication effectiveness.

Step Five: Identifying Effectiveness Criteria

As a result of steps two, three, and four the auditor knows what is to be accomplished by the audit, what will be measured, and how it will be measured. A subsequent and integral part of the audit process is the stipulation of some criteria of success or effectiveness. Through comparison of actual measures with acceptable standards, a judgment can be made about the organization's information-sharing capabilities.

For example, a manager may have various motives for conducting an audit of the movement of memoranda within an organization. She may have experienced complaints and problems about the time consumed preparing memos that reach their destination late—or not at all (problem-solving). Representatives of the firm's data processing department or a computer manufacturer may have suggested the installation of a computer network for an electronic mail system to replace manual distribution (innovation). The audit could be for maintenance purposes, just to ensure that information is flowing in a timely fashion (prevention).

Depending on the purpose, various activities and variables could be measured. The manager may be interested in such measures as the average time to prepare a memo, the average cost to prepare a memo, the accuracy of distribution of memos, the time for distribution of memos, or the actual flow (channels) of distribution.

Appropriate techniques can be developed to measure these activities and variables. But more importantly, the auditor must decide how the measures are to be applied. A decision rule must be developed stating the minimum level of acceptability or "goodness" of each measure. Once the measures are taken they can be compared to the standard. Depending on whether they fall above, at, or below the standard, different actions would be in order.

In the present example the manager could measure the accuracy of distribution of memoranda by tracking them and verifying whether or not they reach their intended destination. Given the importance of the focal unit and the consequences of an undistributed memo (e.g., financial losses, personnel turnover), the manager might set an acceptability limit of 95 percent. This means that as long as 95 percent or more of all memos reach their destination the system would be considered healthy. A measure below 95 percent represents a situation in need of correction.

Likewise the manager could measure the actual time required for distribution of memos by tracking them and observing the time "in flow" from source to destination. She could state the measured time in hours and compute the average number of hours. The manager-auditor might stipulate an acceptable time in terms of a particular range, for example 26–32 hours. If the average actual distribution time is in this range the system is considered to be operating effectively. Otherwise further attention and investigation are in order.

Development of acceptable and meaningful criteria depends on the purpose of the audit, the activities and variables involved, the personal goals and philosophy of the manager conducting the audit, and the current condition of the focal unit. The way in which the criteria are stated would, of course, depend on the actual measures and techniques available for information collection. It is of little value to state effectiveness criteria for which no reasonable measure is possible or for which information is neither available nor accessible.

Step Six: Analyzing and Reporting

After audit information is collected and compiled it must be analyzed carefully in terms of the stated purpose of the audit. We addressed information analysis in Chapter 9 and you are urged to review this information.

Once analysis is completed, conclusions can be drawn regarding the health of the focal unit. In the problem-solving or innovation audit, recommendations are usually in order. The collected information, conclusions, and recommendations must be compiled into an audit report. There are basically three report types: descriptive, explanatory, and prescriptive. Superimposing these report types over the three audit types yields nine combinations. Figure 17–3 shows these combinations with the most likely report type for each audit type.

The maintenance audit usually requires nothing more than a descriptive report indicating the status of the audited system or subsystems. If the focal unit does not meet acceptable standards (i.e., it is not healthy), then explanation or prescription for further study may be in order. In such cases, of course, a more extensive audit and report would be in order.

Problem-solving audits, by their very nature, focus on some unintended and unexplained phenomenon. Most problem-solving audits are conducted by or for individuals who are knowledgeable regarding the

FIGURE 17–3 Audit-Report Combinations

Report Type	Audit Type		
	Prevention	Problem Solving	Innovation
Descriptive_	X		X
Explanatory_		X	X
Prescriptive_		X	X

problem and the focal unit. Consequently, the audit report will focus on an explanation of the phenomenon and prescriptions for action. Descriptive content will be minimal, depending largely on the audience for which the report is prepared.

Innovation audits, because they experiment with the new and the unknown, frequently require extensive description, explanation, and prescription. The content and thrust of the report would depend on the extensiveness and significance of the innovation as well as the interest and knowledge of the readers. A relatively insignificant innovation (e.g., the introduction of colored stationery) may require little description but mainly explanation (e.g., justification) and prescription (recommended action). An innovation with major effects on both personnel and technology (e.g., electronic mail system) might require extensive description and explanation. Likewise, when a report is prepared for readers unfamiliar with, but interested in the innovation the report may require more extensive description and explanation.

In some instances audit reports indicate that communications are in perfect condition. In other instances some action is necessary whether it be corrective or innovative. Before taking action, however, recommendations must be tempered by reality. (Remember our earlier discussion of the physician's ability to prescribe treatment.) The realities of the organization must be used to form the framework for recommending action.

To accomplish this, all reasonable actions should be identified and ranked on the basis of how well they meet certain criteria. Criteria will vary based on the audit unit, the purpose of the audit, and the personalities involved. Criteria may include such considerations as expense involved, professional competencies required, and time necessary to implement.

Frequently, when conducting an audit you conclude that some form of action is required, and this suggests that there must be some type of change. Thus, in this last step it is necessary to address briefly the issue of introducing change.

The specific steps necessary to introduce a particular change in an organization depend on the nature of the action recommended, who it affects, and how. There are two general points to remember when instituting change.

First, the affected individuals must be shown that the action recommended will lead to a higher level of rewards for them. In a textbook on communication, it is well to stress that you cannot expect anyone to believe in such a pronouncement just because you say it is so. Whatever you say must be conveyed in words and sentences that are understandable to the receivers and it must be supported by proof. The individuals involved must be convinced that the change is, in fact, for their benefit and not just beneficial to the organization. They must be convinced enough to accept and carry through the change.

Second, the individuals affected by the change must be convinced that they can accomplish whatever the change requires. Most people are risk averters. They like and need a great deal of certainty and predictability in their environment. Change threatens that need; the individual does not know for sure whether he can accomplish what is being suggested. So it is necessary to convince the individual that he can successfully adapt to the new performance requirements.

Implementation of any plan or action must be fully accepted by the people who are responsible for carrying it out. Therefore, such plans or actions must be carefully and clearly communicated to all concerned individuals. Only in this manner will the plans be acceptable and successful.

SUMMARY

To remain competitive and survive in the long run, an organization must have a healthy communication system for moving information. If an organization's communication system is to remain vital, it must be constantly monitored and improved. One way to maintain such vitality is to conduct periodic communication audits.

An audit is the methodical review, measurement, and analysis of a system's elements to determine how effectively they are functioning. There are at least six distinct steps in the audit process. The first step is to identify the focal unit of the audit. In the most comprehensive audit an entire organizational system can be examined. Frequently, however, it is desirable to conduct an audit on only a part of the organization. Before the audit is conducted it is necessary to clearly define the unit to be studied.

A second key to a successful audit is a statement of the purpose of the audit. There are three different general types of audits: preventive, problem solving, and innovation. Preventive audits are conducted to ensure that a system is operating properly. A problem-solving audit is conducted to identify, measure, and eliminate a particular problem. Innovation audits are conducted to develop and test newer and better methods of communicating.

Once the focal unit is identified and the purpose has been clearly stated for an audit, the next step is to specify the activities and variables to be measured and analyzed. Knowing what is to be measured facilitates step four, which is the collection and treatment of information. There are many different techniques that have been developed for conducting audits or measuring audit information. Content analysis, semantic differentiation, readability analysis, and ECCO analysis are just a few of the many techniques available. The appropriateness of a technique will depend on steps one, two, and three.

Step five consists of identifying criteria to be used in judging the ef-

fectiveness of the communication system. Once a preventive audit is conducted, and you have a measure of how the focal unit is performing, there must be some basis for judging how effective the performance level is. Likewise, criteria would be necessary to decide on the acceptability of problem solutions or the usefulness of an innovation.

Step six in the audit process consists of analyzing audit information, applying the effectiveness criteria and reporting the results. Audit reports may be descriptive, explanatory, or prescriptive, depending on the audit purpose. In those instances where prescription is in order, careful attention should be given to the introduction of any recommended change.

DISCUSSION QUESTIONS

1. Explain an audit in general terms; describe in detail the communication audit. Why is it crucial for an organization and/or its subunits to undergo periodic audits?

2. List and briefly describe each of the six steps in a communication audit.

3. Discuss how the three levels of communication strata could be used in identifying the focal units for a communication audit.

4. What are the three broad purposes of an audit? Compare and contrast them.

5. Why is there an inverse relationship between the frequency of "prevention" and "problem-solving" audits?

6. Chapter 17 had a listing of a representative sample of specific audit purposes using the three levels of communication strata. List four of those specific audit purposes for each of the three strata of communication.

7. Suppose you are in the process of identifying-pertinent variables and activities in an organization-wide communication maintenance audit. Indicate various areas of questioning that you might pursue in order to identify key variables and activities. Give examples of questions you might use.

8. List eight specific techniques of collecting and testing information in a communication audit. Discuss three of those techniques.

9. What are readability tests and why are they used in communication audits? Describe the Gunning Fog Index as an example of a readability test. Discuss the drawbacks of readability tests.

10. What is ECCO analysis? What are some of the drawbacks in the use of ECCO analysis?

11. Compare and contrast the communication log and the shadowing technique. Under what circumstances would each be appropriate?

12. Describe the ICA audit and discuss its advantages.

13. What role do effectiveness criteria play in an audit? Describe how criteria for a communication audit are developed and how they should be used in the audit process.

14. Why would you expect to use different report types for each of the three basic types of audits? Discuss the types of reports most likely to be given for each of the three audit types.

15. Audit results sometimes indicate that corrective action is in order. What factors should be considered in developing specific recommendations for corrective action?

EXERCISES

1. Collect university catalogs, both graduate and undergraduate, from several institutions. Using the Gunning Fox Index, calculate the readability of those catalogs to determine if they are written at the appropriate level.

2. Collect several union newspapers and several company newspapers. Content analyze the newspapers to see if there is a significant difference in the use of certain "key" words or phrases.

3. Design a research project to determine the "actual" and "ideal" images of your institution using one or more of the techniques mentioned in Chapter 17.

NOTES

[1]See, for example, O. Holsti, *Content Analysis for the Social Sciences and Humanities* (Reading, Mass.: Addison-Wesley Publishing, 1969), pp. 150–94.

[2]See, for example, R. Gunning, *The Technique of Clear Writing* (New York: McGraw-Hill, 1952); R. Flesch, *The Art of Readable Writing* (New York: Harper & Row, 1949); G. Klare, *The Measurement of Readability* (Ames, Iowa: Iowa State University Press, 1963).

[3]R. Gunning, *The Technique of Clear Writing* (New York: McGraw-Hill, 1952).

[4]*Readability* (Dallas, Tex.: Micro Power & Light Co., 1982).

[5]C. Osgood, G. Suci, and P. Tannenbaum, *The Measurement of Meaning* (Urbana: University of Illinois Press, 1957).

[6]Ibid.

[7]K. Davis, "Methods of Studying Communication Patterns in Organizations," *Personnel Psychology* 6 (1953); pp. 301–12.

[8]G. Odiorne, "An Application of the Communication Audit," *Personnel Psychology* 7 (1954); pp. 235–43.

[9]G. Goldhaber and P. Krivonos, "The ICA Communication Audit: Process, Status, and Critique," *The Journal of Business Communication* 15 (Fall 1977); pp. 41–55.

SUGGESTED READINGS

BARNETT, GEORGE; DONNA HAMLIN; and JAMES DANOWSKI. "The Use of Fractionation Scales for Communication Audits." Paper presented to the ICA Convention, Minneapolis, May 1981.

GOLDHABER, G. "The ICA Audit: Rationale and Development." Paper presented at a meeting of the Communication Association of the Pacific. Kobe, Japan, 1976.

GOLDHABER, G., and D. ROGERS. *Auditing Organizational Communication Systems: The ICA Communication Audit.* Dubuque, Iowa: Kendall/Hunt Publishing, 1979.

GOLDHABER, G.; H. DENNIS; G. RICHETTO; and O. WIIO. *Information Strategies: New Pathways to Corporate Power.* Englewood Cliffs, N.J.: Prentice-Hall, 1979.

GREENBAUM, HOWARD. "Organizational Communication Systems: Identification and Appraisal." Paper presented at a meeting of the International Communication Association, Phoenix, 1971.

GREENBAUM, HOWARD. "The Appraisal of Organizational Communication Systems." Paper presented at a meeting of the International Communication Association, Atlanta, 1972.

LEVEL, D., and G. R. WATERS. "Experimental Design in Communication Research." *The Journal of Business Communication* 14 (Fall 1976), pp. 7–22.

REDDING, W. CHARLES. "Research Setting: Field Studies." In *Methods of Research in Communication,* ed. Phillip Emmert and William Brooks. Boston: Houghton Mifflin, 1970.

RICHARDS, WILLIAM. *A Manual for Network Analysis: Using the NEGOPY Network Analysis Program.* Palo Alto, Calif.: Institute for Communication Research, Stanford University, 1975.

RUDOLPH, EVAN. "An Evaluation of ECCO Analysis as a Communication Audit Methodology." Unpublished manuscript delivered at the International Communication Association Convention, Atlanta, April 1972.

Appendix A

Timetable for an Organizational

Communication Program

The charts on the following pages illustrate the type of long-range communication program that can be implemented in an organization. The emphasis on media or methods is not intended to be the focus. The content must be considered first, and that varies with the organization and its needs.

This illustrative timetable calls for regular conferences with supervisors, management training sessions, letters to employees, department meetings, monthly newspapers and magazines focusing on selected subjects, and special training sessions for a variety of employees on relevant topics. It does not deal with the day-to-day communication problems encountered in the organization. However, by developing and implementing such a total communications program those problems can be minimized or eliminated.

Month 1

Week

1—Information sessions with supervisors on company organization, resources, responsibilities.

2—Letter from president to employees explaining the forthcoming communication program.

3—Company newspaper or magazine with focus on details of long-range communication program.

4—Special training session with personnel department employees on conducting opinion polls, writing questionnaires, conducting interviews, evaluating results.

Survey and evaluate the communication program: conduct opinion polls, questionnaires, and interviews with top and middle management, first-line supervisors, employees.

Month 2

Week

1—Information sessions with supervisors to cover company policies and procedures.

2—Department meetings to discuss company policies, procedures, rules, regulations, and impact on employees.

3—Company newspaper or magazine with focus on details of special training sessions to be conducted with all levels and subjects.

4—Special training session (e.g., sales) focusing on techniques (closed-circuit TV tape recorders for self-evaluation).

Develop long-range communication programs (one to two years); determine goals, objectives, methods to implement.

Month 3

Week

1—Information sessions with supervisors to discuss sales-production-scheduling aspects of the company.

2—Letter from president to employees explaining sales-production-scheduling aspects with implications for employees.

3—Company newspaper or magazine with focus on sales (volume, price, etc.), production (scheduling problems), suppliers (possible "downtime"), etc.

4—Special training session (e.g., sales) on new research, product design, production, scheduling, pricing.

Initiate or, if in existence, review, evaluate, revise company handbook, orientation materials; involve some representation from employees to determine what they need and what they want to be included.

Month 4

Week

1—Information and training sessions with supervisors on labor-management relationships (grievances, arbitration).

2—Department meetings to discuss labor management relationships, areas of responsibility, federal and state laws.

3—Company newspaper or magazine with focus on federal and state regulations, impact on company and employees.

4—Special training sessions (e.g., for those involved in handling, processing grievances) on company procedures, forms, etc.

Review, evaluate contract with labor organization; determine problem areas and clauses to be discussed for possible negotiation.

Month 5

Week

1—Information session with supervisors on general economic conditions and impact on company, employees, hiring, etc.

2—Letter from president to employees discussing general economic conditions (prelude next meeting).

3—Company newspaper or magazine with details of impact of economic conditions on company and employees

4—Special training session (e.g., office/clerical) explaining word processing center to be implemented.

Month 6

Week

1—Training session with supervisors on leadership styles and impact on employees.

2—Department meetings on financial conditions of company, sales, profits etc.

3—Company newspaper or magazine with abstract or review of annual report.

4—Special department meetings to distribute and explain new (revised) company handbook and orientation materials (completed since month 3).

Month 7

Week

1—Training session with supervisors on interpersonal relations, sensitivity training, communication techniques, etc.

2—Letter from president to employees welcoming and explaining coming open house for employees, families, general public.

3—Company newspaper or magazine with focus on open house, directions, the role of each department, finished product, etc.

4—Conduct open house sessions for employees, families, general public.

Month 8

Week

1—Information session with supervisors on long-range company plans, research and development.

2—Department meetings to explain company plans, new products, plans for future.

3—Company newspaper or magazine with focus on (possible) new plant, products, distribution centers, etc.

4—Special training session (e.g., sales and manufacturing representatives) on new products and advertising.

Month 9

Week

1—Training session for supervisors on interview techniques, types and purpose of interviews.

2—Letter from president to employees explaining forthcoming company survey.

3—Special company newspaper or magazine with company survey (attitude, opinions on varied topics).

4—Special training session with those who recruit (e.g., at college placement services) on interview techniques, knowledge of company products, etc.

Month 10

Week

1—Information and training sessions with supervisors on safety programs.

2—Department meetings on safety programs, problems, reports, accident prevention, medical treatment, compensation, hospitalization, etc.

3—Company newspaper or magazine with complete list of hospitalization coverage, insurance, etc.

4—Special training session with top and middle management on new theories and concepts.

Month 11

Week

1—Training session with supervisors on how to conduct conferences, department meetings, deal with problem solving; review of survey results and implications.

2—Letter from president explaining results of survey (conducted previous month).

3—Company newspaper or magazine reviewing survey; explain suggestion plan to be implemented.

4—Special sessions with those involved in reviewing the previous year and planning next year's program.

Month 12

Week

1—Information session with supervisors to review and plan programs.

2—Department meetings to review and plan programs.

3—Social activities.

4—Final determination and publication of long-range plans for next year.

Appendix B

Sample Employment Interview

Person 1: What time do you have?

Person 2: I have a couple minutes 'til three.

Person 1: I just barely made it for my interview.

Person 2: Who are you talking to today?

Person 1: Fairmont.

Person 2: Fairmont? Aren't they in food distribution?

Person 1: Well, I'm really not sure. I went over to the library today and I couldn't find any brochures on them, so I don't know for sure what type of business they are in.

Person 2: Did you check the brochure file in the Placement Office?

Person 1: I didn't really see going to all that much trouble for it.

Person 2: Oh, I checked back there. I found a brochure on Electro-American. It really helped me get ready to interview.

Person 1: Do you know where Fairmont is located?

Person 2: I'm not sure, I believe it's someplace in Texas. What kind of job are you interviewing for?

Person 1: Oh, I don't really care, I just want a job.

Interviewer:[1] Let's see, I am looking for Bill Brown.

Bill (Person 2): Yes sir.

I: Mr. Brown, I am Harper Johnson from Electro-American. Come back and let's visit for a while.

Comment

A number of questions are probably on your mind as you approach your campus interview. How do I prepare for an interview? What kinds of questions will the recruiter ask? What should I ask? Is reading company literature in advance all that important? What are some points to sell myself?

The importance of the interview cannot be minimized. How you perform, what you say, what you don't say, and what is said to you largely

---

[1]Interviewer will hereafter be designated by "I".

determines how you will invest your college education. It makes sense to approach the interview intelligently and purposefully.

This sample interview cannot begin to tell all there is to know about an interview. Its main purpose is to provide a concise overview of what the average interview is like. The simulated interview presented will give you a realistic impression of what is a typical dialogue between student and interviewer. A typical interview can be broken down into four sections.

In the introductory stage the interviewer attempts to create a relaxed atmosphere and to establish rapport. In the second stage, the interviewer reviews your background and interest. The third stage is primarily a discussion of the employer's opportunities and how you fit in. The fourth stage is the conclusion. During the conclusion the points are clarified and the recruiter explains how and when the next contact will be made, if there is to be one. Now let us look at a typical campus interview.

I: Bill, I see by the college entrance form that I have from the Placement Office that you are a resident assistant at Holt Hall at the university. That is particularly interesting to me—I was an RA at Penn State University in 1968 in a 500-man hall—Hardgraves Hall. I always ask RAs I meet what their main problem has been in their hall.

Bill: There are several in our dorm, but the main problem is probably the use of marijuana. This is fairly common in our dorm and it is hard to stop—like alcohol or something. Everyone knows when someone is smoking and it is difficult to do something about.

I: I see. In '68 when I was a RA, we didn't have problems like alcohol and marijuana. One time some of the boys in the dorm stuffed the cracks under the doors and windows with towels and filled the hall with water and syrup. It's the same kind of things today only now they're expressed differently.

Bill, we want to talk about your background and some of your experiences today and see what you can bring to Electro-American. We'll see how we can match your qualifications with what we have to offer, and we can end the interview with any final questions you have. I prefer to conduct a focused interview—that means that I have some set questions that I will ask you. Feel free to deviate from that at any time. Let's go directly into your background and experience.

Comment

During this introductory stage, Mr. Brown has definitely made a good first impression. He was punctual, well mannered, and well dressed. His firm handshake and alertness showed that he had cultivated confidence beforehand. He was relaxed but did not slouch. His actions were natural—his eye contact was good and he seemed interested and enthusiastic.

The key to this stage is to simply be yourself. All of these things have a considerable effect on the recruiter's first impression.

I: Before we begin with your educational experience, Bill, I see by your college interview form that you have majored in personnel management. Would you tell me why, please?

Bill: I chose personnel management because I enjoy contact with people. Actually, when I started at the university I majored in industrial engineering, but I didn't do extremely well and I lost interest in it rather quickly. The business aspect of some of my courses attracted me and I decided to transfer to business.

I: What have your major courses been in the personnel management field?

Bill: Oh, I would say psychology of business and industry, personnel psychology, business policy, labor problems, personnel problems, and administrative writing and theory.

I: Of these courses, which would you pick as your most challenging course and why?

Bill: I would say psychology of business and industry. We had an excellent instructor, and the class was small enough to interact well. We had a couple of outside projects that were time-consuming, but very informative.

I: Can you expand a little bit on these projects?

Bill: Well, the one I enjoyed most was an analysis of the hiring practices of a local firm. We did this as a group project, and spent a great deal of time at the plant looking at what they did to hire people.

I: Bill, when you got into this kind of project, did you actually get into any evaluation of what you considered to be right or wrong about these hiring practices, or was it just strictly analysis?

Bill: No, sir, just an analysis and comparison of what we had studied.

I: Your minor was finance—that seems an unusual pair, personnel management and finance. Why did you choose finance?

Bill: Well, early in my junior year, I took a finance course as an elective, and it was very interesting to me. Since then, I have taken several courses and have liked them all.

I: O.K. Let's talk for a few minutes about your work experience. Let's pursue the job of resident assistant just a bit further. What are your major areas of responsibility?

Bill: The resident assistant is responsible for programming, motivation, personal guidance, discipline, maintenance, and things like this.

I: Where would you say you spent the most time?

Bill: I would say the majority would be serving as a resource person and probably discipline.

I: What do you mean serving as a resource person? I don't particularly understand that. Would you explain it?

Bill: Keeping abreast of everything that is happening on campus and being able to tell the guys what is going on, where you can get assistance for this or that.

I: Do you feel, Bill, that you have been effective?

Bill: Yes, I do, and I enjoyed the opportunity I had for personal counsel.

I: I see. Let's start then with your work experience in the summer of 19-- to the past summer of 19-- with General Electric in Jonesboro, and for the summers of 19--, 19--, and at Crane in Jonesboro in the summer of 19--. You chose factory labor as your work experience. Why did you choose this type of work experience considering the fact that you are majoring in personnel and minoring in finance?

Bill: I saw little conflict in my summer work and my major. I think my work in the factories gave me a great deal of insight into problems of personnel management. I got an opportunity to view different styles of management on the first-line supervisor level and some I liked and some I didn't like, but I learned a great deal from it and learned the employees' outlook on things. Another reason is that these two jobs are the best paying in the whole area.

I: I want to commend you—I noticed on your interview form that you have earned at least 50 percent of your college expenses. I think that is quite admirable. Let's talk a few minutes about your campus activities and extracurricular activities. I see that you have been active in the Campus Crusade for Christ. I am familiar with some of the writings of Dr. Bill Bright, who, I understand, is founder and present president. Would you tell me please what the student MOB group is?

Bill: That's the student mobilization group—a group of 315 students here on campus that feel like they have the time to dedicate to actually planning and carrying out the Campus Crusade here on our campus.

I: I see. In X number of hours, Bill, tell me how many hours you spend per week in the student MOB group.

Bill: Our meeting each week with the student mobilization group is about one and a half to two hours. Each person in the student mobilization group is required to be in a smaller group called an action group and also lead an action group, plus spend time with members of his action group during the week. The total comes out to about 8 to 10 hours per week.

I: In your work experience you have listed that the number of hours per week as a resident assistant are not set. In the six areas of responsibility you listed to me, approximately how many hours do you spend actually there on the floor?

Bill: The actual physical part of the job can be done in an hour or two a day. But the responsibility of a resident assistant is 24 hours a

day. For that reason, I put "not set." Any time you are there, you are doing an RA's job.

I: I see. Do you feel, Bill, there is any conflict between your job as resident assistant and the time you spend with the student MOB group?

Bill: I feel that I have the ability to cope with it well. A lot of my work in the Campus Crusade was involved with my own men on my own floor in my own dorm so the two fit together really well for me.

I: How do you spend your spare time?

Bill: The majority of my spare time I spend in athletic activities or just around the dorm. I play some basketball and the rest of my spare time would be devoted with my work or with the student mobilization group.

I: I notice that you had been secretary-treasurer of Holt Hall and floor president of the third floor of Holt Hall. Am I correct in assuming that these two positions were not held simultaneously to being an RA?

Bill: Yes, sir, the floor presidency was my freshman year in the dorm and I was secretary-treasurer my sophomore year.

I: Are they elected positions?

Bill: Yes sir, both of them.

I: Let's move into matching your qualifications with what Electro-American has to offer.

Comment

During this stage Mr. Brown has made sure that his strong points were emphasized. He volunteered extra information without being loaded with conceit, and demonstrated the ability to communicate in a clear, logical manner. He was prepared to answer questions about his extracurricular activities, which revealed that he was well adjusted and well able to relate to others. He was also prepared to answer why, where, and when questions concerning his work experience and education. Now let's take a look at the next stage of the interview.

I: Bill, I would be interested in knowing what you picture yourself doing in 10 years.

Bill: I would like to move into a situation where I can, in that length of time, at least have reached a middle management situation. I would like to be able to advance on my own merit as rapidly as possible.

I: Let's talk about Electro-American specifically. I want you to tell me about Electro-American.

Bill: I know that Electro-American is a major electronics corporation that manufactures everything from computers to household appliances and markets those products all over the United States and in fact the world. And in this area you have larger locations, one in Memphis, Tennessee, Oklahoma City, and in Dallas.

I: You are very well informed, and I feel sure that you have read our brochure. This publication has recently replaced an old brochure that was on file in college placement offices for years. I am trying to get a little feedback from students on how effective they feel the brochure is. How did you feel about the brochure?

Bill: It was very interesting, and gave a great deal of insight into all that Electro-American does. I thoroughly enjoyed it.

I: Was there any particular part about the brochure that stood out as being very good or exceptionally poor?

Bill: I was especially interested in the employee relations training program it discussed.

I: Well, good. That's a good way to get into that. I noticed by your application that is what you want to be in. Let me tell you a little about the employee relations training program, and then I will expect you to ask me some questions pertinent to your own situation. We began the program in 19--, as a means of training our personnel people to certain factors and situations in Electro-American that were peculiar only to our situation. In 19--, we began the pilot program with 16 workers and we started out on a 12-week classroom situation which was interspersed with some on-the-job training. We feel that it has been very successful and we have continued it every year since.

Bill: I did have some questions there. In the program—is it classroom instruction, or what kind of training is it?

I: I didn't clarify that, I'm sorry. You start out in the employee relations program. Then, classroom experience. It will be approximately 12 weeks and, as I said, it will be interspersed with some on-the-job training. We have a training center in Dallas, which is located close to the home office and you will be in class up to four hours a day and on the job four hours a day.

Bill: The on-the-job part of the training after the classroom work—will it be in Dallas, is it one location or several, or how does that work?

I: Now, you mentioned in telling me about Electro-American that we have those three major home offices in the South and Southwest. Two of those we use in the employee relations program—Dallas or Memphis. See, what we do, is to trade you off between Dallas and Memphis as we need you in those two locations.

Bill: It sounds very interesting.

I: It is a good program, it is rated very highly among these types of programs by the American Management Association and I feel that all the persons who have been successful in the program have been very happy with what they have learned. I would say that 90 to 95 percent of them have gone on to advance into the executive levels of Electro-American. It has been quite a profitable program. I want to get subjective for a minute. All of these things we have talked about have been objective. Pick out what you would consider your strongest

point, your biggest selling point—the differential advantage that makes Bill Brown better than anybody else. And, at the same time, on the other side of the coin, I want you to pick out your weakest point. The point that may be an impediment to your success in whatever chosen career opportunity. What I want you to do is take your strongest point and sell yourself to me. And then, I want to take that weakest point and make allowance for it and continue to sell yourself to me.

Bill: I would say that my strongest point is my ability to work with people—my ability to establish relationships well. I feel that I can establish and maintain good relationships with people. In my job as a resident assistant I have had the opportunity to develop that ability and I have established many good relationships. That is my strongest point. My weakest point would have to be my lack of ability or lack of patience to do detail. I don't feel that it hinders me that much because I am self-disciplined enough to go ahead and do the paper work. But, my attitude toward it is not very strong.

I: OK. Let's dig those out for a minute. First of all, you say your strongest point is your ability to develop relationships with people quickly and that you do relate well to people. Have you noticed that you may have a tendency to jump to conclusions and to prejudge a situation before you have all the facts in?

Bill: No sir, I don't believe so. I feel like I establish relationships well on any level. I feel like I evaluate people well and I don't jump to conclusions.

I: In other words, you do allow due process, and try to be objective. I think that is certainly a virtue, one that very few people have. Let's dig something out of your weakness. You say you are impatient and intolerant with paperwork. I am sure that the resident assistant's position requires at least some paperwork. Have you found this to be an impediment to your job as an RA?

Bill: No sir, not at all, there is a great deal of paperwork involved, but as I mentioned I am self-disciplined enough to go ahead and do it, I just don't enjoy it very much.

I: Would you say that you could fill that responsibility to the best of your ability and in an efficient manner?

Bill: Quite efficiently.

I: OK. I think that is what I need to know about comparing what you have to offer with what we have to offer. I see our time is getting away. Bill, I want to give you a chance to ask me some questions.

Comment

At this stage, Mr. Brown was prepared to establish immediate as well as long-range objectives. He knew the company's history, products, and locations. Mr. Brown had also prepared questions about the type of work

he would do or the training he would get. He knew why he was interested in this employer. He was well prepared for this stage of matching his career interest with those of the job opening.

Bill: I have a few questions I was interested in asking. Does your company make allowances outside the training program for opportunities in education?

I: Yes, we do and I'm glad that you asked that. Late in the 1970s, we began a pilot program in pursuing graduate study. Of course, there has been an increased emphasis on graduate study in the last few years—especially in business. We provide a program whereby you can select a university of your choice, and a graduate program of your choice, and receive a leave of absence from the company to work toward and receive your masters in business administration. You must have been an employee of the company for five years, and we ask that you fulfill some of your paperwork obligations to the company while you are on the university campus. In return, we pay all of your tuition and living expenses.

Bill: I like that. I gather that everything, promotion and all, is based on merit?

I: Is it based on the merit system? Yes, it certainly is. There are no levels of seniority or anything of that sort in the executive levels of the company. One thing I have found about the employee training program is that we have set a maximum of six months, but what we do is any person can be promoted through the program at his or her own rate. In other words, it is entirely possible that if you were qualified and completed all the criteria that we have for judging you successfully, you could graduate from the program in two weeks.

Bill: One other question about the program. How many people do you accept in your program a year?

I: It is very competitive. We are trying to extract the cream of the crop from the personnel management field. So, therefore, we only take 16 each year. Usually this is divided up into eight in January and eight in July. This is extremely high for the size of our company. The third largest company in the world only takes 30 a year in its executive training program. So, I think we have certainly set a high enough maximum. I will say that last year, we did not even get 16 people. After interviewing and processing all the applications, we didn't feel that we could find 16 qualified applicants. So we only took nine. There is a limit of 16.

Bill: I believe that's all the questions I have right now.

I: I don't think there are any other questions I have for you. I do have one thing I would like you to do for me if you are genuinely interested in Electro-American. I have an application blank that I would like you to fill out. It's about four or five pages. My name and address

are on there and you will need to fill that out within a week and mail it in to my secretary. We will process it and I will be in touch with you fairly soon and we will schedule some mutually convenient appointment times. OK? Bill, it was nice to see you and I enjoyed visiting with you, and I hope to see you soon.

Bill: Thank you.

Comment

In conclusion, some points to remember in preparing for your interview are: First, analyze your strengths and weaknesses, your background, your academic performance, your vocational interests, and your personal aspirations and values. In other words begin to formulate in your own mind not only what you would like to do but also what you are best prepared to do. Next, study your prospective employer. It is imperative that you have some knowledge of their policies, philosophies, and products. Dress in good taste. Although most employers are becoming liberal in their standard of dress and appearance, let basic good taste be your guide. Fourth, be yourself. Your attitude is going to influence the interviewer's evaluation. Don't try to be something that you are not. Simply be yourself. Ask meaningful questions, particularly if you are not clear about the details of the job or the training program or other related concerns.

Name Index

A

Ackoff, R. L., 244
Adler, R. B., 10, 297
Aiken, M., 206
Amos, Nancy, 7
Aronson, E., 388
Athos, A., 182, 204

B

Baird, J. E., 75
Baker, Frank, 204, 205
Baker, Kent, 343
Baker, Russell, 62
Bartunek, J. M., 193
Baty, Wayne, 11
Bavelas, A., 170
Beavin, J., 59
Bednar, David, 4
Bell, C., 387
Bell, D. E., 250
Benne, K., 175
Bennis, W., 387
Berg, D., 266
Berkowitz, L., 170
Berlo, D., 23, 33
Berne, Eric, 152
Berry, P., 193
Birdwhistell, R., 65
Blake, R., 72
Block, C., 193
Bloom, Stuart, 263, 265, 266
Borman, Ernest, 300
Boulton, W., 233
Bowditch, J., 386
Bower, P. G., 253
Brilhart, John, 162
Brooks, W., 64
Broom, H., 277
Brown, C., 58

Burns, T., 206
Byers, Lloyd, 266

C

Camden, Carl, 332
Campion, A., 333
Cannell, C., 325
Carlson, Robert, 341
Carter, N., 218
Cartwright, D., 4, 172
Cheston, R., 366, 367
Christensen, C., 266
Clarke, P., 254
Cohen, Allen S., 112, 171, 173
Colley, C. H., 122
Connelly, J., 114

D

Daft, R., 209, 214, 218
Dauton, Paul, 264
Davies, M. R., 4
Davis, F., 79
Davis, Keith, 309, 409
Davitz, J. R., 73
Davitz, L., 73
Deese, James, 382
Delbecq, A. L., 193, 194
Deutsch, M., 357, 360
Dittmann, A., 69
Dizard, W., 92, 94, 95, 98
Donnelly, J., 358
Drucker, Peter, 5, 231, 282

E

Ekman, Paul, 65
Emery, F., 211
Emmert, P., 64
Endicott, F., 333

F

Fader, Shirley, 340
Feld, Lipman, 335
Fersko-Weiss, Henry, 96
Festinger, L., 172
Fink, S., 112, 171, 172, 175
Fiore, Q., 379
Fisher, B., 192
Flesh, R., 407
Franklin, S., 193
French, W., 387
Friesen, W., 65

G

Gadon, H., 112
Galle, W., 72
Gandz, J., 358
Gaylord, Sarah, 333
Georgopoulus, B., 210
Gibb, Jack, 143, 156, 157
Gibson, J., 358
Giffin, Kim, 361
Glab, Janice, 3
Goebel, Brad, 90
Goldhaber, G., 64, 76, 410
Golen, Steven, 3
Gordon, T., 345
Gordon, W. J., 194
Gottlieb, Marvin, 322
Gratz, Robert, 97
Greiner, L., 184
Grossman, S. R., 193
Gunning, R., 407
Gustafson, D., 193

H

Hackman, J., 386, 387
Hage, J., 206, 214
Hall, E., 70

Subject Index

A

Abstract language, 38
Appraisal interview, 342–45
Assimilating, 136
Attitude, 316
Attribution, 107
Audio aids, 292
Automated office operations, 92

B

Behavior, 381
  changing of, 381
  compliance, 383
  identification, 384
  internalization, 384
  unfreezing/refreezing, 385
Boundary spanning, 215
Bounded rationality, 234

C

Change process, 381
  law of effect, 382
  reinforcement, 382
  role of communication, 386
Changing behavior, 383
Channel overload, 221
Channels of communication, 86
Climate, 316
Closure, 106
Codes of communication, 23
Coherence, 46–47
Communication, 4–10
  as behavior, 8–9
  definition, 10
  models, 11
  styles, 148–50
  & the manager, 5–7
  & the organization, 4

Communication audits, 399
  communication logs, 410
  content analysis, 407
  ECCO analysis, 409
  ICA audit, 410
  interaction analysis, 409
  Odiorn's communication audit, 409
  prevention, 402
  problem solving, 402
  readability test, 407
  reporting, 412
  semantic differentiation, 408
  shadowing, 410
Communication log, 410
Communication objective, 30
Company handbooks, 271
Complaints interview, 345–50
Concept formation process, 26
Concrete language, 37
Conflict management, 356
  definition, 357
  effects, 360
  historical approach, 363
  types, 357
Connotative meaning, 38
Content analysis in audits, 407
Controlling the environment, 216
  contracting, 216
  co-opting, 216
  merging, 216
Counseling interview, 350–53
Culture and nonverbal communication, 79

D

Databases, 239
  bibliographic, 241–42
  factual, 242
  numeric, 242

Debating, 301
Decision making, 8
  behavior cycle, 8–9
  styles, 235
Decoding, 135
Denotative meaning, 38
Detouring, 301
Distractions, 301
  emotional, 301
  mental, 301
  physical, 301
Double bind, 140
Dysphemisms, 39

E

Effective organization communication, 11, 87
Effectiveness, 7–8
Entropy, 204
Episodic communication channels in organizations (ECCO), 409
Euphemisms, 39

F

Facts, 28
Feedback, 141–43, 147, 302
Filtering, 135
Focal unit, 401
  interpersonal, 401
  intrapersonal, 401
  organizational, 401
Forming, 166
Frame of reference, 317
Functionalism, 35

G

Global village, 379
Grammatical structure, 42–46
  active/passive voice, 42

Managerial

Communications

This modern text is designed to prepare you for your future professional career. While theories, ideas, techniques, and data are dynamic, the information contained in this volume will provide you a quick and useful reference as well as a guide for future learning for many years to come. Your familiarity with the contents of this book will make it an important volume in your professional library.

EX LIBRIS